D1193205

Traffic Management

FOURTH EDITION

Laurence M. Olivo

Adrian Knetsch

CONTRIBUTOR
Stewart Flameling

To access the "It's Your Move" Traffic Simulations that accompany this text, go to http://www.emond.ca, create an account, go to My Books, and validate this PIN code:

TM44127856

emond ▪ Toronto, Canada ▪ 2017

1043

Copyright © 2017 Emond Montgomery Publications Limited.

NOTICE & DISCLAIMER: All rights reserved. No part of this publication may be reproduced in any form by any means without the written consent of Emond Montgomery Publications. Emond Montgomery Publications and all persons involved in the creation of this publication disclaim any warranty as to the accuracy of this publication and shall not be responsible for any action taken in reliance on the publication, or for any errors or omissions contained in the publication. Nothing in this publication constitutes legal or other professional advice. If such advice is required, the services of the appropriate professional should be obtained.

We have attempted to request permission from, and to acknowledge in the text, all sources of material originally published elsewhere. If we have inadvertently overlooked an acknowledgment or failed to secure a permission, we offer our sincere apologies and undertake to rectify the omission in the next edition.

Emond Montgomery Publications Limited
60 Shaftesbury Avenue
Toronto ON M4T 1A3
http://www.emond.ca/highered

Printed in Canada.

We acknowledge the financial support of the Government of Canada. Canadä

Emond Montgomery Publications has no responsibility for the persistence or accuracy of URLs for external or third-party Internet websites referred to in this publication, and does not guarantee that any content on such websites is, or will remain, accurate or appropriate.

Vice-president, publishing: Anthony Rezek
Publisher: Mike Thompson
Managing editor, development: Kelly Dickson
Developmental editor: Sarah Fulton
Senior editor: Jim Lyons
Copy editor: Claudia Forgas
Permissions editor: Lisa Brant
Proofreader: Cindy Fujimoto
Indexer: Michael Bunn
Typesetter: Shani Sohn
Cover designer: Tara Agnerian
Cover image: Khram/Shutterstock

Library and Archives Canada Cataloguing in Publication

Olivo, Laurence M., 1946-, author
    Traffic management / Laurence M. Olivo, Adrian Knetsch ; contributor, Stu Flameling. — 4th edition.

Includes index.
ISBN 978-1-77255-076-4 (paperback)

    1. Traffic violations—Canada.   2. Traffic regulations—Canada.   3. Traffic accident investigation—Canada.   I. Knetsch, Adrian, author   II. Flameling, Stu, author   III. Title.

HV8079.5.O45 2017   363.2'3320971   C2016-905273-7

To Joyce, as always — *L.O.*

To my best friend and wife, Evelyn — *A.K.*

Brief Contents

Detailed Contents

1 Introduction

2 The Highway Traffic Act: Defining Terms

3 Licences and Permits

6 Impaired Driving and Other Criminal Code and Highway Traffic Act Offences

7 Collision Investigation

APPENDIXES

List of Figures

Preface

In the late 1990s it was clear that there was a need for a coherent and practical text for highway traffic law in the public safety and police programs at Ontario colleges. In 2000 we met that demand with the first edition of *Traffic Management*, but both the law and police practices regarding highway traffic and motor vehicle offences and regulations are continually evolving and changing. We kept track of those changes with new editions in 2007 and 2011. As the law is an ever-moving target, we have continued to track developments that have led to the fourth edition.

In a text like this, knowledge of both the law and legal procedure as well as knowledge of police practices and procedures is essential to providing students with effective training. In previous editions of *Traffic Management* we had helpful input from an advisory team that featured Tony Altomare (Centennial College), Sergeant Stuart Church (Waterloo Regional Police Service), and Wayne Thomas (Humber College). We also had considerable input from the late Peter Parese, who provided valuable suggestions and materials. All of the professionals involved reviewed previous editions and provided detailed commentary and feedback. Having the benefit of their knowledge and experience in policing and teaching was invaluable in making previous editions and this edition relevant and current.

We would also like to thank those instructors who reviewed the previous edition and provided many helpful suggestions: Rick Bullock (Canadore College), Michael Chesson (Durham College), and Rob Dickie (Algonquin College). Thanks also to Peter Skrypka (Seneca College) and Mike McMurchy (Algonquin College) for their excellent work on the test bank and online traffic simulations, respectively.

In addition to the roles played by the individuals above, Andy Knetsch joined Larry Olivo as co-author of the third edition. Andy's 26 years' experience as a police officer with the Waterloo Regional Police Service and nearly a decade teaching at Conestoga College provided additional guidance on police practices. In this edition, the combination of Andy's skills and practical experience with Larry's legal knowledge and experience along with his three decades of teaching legal subjects at Seneca College has resulted in the creation of a formidable professional team that offers students valuable guidance on policing practicalities.

In addition to updating and tracking legal changes and developments, and changes in police practices and techniques, we have also expanded our focus on practical policing. With the assistance of Stewart Flameling, retired police officer with the Halton Regional Police Service and current *Highway Traffic Act* instructor at Conestoga College, we have developed new case studies and practical exercises that will help students advance professionally, developing their legal knowledge and practical skills.

Laurence M. Olivo
Andy Knetsch
September 2016

For Instructors

For information on obtaining the teaching resources available to those instructors who have chosen this book for their courses, visit the "For Instructors" tab on this book's website at <http://www.emond.ca/traffic4e>. This book also includes free online traffic simulations with self-testing quizzes that are tied to the chapter content, for use by students or instructors. At the front of each book you will find an access code that is valid for six months once it is activated. Contact your Emond representative for more information.

About the Authors

Laurence M. Olivo, BA, MA, JD is a lawyer and recently retired as a professor in the Faculty of Business, Seneca College, where he gained over 30 years' experience in post-secondary teaching, and program and course development in a variety of college programs. His legal practice experience includes civil litigation and family law, as well as policy development work with the Ontario Ministry of the Attorney General. He is the author of more than 15 texts in various areas of law and specialized online courses for use by legal staff and students in post-secondary institutions and employer training programs. He is currently involved in developing legal training materials on a consulting basis, and is a deputy judge of the Ontario Small Claims Court.

Adrian (Andy) Knetsch graduated from Wilfrid Laurier University, Waterloo, Ontario, in 1976 with a degree in political science. He was a member of the Waterloo Regional Police Service from 1976 to 2002, when he retired with the rank of sergeant. During his policing career, Andy served in a variety of capacities, including patrol, community relations, planning and research, and criminal investigations, and received many awards and documentations, including the Ontario Medal of Police Bravery. In 2002 Andy decided to leave the great profession of public policing to become a college professor at Conestoga College, in Kitchener, Ontario where he remained until 2010. During his teaching career, he taught students in political science, ethics, traffic management, interviewing and investigations, and police preparation courses. As a teacher, Andy sought to challenge his students and to instill in them a philosophy of never settling for "second best" and always treating others with dignity and respect.

Stewart Flameling (contributor) is an instructor at Conestoga College where he teaches traffic management, among other courses. He served with the Halton Regional Police Service, including in the traffic division, for 33 years. Stewart has also taught at the Ontario Police College.

Introduction

1

LEARNING OUTCOMES

After completing this chapter, you should be able to:

- Appreciate the breadth and complexity of the law relating to traffic management and motor vehicle law.
- Understand the importance of the Ontario *Highway Traffic Act* (HTA) to motor vehicle law.
- Understand the relationship between the HTA and the regulations made under it.
- Understand the importance of filling out tickets and summonses accurately, and the consequences of failing to do so.
- Find provisions of statutes, regulations, amendments, proposed legislation, and previous versions of current legislation on the Ontario e-Laws and federal Justice Laws websites.
- Locate topics in a consolidated version of the HTA using the table of contents, index, table of contents for the regulations, and the *General* regulation.

Overview of the Law Governing Traffic Management

The law governing motor vehicles is both broad and complex. It is broad because it covers many aspects of and activities related to motor vehicles. And it is complex both because of the subject matter and because of the overlap between the provincial and federal jurisdictions that govern motor vehicle law.

The breadth of motor vehicle law can be appreciated simply by looking at what is included among the topics covered by the Ontario *Highway Traffic Act* (HTA):

- establishment and operation of government offices and departments to administer motor vehicle law,
- vehicle permits,
- parking permits,
- licensing of drivers and driving instructors,
- licensing and regulation of garages and storage facilities,
- vehicle and equipment requirements and standards,
- vehicle loads and dimensions,
- vehicle weight,
- vehicle rates of speed,
- rules of the road,
- regulation of toll highways,
- regulation of medical transportation services,
- off-road vehicles,
- civil liability issues involving motor vehicles,
- municipal bylaws regarding motor vehicles,
- suspension for failure to pay judgments or meet support obligations,
- accident records and reporting,
- photo-radar system evidence,
- red light cameras, and
- traffic enforcement rules (including procedure, arrest, and penalties).

In addition to the topics covered by the HTA, more motor vehicle topics are covered by other legislation. Under federal law, Canada's *Criminal Code* (CC) deals with more serious vehicle operating offences such as dangerous operation of a vehicle and impaired driving. There are also federal laws that govern vehicle safety requirements, some of which overlap with or complement provincial rules.

Considering the range of motor vehicle topics covered by different laws, it is not surprising that this area of law can be quite complex. For example, the many types of vehicles and the varied uses to which they may be put create complicated licensing and permit systems both for vehicles and for those who operate them. As well, some of the equipment and safety requirements for vehicles have resulted in the implementation of detailed rules that incorporate engineering terms and concepts that are only easily understood by experts. And because the federal and provincial laws that cover an activity occasionally overlap, it can be complex to sort out a potential jurisdictional conflict and decide which law is appropriate to a situation.

Consider the provincial offence of careless driving and the federal offence of dangerous operation of a motor vehicle. The HTA offence of careless driving (s 130) requires proof that the accused drove "without due care and attention or without reasonable consideration for other persons using the highway." The CC offence of dangerous operation of a motor vehicle requires proof that the accused operated "a motor vehicle in a manner that is dangerous to the public, having regard to all the circumstances, including the nature, condition and use of the place at which the motor vehicle is being operated and the amount of traffic that at the time is or might reasonably be expected to be at that place" (s 249 (1)(a)). The grounds for laying a charge are determined by the circumstances involved in the incident. Generally, the greater the departure from ordinary negligence in the direction of an intentionally dangerous act, the more likely that a CC charge will be laid.

WHAT DOES THE LAW SAY?

Criminal Code

249(1) Every one commits an offence who operates
   (a) a motor vehicle in a manner that is dangerous to the public, having regard to all the circumstances, including the nature, condition and use of the place at which the motor vehicle is being operated and the amount of traffic that at the time is or might reasonably be expected to be at that place;

Highway Traffic Act

Careless driving

130. Every person is guilty of the offence of driving carelessly who drives a vehicle or street car on a highway without due care and attention or without reasonable consideration for other persons using the highway and on conviction is liable to a fine of not less than $400 and not more than $2,000 or to imprisonment for a term of not more than six months, or to both, and in addition his or her licence or permit may be suspended for a period of not more than two years.

You might wonder why an offence in relation to motor vehicles cannot be dealt with by a single piece of legislation but instead is addressed by two different laws that may both apply to a particular situation or incident. The reason is that under the *Constitution Act, 1867*, the division of law-making power between the provinces and the federal government may result in overlaps. In the case of motor vehicle law, the courts have sorted out, in most cases, where the jurisdictional boundaries lie. For us, it is enough to know that more serious, harmful acts are usually characterized as criminal acts, over which the federal government has jurisdiction, and are covered by the CC. Those acts that are less serious and that can be characterized as regulatory offences involving breaches of a regulatory system within a province come within the province's jurisdiction and are covered by its provincial traffic act. There are of course grey areas where the boundary between provincial and federal jurisdiction is not always clear, but we can leave this issue to constitutional lawyers and the courts to sort out.

In this introductory text, our focus will be on matters that police officers commonly deal with or need to know about in day-to-day law enforcement: vehicle and operator permits, equipment requirements, rules of the road, HTA offences, HTA charging procedures and penalties, CC driving offences, and the duties of drivers involved in motor vehicle collisions. We will begin by learning how to find our way through and use the HTA. Once you have learned how to do so, you will find that the techniques used can be applied to finding your way through other legislation—such as the CC—that we examine later in this text.

The Relationship Between a Statute and Its Regulations, or "The Devil Is in the Details"

regulations
rules made by Cabinet (although actually by ministry officials under the authority of a statute) that deal in more detail with matters covered by the statute itself. To be legitimate, the power to authorize and create a regulation must be found in a specific statute's regulation-making powers, usually set out at the end of a statute.

A statute (that is, a law) like the HTA sets out general legal principles, but it does not usually deal with technical details. Instead, the technical details are dealt with in **regulations**. The statute will contain a section or sections that allow the government to make regulations that deal with specific technical areas described in the section of the statute that creates a regulation-making power. For example, s 56 of the HTA authorizes the demerit point system, but the details of the demerit point system—how many demerit points are deducted for each offence—are located in Ontario Regulation (O Reg) 339/94. Another example of a regulation that supports the Act with technical details pertains to seat belts. Sections 106(2) to (4) of the Act stipulate that both the driver and passengers in a motor vehicle shall wear the complete seat belt assembly when driving on a highway (in the case of certain young passengers, the passenger must be secured by a child seating system or child restraint system). The technical details are contained in Regulation 613, *Seat Belt Assemblies*, which lists certain exemptions for police officers, prisoners in custody, ambulance attendants, firefighters, and others.

Examples of a Statutory Provision and the Authority to Make Regulations Under That Provision and the Regulation Enacted

Sections 68.1(1) to (11) of the HTA state the following:

Speed-limiting systems
Required use by commercial motor vehicles
   68.1(1) No person shall drive, or permit the operation of, a commercial motor vehicle on a highway unless the vehicle is equipped with a speed-limiting system that is activated and functioning in accordance with the regulations.

Same
   (2) Except as authorized by the regulations, no person shall,
      (a) deactivate, or permit a person to deactivate, a commercial motor vehicle's speed-limiting system; or
      (b) modify, or permit a person to modify, a commercial motor vehicle's speed-limiting system such that it ceases to function in accordance with the regulations.

Tampering device prohibited
   (3) No person shall drive, or permit the operation of, a commercial motor vehicle on a highway if the vehicle is equipped with, has attached to it or carries,
      (a) a prescribed device or prescribed equipment; or
      (b) another device or equipment that is designed to disguise the fact that the vehicle is not equipped with a speed-limiting system that is activated and functioning in accordance with the regulations.

Verifying compliance
   (4) A police officer or officer appointed for carrying out the provisions of this Act, in exercising his or her powers under section 82 or 216.1, may require that the driver or other person in charge of a commercial motor vehicle,
      (a) provide the officer with access to the vehicle's computer system in order to retrieve and read any information relevant to the activation and functioning of the vehicle's speed-limiting system;
      (b) surrender to the officer any device or equipment carried in the vehicle that operates as part of the vehicle's speed-limiting system; and
      (c) surrender to the officer any records that the driver is required by the regulations to carry with him or her while driving the vehicle.

Same

(5) A driver or other person in charge of a commercial motor vehicle shall comply with any requirement made under subsection (4) by a police officer or officer appointed for carrying out the provisions of this Act.

Seizure of tampering device

(6) If a police officer or officer appointed for carrying out the provisions of this Act finds a device or equipment prohibited by subsection (3) in the course of any inspection of a commercial motor vehicle, he or she may detach, if necessary, and seize any such device or equipment.

Sale of tampering devices prohibited

(7) No person shall sell, offer or advertise for sale a device or equipment prohibited by subsection (3).

Offence

(8) Every person who contravenes or fails to comply with subsection (1), (2), (3), (5) or (7), or a regulation made under this section, is guilty of an offence and on conviction is liable to a fine of not less than $250 and not more than $20,000.

Evidentiary presumption

(9) In any proceeding under this section and in the absence of evidence to the contrary, proof that a commercial motor vehicle was driven on a highway at a speed equal to or greater than the speed prescribed for the purpose of this subsection is proof that the vehicle was not equipped with a speed-limiting system that was activated and functioning as required by subsection (1).

Forfeiture of tampering device

(10) Where a person is convicted of an offence under subsection (3), any device or equipment seized under subsection (6) by means of which the offence was committed is forfeited to the Crown.

Regulations

(11) The Lieutenant Governor in Council may make regulations,

(a) defining "commercial motor vehicle" for the purposes of this section;[1]

(b) prescribing standards for speed-limiting systems;

(c) governing the activation and functioning of speed-limiting systems, including prescribing and governing the speed at which speed-limiting systems must be set and prescribing different speed settings for different circumstances;

(d) prescribing devices and equipment for the purpose of clause (3)(a);

(e) governing methods to verify compliance with this section and the regulations, including prescribing devices and software to be used to retrieve and read information in computer systems;

(f) prescribing the speed for the purpose of subsection (9);

(g) requiring and governing the inspection and maintenance of speed-limiting systems;

(h) governing records to be kept and submitted in relation to the inspection, maintenance, activation and functioning of speed-limiting systems;

(i) governing records to be kept and carried by drivers in relation to the activation and functioning of speed-limiting systems;

(j) exempting any person or class of persons or any commercial motor vehicle or class of commercial motor vehicles from any requirement or provision of this section or of a regulation made under this section and prescribing conditions and circumstances for any such exemption.

---

1 On January 1, 2017, the day named by proclamation of the Lieutenant Governor, clause (a) is repealed. (See: 2014, c 9, Sched 2, ss 25, 47)

On page 540 of the index to MacBeth Publishing's *The Ontario Highway Traffic Act—Cross Referenced to Selected Regulations, 2016 Edition* (St Catharines, Ont: MacBeth, 2016) (MacBeth 2016) (see Figure 1.1, later in this chapter), the entry "Speed-limiting systems S-68.1" (referencing s 68.1 of the HTA) directs you to page 116, where s 68.1 can be found. Under s 68.1(11) (on page 251), you will see a reference to Regulation 587, ss 12-18 (reproduced below).

> For quick reference, mark the regulations index in your copy of the HTA with a sticky note (page 245 of MacBeth 2016).

Speed-Limiting Systems

12. For the purposes of section 68.1 of the Act,

"commercial motor vehicle" means a commercial motor vehicle as defined in subsection 1(1) of the Act.

13(1) A commercial motor vehicle is exempt from subsections 68.1(1), (2), (3) and (6) of the Act if it is,

  (a) a bus;

  (b) a mobile crane;

  (c) a motor home;

  (d) a vehicle manufactured before 1995;

  (e) a vehicle with a manufacturer's gross vehicle weight rating under 11,794 kilograms; or

  (f) an ambulance, a cardiac arrest emergency vehicle, or a fire apparatus.

(2) For the purposes of clauses 1(d) and (e), the date that a commercial motor vehicle was manufactured and its manufacturer's gross vehicle weight rating shall be deemed, in the absence of evidence to the contrary, to be,

  (a) the date and weight on the commercial motor vehicle's compliance label; or

  (b) where a commercial motor vehicle does not have a compliance label affixed or the label is illegible, a document from the vehicle's manufacturer that is carried by the driver and that references the vehicle's vehicle identification number and indicates its year of manufacture and gross vehicle weight rating.

(3) A commercial motor vehicle is exempt from subsection 68.1(1) of the Act if,

  (a) it is not equipped with an electronic control module capable of being programmed to limit vehicle speed;

  (b) it is engaged in providing relief in an emergency, being a situation or impending situation that constitutes a danger of major proportions to life, property or the environment, whether caused by forces of nature, an accident, an intentional act or otherwise; or

  (c) it is operated by or on behalf of a municipality, road authority, public utility or of the government of Ontario or of Canada while responding to a situation or impending situation that constitutes an imminent danger, though not one of major proportions, to life, property or the environment, whether caused by forces of nature, an accident, an intentional act or otherwise.

(4) A driver of a commercial motor vehicle is exempt from subsection 68.1(1) of the Act if the vehicle is leased for 30 days or less by an individual for the transportation of the goods kept for the individual's personal use.

14(1) The speed-limiting system of a commercial motor vehicle shall be properly set at a maximum speed of 105 kilometres per hour.

(2) A speed-limiting system is properly set for the purposes of subsection (1) if it prevents a driver, by means of accelerator application, from accelerating to or maintaining a speed greater than permitted under subsection (1).

(3) The maximum speed under subsection (1) shall be set by means of the electronic control module that limits the feed of fuel to the engine.

(4) A commercial motor vehicle is exempt from subsection (3) if it is equipped with an equally effective system, not dependent on the electronic control module, that allows limitation of vehicle speed, remotely or not, but does not allow the driver to deactivate or modify the system in Ontario so that it does not comply with subsections (1) and (2).

15(1) A speed-limiting system shall be in good working order.

(2) Without limiting the generality of subsection (1), all aspects of a commercial motor vehicle's computer system or systems, computer programs, components, equipment and connections that are capable of playing a role in preventing a driver from increasing the speed of a commercial motor vehicle beyond a specified value shall be in good working order.

16. A commercial motor vehicle's electronic control module shall contain information that accurately corresponds with any component or feature of the vehicle referred to in the module, including information regarding the tire rolling radius, axle gear ratio and transmission gear ratio.

17. The prescribed speed for the purposes of subsection 68.1(9) of the Act is 115 kilometres per hour.

18. The following devices are prescribed for the purposes of clause 68.1(3)(a) of the Act:

1. A device that causes inaccurate information to be transmitted to the electronic control module about a commercial motor vehicle's actual speed.

2. A device that causes inaccurate information to be sent to the electronic control module about the revolutions per minute of the engine.

Organization of Statutes and Regulations Online

In order to understand how to find sections of the HTA and the regulations made under its authority, we need to know how they are organized. Prior to 1990 in Ontario, the province revised and published a printed update of all statutes and regulations on a periodic basis, usually once every ten years. Since 1990, the province has stopped doing periodic printed revisions, and has put all statutes and regulations on its e-Laws website, where the latest and most up-to-date version can be accessed (see the HTA at <https://www.ontario.ca/laws/statute/90h08>).

While the printed versions of the **Revised Statutes of Ontario** and **Revised Regulations of Ontario** may have gone the way of the dodo, the statutory citation system used almost 30 years ago is still in use today. For example, the HTA is still cited as RSO 1990, c H.8, which is the short form for *Revised Statutes of Ontario* 1990, chapter H.8. An amendment to the HTA might be cited as 2009, c 4, which refers to an amending statute—in this case, one passed in the 2009 legislative session as the 4th statute of that session of the legislature. Similarly, statutes that have been passed as entirely new legislation since 1990 are cited by the year in which they became law and with the number indicating their place in the chronological list of statutes passed in that legislative session: for example, *Heritage Hunting and Fishing Act, 2002,* SO 2002, c 10.

The regulations citation system is similar. The regulation for seat belt assemblies under the HTA is cited as RRO 1990, Reg 613, meaning that it is the 613th regulation in the *Revised Regulations of Ontario* 1990. If this Regulation were amended after 1990 by a later

Revised Statutes of Ontario and Revised Regulations of Ontario the printed versions of the government of Ontario's revised statutes and revised regulations as of the date of publication. Statutes and regulations repealed since the last revision are removed from the current version, and amendments and new statutes are added. With the advent of the Internet, revisions are no longer published in books but are posted to the province's e-Laws online database for statutes and regulations at <https://www.ontario.ca/laws>.

regulation, that amending regulation might be cited as O Reg 236/09, meaning that it was the 236th Ontario regulation passed in 2009. An entirely new regulation passed after 1990 would be cited in the same way as an amended regulation.

Now that you know that you can find the most up-to-date versions of statutes and regulations on the e-Laws website, finding amendments will be easy. The information is posted quickly, putting the current law at your fingertips. In addition, if you want to see what the law *was* at a particular time or read through proposed or amended statutes and regulations, you can do that as well.

When you search for the current version of the HTA on the e-Laws website, you will get the 1990 revised version updated to include all amendments, up to the "e-Laws currency date," which is the last time the Act was updated. The HTA web page also shows the dates of and provides a link to past amendments to the Act. This information eliminates the need to look through paper statute books for amendments since 1990. It also allows you to update any printed version of the Act you might be using. The Act in its current form, including indications of amendments not yet proclaimed, is now all in one place, making finding the information you need much easier than before the law went online.

Finding regulations on the e-Laws website is also easy. When you find the statute you are looking for, if you select the "Regulations under this Act" tab at the top of the page, you will see a list of all the current regulations. By selecting a regulation, you will get the up-to-date text, including any amendments to that regulation. If you wish to check to see if a regulation has been revoked, you can do so by returning to the Act and selecting the "Revoked/spent regulations under this Act" tab.

Similarly, federal statutes no longer go through the revision process (the last print revision was in 1985). If you are looking for provisions of statutes, regulations, amendments, proposed legislation, previous versions of current legislation, and so on, they are available on the Justice Laws website maintained by the Department of Justice (<http://laws.justice.gc.ca>).[2]

Now that we have an idea of how statutes and regulations are organized, let us consider how we locate topics under the HTA and its regulations.

Using e-Laws

1. Go to the e-Laws website at <https://www.ontario.ca/laws>.

2. On the left side of the homepage, ensure that the "Browse" tab is activated and that "Consolidated law" and "Current" are selected. These are the default settings (see the figure here).

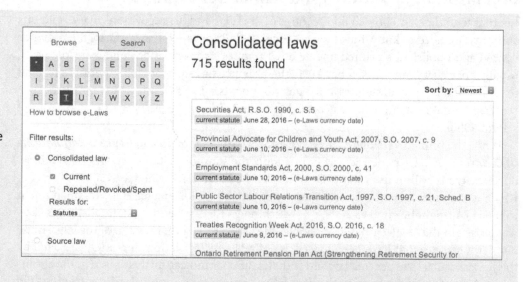

---

2 For more information on how to use the standard sources for finding and updating statutes and regulations, including electronic sources, see M Kerr, J Kurtz & A Blatt, *Legal Research: Step by Step*, 4th ed (Toronto: Emond Montgomery, 2015); and Mary Ann Kelly, "Legal Research: An Introduction" in L Olivo, ed, *Introduction to Law in Canada* (Toronto: Captus Press, 2014).

3. Under Browse, select the letter "H."

4. In the list of statutes, scroll down to the *Highway Traffic Act* and select it. The current version of the HTA will open, which includes a list of amendments passed but not yet in force (if any). See the figure here.

If you select the tab "Regulations under this Act," you will get a list of all of the regulations made pursuant to the HTA. From that list, you can open any of the HTA regulations.

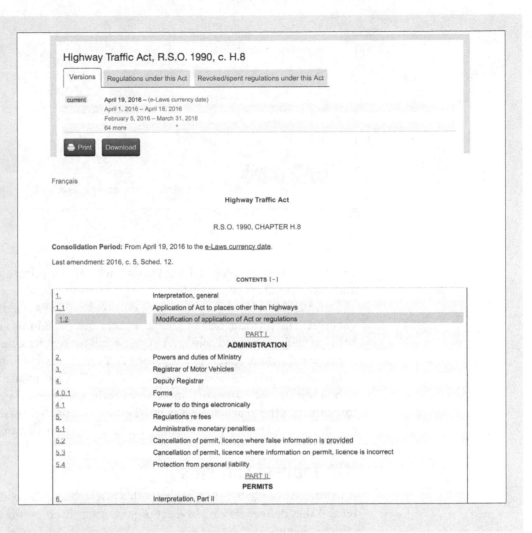

Locating Topics in the HTA and Its Regulations: The Use of a "Pocket Book" Consolidation on the Job

Police officers frequently use the HTA and need to be familiar with many parts of the Act and its regulations. As a result, a number of "pocket book" versions of the Act are available, and they include some or all of the Act's regulations, complete with a table of contents and a subject index (for example, MacBeth 2016, cited earlier; see Figures 1.1 and 1.2). The **consolidated** HTA is amended or revised as of the time of publication and includes regulations that are also up to date as of the time of publication. Consolidated versions of the HTA are published on an annual basis. Because police often still use and refer to these printed versions of the HTA, your instructor will specify which of the consolidated versions you should use.

If you are using a printed consolidated version, note the date to which it is current. In some circumstances, it may be necessary to update the statute or the regulations to be sure there have been no changes since the publication of the consolidated version you are using. This update is easy to do by visiting the e-Laws website and selecting the HTA link. On the opening page of the HTA, you will see a list indicating the dates of the most recent update both of the statute and the regulations, as well as previous updates (see the figure below).

consolidated statutes and regulations
the current version of statutes and regulations that includes all amendments and revisions made to the original content; the printed consolidated version is current as of the time of publication, whereas the online consolidated version includes the most recent amendments and revisions; Ontario's e-Laws website lists the latest consolidation date for any statute, along with all previous consolidations

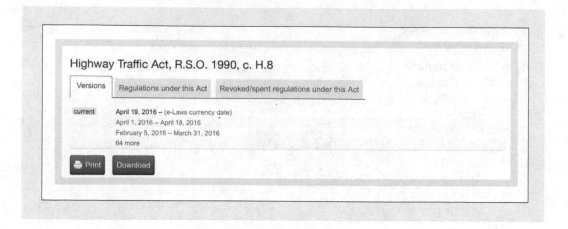

From there, you can pick up from the date where your printed version of the HTA left off, and note the subsequent updates.

In time, the printed versions of the consolidated HTA will likely be replaced by ebook versions. The introduction of ebook readers such as Kindle and the use of iPhones and iPads as well as onboard computer systems will make it feasible for officers to easily access the Internet, where statutes such as the HTA can be easily found in their current versions. While the printed consolidated versions of the HTA are updated annually, the HTA and its regulations may be amended more frequently, with several new provisions coming into force during the year between printed editions. For that reason, having ready access to e-versions of statutes and regulations is crucial to effective traffic enforcement.

HTA Table of Contents

A printed consolidated HTA begins with a brief table of contents (often simply titled "Contents") that defines its part-by-part organization. Each part is titled and lists the page on which it begins.

An excerpt from the table of contents for the e-Laws version of the HTA follows. The table of contents lists the part titles of the HTA as well as the section titles within each part and their section numbers. For instance, in the excerpt below, "Powers and duties of Ministry" is found in s 2 of part I, "Administration." Note that just the sections are listed, not the subsections, clauses, or subclauses. This means that the table of contents gives you a general overview of how the Act is organized, but it is only a partial aid in locating topics; it merely skims the surface. Note that in the excerpt below, the numbers in the right column refer to section numbers of the Act, not page numbers.

Excerpt: Table of Contents of the HTA (e-Laws)

PART I

ADMINISTRATION

2.	Powers and duties of Ministry
3.	Registrar of Motor Vehicles
4.	Deputy Registrar
4.0.1	Forms
4.1	Power to do things electronically
5.	Regulations re fees

HTA Index

A more specific aid is the index at the back of MacBeth 2016, beginning on page 495. This index to the Act is a more detailed list of subjects by pointer words, which are arranged alphabetically by subject. For example, one set of pointer words is "Licence Plates." Listed alphabetically under this heading are subheadings that are more specific pointer words, along with the section and subsection where more specific topics can be located. For example, under the entry "Licence Plates," you will find the subheading "validation sticker," with several subtopics under it, including "deface, alter, misuse S-12, 14" and "location on plate R-628 9(1)."

> **Excerpt from the HTA Index (MacBeth 2016)**
>
> Licence Plates
>
> ...
>
>   validation sticker
>   deface, alter, misuse S-12, 14
>   issue validation by Ministry S-7(7)
>   location on plate R-628 9(1)
>   must have S-7(1)

The consolidated index also identifies any relevant regulation that is associated with a section of the HTA. Finding relevant regulations is discussed in more detail below.

Abbreviated Forms for HTA Offences

The Ontario *Provincial Offences Act* makes writing HTA tickets easier for an officer by permitting the offence to be described by section number and an appropriate abbreviated description. This format is referred to as the "abbreviated form" or "short form" of the offence.

The abbreviated forms can also be used like an index or table of contents to quickly find an offence, together with its section number.

The abbreviated forms are authorized by the *Provincial Offences Act*, and are found in Schedule 43 (*Highway Traffic Act*) to RRO 1990, Reg 950, *Proceedings Commenced by Certificate of Offence*. You can look up this Act and schedule on the e-Laws website and download the abbreviated forms; MacBeth and other publishers also produce pocket book versions that officers can carry and use.

> **Examples of Abbreviated Forms Applicable to the HTA**
>
> | | |
> |---|---|
> | Fail to notify change of name | s 9(2) |
> | Red light—fail to stop | s 144(18) |
> | Follow too closely | s 158(1) |

Table of Contents for the HTA Regulations

The table of contents for the HTA regulations in a consolidated version of the HTA usually follows the main body of the Act. For example, in MacBeth 2016, the table of contents for the regulations is found on page 245. It consists of the titles of all HTA regulations, and it is arranged alphabetically like an index, but is much shorter.

If a topic covered by the Act is very detailed, there may be a regulation that also discusses it. For example, you stop a motorcycle operator who is wearing an odd-looking piece of headgear that the operator claims is a regulation helmet. You might start looking for information on motorcycle helmets that meet required legal specifications. You would find that this topic is dealt with under s 104(1) of the Act, and by scanning the table of contents for the regulations, you would find that this topic is also dealt with under Regulation 610.

Excerpt from the Table of Contents for the HTA Regulations (MacBeth 2016, p. 245)

Regulations under the Highway Traffic Act

...

In this example, Regulation 610 of the *Revised Regulations of Ontario* 1990 is found on page 265 of the consolidated version of the HTA.

HTA General Regulation

If a topic of fine detail is not described in the table of contents for the regulations, it may be covered in the *General* regulation (MacBeth 2016, page 256). The *General* regulation (RRO 1990, Reg 596, as amended by O Regs 537/97 and 213/03) is a mix of miscellaneous topics. For example, if you were searching for the regulation that covers the amount of damage to property that requires the police to complete a motor vehicle collision report, you would not find it described in the table of contents for the regulations. However, if you turned to the page on which the *General* regulation is found and scanned the headings, you would find the heading "Damage to Property Accident Report."[3]

Example of a Provision in the General Regulation

11. For the purpose of subsection 199(1) of the Act, the prescribed amount for damage to property is $2,000.

Finding Regulations in the Index

If you look up a more detailed topic in the index, you will find references not only to sections of the Act, but also to the details set out in a relevant regulation that deals with the topic covered by the section of the Act. For example, in MacBeth, if you look up "Vehicle, Dealers-Garages-Wreckers" and then the subtopic "engine serial number" in the index, you are referred to both s 60(3) of the Act and Regulation 595(4). Section 60(3) sets up a general prohibition on altering engine serial numbers, while Regulation 595(4) sets out specific rules for garages to maintain a record of serial numbers. For another example, see "Speedometer" in Figure 1.1.

---

3 Dollar amounts are often described in regulations rather than in the statute because regulations can be quickly changed to reflect the impact of inflation.

Finding a Topic in a Consolidated HTA

To find a topic in your consolidated HTA, follow these steps:

1. If your topic is general, check the detailed table of contents, which lists general topics covered by the Act.

2. If you cannot find your topic, check the headings in the index, which provides a more detailed list of topics.

3. If your topic is very detailed, also check the table of contents for the regulations.

4. If you cannot find your topic in the table of contents for the regulations, turn to the *General* regulation and look for it in the section headings.

5. If you cannot find your topic in the *General* regulation, check the headings and sub-headings in the index for topics that refer you to specific sections of the regulations. Also check the "definitions" at the beginning of each part. For example, the definition of "full trailer" appears in part VII, Load and Dimensions, s 108 of the HTA.

To make it easier to look things up in your copy of the consolidated HTA, place a sticky note at the beginning of the table of contents, the index, the table of contents for the regulations, and the *General* regulation.

Correctly Identifying or Citing Sections of Acts and Regulations

Once you have found a section of a statute or regulation, you have to know how to identify or cite the section. You will note in your consolidated HTA that every section has a numeric identification system so that every rule can be identified by a series of numbers and letters.

Care should be taken in recording the correct alphanumeric code, particularly for offences. If you make an error in recording the code for an offence against a defendant so that it describes an offence that the defendant did *not* commit, the offence may not be processed by the court office; or, if it reaches trial, it may be dismissed.

For example, if you stop a motorist whose car does not display licence plates, you will probably wish to charge the motorist with failing to display licence plates under s 7(1)(b)(i). However, if in issuing the ticket you accidentally write s 7(1)(b)(ii), you will have charged the motorist with the offence of failing to have historic licence plates on his or her vehicle, which is not the proper offence, and the charge, as recorded, may be dismissed.

PROFESSIONAL PRACTICE

Check Your Tickets and Summonses

Always review any submitted documentation, including provincial offence tickets or summonses. If you fill them out incorrectly, your paperwork may cause you to lose cases in court. Moreover, from a professional standpoint, incorrect paperwork points to a lower level of competency and a lack of professionalism that will reflect negatively on you as well as your police service. Keep in mind that you are constantly being evaluated by supervisors.

Accountability is critical for an officer; when giving testimony, whether in traffic court or criminal court, an officer has only his or her credibility to rely on. Once credibility is lost, it is difficult—and in some cases, impossible—to regain.

FIGURE 1.1 Finding Regulations in the Index

S *Highway Traffic Act*

540

FIGURE 1.2 Components of the Highway Traffic Act

The Ontario Highway Traffic Act

Cross Referenced to

Selected Regulations

2016 Edition

MacBeth Publishing Ltd.

MACBETH@MACBETHBOOKS.COM

1

FIGURE 1.2 Components of the Highway Traffic Act *continued*

Highway Traffic Act

Contents

3

FIGURE 1.2 Components of the Highway Traffic Act *continued*

Regulations

under the Highway Traffic Act

[This is page 245 of MacBeth's *The Ontario Highway Traffic Act, 2016.*]

FIGURE 1.2 **Components of the Highway Traffic Act** *concluded*

Highway Traffic Act   A

Index

A

Abandoned vehicle
    abandoned or unplated S-170(7) 196
    abandoned or unplated S-221 243
    cars stored, parked S-60(4) 108
Accessible Parking
    Courts to report conviction S-210(4) 234
    fictitious-altered-fraudulently obtained S-27 44
    permit, regulation S-30 45
Accessible Parking Permit
    accessible parking rules S-26 to 29 44
Accident
    amount of damage to report 259
    amount of damage to report S-199 219
    amount of damage to report S-201 222
    claims fund, mentioned S-198(2) 216
    damage claim, time limit S-206 233
    onus on driver or owner, negligence S-193 213
    provide assistance, information, remain S-200 222
    recovery from injuries, penalties no bar S-209 234
    report completion, police S-205 224
    reports by;
        blank forms S-205 224
        charitable institutions S-202(2) 222
        Crown Attorneys S-202 222
        driver, passengers, damage amount R-596-11 259
        driver, passengers S-201 222
        driver S-199 219
        hospital and other officials S-202 222
        Police S-199 to 202 219
Address
    driver's licence, change R-340/94-33 416
    notice of change, CVOR certificate S-18 39
    notice of change, owner, lessee S-9(2-4) 32
    provide at accident S-200 222
    provide to Police S-33 49
    provide to police S-218 241
Affidavits
    administration R-7(23) 24
    false statement, make in S-9(1) 32

495

General Considerations in Interpreting and Applying the Acts and the Regulations

Some offences under the HTA can be committed anywhere, but others can only be committed on a highway. Offences can be committed in some cases by anyone, but in others only by a driver, and still others only by an owner (and some may be committed by drivers and owners).

For example, s 32(1) of the HTA states the following:

> No person shall drive a motor vehicle on a highway unless the motor vehicle is within a class of motor vehicles in respect of which the person holds a driver's licence issued to him or her under this Act.

It is clear that everyone who drives a motor vehicle on a public highway must be properly licensed. So, "anyone" may commit the offence described in s 32(1) HTA, but only when driving on a highway. If you do not have a licence but wish to drive a car on private property, you may do so without violating the HTA.

CHAPTER SUMMARY

The law governing motor vehicles in Ontario is found in various pieces of legislation, including the Ontario *Highway Traffic Act*, the *Criminal Code* of Canada, and a variety of other federal laws, some of which overlap with or complement provincial rules. While a statute such as the HTA sets out general legal principles, regulations provide the related technical details; for example, the HTA authorizes the demerit point system, while Regulation 339/94 sets out how many points are deducted for each offence.

The HTA and its associated regulations may be found in pocket book consolidated versions of the Act and regulations, which officers use on the job, or they may be accessed online at the Ontario e-Laws website. If you are using a consolidated version, you must update the statute and regulations to make sure that there have been no changes since the publication of the version you are using; all amendments are reflected on the e-Laws website, allowing you to access current laws quickly and easily.

You must know how to locate a topic (for example, obstruction of licence plates) in a consolidated HTA, and you must *always* ensure that you record the section and subsection numbers and letters accurately when recording the code for an offence on a ticket. Failure to do so may result in the offence not being processed by the court, or, if it reaches trial, may result in the charge being dismissed.

ON THE SCENE

Abandoned Vehicle on Roadway

Scenario

On [use today's date and time: DD/MM/YYYY at HR:MIN a.m./p.m.], Constable (Cst.) Andrew Schmidt, Badge #313, of the London Police Service, responded to 154 Green Street, London, Ontario as a result of two complaints that police dispatch had received regarding a vehicle that was blocking traffic on the roadway. Upon arrival, the officer noted a brown-coloured Dodge Charger, Ontario Licence ABCD123 parked on the eastbound lane of Green Street and affecting eastbound traffic flow.

Cst. Schmidt advised dispatch of the licence plate number of the vehicle and the location of the traffic stop. Cst. Schmidt, upon checking the vehicle, noted that there was no driver present nor was anyone standing near the vehicle. The vehicle was hindering eastbound traffic and posed a public danger.

What Actions Should the Officer Take?

1. Should Cst. Schmidt seize the vehicle? What is the Act/section that will authorize him to seize the vehicle?

2. Should Cst. Schmidt have dispatch call the owner and wait until he or she arrives, or should he have the vehicle towed and have dispatch notify the registered owner why and where the vehicle was towed? Should he leave the scene knowing that the tow truck will come? What would be the possible consequences of such a decision? Should he remain until the tow truck responds and then leave?

3. What should Cst. Schmidt do if, while waiting for the tow truck, dispatch advises patrol units that a bank robbery has just occurred a block away? What would be the most responsible course of action? Should he advise dispatch that he is responding? Explain your answer.

KEY TERMS

consolidated statutes and regulations, 9

regulations, 4

Revised Statutes of Ontario and *Revised Regulations of Ontario*, 7

WEBSITES

- Province of Ontario e-Laws site for all statutes and regulations <https://www.ontario.ca/laws>
- How to use the province of Ontario e-Laws site <https://www.ontario.ca/laws/about-e-laws>
- Government of Canada site for federal statutes and regulations <http://laws.justice.gc.ca/eng>

REVIEW QUESTIONS

True or False?

In the space provided next to each statement, place a "T" if the statement is true or an "F" if it is false.

1. Statutes are federal laws, and regulations are provincial laws.   _____

2. Statutes provide details that are not included in the regulations.   _____

3. An "abbreviated form" or "short form" of an offence is the form used for writing a ticket.   _____

4. The *General* regulation to the *Highway Traffic Act* is a mix of miscellaneous topics.   _____

5. If an officer who has stopped a car with licence plates that are covered up is distracted by the defendant and mistakenly writes "s 7(1)(b)(ii)" on a ticket instead of "s 7(1)(b)(i)," the charge may be dismissed.   _____

6. The *Highway Traffic Act* applies equally to private and public roads.   _____

Short Answer

Briefly answer the following questions.

1. **a.** What are the places to search for a particular topic such as speed-measuring warning devices in a consolidated *Highway Traffic Act*?

   b. What are the best places to search for information about speed-measuring warning devices if you are using the e-Laws version of the HTA?

2. Using the HTA index and table of contents, find all the statute sections and regulations dealing with the following:

   a. automobile trailers

   b. fines for speeding offences

   c. motorcycle helmets

   d. lighting on bicycles

3. The HTA, RSO 1990 version is updated in the province's online database, e-Laws. Why is it easier to check amendments in e-Laws than in the updated printed versions? What are some other benefits of the e-Laws website?

The Highway Traffic Act: Defining Terms

2

LEARNING OUTCOMES

After completing this chapter, you should be able to:

- Distinguish between the various definitions of "vehicle" in the Ontario *Highway Traffic Act* (HTA) and understand the reasons for the variations in the definitions.

- Understand the definitions of "highway," "roadway," and related terms used in the HTA and the reasons for those definitions.

- Understand the definitions of "stopping," "standing," and "parking" in the HTA.

- Appreciate that although the definitions discussed in this chapter are key definitions, there are others in the HTA that you will need to look up from time to time.

Introduction

This chapter discusses some key definitions used in the Ontario *Highway Traffic Act* (HTA). These definitions include conveyances (modes of transportation) of various kinds, such as

- vehicle (s 1);
- motor vehicle (s 1);
- commercial motor vehicle (s 1);
- trailer (s 1);
- bus (s 1); and
- school bus (s 175(1) and RRO 1990, O Reg 612).

Some definitions are about geographical elements over which conveyances travel, such as

- crosswalk (s 1);
- highway (s 1);
- intersection (s 1);
- King's Highway (s 1);
- pedestrian crossover (s 1); and
- roadway (s 1).

Other definitions are about stopping conveyances on highways, such as

- parking (s 1);
- standing (s 1); and
- stopping (s 1).

Highway Traffic Act Definitions

Vehicle, Section 1

The definition of **vehicle** includes motor vehicles, such as cars, trucks, trailers, farm tractors, and road-building machines (for example, steam rollers and graders). The definition also includes vehicles that operate by any other form of power, including muscular power, such as bicycles and horse-drawn carriages. In the case of *R v Yick* ([2004] OJ No 4166 (QL) (Prov Ct)), the Ontario Provincial Court found that a person on the roadway using Rollerblades was operating a vehicle, as defined in the HTA, and could be convicted of failing to stop at a stop sign. The definition of "vehicle" is used in connection with the "rules of the road" and is very broad, so that drivers of a wide variety of vehicles can be made subject to the rules of the road.

Motor Vehicle, Section 1

The definition of **motor vehicle** includes automobiles, snowmobiles, street cars, motor-assisted bicycles (mopeds), and motorcycles (which includes motor scooters), unless otherwise indicated in the HTA. While the definition includes motorized bicycles, *power-assisted* bicycles are classed with bicycles, generally, as vehicles. A power-assisted bicycle has a rechargeable, battery-run electric motor that assists the rider to pedal up steep grades, but does not become a sole source of power. Power-assisted bicycles are used in public bike

vehicle
includes a motor vehicle, trailer, traction engine, farm tractor, road-building machine, bicycle, snowmobile, street car, or any vehicle drawn, propelled, or driven by any kind of power, including muscular power

motor vehicle
includes an automobile, a motor-assisted bicycle (moped), or a motorcycle (including a motor scooter), unless otherwise indicated in the HTA, as well as any other vehicle propelled by anything other than muscular power; farm tractors, self-propelled implements of husbandry (such as reapers and combines), road-building machinery, and traction engines are not considered motor vehicles

rental programs in many European cities, and have been introduced in bike rental schemes in some urban areas in Canada. The key to treating power-assisted bicycles as vehicles rather than as motor vehicles is that the bicycle can be pedaled using muscular power, a point made clear by the Ontario Court of Appeal in the case of *R v Pizzacalla* (2014 ONCA 706). In this case, what appeared to be a power-assisted bike with pedals was classed as a motor vehicle because the pedals, although attached, were unusable. Also in this case, because Mr. Pizzacalla was found to be driving a motor vehicle rather than a vehicle, and as he had been disqualified from driving a motor vehicle for 3 years, he could be charged with driving while disqualified under s 259(1) of the *Criminal Code* (CC). If the bike had been merely power-assisted and, therefore, classed as a vehicle, he could have driven it about all he liked, whether he had a valid driver's licence or not.

Although the definition of "motor vehicle" includes other vehicles propelled by anything other than muscular power, it does not include the following:

- **f**arm tractors,
- self-propelled **i**mplements of husbandry (SPIH) (farm equipment such as reapers and combines),
- **r**oad-building machinery, and
- **t**raction engines (tractors).

You can remember which vehicles are excluded by using the mnemonic device "firt."

The definition of "motor vehicle," with the "firt" exclusions, is generally used for rules regarding vehicle permits, driver's licences, and equipment requirements under the HTA. It is narrower and more restrictive than the definition of "vehicle." The "firt" exclusions are regulated under other legislation, or are left unregulated.

Commercial Motor Vehicle, Section 1

A commercial motor vehicle is a vehicle that has a truck or delivery body attached to it. "Delivery body" is not defined by the HTA, but it can be assumed that it is a vehicle primarily for carrying cargo or objects rather than people. Other vehicles specifically included in the definition are as follows:

- ambulances,
- hearses,
- fire apparatus,
- buses, and
- tractors used for hauling on highways.

The definition of "commercial motor vehicle" is not based on the purpose or function of the vehicle, but on its structure and physical description. Therefore, if someone uses a hearse as a domestic family vehicle, it is still defined as a commercial vehicle because of its structure and physical description. This definition is used in the HTA to describe the type of motor vehicle that requires commercial motor vehicle licence plates. Commercial plates have a different colour (black, rather than blue, on a white background) and the number sequencing is different from that for passenger motor vehicles. With respect to vans, if there is a seating capacity of four or more, the van is considered a passenger motor vehicle; if there are fewer than four seats, the van is considered a commercial motor vehicle. If a van has more than ten seats and is used for transporting people, it is considered a commercial vehicle, but will also be defined as a bus.

Trailer, Section 1

A trailer is any vehicle drawn on a highway by a motor vehicle, but it excludes the following:

- a **m**otor vehicle being towed,
- a **m**obile home designed and used as a residence or working accommodation that exceeds 2.6 m in width *or* 11 m in length,
- an **i**mplement of husbandry (for example, a hay wagon),
- a **s**ide car on a motorcycle, and
- any device or apparatus not designed to **t**ransport persons or property and that is temporarily drawn on a highway (for example, a portable cement mixer).

You can remember which vehicles are excluded by using the mnemonic device "mmist."

The definition of "trailer" describes vehicles that require trailer plates. Such vehicles must be pulled by a motor vehicle and pulled on a highway. If the vehicle does not fit the definition or is one of the exceptions, it does not require trailer plates.

Bus, Section 1

A bus is a motor vehicle designed and used for carrying ten or more passengers. This definition is used for the purpose of determining who must have a bus driver's licence.

School Bus, Section 175(1) of the HTA, and O Reg 612

As in the definition of "bus," the definition of "school bus" has two parts: a definition by physical description and a definition by use. A school bus is chrome yellow in colour. It has the words "SCHOOL BUS" marked on the front and rear and the words "DO NOT PASS WHEN SIGNALS FLASHING" on the rear. It also has red flashing lights at the front and rear. A school bus is used for transporting children anywhere for any reason, or transporting developmentally handicapped adults to or from a training centre. Buses that fit this definition must meet the safety equipment requirements and the rules for operation of safety equipment for the loading or discharging of passengers, and drivers must meet licensing requirements specific to school buses.

Highway, Section 1

road allowance
a continuous strip of land dedicated for the location of a public highway, usually one chain (66 feet) wide; the actual roadway may be considerably narrower, but the whole width of the road allowance constitutes the highway, within the meaning of the HTA

chain
a surveyor's measure, consisting of a chain or line that is 66 feet long

The term "highway" is described very broadly and includes a common and public highway, street, avenue, parkway, driveway, square, place, bridge, viaduct, or trestle that is intended for or used by anyone to pass over in a vehicle. It includes not only the space over which the vehicle moves, but also the land on either side of the roadway between the lateral property lines. In many parts of the province, **road allowances** that constitute the highway are usually one **chain** (66 feet) wide (33 feet on either side of the centre of the roadway). In some cases, where the roadway is narrower than the road allowance, private property owners may have encroached on the highway where it is not clearly delineated, by planting lawns or shrubs on what is technically the road allowance and part of the highway.

For practical reasons, on city streets, the highway includes the sidewalks on either side or, if there is no sidewalk, the shoulder or verge of the road up to the property line of properties adjacent to the highway. The illustrations in Figure 2.1 will help you see that the highway consists of more than just the roadway itself.

FIGURE 2.1 Highways

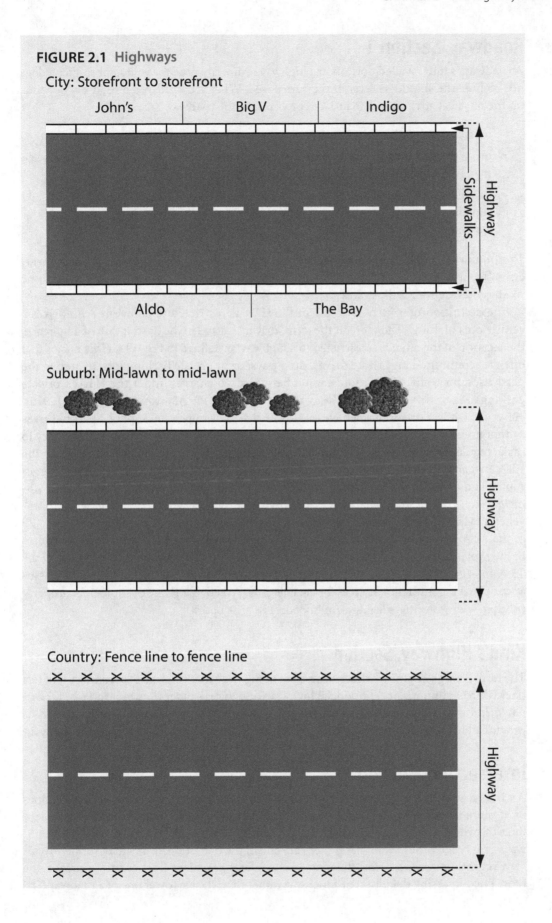

Roadway, Section 1

A roadway is the travelled portion of a highway ordinarily used for vehicular traffic; it does not include the shoulders, even if they are paved. What is considered a roadway depends on the physical attributes of the road. For example, the roadway is

- on a city street, the paved portion between the curbs on either side;
- on a street where there is no curb, the paved portion between the edges of the pavement on either side of the travelled portion; and
- on a gravel or snow-covered road, the travelled portion (note that this kind of road can change width, depending on how much of the right of way is gravelled or cleared of snow).

To summarize, a roadway is the travelled part of a highway. Where there are median dividers and exit and entrance ramps, a highway, like Highway 401, can include more than one roadway, as Figure 2.2 illustrates.

The definition of a "driver" in s 1 of the HTA is restricted to someone who drives a vehicle on a highway. Therefore, if the term "driver" is used in the description of an offence, the location of the offence is restricted to a highway, as defined in the HTA. This means that offences committed on private drives, driveways, or in private parking lots, including the parts used for traffic circulation, cannot be subject to charges under the HTA; a private parking area or drive is not a highway under the HTA (*R v Mansour*, [1979] 2 SCR 916). However, while a driver of a vehicle on private drives or in private or public parking areas cannot normally be charged under the HTA, s 1.1 of the HTA now permits the Ministry to make regulations providing that the HTA, or a section of it, or a regulation made under the HTA, can apply to a specified place (or classes of places) that is not a highway. Also, charges can be laid under other legislation. For example, under section 425(1) of the Ontario *Municipal Act, 2001*, a municipality may pass bylaws that provide that a person who contravenes a bylaw of the municipality passed under this Act is guilty of an offence. Section 429 of the Act permits the municipality to enforce bylaws with fines, following the procedures in the *Provincial Offences Act*. An example of the exercise of this power may be found in the *Toronto Municipal Code*, 2015, c 915, article 3, section 915-5(B), which allows for the issuance of parking infraction notices for cars illegally parked on private or municipal property (<http://www.toronto.ca/legdocs/municode/1184_915.pdf>).

King's Highway, Section 1

The term "King's Highway" describes a class of highway that consists of secondary and tertiary (third in importance) provincial highways designated under the Ontario *Public Transportation and Highway Improvement Act*. These highways are commonly known as provincial highways and are identified by numbered route signs posted along the highway.

Intersection, Section 1

An intersection is the area of the highway that falls within the extension of the curb lines or, if there is no curb, it is the area that falls within the extension of the lateral boundary lines of two or more highways that join one another at an angle, whether or not the highways cross each other. Note that if there are curbs, the definition seems to describe a roadway, yet if there are no curbs, the reference to lateral boundary lines seems to suggest the more encompassing definition of a highway rather than the narrower one of a roadway. The

FIGURE 2.2 Highway with Two Roadways

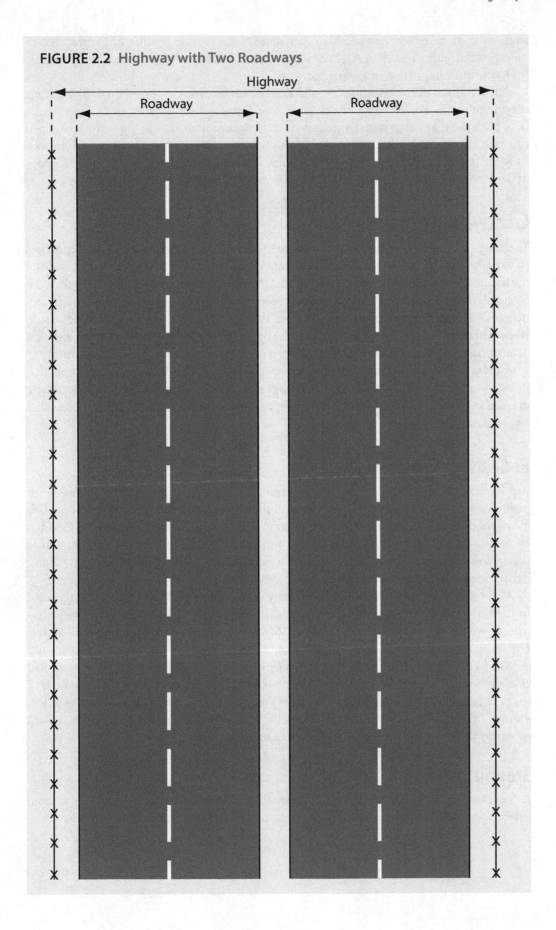

angle of an intersection can be oblique or acute (as in the top portion of Figure 2.3), although we usually think of intersections as two highways crossing each other at right angles (as in the bottom portion of Figure 2.3).

The definition of "intersection" provides an important reference point for defining some driving offences. For example, the definition of "intersection" is invoked to describe the legal placement of a stop sign. Stop signs used in plaza or mall exits to highways are on private property and are, therefore, probably only advisory. Charges might not be laid successfully for failing to stop at such signs, although as noted previously, s 1.1 of the HTA does make it possible to have provisions of the HTA apply in places other than highways.

Crosswalk, Section 1

There are two kinds of crosswalks: marked crosswalks and unmarked crosswalks. Unmarked crosswalks are defined as that part of a roadway at an intersection that forms the area within the boundary created by the connection of the lateral lines of the sidewalks on opposite sides of the highway. More simply, an unmarked crosswalk exists only where there is an intersection with sidewalks on opposite sides; one of the sidewalks, if it were to continue, would cross the road to meet another sidewalk on the opposite side (see Figure 2.4). This definition determines the place at an intersection where a pedestrian may safely cross the highway.

A marked crosswalk is any portion of a roadway, at an intersection or elsewhere, distinctly set out for pedestrian crossing by signs or markings on the roadway. Because a marked crosswalk can be posted at places other than intersections, the law requires that crosswalks be marked (see Figure 2.5).

Pedestrian Crossover, Section 1

A pedestrian crossover is any portion of a roadway designated by a municipal bylaw for pedestrian crossing by signs on the highway and by lines or other markings on the surface of the roadway, as prescribed by the regulations. This type of crossing is generally found in large cities, and there are prescribed stopping and passing requirements with respect to these crossovers that do not apply to ordinary crosswalks. Usually, crossovers have signs, lights, or both suspended over the roadway, although these are not required by law.

A pedestrian crossover may be found at any point on any roadway and is distinguished from a crosswalk by having overhead, illuminated signs with special markings, where pedestrians have the right to cross the road. In 2016, ss 140 and 176 of the *Transportation Statute Law Amendment Act (Making Ontario's Roads Safer)* made it an offence for drivers and cyclists to drive through a pedestrian crossover or school crossing until all pedestrians had cleared the crossover. Previously, it was permissible to proceed if the pedestrian was clear of the vehicle. The rationale behind the change in the law is to ensure that all drivers have a clear view of the entire crossover. The change in the law follows a recommendation in a 2012 report by the Ontario Coroner's Office on pedestrian road fatalities.

Stopping, Section 1

A "no stopping" area on a roadway indicates that a vehicle may not stop for any reason, except to avoid traffic or when required by the police, traffic signs, or traffic signals.

FIGURE 2.3 **Intersections**

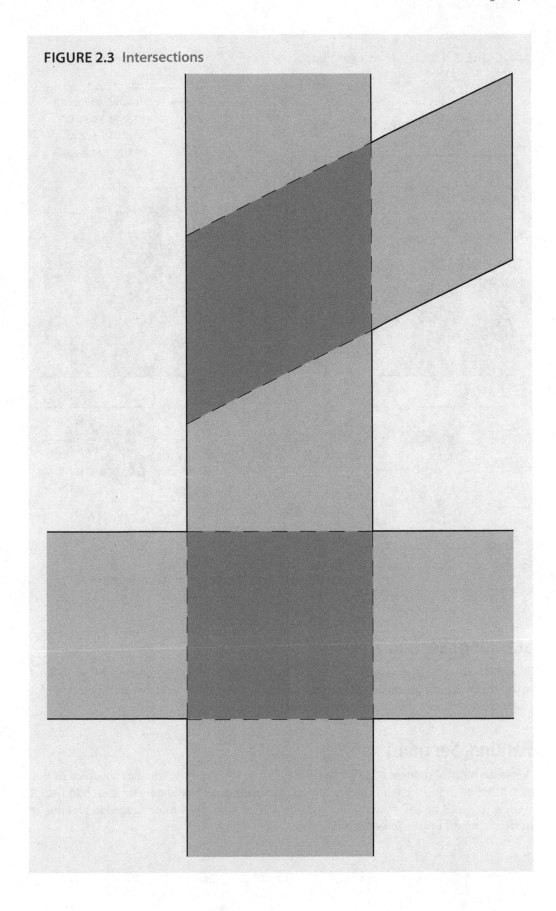

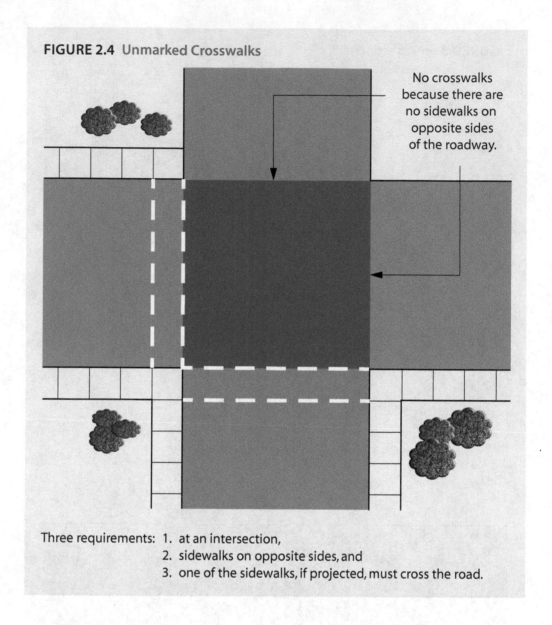

FIGURE 2.4 Unmarked Crosswalks

No crosswalks because there are no sidewalks on opposite sides of the roadway.

Three requirements: 1. at an intersection,
2. sidewalks on opposite sides, and
3. one of the sidewalks, if projected, must cross the road.

Standing, Section 1

A "no standing" sign means that a vehicle may not stop, except while engaged in picking up or dropping off passengers. Standing does not mean that a vehicle can stay to wait for passengers who are going to be picked up or dropped off.

Parking, Section 1

A "no parking" sign means that a vehicle may not be left standing, whether occupied or not, except when standing temporarily to pick up or drop off passengers or merchandise. A vehicle may not be left standing in a "no parking" area except while engaged in picking up or dropping off passengers or merchandise.

FIGURE 2.5 Marked Crosswalks

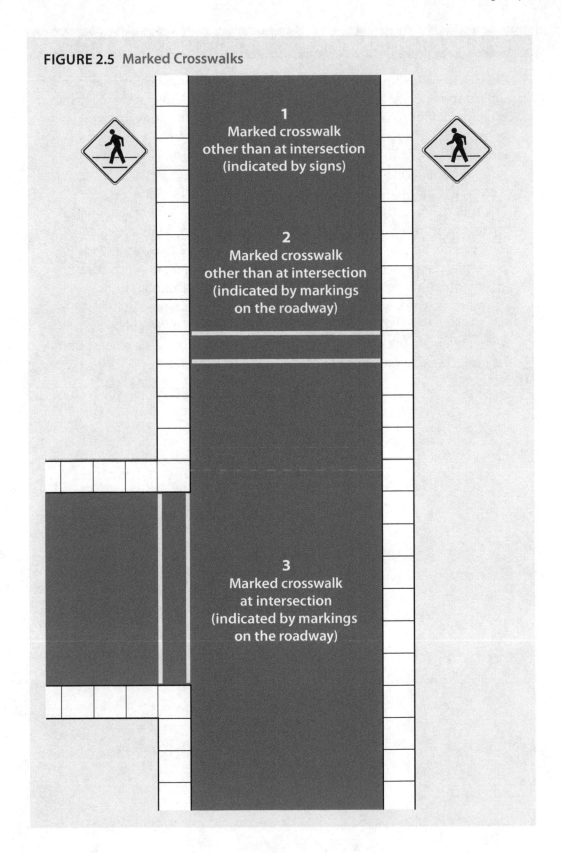

CHAPTER SUMMARY

The HTA includes a number of basic terms and definitions that you need to understand and apply to driving and permit offences. Some of these relate to defining different kinds of conveyances—namely, the general term "vehicle," and its subcategories (that is, "motor vehicle," "commercial motor vehicle," "trailer," "bus," and "school bus"). The division of "vehicle" into subcategories is generally related to operator licensing requirements and, in the case of commercial vehicles and buses, to equipment requirements.

Other definitions in the HTA relate to geographical elements over which conveyances travel—namely, the general term "highway" and its related components ("roadway," "King's Highway," "intersection," "crosswalk," and "pedestrian crossover"). Still others cover the various ways in which conveyances stop on highways ("stopping," "standing," and "parking").

You must know the definitions for these terms as provided in the HTA, including any exceptions. These terms provide the necessary context for driving offences and collision investigation that concern police officers, and they will be explored in greater detail throughout this book.

ON THE SCENE

Driving a Riding Mower on a Roadway

Scenario

Constable (Cst.) Charlene Smith, Badge #127, of the London Police Service, Ontario, is on routine patrol [use today's date and time: DD/MM/YYYY at HR:MIN a.m./p.m.] on John Street in London, Ontario.

   Mr. Duff McDuff, age 75, has purchased a brand new 18 HP John Deere riding mower. After mowing his lawn, he decides to go for a ride through town. McDuff proceeds northbound on John Street and carefully drives close to the curb. People are driving by, honking and waving at McDuff. McDuff approaches the T intersection of John Street and Edward Street. McDuff, while making his right or eastbound turn onto Edward Street, looks up and down Edward Street and observes no other traffic. There is a stop sign on John Street at its intersection with Edward Street, but McDuff does not slow down; he makes a manual right-hand turn signal and proceeds onto Edward Street. No sooner has McDuff turned the corner when he hears a short "blast" from a police siren and pulls onto the south sidewalk. McDuff becomes irate that he has been stopped and lets Cst. Smith verbally "have it." He tells her that he has done nothing wrong, that she is wasting her time, that she should be going after "real crooks," and that she should go and have some more coffee at the local restaurant. When Cst. Smith asks him to identify himself, McDuff refuses to tell her who he is.

What Actions Should the Officer Take?

1. McDuff is visibly upset. What should Cst. Smith do?

2. What offence(s), if any, has McDuff committed?

3. Consider the attitude of McDuff toward Cst. Smith. Does that make a difference in laying a charge? Should it?

4. Can Cst. Smith arrest McDuff? If yes, on what grounds? What is the charge(s)?

5. What if McDuff does not have a proper driver's licence?

6. Is there any legal obligation on Cst. Smith's part to allow McDuff to drive home? Would she have grounds to tow the riding mower?

KEY TERMS

chain, 26

motor vehicle, 24

road allowance, 26

vehicle, 24

CASES AND WEBSITES

- *R v Mansour*, [1979] 2 SCR 916
- *R v Pizzacalla*, 2014 ONCA 706
- *R v Yick*, [2004] OJ No 4166 (QL) (Prov Ct)
- Pedestrian road safety information, online: <http://www.mto.govon.ca/english/safety/pedestrian-safety.shtml>
- *Toronto Municipal Code*, c 915, online: <http://www.toronto.ca/legdocs/municode/1184_915.pdf>

REVIEW QUESTIONS

True or False?

In the space provided next to each statement, place a "T" if the statement is true or an "F" if the statement is false.

Under the HTA:

1. A roadway includes shoulders. _____

2. A bicycle is a vehicle. _____

3. A self-propelled farm harvester is a motor vehicle as defined in the HTA. _____

4. A manure spreader, which is drawn along a highway by a truck, is a trailer. _____

5. The only exception to prohibited parking is for picking up or dropping off passengers. _____

6. A streetcar is a motor vehicle. _____

7. A portable cement mixer, which is pulled by a dump truck, is a trailer. _____

8. A road grader is not a motor vehicle. _____

9. When a motor vehicle with a designed seating capacity of 14 people is carrying 7 people, the motor vehicle is considered a bus as defined in the HTA. _____

10. In a residential area, the boulevard and sidewalk on either side of the roadway are considered part of the highway. _____

11. A compressor, which is pulled by a half-ton truck, is a trailer. _____

12. A highway is all the area between the lateral property lines of the road allowance. _____

13. A motorcycle, a motor-assisted bicycle, a motor home, and a self-propelled cement truck are all motor vehicles as defined in the HTA. _____

14. An exception to prohibited stopping is the temporary loading or unloading of cargo. _____

15. A pedestrian crossover is only required to be designated by signs and a bylaw to be lawful. _____

16. A chrome-yellow bus with the words "SCHOOL BUS" on the front and rear and "DO NOT PASS WHEN SIGNALS FLASHING" on the rear that is used for transporting a children's hockey team to a weekend tournament is a school bus. _____

17. A crosswalk must be indicated by lines painted on the roadway. _____

18. A driver is permitted to discharge or pick up passengers in a "no stopping" zone. _____

Short Answer

Briefly answer the following questions.

1. How does a marked crosswalk differ from an unmarked crosswalk, and how do both differ from a pedestrian crossover?

2. List four vehicles with motors that are excluded from the HTA definition of "motor vehicle."

3. Can you be charged under the HTA for driving 80 km/h in the traffic circulation area of a private parking area in a plaza? Why or why not?

4. What is the difference between a highway and a roadway under the HTA?

5. If a half-ton truck is used only for personal use, can it be classed as a passenger motor vehicle rather than a truck?

6. What towed vehicles are excluded from the definition of "trailer" in the HTA?

7. Is a trailer that is pulled by a bicycle considered a trailer within the meaning of the HTA? Explain.

8. Can an unmarked crosswalk be located on a highway, 250 m from an intersection? Explain.

9. Is a highway always the same width as a road allowance? Explain.

10. Harry is driving northbound, approaching a crossover where the overhead lights are flashing, indicating a pedestrian is crossing. He sees the pedestrian has crossed the northbound lane and is on the far side of the crossover so that the road ahead of him is clear.

    a. Is it permissible for him to proceed so long as the pedestrian is on the far side of the road?

    b. Would your answer be different if this were a school crosswalk?

    c. Would your answer be different if this were a crosswalk as defined in the HTA?

DISCUSSION QUESTIONS

In *R v Yick*, the accused was convicted of failing to stop at a stop sign while rollerblading in the roadway. The court held that roller skates came within the definition of "vehicle" under the HTA. The brief oral decision on the case is set out below.

AUGUST J (orally):

[1] MS. PETERKIN: Good afternoon, Your Honour. For the record, the name is Peterkin, first initial K. Appearing on behalf of the City of Toronto. We can deal with number one-four, Winson-Wei Yick.

[2] MR. McKINNON: Yes. Good afternoon Your Honour. For the record, my name is McKinnon, first initials T.J., appearing as agent on behalf of the appellant who is not present before Your Honour's court, with your permission. Your Honour, this is a defence appeal for the conviction of disobey stop sign, fail to stop. The trial was held on January sixth, 2003, in C court. At that trial it was revealed that the defendant at that time, the appellant in this case, was roller-blading down the street. And the officer waved the appellant over and issued a Provincial Offences Notice to the appellant for the offence of disobey stop sign, fail to stop. Under that section, Your Honour, I would submit that the prosecution has the burden of proving that number one, the appellant was driving as it cites in s 136(1).

[3] THE COURT: Is that in dispute?

[4] MR. McKINNON: Pardon me?

[5] THE COURT: Is that in dispute?

[6] MR. McKINNON: That he was driving the Roller Blades?

[7] THE COURT: Yes.

[8] MR. McKINNON: Yes, Your Honour. The crux of this appeal basically is that the Roller Blades, I would submit, are not classified as a vehicle, that you cannot drive Roller Blades, that they would be similar to skates or shoes or skis, something of that nature. I would submit that the intent of the law would be to prohibit vehicles, scooters, motorcycles, things of that nature. And that someone using Roller Blades would be the same as people in Nathan Phillips Square skating on the rink over there. I would submit that they are not driving or operating vehicles on the ice rink. I would say that Roller Blades would be very similar to shoes or boots and that you strap them on your feet, that they are part of your apparel. And I would submit that someone standing in Roller Blades would not be in a vehicle or operating a vehicle. That's the appeal.

[9] MS. PETERKIN: Your Honour, I would … submit to the Court that I differ quite to the contrary, that notwithstanding first of all that it was never argued about the roller-blading not being a vehicle, I have provided some excerpts from the *Highway Traffic Act* as well as the *Oxford English Dictionary* and the *Black's Dictionary*. If I can pass up some information to Your Honour and as well as to Mr. McKinnon as well. I first highlighted the section itself,

being 136(1)(a) from the *Highway Traffic Act*, which reads, "Every driver or streetcar operator approaching a stop sign at an intersection shall stop his or her vehicle or streetcar at a marked stop line, or if none, then immediately before entering the nearest crosswalk, or if none, then immediately before entering the intersection." I have further provided an excerpt for the *Black's Law Dictionary* with a definition of driving, which indicates, "To urge forward under guidance; compelled to go in a particular direction; urge onward and direct the course of." Further to that, the definition of "driver" in the *Highway Traffic Act*, which is an essential element in the charge before us today, indicates—means, "a person who drives a vehicle on a highway." In the transcript before you on page—I believe it's line four, it clearly indicates. ...

[10] THE COURT: What page?

[11] MS. PETERKIN: Sorry. Page four, line 25. The officer indicates in his evidence that, "I observed a male roller-blading southbound on Beverly Street in the curb lane at a very fast pace. The male roller-blader went right through the intersection where there is a marked stop line for southbound traffic." I would submit there that the roller-blader was in fact on the highway, on the curb lane, which is a travel portion of the roadway by vehicles. I further went on to give a copy of the definition of "vehicle" from the *Highway Traffic Act*, which is different. There is a difference between a motor vehicle and a vehicle. And in the charge before us today it indicates, "vehicle," which includes a motor vehicle, trailer, traction engine, farm tractor, road-building machine, bicycle, and any vehicle drawn, propelled or driven by any kind of power including muscular power. And I'm submitting that roller-blading or in-line skating would fall in the definition of "vehicle," including "muscular power." It's quite obvious that the muscles being used amongst many, but certainly would be the leg muscles. And also further and lastly I have provided a definition of vehicle not only from the *Highway Traffic Act*, but also from the *Oxford English Dictionary*, that indicates, "A material, means, channel or instrument by which a substance or some property of matter is conveyed or transmitted from one point to another." And it also further goes on to mean, "A means of conveyance provided with wheels, or runners and used for the carriage of persons or goods." I'd respectfully submit that the defendant was roller-blading on [a] highway in the curb lane. He was on a means of conveyance. He was being transported by the Roller Blades, which in fact have wheels. And under those circumstances I would respectfully submit that roller-blading would fall in the definition of vehicle as I've provided today and that there was no error in law in the trial before the Court, and that the appeal should be dismissed.

[12] THE COURT: Thank you. Any reply?

[13] MR. McKINNON: Just briefly. I'm not sure if Your Honour's copy of the *Oxford English Dictionary* is highlighted as mine was, but after the highlighting for the first part, "A material, means, channel or instrument by which a substance or some property of matter, as sound or heat, is conveyed or transmitted from one point to another."

And after that it says, "1615." Now I can't be sure what that "1615" means, but it sounds to me like a year, maybe when that definition was made. I would submit that they would have no comprehension of Roller Blades. I would submit that the muscular power is too broad in its wording and that my shoes are propelled forward by muscular power. By my friend's submission if I were to run through a stop sign my shoes would propel me through there by muscular power. I would submit that the Roller Blades should not be looked at as a vehicle, that they are part of someone's apparel, that they are basically footwear. Now they have wheels on the bottom but they are footwear, I would submit. And again, skates, I would submit if you're skating down the road that you would not contravene this section. I would submit that the reason why it includes muscular power is for things like bicycles, for scooters. Those things I would submit are vehicles and I concede that. However I would ask Your Honour to accept that Roller Blades are footwear and apparel and are not vehicles. And I'd ask Your Honour to allow the appeal and enter an acquittal.

[14] THE COURT: All right. Thank you. I choose to accept the submissions of the prosecution and I do not agree with the position taken by the appellant. And therefore the appeal is dismissed and the conviction and sentence are affirmed. ...

---

1. **a.** Consider the opposing arguments made by counsel. Are there legitimate practical reasons for this decision, or is this a case of *de minimis non curat lex* (the law does not concern itself with trifling matters)?

   b. Would it have made any difference to the outcome of this case if Mr. Yick had been rollerblading on the sidewalk rather than in the roadway?

   c. Would it have made any difference to the outcome of this case if Mr. Yick had been skateboarding in the roadway?

2. Babette has a four-wheel vehicle that seats one person and has a flat, horizontal deck behind the seat. It also has a mast and a sail; there is no motor. Using wind power, she is able to drive around the city. Does she require a vehicle permit under s 7(1) of the HTA? If so, what kind?

3. Babette has added a larger deck and seating for 11 passengers to her wind-driven vehicle. She has accepted a contract for driving children to and from school. Discuss how this vehicle should be classified.

4. If a person driving in a Walmart store's parking lot drives through a stop sign located in that parking lot, could the driver be charged under s 136(1) of the HTA? If yes, what charges may apply?

Licences and Permits

3

LEARNING OUTCOMES

After completing this chapter, you should be able to:

- Explain the difference between restricted and non-restricted vehicle permits.
- Describe arrestable without warrant offences involving the unlawful use of plates, permits, and validation tags.
- Identify the vehicle classes set out in the Ontario *Highway Traffic Act* (HTA).
- Describe graduated/restricted driver's licences and non-graduated driver's licences and the conditions associated with them.
- Explain the requirements for vehicle insurance under the Ontario *Compulsory Automobile Insurance Act* (CAIA), and the related offences under this Act.

Introduction

In this chapter, we examine the requirements of the permit system for licensing different classes of vehicles, and the requirements for different classes of operator's licences.

Vehicle Permits

The permit is the document that licenses a vehicle to be used on the highways of the province and authorizes the attachment of metal number plates to that vehicle. There are two parts to a permit: the vehicle portion and the plate portion.

A sample motor vehicle permit (front).

Source: Publications Ontario © Queen's Printer for Ontario, 2016. Reproduced with permission.

A sample motor vehicle permit (back).
Source: Publications Ontario © Queen's Printer for Ontario, 2016. Reproduced with permission.

The statutory basis for the requirement of permits is s 7 of the Ontario *Highway Traffic Act* (HTA). It reads as follows:

7(1) No person shall drive a motor vehicle on a highway unless,

(a) there exists a currently validated permit for the vehicle;

(b) there are displayed on the vehicle, in the prescribed manner,

(i) number plates issued in accordance with the regulations showing the number of the permit issued for the vehicle, or

(ii) number plates described in subsection (7.2) [re self-propelled implements of husbandry] if the vehicle is an historic vehicle and the Ministry has issued a currently validated permit for it; and

(c) evidence of the current validation [**valtag**] of the permit is affixed, in the prescribed manner, to,

(i) one of the number plates mentioned in subclause (b)(i) displayed on the vehicle, or

valtag
a vehicle permit renewal sticker that shows that a permit has been renewed and is up to date; must be properly affixed as required under the HTA

(ii) to a mini-plate attached to the number plate exposed on the rear of the vehicle, if number plates described in subsection (7.2) are displayed on the vehicle.

• • •

7(5) … [E]very driver of a motor vehicle on a highway shall carry,

(a) the permit for it or a true copy thereof; and

(b) where the motor vehicle is drawing a trailer, the permit for the trailer or a true copy thereof,

and shall surrender the permits or copies for inspection upon the demand of a police officer.

While most permits and plates in the province are issued as permanent plates with no restrictions, there are a number of situations where they may be issued for temporary purposes, or may be restricted.

Summary of Permit Requirements

HAVE: Any driver of a motor vehicle on a highway must have a permit for the motor vehicle that authorizes the number plates on that vehicle.

DISPLAY: Except in the case of temporary permits and motorcycles, there must be two number plates—one affixed to the front and one affixed to the rear—of a motor vehicle operated on a highway, and the rear plate must be currently validated in the upper right corner of the plate. Motorcycle owners must affix only one number plate to the rear of their motorcycles.

SURRENDER: The driver of a motor vehicle on a highway must carry the permit or a true copy of it in the motor vehicle and surrender it to a police officer for inspection on demand.

Restricted Permits

The system for obtaining temporary plates changed in 2008. While the system for dealer and service plates remains largely unchanged, the six- and ten-day permits previously used in a variety of situations have been replaced by temporary vehicle registration and special permits.

Temporary Vehicle Registration

Currently, all Ontario passenger and unladen commercial motor vehicles, motorcycles, and low-speed motorcycles are eligible for temporary vehicle registration. This type of registration allows unregistered vehicles to be driven for certain purposes, such as to licensing offices, to garages to satisfy safety standards, or to meet Drive Clean (emissions testing) requirements, and for other necessary, short-term purposes. Newly transferred vehicles that require temporary vehicle registration must be registered and plated in the new owner's name prior to temporary registration being issued, and owners must pay outstanding 407 ETR fines, parking tickets, and cheques marked NSF (non-sufficient funds) before being granted permanent registration. If a new owner can meet all registration requirements, a regular registration will be issued; temporary vehicle registration will be issued where full registration cannot be issued for the reasons referred to above.

Temporary vehicle registration consists of a "T" validation sticker that must be placed on the upper right corner of the vehicle's licence plate. On a motor vehicle, the sticker is placed on the rear plate, and for a truck it is placed on the front plate. The sticker is valid for ten days from the date of issue. In a 365-day period, all passenger and unladen commercial motor vehicles are eligible to obtain a maximum of two such registrations per vehicle.

The following example illustrates a situation where temporary vehicle registration would be necessary. Siobahn purchased a vehicle from Hari in a private sale. The vehicle is not roadworthy and must be taken to a garage for required work that will enable it to meet safety standards certificate requirements. Siobahn registers the vehicle and obtains plates, but because the vehicle does not have a safety standards certificate, Siobahn obtains a temporary vehicle registration and puts the "T" marker in the upper right corner of the plate so that she can lawfully drive the vehicle to a garage to be repaired within the next ten days.

Special Permits

Where temporary vehicle registration is not suitable (for example, for out-of-province vehicles or laden commercial vehicles), a special permit must be obtained instead. For example, in order to make it roadworthy, Jason needs to move a laden commercial vehicle that he just bought to a garage for repairs. Because it is a laden vehicle, it is not eligible for a temporary vehicle registration, and Jason will instead require a special permit.

If a commercial vehicle is registered in Ontario and has a higher gross vehicle weight than indicated on the plate portion of the permit, a special permit may be used. A special permit will also allow a vehicle to operate in Ontario on a continuous trip that begins and ends at a point outside Ontario (known as "corridor movement"). A special permit consists of a decal that must be displayed in the windshield of the vehicle, and is valid for ten days. In a 365-day period, motor vehicles and unladen commercial motor vehicles are allowed two permits per vehicle, while laden commercial motor vehicles are allowed an unlimited number.

WHAT DOES THE LAW SAY?

RRO 1990, Reg 628, Vehicle Permits, Section 12

Restricted Permits

12(1) A special permit that is valid for 10 days may be issued for the following motor vehicles:

1. A commercial motor vehicle.

2. A motor vehicle or trailer owned by a manufacturer or dealer in motor vehicles or trailers.

3. A motor vehicle or trailer bought at an auction if the Ministry has authorized the issuance of special permits at the auction.

4. A motor vehicle or trailer that is entering Ontario solely for the purpose of passing through Ontario.

5. A motor vehicle or trailer that is being taken out of Ontario.

6. A motor vehicle that is a roadworthy prototype vehicle.

(2) A special permit shall not be issued if the applicant has not complied with subsection 11(2) of the Act.

(3) A person to whom a special permit is issued for a vehicle may be issued only one further special permit for the same vehicle in any 12-month period.

(4) Subsection (3) does not apply in respect of a special permit for which the fee prescribed under subparagraph 15 iv, v, vi or vii of subsection 17(1) is paid.

(5) A special permit shall be affixed in a clearly visible position,

(a) to the windshield of a motor vehicle; or

(b) in the case of a special permit issued for a trailer, to the windshield of the motor vehicle drawing the trailer.

(6) Despite subsection (5), if a special permit provides for another method for affixing or carrying the special permit, it shall be affixed or carried as stated and not as provided by subsection (5).

(7) A special permit shall not be issued for a motor vehicle or trailer if the permit for the motor vehicle or trailer is marked "unfit motor vehicle" or "unfit" or, in the case of a permit issued by another jurisdiction, the equivalent of unfit in that jurisdiction.

(8) A special permit shall not be issued for a motor vehicle or trailer if the permit for the motor vehicle or trailer indicates that it is classified as irreparable or salvage or, in the case of a permit issued by another jurisdiction, the equivalent of irreparable or salvage in that jurisdiction.

(9) A special permit shall not be displayed on a laden commercial motor vehicle unless the fee paid for the special permit was the fee prescribed by subparagraph 15 v, vi or vii of subsection 17(1).

(10) Subsection (9) does not apply to a special permit issued for a trailer if,

(a) the trailer is drawn by a motor vehicle for which the vehicle permit was not issued under this section; and

(b) the trailer and the motor vehicle drawing it are in compliance with subsection 121(1) of the Act.

(11) Clauses 7(1)(b) and (c) of the Act do not apply in respect of a motor vehicle for which a special permit is issued while the special permit is valid.

(12) Clause 7(4)(b) of the Act does not apply in respect of a trailer with a valid special permit.

(13) Section 2 does not apply to the issuance of a special permit.

Dealer and Service Permits and Plates

Dealer and service permits (O Reg 628, s 13) and plates are issued to

- manufacturers of motor vehicles or trailers;
- dealers in motor vehicles or trailers;
- persons engaged in the business of repairing, customizing, or modifying motor vehicles or trailers; and
- persons engaged in the business of transporting motor vehicles or trailers.

Dealer and service permits and plates may be used only

- on a vehicle for sale that is owned by the permit holder;
- to fix, test, or modify a vehicle by the person who owns the permit; or
- on a vehicle being transported by a person engaged in the business of transporting vehicles.

The permit and plates may not be used on a new vehicle that is being rented. Only one plate is issued, with red letters and numbers on a white background. The plate must be attached in a conspicuous position on the rear of the rear-most vehicle being towed or driven on a highway. This requirement suggests that the permit may apply to more than one vehicle, if they are linked together for transit. Dealer plates must be validated, and the val-tag shall be affixed to the upper right corner of the plate.

A sample valtag.
Source: Publications Ontario
© Queen's Printer for Ontario, 2016.
Reproduced with permission.

Non-Restricted Permits

We can now look at the requirements for permits and number plates in the ordinary course of events, and we will do this for a number of common vehicle-transfer and vehicle-acquisition situations. Number plates are issued to the person rather than the vehicle, which means that plates can be transferred by an owner from one vehicle that he or she owned to another that he or she has bought. This means that if you buy a used or new car, you can transfer the plates to it from the car you previously owned, provided that you follow the rules prescribed in the legislation.

Seller's Obligations: HTA, Section 11(1)

The seller, on selling a motor vehicle, is not obliged to notify the Ministry of Transportation, but is obliged

- to remove the number plates from the vehicle;
- to retain the plate portion of the permit; and
- on delivery of the vehicle to the new owner,
    - to complete and sign the transfer application on the back of the vehicle portion of the permit, including the date of delivery, and
    - to give this portion of the permit to the new owner.

The seller may retain the plates that he or she has removed from the vehicle that is being sold and affix them to another car that he or she owns under certain circumstances described in the HTA and its regulations (HTA, s 11(3); O Reg 628, s 10)). The newly acquired motor vehicle must be similar to the class of vehicle from which the plates have been removed—that is, you can transfer a plate from one passenger automobile to another passenger automobile, but not from a passenger automobile to a commercial vehicle. In addition, you must meet the following requirements set out in O Reg 628, s 10(1):

1. The number plate must show current validation.
2. The driver must have in his or her possession the following documents:
    a. The vehicle portion of the permit issued for the vehicle that is being driven, with the transfer application completed on the back, signed by both seller and purchaser. If the motor vehicle is new and has not had a previous owner or lessee, a copy of the bill of sale or other ownership document or a leasing document may be substituted for the vehicle portion of the permit issued for the vehicle (O Reg 628, s 10(4)).
    b. The plate portion of the permit corresponding to the plates that were transferred to the vehicle.
    c. A valid safety standards certificate—that is, one issued within 36 days of the transfer. This is not required if the vehicle is new (O Reg 628, s 10(1)(c)).

Buyer's Obligations: HTA, Section 11(2)

The buyer is obliged to apply for a new permit within six days of becoming the owner of a motor vehicle or trailer for which a permit was previously issued to someone else. In general, if a person wants to take the number plates off one motor vehicle and transfer the plates to another motor vehicle, he or she should get a new registration permit authorizing the "old" plates to be used on the "new" motor vehicle before attaching the old plates to the new motor vehicle.

The following scenarios illustrate some of the most common situations that might involve switching plates. Note that for some of the situations, switching plates is prohibited.

Transferring Plates from One Vehicle That You Own to Another Vehicle That You Own

Where you own two vehicles at the same time, you cannot use the six-day temporary use of plates provision because the plates are not from a vehicle that you no longer own, nor are they being transferred to a vehicle that you have purchased in the last six days. In this case, you must apply for a new permit authorizing the use of the plates on the vehicle before you can attach the plates to it and drive on the highway. Also, if you do this, you cannot transfer the plates back to the original vehicle by relying on the six-day temporary use rule.

Transferring Plates from One Vehicle That You Have Just Sold to Another Vehicle That You Have Owned for a Period of Time Prior to the Sale of the Other Vehicle

Where you owned two vehicles at the same time and sold one, you cannot use the six-day temporary use of plates provision if you did not obtain ownership of the vehicle to which you propose to transfer the plates within the last six days. Again, you can only resort to the six-day temporary use of plates provision if you bought the vehicle in the last six days and are using the plates within that six-day period. If stopped by the police, you will have to produce the old plate portion, the new vehicle portion, and a valid safety standards certificate. For example, Raj bought a Ford on January 3 and a Toyota on March 2; on April 3, he sold the Toyota. Raj removed the plates from the Toyota and would like to attach them to the Ford. He cannot do this, however, because he did not buy the Ford in the last six days before April 3.

Transferring Plates by a Dealer Selling a "Demo" Model with Regular, Rather Than Dealer, Plates to Another Vehicle That the Dealer Bought in the Last Six Days

If you are a dealer, you cannot undertake this transfer because dealers or other persons entitled to use "dealer" plates are not entitled to take advantage of the six-day temporary use of plates provision. In this case, the dealer would have to apply for a new permit authorizing the use of plates on the car before it can be operated on the highway.

Transferring Plates from a Vehicle You Previously Owned to a Brand-New Vehicle Where You Are the First Owner or Lessee

Where you have sold one vehicle and then bought or leased another brand-new vehicle from a dealer, you *can* take advantage of the six-day temporary use of plates provision for six days from the date of purchase, after which you must obtain a new permit from the Ministry of Transportation. In general, a dealer will obtain the new permit as a courtesy for a new owner, although this ability to obtain a permit in the name of someone else is a cause for some concern because it makes it difficult to determine who actually owns a vehicle if a driver is stopped for a driving offence or if the vehicle is stolen and then recovered. During the six-day period, you are required to carry the plate portion of the old permit, a bill of sale, or a copy of the lease in lieu of the vehicle portion of the permit, since this car, because it is new, has never had a permit. No safety standards certificate is required because the car is new.

Arrestable Without Warrant Offences

Plate and Permit Offences

Section 12(1) of the HTA sets out several offences involving the unlawful use of plates and permits. A person may be arrested for offences under s 12 without a warrant. If a person is convicted of a s 12 offence, he or she is liable to a fine of between $100 and $1,000, to imprisonment for not more than 30 days, or to both a fine and imprisonment. In addition, the convicted offender may have his or her licence suspended for up to six months.

Defacing or Altering Plates or Permits: HTA, Section 12(1)(a)

It is an offence to alter or deface any number plate, permit, or valtag.

Use of Defaced Plates or Permits: HTA, Section 12(1)(b)

In addition to altering or defacing, the use of an altered or defaced number plate, permit, or valtag is prohibited.

Unauthorized Removal of Number Plate: HTA, Section 12(1)(c)

It is an offence to remove a number plate from a vehicle or a trailer without the authorization of the permit holder. This offence is commonly related to the theft of a number plate.

Use of Unauthorized Number Plate: HTA, Section 12(1)(d)

It is an offence to use or permit the use of a number plate on a vehicle other than the number plate authorized for use on that vehicle. Section 12(1)(d) can be invoked to charge someone who abuses the six-day temporary use rule.

Unauthorized Use of Valtag: HTA, Section 12(1)(e)

It is an offence to use or permit the use of a valtag on a number plate displayed on a motor vehicle that is not the valtag furnished by the Ministry of Transportation for that vehicle.

Use of Valtag or Plate Contrary to the HTA and Regulations: HTA, Section 12(1)(f)

Anyone who uses or permits the use of a number plate or valtag other than in accordance with the HTA and the regulations is guilty of an offence. This provision can be invoked for any future amendments to the legislation and for amended or new regulations.

WHAT DOES THE LAW SAY?

HTA, Section 217(2)
Arrests without warrant
   217(2) Any police officer who, on reasonable and probable grounds, believes that a contravention of any of the provisions of subsection 9(1), subsection 12(1), subsection 13(1), subsection 33(3), subsection 47(5), (6), (7) or (8), section 51, 53, subsection 106(8.2), section 130, 172 or 184, subsection 185(3), clause 200(1)(a) or subsection 216(1) has been committed, may arrest, without warrant, the person he or she believes committed the contravention.

SECTIONS	DESCRIPTION OF OFFENCE	A = Anywhere H = Highway
9(1)	Knowingly makes false statement in writing to ministry (MTO)	A
12(1)(a)	Deface or alter a number plate, evidence of validation, or permit	A
12(1)(b)	Use/permit use of defaced/altered plate, validation, or permit	A
12(1)(c)	Without holder's authority remove number plate from motor vehicle or trailer	A
12(1)(d)	Use/permit use of number plate not authorized by MTO for that vehicle	A
12(1)(e)	Uses/permits use of evidence of validation upon a number plate displayed on a motor vehicle other than evidence furnished by the MTO in respect of that motor vehicle	A

SECTIONS	DESCRIPTION OF OFFENCE	A = Anywhere H = Highway
12(1)(f)	Uses/permits the use of a number plate or evidence of validation other than in accordance with this Act and/or regulations	A
13(1)	Expose a number in such a manner to confuse the identity of a number plate	A
33(3)	When unable or refusing to surrender driver's licence, fail to give reasonable identification	H
47(5)	Unlawful possession or applying for an owner's permit (own name) when permit suspended or cancelled	A
47(6)	Applying for, procuring or possession of a driver's licence when suspended or cancelled	A
47(7)	Applying for or procuring a C.V.O.R. certificate while certificate suspended	A
47(8)(a)	Operate commercial motor vehicle where fleet limitation certificate not carried when fleet limitation imposed	H
47(8)(b)	Operate commercial motor vehicle when his or her permit or certificate is under suspension	H
51	Drive a motor vehicle the permit for which is suspended or cancelled	H
53	Drive a motor vehicle or streetcar while driver's licence suspended	H
106(8.2)	Passenger fail to identify	H
130	Drive a vehicle or streetcar carelessly	H
172	Drive a motor vehicle in a race or on a bet or wager	H
184	Wilfully remove, deface, interfere with notice or obstruction lawfully on a highway	H
185(3)	Refuse to accompany a police officer off a highway prohibited to pedestrians	H
200(1)(a)	Every person in charge of a vehicle or streetcar who is directly or indirectly involved in an accident on a highway shall remain at or immediately return to the scene	H
216(1)	Driver . . . fail to stop immediately when requested or directed by a police officer who is in lawful execution of his duty and readily identifiable	H
217(3.1)	On reasonable grounds believes that a person has contravened subsection 177(2) (Stopping or approaching vehicle on roadway) if the officer directed the person not to engage in the activity or on reasonable grounds believes arrest is necessary to establish identity	H
218(4)	Every person in charge of a bicycle who is required to stop by a police officer shall correctly identify himself or herself	A

Source: *Provincial Offences Wording and Fines* (St Catharines, Ont: MacBeth, 2016) at 10-11.

WHAT DOES THE LAW SAY?

HTA, Section 14(1)

Improper number plate

14(1) Where a police officer or an officer appointed under this Act has reason to believe that,

(a) a number plate attached to a motor vehicle or trailer,

(i) has not been authorized under this Act for use on that vehicle,

(ii) was obtained by false pretences, or

(iii) has been defaced and altered;

(b) evidence of validation of a permit displayed on a motor vehicle

(i) was not furnished under this Act in respect of that motor vehicle,

(ii) was obtained by false pretences, or

(iii) has been defaced or altered; or

(c) a permit carried by a driver of a motor vehicle,

    (i) was not authorized under this Act in respect of that motor vehicle,

    (ii) was obtained by false pretences, or

    (iii) has been defaced or altered,

the officer may take possession of the number plate, evidence of validation or permit and retain it until the facts have been determined.

DISCUSSION POINT

It is 11 p.m. in a quiet industrial complex. You stop a car with what appears to be one adult male inside it. The area of the traffic stop is dark and, as you approach the vehicle, you notice that the validation sticker on the rear licence plate has been tampered with. What should you do? What steps will help ensure your safety?

Seizure of Evidence of a Section 12 Offence: HTA, Section 14(1)

This section authorizes the seizure of evidence of an offence under s 12(1) of the HTA. It says that a police officer may seize the number plate, valtag, or permit, and retain it until the facts in issue have been determined if the officer has reason to believe that a number plate, valtag, or permit

- is not authorized for that vehicle,
- was obtained by false pretences, or
- is defaced or altered.

This means that the items seized may be held until the trial has ended and the time for launching an appeal has elapsed. If an appeal is launched, the items may be held until the appeal is dismissed.

PROFESSIONAL PRACTICE

Handling Seized Plates

After an officer seizes plates, it is critical that possession and continuity be maintained. To this end, officers should do the following:

- Note the time and location where the plates were seized in their notebook.
- Note the vehicle information, and any discussion with the driver and any passengers in their notebook.
- Attach a property tag to the plate, place it in property lock-up, and note the time. In addition, if there is a main property registry, record the particulars there as well.
- If the plate is required for court purposes, sign out the evidence.

Vehicle Classes

Ontario Regulation 340/94, *Drivers' Licences* under the HTA outlines the classes of licences and motor vehicles (A, B, C, D, E, F, G, and M), and sets out the vehicles that drivers with a particular class of licence may operate. Motor vehicle classes for vehicles other than passenger automobiles are determined by passenger capacity, purpose, or weight, in the case of buses, and by weight in all other types of commercial vehicles. These classifications are used to determine the type of vehicle permit required and the class of licence that an operator must possess to operate a motor vehicle in each class.

A number of definitions are necessary in order to understand the classifications in O Reg 340/94:

gross weight
the total weight of the motor vehicle, its trailer, and the load it is carrying; can be determined only by weigh scales used by the Ministry of Transportation

- The **gross weight** is the weight of the motor vehicle, its trailer, and its load, and can be determined only by weigh scales of the type that you see on 400-class highways (highway 401, 407, etc.).
- The **towed weight** is the weight of the trailer and its load.
- The **total weight** is determined from *either* the gross weight of the motor vehicle, trailer, and load *or* the registered gross weight of the motor vehicle, whichever is more.

towed weight
the weight of the trailer and its load

The **registered gross weight** is printed on the permit for commercial motor vehicles. This is the weight for which the owner has prepaid the government for hauling loads on the highway—a form of tax for highway carriers to defray the cost of repairing the damage caused to the roadway by heavy commercial vehicles. Generally, the registered gross weight is used to determine the class of the motor vehicle, even if it is empty and weighs far less than the registered gross weight. If, however, the truck is loaded, and the actual gross weight according to the weigh scales exceeds the registered gross weight, the larger weight is used to determine the motor vehicle class, and the driver or owner can be fined for exceeding the weight for which he or she has prepaid. The registered gross weight allows enforcement officers to determine the class of motor vehicle simply by checking the permit.

total weight
determined from *either* the gross weight of the motor vehicle, trailer, and load or the registered gross weight of the motor vehicle, whichever is more

The registered gross weight always applies to a motor vehicle, not a trailer. The registered gross weight for a truck tractor (the tractor of a tractor-trailer combination) will always exceed 11,000 kg because of the size it needs to be to pull heavy loads. This means that even when the truck tractor is being operated independently without a trailer, the registered gross weight will exceed 11,000 kg. (As Figure 3.1 shows, this means the driver of such a vehicle would need a class D driver's licence.) The moment that the driver hooks the trailer onto his vehicle, the total weight of the trailer and its load must be considered. The permit for the trailer has the empty vehicle weight printed on it. If the empty weight of the trailer is not more than 4,600 kg, the driver still only needs a class D driver's licence. When the trailer is loaded so that the total weight of the trailer and its load exceeds 4,600 kg, the driver needs a class A driver's licence.

registered gross weight
the weight of the vehicle and the load set out in the motor vehicle permit; the owner has prepaid the government to have the legal right to haul loads of that size in that vehicle on the highway

A motor vehicle is a bus if it has at least 10 permanent passenger seats. Buses are classed (B, C, E, or F) according to how many passenger seats they have and the purpose for which they are used; buses with 24 or fewer passenger seats are in a different class from buses with more than 24 passenger seats. The two types of buses require different skills to operate and, therefore, require different driver's licences. The main reason for differentiating between "big" and "little" buses when the buses in question are school purposes buses is to ensure that school purposes bus drivers have been criminally screened.

It is important to note that a vehicle is not considered a bus for the purpose of driver's licence requirements unless the bus has at least one passenger. If there are no passengers on board, the weight of the bus is used to determine the class of driver's licence required by the driver. If, for example, a school bus carrying no passengers on a highway weighs 9,000 kg, the driver needs only a class G driver's licence to drive the bus lawfully on the highway. If a large bus carrying *no* passengers on a highway weighs 17,000 kg, the driver needs a class D driver's licence to drive the bus lawfully on the highway.

Figure 3.1 explains the classes of vehicles, with examples, as set out in O Reg 340/94, s 2(1). Use it as a guide to determining the missing classes of driver's licence in Figure 3.2.

FIGURE 3.1 Vehicle Classes and Descriptions

Class of Licence	Class of Motor Vehicle	Example	Other Classes of Motor Vehicle Licencee Authorized to Drive
Class A	Class A—any combination of a motor vehicle and towed vehicles where the towed vehicles exceed a total gross weight of 4,600 kilograms, but not a bus carrying passengers	Moving van	Class D and G
Class B	Class B—any school purposes bus having a designed seating capacity for more than 24 passengers	Large school bus	Class C, D, E, F and G
Class C	Class C—any bus having a designed seating capacity for more than 24 passengers, but not a school purposes bus carrying passengers	Coaches and city buses	Class D, F and G
Class D	Class D—any motor vehicle exceeding 11,000 kilograms gross weight or registered gross weight, and any combination of a motor vehicle exceeding a total gross weight or registered gross weight of 11,000 kilograms and towed vehicles not exceeding a total gross weight of 4,600 kilograms, but not a bus carrying passengers	Dump truck	Class G
Class E	Class E—any school purposes bus having a designed seating capacity for not more than 24 passengers	Small school bus	Class F and G
Class F	Class F—any ambulance, and any bus having a designed seating capacity for not more than 24 passengers, but not a school purposes bus carrying passengers*	Ambulance, police paddy wagon	Class G
Class G	Class G—any motor vehicle not exceeding 11,000 kilograms gross weight or registered gross weight and any combination of a motor vehicle not exceeding a total gross weight or registered gross weight of 11,000 kilograms and towed vehicles where the towed vehicles do not exceed a total gross weight of 4,600 kilograms, but not, (a) a motorcycle or motor assisted bicycle; (b) a bus carrying passengers; or (c) an ambulance in the course of providing ambulance service as defined in the *Ambulance Act*	Passenger car, van, light truck	
Class G1	Class G1—any motor vehicle in Class G and any combination of a motor vehicle in Class G and towed vehicles, except, (a) Class D farm vehicles deemed to be Class G vehicles under subsection 2 (3); (b) Class F vehicles deemed to be Class G vehicles under subsection 2 (4); (c) a vehicle equipped with air brakes		

* If the vehicle is not carrying passengers, the basis for classification is weight.

FIGURE 3.1 Vehicle Classes and Descriptions *concluded*

Class of Licence	Class of Motor Vehicle	Example	Other Classes of Motor Vehicle Licencee Authorized to Drive
Class G2	Class G2—any motor vehicle in Class G and any combination of such a vehicle and towed vehicles, except a vehicle equipped with air brakes		
Class M	Class M—a motorcycle, including a limited-speed motorcycle, and a motor assisted bicycle		subject to Class G1 conditions, any motor vehicle in Class G1 and any combination of such a vehicle and towed vehicles
Class M1	Class M—a motorcycle, including a limited-speed motorcycle, and a motor assisted bicycle		
Class M2	Class M—a motorcycle, including a limited-speed motorcycle, and motor assisted bicycle		subject to Class G1 conditions, any motor vehicle in Class G1 and any combination of such a vehicle and towed vehicles

NOTES

1. A Class D or G motor vehicle that is designed and used as a tow truck shall be deemed not to be a Class A motor vehicle when it is towing a disabled or unsafe motor vehicle or trailer on a highway. O Reg 340/94, s 2(2).

2. A Class D motor vehicle shall be deemed to be a Class G motor vehicle if,

   a. it is owned or leased by a farmer and used for his or her personal transportation or the transportation of farm products, supplies or equipment without compensation to or from a farm; and

   b. the fee paid for the vehicle permit was determined under Schedule 2 to Regulation 628 of the Revised Regulations of Ontario, 1990. O Reg 340/94, s 2(3).

3. A Class F motor vehicle shall be deemed to be a Class G motor vehicle when being operated by,

   a. a police officer in the performance of police duties; or

   b. a peace officer who, in the course of his or her duties, is transporting prisoners or other persons held in custody. O Reg 340/94, s 2(4).

4. A Class F motor vehicle, other than an ambulance or car pool vehicle as defined in the Public Vehicles Act, with a designed seating capacity of not more than 11 passengers that is used for personal purposes without compensation shall be deemed to be a Class G motor vehicle. O Reg 340/94, s 2(5).

5. No driver's licence provides authority to drive a motor vehicle equipped with air brakes unless the licence bears an air brake endorsement. O Reg 340/94, s 2(6).

Source: Adapted from O Reg 340/94, s 2(1).

FIGURE 3.2 What Class of Driver's Licence Is Required by the Drivers of These Vehicles?

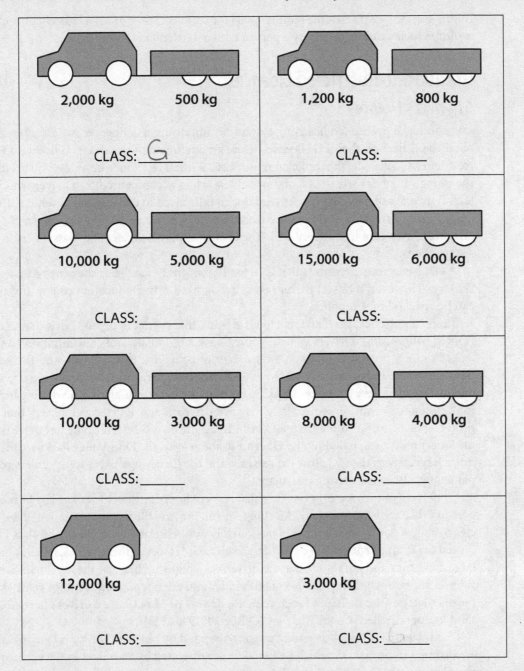

2,000 kg 500 kg	1,200 kg 800 kg
CLASS: _G_	CLASS: _____
10,000 kg 5,000 kg	15,000 kg 6,000 kg
CLASS: _____	CLASS: _____
10,000 kg 3,000 kg	8,000 kg 4,000 kg
CLASS: _____	CLASS: _____
12,000 kg	3,000 kg
CLASS: _____	CLASS: _____

Remember:

1. If the towed weight is more than 4,600 kg, a class A licence is required.
2. If the towed weight is not more than 4,600 kg, the vehicle weight is considered.
3. If the vehicle weight is more than 11,000 kg, a class D licence is required.
4. If the vehicle weight is not more than 11,000 kg, a class G licence is required.

Driver's Licences

In this section, we discuss the requirements for various classes of driver's licences, and what motor vehicles can be driven by a person with a particular class of licence.

Graduated/Restricted Licences

G1 Driver's Licence

Ontario has a graduated licensing system for obtaining a G licence. A person must first obtain a G1 licence, then a G2 licence, before graduating to the final class G licence. In order to obtain a G1 licence, the applicant must pass a written test. Once he or she obtains the G1, the person may drive a class G motor vehicle when accompanied by a driver who has at least four years of driving experience and who is licensed to drive a class G vehicle. This accompanying driver must ride in the front passenger's seat beside the G1 driver. No other passenger may ride in the front seat. The back seat may hold as many passengers as there are seat belts.

A G1 driver must remain at that level for 12 months before he or she can graduate to the G2 level. However, if the G1 driver takes a recognized driver-education course, this period can be reduced by 4 months.

There are restrictions that apply to G1 drivers that do not apply to G drivers in general (O Reg 340/94, s 5). Drivers generally must have a blood alcohol concentration (BAC) of less than 0.05 percent. However, a G1 driver must have a BAC of zero, and the accompanying driver must have a BAC that is less than 0.05 percent. Accompanying drivers 21 and under must have a 0 percent BAC. G1 drivers also are prohibited from driving between midnight and 5 a.m. Moreover, they may not drive on any 400-series highway that has a posted speed limit of more than 80 km/h. In addition, a G1 driver may not drive on any urban expressways, including the Queen Elizabeth Way, the Don Valley Parkway, the Gardiner Expressway, the E.C. Row Expressway, and the Conestoga Expressway, unless accompanied by a licensed driving instructor.

G1 drivers may drive any class G vehicle, except heavy farm vehicles used by farmers for personal-use transportation and for shipping and moving their crops to market; these vehicles usually have "farm" number plates. Such heavy vehicles would usually be class D, but, if used for farm purposes, are deemed to be class G. However, these vehicles do not include large combines and harvesters that are driven on a highway, because these vehicles are considered self-propelled implements of husbandry and are not defined as motor vehicles. This means that, despite the size of such vehicles, drivers need not have a driver's licence of any kind to operate them on the highway (O Reg 340/94, s 2(3)).

Class F vehicles—such as paddy wagons operated by police officers, and ambulances—are deemed to be class G vehicles when they are operated by an officer in the performance of police duties (O Reg 340/94, s 2(4)).

G2 Driver's Licence

In order to progress to the G2 class, the G1 driver must pass a road test. A driver who passes the G2 test enters that level and must remain at that level for a minimum of 12 months. Like G1 drivers, G2 drivers must have a BAC of zero. G2 drivers, however, may drive alone, and without an accompanying qualified class G driver.

Recent restrictions placed on G2 drivers under the age of 20 aim to discourage joyriding among this group. Between the hours of midnight and 5 a.m.:

- for the first six months, G2 drivers under the age of 20 may not carry more than one passenger under the age of 20 unless other passengers are members of the novice driver's immediate family, and
- after the first six months, G2 drivers under the age of 20 may carry up to three passengers under the age of 20, although they can exceed that number if the other passengers are members of the novice driver's immediate family (O Reg 390/94, ss 6(1) and (1.1)).

At other times, G2 drivers may have as many passengers as there are operable seat belts in the vehicle. The above passenger restrictions do not apply if the G2 driver is accompanied by a full G-licensed driver (with at least four years' driving experience) in the front seat, or if the passengers are immediate family members.

G2 drivers may drive any class G vehicle, as set out in Figure 3.1, except vehicles equipped with air brakes, which require training and a test.

After 12 months, the G2 driver may take a comprehensive road test and obtain the G licence. The G2 driver has five years from the time he or she obtained the G1 licence to take the comprehensive road test for the G licence. If the person does not apply to take the test within five years of obtaining the G1 licence, he or she must start over again and apply for a G1 licence.

G Driver's Licence

Once the basic G class licence has been obtained, a class G driver can drive a class G motor vehicle, as set out in Figure 3.1. In addition, class G drivers can learn to drive any other class of vehicle as long as they are accompanied by a driver who is licensed to drive that particular class of vehicle.

The Graduated Licensing System for Obtaining a G Licence

The only differences between a class G2 and a class G licence are that for the G2 licence,

- the driver's blood alcohol level must be zero, and
- the number of passengers must be limited to the number of operable seat belts, but additional restrictions apply to drivers under age 20 between the hours of midnight and 5 a.m. in certain circumstances.

M1 Driver's Licence

Anyone who wishes to drive a motorcycle must obtain a class M licence. Like the class G licence, the class M licence is obtained through a graduated licensing system; the driver must obtain the M1 and then the M2 before obtaining the M licence. To obtain the M1 licence, the applicant must pass a written test that will permit the applicant to learn to drive a motorcycle. An M1 licence lasts for a minimum of 60 days and is valid for only 90 days. This means that the licence holder cannot take the road test for the M2 for at least 60 days from the date that the M1 was issued, even if the licence holder has taken a motorcycle safety course. However, the licence holder must take the test within 90 days; if he or she does not, the licence holder must apply for an M1 licence again.

There are specific operating conditions for M1 drivers (O Reg 340/94, s 7). The driver

- cannot carry any passengers on the motorcycle;
- must drive the motorcycle only during the daytime (one half-hour before sunrise to one half-hour after sunset);
- cannot drive on highways with speed limits in excess of 80 km/h, except highways 11, 17, 61, 69, 71, 101, 102, 144, and 655; and
- must pass a road test to progress to the M2 licence, either through an approved motorcycle safety course or through a Ministry road test (O Reg 340/94, ss 28(8) and 28(12)).

M2 Driver's Licence

Once the driver has passed the road test, he or she progresses to the M2 level, where he or she must remain for a minimum of 22 months. This period may be reduced to 18 months if the M2 licence holder completes an approved motorcycle safety course, which can be taken at any time while the driver is classed as an M1 or M2 licence holder.

The night time driving restriction is lifted for M2 drivers, but the M2 driver must have a BAC of zero—as must any driver with any class of licence who is 21 years of age or under. Once the driver has completed the minimum M2 licence period, he or she may take a comprehensive road test to qualify for a class M licence.

Holders of an M2 driver's licence can also drive a class G motor vehicle, but only under the conditions that apply to a class G1 driver's licence.

M Driver's Licence

Once an M2 driver has passed the comprehensive road test and has become an M licence holder, he or she may lawfully drive any motorcycle and may also drive a class G vehicle, but only under the conditions that apply to a class G1 driver.

Duration of Graduated Driver's Licences

G1	Lasts a minimum of 12 months (8 months, if lessons taken) and a maximum of 5 years.
G2	Lasts a minimum of 12 months and is valid for the remainder of the 5-year period for which the G1 licence was valid.
M1	Lasts a minimum of 60 days and a maximum of 90 days.
M2	Lasts a minimum of 22 months (18 months, if safety course taken) and a maximum of 5 years.

Penalties for Violating Conditions of a Graduated G or M Licence

If a person is convicted of violating the conditions of a graduated licensing system, he or she will be notified that his or her driver's licence has been suspended. The suspension will last for 30 days from the date that the licence is surrendered, or two years from the date that the licence is suspended if it is not surrendered.

Although there have been some problems with the graduated system—long waits for road tests, for example—there is evidence that jurisdictions using graduated licensing systems boast a reduction in collisions among young drivers. Furthermore, the reduction in collisions has occurred across the spectrum of drivers, regardless of age.

However, despite the introduction of the graduated system, statistics indicate that drivers aged 16 to 25 continue to have a very high risk of involvement in accidents that result in serious injury or death. While the graduated system may help in gradually introducing young drivers to the responsibilities of driving, it cannot cancel out the age-related factors of immaturity and inexperience. Consider the following statistical findings reported on the website for Mothers Against Drunk Driving (MADD) at madd.ca:

- Young people have the highest rates of traffic death and injury per capita among all age groups and the highest death rate per kilometre driven among all drivers under 75 years of age. More 19-year-olds die or are seriously injured than any other age group.

- Motor vehicle crashes are the leading cause of death among 16- to 25-year-olds, and alcohol and/or drug impairment is a factor in 55% of those crashes.

- 16- to 25-year-olds constituted 13.6% of the population in 2010, but made up almost 33.4% of the alcohol-related traffic deaths in that year.[1]

Drivers over 80 Years of Age

Young drivers are not the only drivers who receive close attention around licensing. Older adult drivers are also carefully checked because of concerns that diminished physical and mental abilities could raise the risk of accident and injury.

Regardless of class of licence, every driver who is 80 years old or older must renew his or her licence every two years. The renewal process requires that the older adult attend a renewal session to check vision and a 45-minute interactive session that includes an update on recent changes to traffic laws. There may also be a review of the older adult's driving record. An individual who does not satisfy all of the requirements to renew his or her licence will have the licence cancelled.

Non-Graduated Driver's Licences

Once a driver has obtained a G licence, he or she may go on to obtain other licences to drive other classes of vehicles. There is no graduated system for these licences; the only requirement is that a learner have an accompanying driver with a class of licence for driving that class of vehicle. For example, a person seeking a class A licence must have a person with a valid class A licence with him or her while driving a class A vehicle.

The criteria that must be met to obtain licences other than G or M are set out in O Reg 340/94 and vary with the licence. Road tests generally are not required, but an application form must be completed indicating that skill requirements (and in some cases, vision and hearing standards) have been met. (See also Figure 3.1.)

Class A Licence

A driver with this licence may drive either

- a class A vehicle, which is any combination of a motor vehicle and towed vehicles where the towed vehicles exceed a total gross weight of 4,600 kg, but does not include a bus carrying passengers (which requires a B, C, E, or F driver's licence, depending on the size of or purpose of the bus); or

- a class D or G vehicle (O Reg 340/94, s 2(1), table).

---

1 MADD Canada, "Youth and Impaired Driving," online: MADD Canada <http://madd.ca/pages/impaired-driving/overview/youth-and-impaired-driving>.

Class B Licence

A driver with this licence may drive

- any school purposes bus with a designed seating capacity for more than 24 passengers; and
- any class C, D, E, F, or G vehicle.

Class C Licence

A driver with this licence may drive

- any bus with a designed seating capacity for more than 24 passengers, but not a school purposes bus carrying passengers; and
- any class D, F, or G vehicle.

Class D Licence

A driver with this licence may drive

- any motor vehicle that exceeds 11,000 kg total gross weight or registered gross weight;
- any combination of a motor vehicle exceeding 11,000 kg total gross weight or registered gross weight and towed vehicles not exceeding a total gross weight of 4,600 kg; and
- any class G vehicle.

However, a D licence holder may not drive a bus carrying passengers that otherwise might fit the class D definition. A bus that weighs over 11,000 kg cannot be classified as a class D vehicle once a passenger climbs aboard. Once a passenger is on board, the driver requires the appropriate bus licence.

Class E Licence

A driver with this licence may drive

- any school purposes bus with a designed seating capacity of 24 passengers or less; and
- any class F or G vehicle.

Class F Licence

A driver with this licence may drive

- any ambulance;
- any bus with a seating capacity of not more than 24 passengers; and
- any class G vehicle.

However, an F licence holder may not drive a school purposes bus carrying passengers.

Air Brakes

The Ministry of Transportation requires licence holders to have a Z endorsement on their licence in order to drive a vehicle equipped with air brakes. The Z endorsement on any class of driver's licence authorizes the holder of the licence to drive the class of vehicle he or she is otherwise permitted to drive if it is equipped with air brakes. The endorsement is not a separate class of licence; rather, it is in addition to the existing class of driver's licence. For example, the holder of a D licence who obtains an air-brake endorsement will receive a DZ licence, showing that he or she can drive a class D vehicle equipped with air brakes. To obtain a Z endorsement, the applicant must attend classroom instruction and pass an examination.

Calculating Which Classes of Motor Vehicle a Driver Is Licensed to Drive

THE "BIG EDDIE" ACRONYM	
B	(Big)
E	(Eddie)
C	(Can)
F	(Fool)
A	(All)
D	(Dumb)
G	(Goats)

There is an easy way to calculate all the classes of motor vehicles that a driver is legally licensed to drive on a highway in Ontario: use the "Big Eddie" acronym, set out in the box at right. The acronym is used to help remember the order of letters in the right-hand column.

To calculate all the classes of motor vehicles that a driver is legally licensed to drive on a highway in Ontario, use the table in the box below and follow these steps:

1. Note the class letter of the driver's licence in the driver's possession.
2. Locate the letter in both of the columns.
3. Position your pen so that it joins the same letter in both columns.
4. The driver can legally drive the class of motor vehicle for which he or she is licensed and any class of vehicle for which there is a letter in both columns below the pen.

Example of How to Use the "Big Eddie" Technique

THE DRIVER'S LICENCE CLASS	THE "BIG EDDIE" ACRONYM	
A	**B**	(Big)
B	**E**	(Eddie)
C	**C**	(Can)
D	**F**	(Fool)
E	**A**	(All)
F	**D**	(Dumb)
G	**G**	(Goats)

The driver can legally operate class D vehicles and class G vehicles (G is the only letter that appears in both columns below the pen). Similarly, a driver with a class E licence can legally operate class E, F, and G vehicles (F and G appear in both columns below the pen).

An exemption to these restrictions exists for police officers in the following situation. An officer with *any* class of "Big Eddie" licence (B, E, C, F, A, D, or G) may drive any class of motor vehicle, including those equipped with air brakes, except for a motorcycle, on a highway *in an emergency in the course of his or her duty*. For example, a police officer with a class G licence is allowed to drive a large bus in an emergency. Similarly, a mechanic is also permitted this liberty while road testing a vehicle in the course of servicing it. Again, motorcycles are excluded.

Driver's Licence Offences: HTA Sections 32 and 33

Once a licence is issued, in addition to driving within the licence restrictions, the licence holder is required to have the licence in his or her possession when driving, and to surrender it for inspection by a police officer or other designated person.

Instead of the traditional driver's licence, some drivers may have an enhanced licence, which combines a driver's licence with proof of Canadian citizenship. A person who has applied for and obtained a combined photo card must surrender his or her previous Ontario driver's licence. The enhanced licence may be used by Canadian citizens to enter the United States from Canada by road or by boat, but not by air without producing a passport. For our purposes, the combined photo card has the same force and effect as a driver's licence (*Photo Card Act, 2008*).

Section 32(1) of the HTA says that no person shall drive a motor vehicle on a highway unless the motor vehicle is within a class of motor vehicles for which the person holds a valid driver's licence. If a licence holder is convicted of driving a class of vehicle that he or she is not entitled to drive, he or she is subject to a fine of not less than $200 and not more than $1,000. If a streetcar is driven on a right of way that is on a highway, even though it is not a motor vehicle within the HTA definition, the operator must nevertheless have a driver's licence (s 32(2)).

Section 33(1) of the HTA requires every driver of a motor vehicle or streetcar to carry a driver's licence at all times while in charge of a motor vehicle, and to surrender it for reasonable inspection on the demand of a police officer or an officer appointed for carrying out the provisions of the HTA. If a person is unable or refuses to surrender his or her driver's licence in accordance with s 33(1) or (2), the person shall give reasonable identification of himself or herself, and, for the purposes of s 33(3), his or her correct name and address shall be deemed to be reasonable identification. Failure to comply with s 33(3) can lead to an arrest.

Arrest Authority: Failure to Identify

- A person cannot be arrested for failing to have or failing to surrender a driver's licence, but a person can be charged.
- A person can be arrested for failing to identify himself or herself after failing or refusing to surrender his or her driver's licence.

The authority to arrest is for failing to *identify*, and is intended to secure the person until he or she can be identified.

If an individual is driving a motor vehicle on a highway, the individual is lawfully required to identify himself or herself if a police officer demands this information. This is one of the few instances when an individual is lawfully required to identify himself or herself to a police officer. If an officer asks the person to identify himself or herself and the person tells the officer orally who he or she is, the officer cannot arbitrarily decide that the driver is not who he or she claims to be (HTA, s 33(3)). The officer must have reasonable proof that the person is lying in order to arrest the person. This proof may require some investigation. Remember that the individual has the right to remain silent and is not obliged to answer these investigative questions, and refusal to answer the questions is not proof that the person is lying. The refusal may lead to suspicion, but the officer needs more than suspicion for grounds to make an arrest.

If the driver is arrested for failing to identify himself or herself, he or she is released once the correct identification has been obtained. With the name and address, the driver can be given a ticket for failing to surrender his or her driver's licence and for failing to identify himself or herself.

Non-Ontario Plates and Licences

The issuance of Ontario plates and licences is tied to provincial residence. Only residents of the province may apply for vehicle permits and licences. Non-residents may, in general, drive vehicles on Ontario highways for limited periods of time. For these purposes, s 15 (plates) and s 34 (permits) of the HTA distinguish between residents of another province and residents of another country. The non-resident exemptions and conditions are set out in Table 3.1.

TABLE 3.1 Non-Resident Plate and Licence Exemptions Under the HTA

	AUTHORITY TO DRIVE IN ONTARIO			
	WITH OUT-OF-PROVINCE PLATES (SECTION 15)		**WITH OUT-OF-PROVINCE DRIVER'S LICENCE (SECTION 34)**	
	Non-Ontario resident	*New Ontario resident*	*Non-Ontario resident*	*New Ontario resident*
From other province	In general, one who resides in another province and who does not reside in or carry on a business in Ontario for more than six consecutive months in a calendar year is exempt from Ontario plate and licence requirements.	One who no longer resides in another province and is a new resident of Ontario must obtain Ontario plates within 30 days. Needs SSC.	One who resides in another province and who is at least 16 years old and has a valid driver's licence from that province can use his or her driver's licence so long as it is valid.	One who no longer resides in another province and is a new resident of Ontario must obtain an Ontario driver's licence within 60 days.
From other country	In general, one who resides in another country and who does not reside in or carry on a business in Ontario for more than three months in a calendar year is exempt from Ontario plate and licence requirements.	One who no longer resides in another country and is a new resident of Ontario must obtain Ontario plates within 30 days. Needs SSC.	One who resides in another country and who is at least 16 years old and has a valid driver's licence from that country can use his or her driver's licence in Ontario for no more than three months in a calendar year.	One who no longer resides in another country and is a new resident of Ontario must obtain an Ontario driver's licence within 60 days.

SSC = safety standards certificate.

Non-Resident Exemptions and Reverse-Onus Requirements

With the application of the *Canadian Charter of Rights and Freedoms* to criminal or quasi-criminal proceedings, the accused is no longer required to prove anything under a **reverse-onus clause** in a statute, because reverse-onus rules have been held to be contrary to the Charter. An example of a reverse-onus clause in criminal law follows: in circumstances where the Crown proved that a person was inside a premises unlawfully, the accused was presumed to have been there for the purpose of committing an indictable offence. It was then up to the accused to prove that he or she was not there for the purpose of committing an indictable offence. Under the Charter, however, the Crown must now prove every element of the offence, without the accused having to prove anything.

However, s 47(3) of the *Provincial Offences Act* places the **burden of proof** on the accused to show that an exemption under s 15 or s 34 of the HTA operates in his or her favour. Although this is clearly a reverse-onus clause, the courts in Ontario have accepted that driving is a privilege rather than a right, so the reverse-onus provision is deemed lawful. This means that a driver in Ontario is presumed to require an Ontario driver's licence and Ontario number plates and that the onus is on the person to prove entitlement to the exemptions in ss 15 and 34.

reverse-onus clause
a provision in a statute that shifts the burden of proof from the person who normally bears it to a named person in a specific situation. For example, in criminal law, a reverse-onus clause may shift the burden of proof from the Crown to the accused, once the Crown proves a specific fact that triggers the shift of the burden of proof to the accused to rebut the presumed fact or prove a specific fact

burden of proof
describes the duty or obligation of a person to offer evidence to support or establish a fact

Compulsory Automobile Insurance Act

In addition to having the appropriate vehicle permits and licences, every owner of a motor vehicle registered in Ontario must maintain an insurance policy on the motor vehicle that conforms to the minimum insurance coverage requirements under the Ontario *Compulsory Automobile Insurance Act* (CAIA). All of the CAIA charges except for s 3(1) are no set fine (NSF), meaning that the officer writes a Part III summons; a Provincial Offence Notice (PON) would be written for s 3(1), as there is an associated fine.

Failure to Have Insurance

Under s 2(1) of the CAIA, no owner or lessee of a motor vehicle shall operate, or allow to be operated, a motor vehicle that is not insured. This section places the obligation to insure squarely on the owner or the lessee of the vehicle (unless the lessor maintains the necessary insurance). Section 2(3) sets out stiff penalties for contravention of s 2(1), and defines as a further offence the production of a false insurance card for inspection by the police that purports to show that the vehicle is insured when it is not. Fines of between $5,000 and $25,000 for a first offence, and between $10,000 and $50,000 for a subsequent offence, are steep enough that it is cheaper to maintain an insurance policy than to risk operating an uninsured vehicle. The offender, as defined in this section, is the owner or lessee of the vehicle. Charges would be laid under the offence section, s 2(3).

Failure to Surrender Insurance Card

Under s 3(1) of the CAIA, an operator of a motor vehicle shall have an insurance card for that motor vehicle in the vehicle, or an insurance card showing that he or she is insured on another contract of motor vehicle insurance other than the one for the car that is being driven. If the operator of the vehicle is not the owner, and he or she produces his or her own insurance card rather than the one for the car he or she is driving, this does *not* relieve the owner of the vehicle that has been stopped of the responsibility for insuring the motor vehicle. The operator is obliged to surrender either his or her own card, or the owner's insurance card, for inspection by the police on request. A person who fails to produce either insurance card is guilty of an offence and may be fined up to $400 under s 3(3) of the CAIA. The offender, according to this section, is the operator of the vehicle. Charges would be laid under the offence section, s 3(3) of the CAIA.

If a driver produces an insurance card for a motor vehicle other than the one he or she is driving, the police should check with the owner to see whether the vehicle is, in fact, insured. Normally, a police request for an insurance card is made of a driver after a traffic stop or collision. The officer may ask the owner, even if the owner is not at the scene (for example, if the owner is at home), to surrender the insurance card, via dispatch. If the owner cannot or will not do this, the owner may be charged with permitting the operation of the vehicle without insurance, contrary to s 2(1)(b) of the CAIA. Case law is clear that, even if the owner is in his or her own home, the owner must produce the card or be charged with the offence. At the officer's request, an original (*not* a copy) motor vehicle liability insurance card must be produced for the vehicle in question.

Failure to Disclose Particulars of Insurance

Under s 4(1) of the CAIA, an operator of a motor vehicle on a highway who is directly or indirectly involved in a collision shall, on request of any other person involved, disclose to that person the particulars of the contract of motor vehicle insurance that insures the motor vehicle. These particulars are identified in s 4(2) of the CAIA as follows:

(a) the name and address of the insured,

(b) the make, model and serial number of the insured vehicle [identified by the vehicle identification number (VIN)],

(c) the effective date and expiry date of the contract,

(d) the name of the insurer,

(e) the name of the insurer's agent, if any [some insurance is sold directly without an agent], and

(f) the policy number of the contract.

Failure to disclose particulars when requested can lead to a charge under s 4(3), with a fine of up to $400 on conviction.

Short Form Wordings: Compulsory Automobile Insurance Act

ITEM	WORDING	SECTION	FINE
	Owner operate motor vehicle on a highway—no insurance	2(1)(a)	N.S.F.
	Owner cause operation of motor vehicle on a highway—no insurance	2(1)(b)	N.S.F.
	Owner permit operation of motor vehicle on a highway—no insurance	2(1)(b)	N.S.F.
	Owner surrender false evidence of insurance	2(3)(b)	N.S.F.
1.	Fail to surrender suspended driver's licence	2(6)	$25.00
2.	Refuse to surrender suspended driver's licence	2(6)	$25.00
3.	Fail to have insurance card	3(1)	$50.00
4.	Fail to surrender insurance card	3(1)	$50.00
5.	Fail to disclose particulars of insurance	4(1)	N.S.F.
	Make false statement	13(2)	N.S.F.
	Knowingly have false insurance card	13.1(1)(a)	N.S.F.

ITEM	WORDING	SECTION	FINE
	Knowingly have invalid insurance card	13.1(1)(a)	N.S.F.
	Knowingly use false insurance card	13.1(1)(b)	N.S.F.
	Knowingly use invalid insurance card	13.1(1)(b)	N.S.F.
	Knowingly sell false insurance card	13.1(1)(c)	N.S.F.
	Knowingly sell invalid insurance card	13.1(1)(c)	N.S.F.
	Knowingly give false insurance card	13.1(1)(c)	N.S.F.
	Knowingly give invalid insurance card	13.1(1)(c)	N.S.F.
	Knowingly deliver false insurance card	13.1(1)(c)	N.S.F.
	Knowingly deliver invalid insurance card	13.1(1)(c)	N.S.F.
	Knowingly distribute false insurance card	13.1(1)(c)	N.S.F.
	Knowingly distribute invalid insurance card	13.1(1)(c)	N.S.F.

N.S.F. = no set fine.

Source: *Provincial Offences Wording and Fines* (St Catharines, Ont: MacBeth, 2016) at 104.

CHAPTER SUMMARY

All drivers who operate a motor vehicle on a highway must have a permit for the vehicle that authorizes the number plates on that vehicle. Permits are either limited and restricted, or non-restricted and permanent. Restricted permits include temporary registration and special permits, and dealer and service permits and plates. The HTA outlines the actions that individuals who buy and sell motor vehicles must take, and when, with respect to plates and permits; it also lists the offences with respect to permits and plates—for example, defacing or altering plates and permits, unauthorized removal of a number plate, use of an unauthorized number plate, and unauthorized use of a valtag. Persons may be arrested for such offences without a warrant, and are subject to fines and/or imprisonment as outlined in the Act.

All vehicles fall into one of several classes: A, B, C, D, E, F, G, or M. The classes and their descriptions are outlined in O Reg 340/94. Motor vehicle classes for vehicles other than passenger automobiles are determined by passenger capacity (in the case of buses), purpose, or weight, and by weight in all other types of commercial vehicles. Sometimes, the purpose of a commercial vehicle alters the class into which it falls. In addition to vehicle classes, there are different classes of driver's licence, and drivers must possess the appropriate licence to operate a vehicle in a particular class. The "Big Eddie" acronym is a useful tool for determining which vehicles the holder of a particular licence may lawfully drive. Graduated licensing systems are in place for obtaining class G and class M licences, and drivers at various stages of the licensing process face various restrictions. Drivers who obtain a G licence may obtain licences to drive other classes of vehicles. There is no graduated system for these licences, but learners must have an accompanying driver with a class of licence for driving that class of vehicle. Drivers of vehicles equipped with air brakes must have a Z endorsement on their licence, obtained through classroom instruction and an exam.

Licence holders must drive within the restriction of their licence, and must have the licence in their possession while driving. When requested to surrender their licence to a police officer, individuals must do so, or may face charges. After failing to surrender their licence and subsequently failing to identify themselves to an officer, individuals may be arrested and detained until the correct identification information has been obtained. All owners of motor vehicles registered in Ontario must maintain an insurance policy on the motor vehicle that conforms to the minimum insurance coverage requirements under the CAIA. The Act sets penalties for various offences against the Act—for example, operating or allowing to be operated a vehicle that is not insured, or producing a false insurance card for inspection.

ON THE SCENE

No Rear Licence Validation Sticker/ Expired Licence

Scenario

Constable (Cst.) Jillian Brocco, Badge #377, Platoon #5 on [use today's date and time: DD/MM/YYYY] at 11:00 a.m. is eastbound on Brown Avenue in Kitchener, Ontario on routine patrol in marked police cruiser #123. Cst. Brocco notes while following an eastbound brown Chevrolet Malibu, Ontario licence plate EFGH123, that the valtag on the rear licence plate has expired. Cst. Brocco stops the vehicle, without any problems, in front of 123 Brown Avenue. The driver shows the officer the Ministry of Transportation validation sticker and indicates that he had forgotten to place the valtag on the rear licence plate. While speaking with the male driver, the officer notices an adult female passenger seated in the right front wearing a seat belt. The driver breaks into tears and states, "I am sorry, but my licence has expired." The driver surrenders the expired licence to Cst. Brocco, then provides upon request the ownership and valid insurance for the vehicle. The driver indicates that he is the owner of the vehicle. When asked his name, he identifies himself verbally as James Robert Thurston, date of birth April 17, 1995 of 35 Greenwell Street, Kitchener, Ontario, N1H 4R5, home phone: 519-555-4567, Driver's Licence# T5809-12219-50417. Thurston, at this time, was not attending school and was unemployed.

What Actions Should the Officer Take?

1. Should Cst. Brocco arrest Thurston because his licence has expired?

2. Should Cst. Brocco tell Thurston and his passenger to get out of the car to search the interior of the vehicle?

3. Should Cst. Brocco allow Thurston to drive home as he lives "just around the corner"?

4. Should Cst. Brocco check the driver on the Canadian Police Information Centre (CPIC) to confirm the driver's identity?

5. Should Cst. Brocco charge Thurston or just give him a warning because he is being honest?

KEY TERMS

burden of proof, 63

gross weight, 52

registered gross weight, 52

reverse-onus clause, 63

total weight, 52

towed weight, 52

valtag, 43

CASES AND WEBSITES

- *R v Bray*, 2010 ONCJ 98
- Information about the screening process for drivers 80 years of age and older <https://www.ontario.ca/page/renew-g-drivers-licence-80-years-and-over>
- Overview of driver licensing and vehicle registration requirements <https://www.ontario.ca/page/driving-and-roads>

REVIEW QUESTIONS

True or False?

In the space provided next to each statement, place a "T" if the statement is true or an "F" if the statement is false.

1. Temporary and special permits are valid throughout the province of Ontario. _____

2. A mechanic who has been issued a dealer and service plate is permitted to use the plate on any motor vehicle that the mechanic is repairing. _____

3. Everyone who drives a motor vehicle on a highway in Ontario must have a permit for the motor vehicle and surrender the permit or a true copy at a police officer's request. _____

4. The buyer of a motor vehicle must apply to the Ontario Ministry of Transportation for a new permit within six days of becoming the owner, even if the new owner does not plan to operate the motor vehicle on the highway. _____

5. It is lawful to take the plates off a motor vehicle that you own and affix them to another motor vehicle of the same class that you have just purchased within six days and drive that motor vehicle on the highway as long as you carry the prescribed documents and surrender them at a police officer's request. _____

6. If any of the requirements for the six-day temporary use of plates are violated, the plates are not lawfully authorized for use on the vehicle and the plates can be seized and the driver arrested. _____

7. It is an arrestable offence to alter a permit or a number plate. _____

8. A driver with a class B driver's licence can lawfully drive any bus on a highway. _____

9. The holder of a class M2 driver's licence cannot drive at night or on any road with a speed limit above 80 km/h. _____

10. A driver with a class F driver's licence can lawfully drive class D and G vehicles on a highway. _____

11. A school bus with a weight of 10,000 kg when empty can be lawfully driven on a highway by a driver with a class G licence if the 20-seat bus has no passengers. _____

12. A driver with a class B driver's licence could lawfully drive a tractor-trailer combination on a highway because a class B driver's licence is the "top" licence. _____

13. Ambulances are considered to be class F vehicles. _____

14. Class B and E vehicles are school purposes buses and applicants for these classes of driver's licence are criminally screened. _____

15. A person with any class of driver's licence that is determined by weight cannot lawfully drive any bus that is transporting passengers on a highway. _____

16. To lawfully pull on a highway a trailer with a weight of 2,000 kg, the driver of a 5,000 kg motor vehicle would require at least a class D driver's licence. _____

17. The holder of a class G1 driver's licence must be accompanied by a driver with at least four years' driving experience and at least a class G driver's licence. _____

18. An M1 driver's licence is only valid for 90 days. _____

19. The holder of an M2 driver's licence can drive any motor vehicle on any highway. _____

20. The holder of a class M driver's licence can lawfully drive a class G vehicle under the conditions that apply to a class G1 driver's licence. _____

21. The holder of a class G2 licence who is over age 21 can have a trace percentage of alcohol in his or her blood. _____

22. A 19-year-old who has held a class G2 licence for seven months may drive at 4 a.m. with two friends, both aged 18, in his or her car. _____

Short Answer

Briefly answer the following questions.

1. What are you required to do with the plates and permit of a vehicle that you are selling?

2. Where would you expect to find the valtag on a passenger vehicle? On a commercial vehicle?

3. What are the conditions precedent that must be met to acquire the following?

   a. Temporary vehicle registration.

   b. A special permit.

   c. Dealer and service permits and plates.

4. State the class of driver's licence that would be required in the following situations:

   a. A Greyhound bus (seating capacity is 48) that has been hired by a school board for a high school ski trip on a weekend.

   b. A motor vehicle pulling a trailer with a weight of 5,000 kg, where the total weight of the motor vehicle and trailer is 15,000 kg.

5. Explain the circumstances in which the following reclassifications occur:

   a. The classification of a class D farm truck as a class G vehicle.

   b. The classification of a class D and G tow truck as a class G vehicle when towing a disabled vehicle.

   c. The classification of a class F bus as a class G vehicle.

Discussion Questions

1. Orestes Smith has plates that were first issued in 1988. Each time he purchased a new car, he elected to transfer the plates from the old car he sold to the new car. It is now 2016. The plates are rusting, and most of the paint had worn off. Too cheap to buy new plates, Orestes bought a can of white paint and a can of dark blue paint. He repainted both plates, with a white background and blue numbers and letters. The blue letters are very slightly different in tone from the original blue letters. The plates are more legible than they were prior to being repainted, although it is obvious on close inspection that they are old plates that have been repainted. A police officer sees the painted plates and charges Orestes under s 12(1)(a) of the HTA.

   Discuss the arguments in favour of, and against, conviction.

2. As the result of a stolen vehicle investigation, under the HTA an officer seized a car's front and rear licence plates. It is the officer's last shift before going on holiday for two weeks. Because the officer was in a hurry, he decided to leave the plates in his locker. What will happen to the continuity of the investigation? What would happen if a supervisor, at the request of a detective, were asked to look for a notebook containing information regarding an entirely unrelated criminal investigation, and the supervisor opened the officer's locker and observed the plates? Does the officer's laziness and negligence fall under the *Police Services Act* (RSO 1990, c P.15)? Was this a "career advancing" action?

Who Is the Owner for Registration Purposes?
R v Bray, 2010 ONCJ 98

Issues can arise about who is entitled to use a set of plates, and where they may be used. And it can get complicated. In *R v Bray*, the defendant, who operated an auto-towing service and a scrapyard, was charged with using a number plate from his sister's Volkswagen on a Toyota that he had purchased. He stated that his sister was in the process of transferring the ownership of the Volkswagen to him and that she could be deemed to be the common law owner of the Toyota, even though no paperwork had been filled out to change the registration of the Volkswagen, which was legally in her name. He also stated that she intended to buy the Toyota that he had obtained to formally transfer to her, so she could be considered the common law owner if not the legally registered owner of the Toyota. In brief, Bray's sister, Sandra, argued that she was the "owner" of both vehicles within the meaning of the HTA, which does not distinguish between legally registered owners and those who might be considered owners at common law by having a sufficient interest in or connection to a property—in this case, a vehicle.

While driving the Toyota, Bray was involved in an accident. The responding officer, in checking the registration, discovered that Ministry records showed the plates on the Toyota were assigned to the Volkswagen. Bray was charged under s 12(1)(d) of the HTA with using a number plate on a vehicle other than a number plate authorized for use on that vehicle.

The court held that this offence was one of strict liability: the prosecutor only needed to prove the commission of the offence beyond reasonable doubt; that is, that the plates on the Toyota had been assigned to the Volkswagen. Once that was done, there was no need to prove criminal intent, negligence, or the absence of due diligence by Bray.

Bray's defence, however, was not based on an absence of criminal intent or negligence or due diligence but on s 11(3) of the HTA, which permits removal of a plate from a vehicle one no longer owns, to attach it to another vehicle of the same class one does own, provided that the prescribed requirements are followed.

1. Do you think Bray complied with s 11(3) of the HTA based on this account and on the judge's findings of fact set out below?

[54] Accordingly, based on the totality of the evidence before me, I make the following findings of fact pertaining to the issue of the ownership of the subject motor vehicles:

1. that as of the 4th day of October, 2008, Sandra Lee Bray was shown on the records of the Ontario Ministry of Transportation, as the registered owner of a 1991 Volkswagen CPA, motor vehicle, bearing vehicle identification number WVWG-B0319ME006014, for which the "number" plate AZPE490 was authorized;

2. that in or about mid-August 2008, Sandra Lee Bray delivered her Volkswagen vehicle to the wrecking yard operated by her brother, Robert Bray and surrendered possession of the vehicle at that time;

3. that at the time that Sandra Lee Bray surrendered possession of the Volkswagen, she removed the licence plates attached to the vehicle, being "number" plate AZPE490 and retained possession of those plates until October 4th, 2008;

4. that as of October 4th, 2008, the defendant retained possession of the said Volkswagen vehicle in his wrecking yard and was, at that time, in possession of the ownership documents for the said vehicle in the name of Sandra Lee Bray;

5. that on the 22nd day of September 2008, the defendant's company, Bray Auto Truck Center Inc. purchased a Toyota motor vehicle, bearing vehicle identification number 2T1BR12E2XC754305, from Georgetown Chevrolet;

6. that on or about the 2nd or 3rd day of October, 2008, the ownership for the said Toyota vehicle was formally transferred and registered with the Ontario Ministry of Transportation in the name of the defendant;

7. that the defendant purchased the Toyota on September 22nd, 2008, for his sister Sandra Lee Bray;

8. that on or about September 22nd, 2008, Sandra Lee Bray entered into a verbal agreement with the defendant to purchase the Toyota from him;

9. that in entering into this agreement, the parties agreed on a purchase price, but did not record any details of the agreement in a document;

10. that during the week prior to October 4th, 2008, Sandra Lee Bray placed a telephone call to her insurance company pertaining to the subject Toyota vehicle;

11. that further to the purchase agreement between Sandra Lee Bray and the defendant, on October 4th, 2008 the defendant drove the Toyota to the residence of Sandra Lee Bray, in Oakville, Ontario;

12. that as of October 4th, 2008, Sandra Lee Bray had not given any money to the defendant for the purchase of the Toyota vehicle;

13. that as of October 4th, 2008, no "paperwork" had been "filled out" evidencing the purchase of the Toyota vehicle by Sandra Lee Bray from the defendant;

14. that as of October 4th, 2008, Sandra Lee Bray was in possession of the Toyota vehicle;

15. that as of October 4th, 2008, Sandra Lee Bray subjectively considered herself to be the owner of the Toyota vehicle based on the informal, verbal agreement which she entered into with the defendant, on September 22nd, 2008.

2. Hindsight is wonderful. Is there anything Bray could have done prior to the accident to avoid being convicted?

Rules of the Road

4

LEARNING OUTCOMES

After completing this chapter, you should be able to:

- Determine the speed limits that can apply to a highway, depending on location, type, and class of roadway; use of roadway; and other relevant factors.
- Identify and understand the basic rules of the road.
- Identify what equipment is mandatory on different classes of vehicles.
- Describe the victim surcharge, its purpose, and how it is calculated.
- Understand the purpose of the demerit point system.

Introduction

This chapter covers the *Highway Traffic Act* (HTA) rules regulating speed that are set out in part IX (ss 128 to 132), the rules of the road set out in part X (ss 133 to 191.0.1), the key equipment requirements set out in part VI (ss 61 to 107), and the demerit point system for HTA driving offences (O Reg 339/94).

Before exploring these topics, it must be noted that police officers across Canada have been injured and killed in the line of duty while enforcing the rules of the road and conducting routine traffic stops. It is critical that all officers appreciate the following fundamental point: *there is nothing "routine" about a traffic stop—ever.* The Honour Roll on the Police Association of Ontario's website (<http://www.pao.ca>) contains biographies, photographs, and stories of officers who have given their lives in the service of the people of Ontario. Although the risks that officers face on a daily basis cannot be eliminated, thorough preparation is the key to reducing them (see the "Professional Practice" box).

PROFESSIONAL PRACTICE

Officer Preparation

The moment police officers become complacent in their professional practice is the moment their lives and the lives of others may be in danger. You must *always* be on guard and *never* take anything for granted. Minimizing risks involves asking yourself the questions below and planning accordingly. All of the questions are included in the larger question: "Do I have all of my equipment with me, is it in working order, and am I prepared to use it with confidence?"

- *Do I have all of the proper documents, and in sufficient quantities?*   For example, if your Provincial Offence Notice book has only a few tickets left, obtain another book to ensure that you have enough tickets for use during your tour of duty.
- *Are there sufficient pages remaining in my notebook, or do I need to obtain a new one?*
- *Do I have my HTA/Criminal Code/charge wording?*
- *Do I know my use-of-force options, and am I prepared to use one or more?*   If a situation arose that I profiled as "causing bodily harm" or "causing death," would I be able to use the appropriate level of force?
- *Do I have my utility knife on me?*   A utility knife is a great tool for extracting people who are trapped by seat belts.
- *Is my flashlight working properly, and do I have extra batteries?*   Not only is a flashlight necessary during a midnight shift, but you may need it at other times—for example, looking for break-and-enter suspects in the darkened basement of an abandoned building.

- *Where is my handcuff key?*
- *Do my pens work in all kinds of weather?*

Before setting out, conduct an external and internal check of the cruiser; report immediately to your supervisor any damage to the outside of the vehicle, and make notes. When conducting the internal check, ensure that you lift the rear seat of the cruiser in addition to looking under the front seats. Maybe you will not find anything—but it is possible that there may be drugs or weapons that an arrested person managed to "stash" under the rear seat. Make notes regarding the results of your search, and report any items you located to your supervisor. (A related reminder is to always ensure that *you* check the back seat after each arrest and at the end of *your* tour of duty.) Always note the cruiser mileage at the beginning and the end of your tour of duty, and always check your cruiser headlights/siren/emergency lights prior to beginning your shift. If the gas tank needs to be filled, do so before taking calls.

Ensure that you take an inventory of the emergency equipment in your cruiser trunk and that you have the necessary items, such as a reflective vest, emergency first aid kit, rope, pylons, hard hat, and measuring tape. If the yellow "Police Line Do Not Cross" tape is missing, make sure that you obtain a new roll. Ten minutes after being 10-8 ("in service"), you may be heading to a reported fatality accident. Having to ask another officer to respond with tape is not professional.

DISCUSSION POINT

Showing initiative when enforcing the rules of the road sometimes leads to positive—and unexpected—outcomes. What might some examples be?

Rate of Speed: HTA, Part IX

Standard Speed

The standard speed on highways within a municipality or a built-up area is 50 km/h (HTA, s 128(1)(a)). If the highway is in a municipality, but not in a built-up area, the speed limit is 80 km/h (s 128(1)(b)). On a controlled-access highway, whether it is within a municipality or built-up area, the speed limit is 80 km/h (s 128(1)(c)). However, the minister, under s 128(7)(b), may make regulations prescribing a speed limit that exceeds 80 km/h on any King's Highway, and that is the case for most of the 400-series highways (for example, Highway 401), which have speed limits of 100 km/h. The Ministry may also set speeds for designated highway construction zones (s 128(8)) and for provincial parks (s 128(7)(a)). It may also, under s 128(7)(c), set limits in areas that are not within municipalities. However, local municipalities[1] have been given broad powers under the HTA to pass bylaws to determine speeds in certain conditions and circumstances (s 128(1)(d)):

1. On a highway that passes through the territorial jurisdiction of the municipality (s 128(2)), the speed may be set by the municipality at any speed up to 100 km/h, and different rates of speed may be prescribed for different times of day.

2. On highways within the municipality's jurisdiction that adjoin a school entrance, the speed may be reduced from the speed otherwise prescribed for 150 m on either side of the school entrance during the designated times (s 128(5)).

3. On bridges within a municipality's jurisdiction, the speed may be set by the municipality (s 128(6)).

In addition to prescribing maximum speeds on highways, the Ministry may, by regulation, also prescribe speeds for different types of motor vehicles. When a municipality, under a bylaw, or the Ministry, by regulation, has posted a speed for the highway, it is not valid and enforceable until the bylaw or regulation is posted and made public. Note that the validity of the speed limit does depend on the presence of, or the erection of, speed limit signs (HTA, ss 128(8) and (10)). If the bylaw or regulation is properly proclaimed and valid, the speed limit it prescribes takes precedence over the limits set out in s 128(1)(a), and it is enforceable from that time, provided that speed limit signs have been erected.

Whatever the speed limit, the HTA exempts fire trucks, police vehicles, and ambulances from posted speed limits in the following circumstances (HTA, s 128(13)):

- Fire trucks are only exempt when responding to a fire or emergency, not when returning from one.
- Police vehicles are only exempt when being used in the lawful performance of a police officer's duties.
- Ambulances are only exempt when responding to an emergency or transporting a patient in an emergency.

Remember that the exemption attaches to the use of the vehicle, and not merely to the vehicle itself.

---

1 "Municipality," as used here, includes cities, towns, incorporated and unincorporated villages, and police villages. Note that the city of Toronto has been given separate powers in the HTA to regulate speed under the *Stronger City of Toronto for a Stronger Ontario Act*, SO 2006, c 11.

Speeding Offences

Violations of s 128 of the HTA, or regulations or bylaws made under its authority, may result in fines that increase progressively, depending on how much beyond the speed limit the person was driving (ss 128(14) and (15)).

Speeding Fines

SPEED	FINE
Less than 20 km/h over the limit	$3.00 for each km/h over the speed limit
Between 20 and 29 km/h over the limit	$4.50 for each km/h over the speed limit
Between 30 and 49 km/h over the limit	$7.00 for each km/h over the speed limit
50 km/h or more over the limit	$9.75 for each km/h over the speed limit*

* The court may also suspend the person's driver's licence for a period of up to 30 days. (It should be noted that speed in excess of 50 km/h over a posted speed limit may constitute the separate HTA offence of "racing" (HTA, s 172), for which the consequences are an immediate administrative seven-day suspension, with further suspension of up to two years upon conviction. See the discussion of "street racing" (a *Criminal Code* offence) under the heading "Street Racing Under the Criminal Code," below.)

facts in issue
all of the elements
of an offence

These fines are doubled if the offence occurs on a part of a highway that has been designated as a "construction zone" by the province or by a municipality (where the highway is under municipal jurisdiction). The construction zone must be properly marked by signs (HTA, ss 128(8), (8.1), (8.2), (10), and (10.1)).

PROFESSIONAL PRACTICE

Speeding Charges—Facts in Issue

When a Provincial Offence Notice (PON) is issued for speeding, the following **facts in issue** should be recorded for court purposes:

- The type of radar used: make/model, serial number, and condition of the radar equipment before, during, and after use.

Radar Testing

Some controversy surrounds how radar accuracy and reliability should be tested by officers. For many years, the devices were tested with a tuning fork of the type used for musical instruments. However, a tuning fork test can be difficult to do, and many police forces, including the Ontario Provincial Police (OPP) have switched to other tests. However, some forces, including the Royal Canadian Mounted Police (RCMP), continue to use tuning forks to test their radar equipment on the grounds that, if used properly, they provide a reliable test to prove in court that the radar device was accurately recording an accused's speed. This point is not lost on defence lawyers. The tuning fork has not become obsolete; in fact, it may become popular once again. For more information on radar testing, see the websites cited at the end of this chapter.

- Whether the officer was moving or parked; the location and direction of the cruiser; and, if it was mobile, the cruiser's speed.
- Whether the cruiser was marked or not, and its identification number.
- Weather conditions, noting any weather changes during the tour of duty.
- Road conditions (for example, dry, wet, or snow covered).
- A description of the grade of the roadway and the officer's location (for example, a two-lane paved roadway; officer located at the bottom or top of a hill).
- The existence of any other traffic and/or pedestrians in the area.
- The location of posted speed and construction signs.
- The approximate distance when and where the offender was first observed and when "clocked."
- The distance travelled before the driver was stopped, and the specifics regarding where the driver was stopped. In addition, the tracked speed when "pacing" or following other drivers.
- The zoning classification of the area.
- The speed of the offender's vehicle, and whether the charge was reduced.

- Whether the roof lights and/or siren were activated.
- Whether the officer lost sight of the vehicle and, if so, for how long.
- Whether the offender provided all particulars (driver's licence, insurance, and registration). If not, whether additional charge(s)/warnings were issued. If so, cross-reference to the other PON(s)/part IIIs should be recorded.
- Whether the driver was shown the speed on the radar unit.
- The attitude of the driver, and *any conversation* with the driver (must be recorded as soon as possible in the officer's notebook).
- The number of occupants in the vehicle.

Officers should never make assumptions. Always check drivers in the system, because there may be an outstanding warrant, or the driver may be suspended or prohibited from driving. The officer may ask the passenger(s) for identification as well, but do not insist if there are no grounds that require the passengers to produce identification.

The facts in issue should be written in one of the following places:

1. On the back of the officer's copy of the PON. Space limitations may make reading the facts difficult later. A defence lawyer may ask to see the back of the officer's copy of the ticket, and if a reasonable doubt is raised regarding the credibility of the notes or the lack of knowledge on the officer's part while giving testimony, then the charge is likely to be dismissed.

2. In the officer's notebook, with a cross-reference to the notebook number and page number recorded at the top of the officer's copy of the PON ticket. This gives the officer space to write down the particulars, especially if there are more charges, and increases the professionalism of the notes.

When issuing tickets, remember that it is better to issue five tickets with all of the necessary information than to issue ten incomplete ones and hope that everyone pleads guilty. The following point cannot be stressed enough: the officer must *take his or her time* in completing notes before resuming patrol duties.

These fines are also doubled if the offence occurs on a part of a highway designated as a "community safety zone" or as a "construction safety zone" by the province or by a municipality (where the highway is under municipal jurisdiction). A community safety zone can be created under s 214.1 of the HTA, where "public safety is of special concern on that part of the highway." For example, a stretch of highway where there have been frequent serious collisions due to excessive speed might attract this designation, as could a stretch of highway near a seniors' residence, where risk to residents is high. A construction safety zone can be created under ss 128(8) and (8.1) where people are working on construction sites on or adjacent to a highway.

Breach of other provisions of the HTA, including most of the rules of the road in part X, will also double fines in a community safety zone (HTA, s 214.1(6)).

Although the law is primarily concerned about excessive speed, s 132 of the HTA also prohibits driving a motor vehicle at "such a slow rate of speed as to impede or block the normal and reasonable movement of traffic," except where a slow rate of speed is necessary for safe operation (for example, because of adverse weather conditions, or where the vehicle is involved in road maintenance). How slow is slow? There is no minimum limit set, and reference should be made to the maximum speed posted and the test set out in s 132(1): Is the driver impeding or blocking normal and reasonable traffic flow?

Careless Driving: HTA, Section 130

In addition to speeding, another broadly described offence in part IX is careless driving, which is defined as driving on a highway "without due care and attention" or "without reasonable consideration for other persons using the highway" (see the "Careless Driving" and "Aggressive Driving and Road Rage" boxes below).

On conviction, the driver can be liable to a fine of between $400 and $2,000 or to imprisonment for a term of up to six months, or to both a fine and imprisonment. In addition, the person's licence may be suspended for up to two years. Note that there are no specific acts that constitute this offence and that it is subjectively defined; in deciding whether a driver is guilty of careless driving, the court asks what a *reasonable person* would consider to be an act of driving "without due care and attention" or "without reasonable consideration for other persons using the highway."

Note that the intent required to support a careless driving charge under the HTA differs from the intent required to support a charge of dangerous driving or of criminal negligence in the operation of a motor vehicle and other *Criminal Code* (CC) offences. Generally, under the HTA there need be no more than simple, inadvertent negligence or carelessness, regardless of the driver's intent, where the act alone is objectively assessed against what the reasonable and prudent driver would have done in the circumstances.[2] In the case of criminal negligence, by way of contrast, the required intent has been defined as a reckless or wanton disregard for the lives and safety of others—the driver has considered the risk, and demonstrated a positive acceptance of it without regard for the consequences. Although this does not amount to a positive intention to do harm, it is more than off-handed carelessness or mere indifference to consequences.[3]

Dangerous driving, criminal negligence, and other CC driving offences are discussed at length in Chapter 6.

Careless Driving

Case #1

Domingo Martinez was driving his car south on the 8th Line in the Township of Halton Hills. It was daylight and visibility was good. The road on which he was driving was straight and dry. He was driving at about 50 km/h on a road where the speed limit was 70 km/h. He was proceeding toward the 10th Sideroad, an east–west, through highway. Traffic proceeding south on the 8th Line is required to stop at the 10th Sideroad. There was a clearly visible "stop ahead" warning sign on the 8th Line about 160 m north of the 10th Sideroad.

As Martinez drove south on the 8th Line, he entered the intersection without stopping. A van was proceeding through the intersection from the west. Martinez was more than halfway through the intersection before he applied his brakes. Martinez's car collided with the rear quarter panel of the van, causing the van to flip between five and seven times. The driver, the sole occupant of the van, died as a result of head injuries he sustained in the accident.

Martinez was originally charged with dangerous driving causing death contrary to s 249(4) of the CC. At his preliminary hearing, he elected trial by a General Division (now Superior Court) judge sitting without a jury. After some evidence was heard, with the Crown's concurrence, he entered a plea of guilty to careless driving contrary to s 130 of the HTA.

(*R v Martinez*, 1996 CanLII 663 (Ont CA))

Case #2

On November 13, 2002 at about 6:30 a.m., Michael Hutchings was driving his motor vehicle at about 65 km/h eastbound on Dixon Road between Kipling Avenue and Islington Avenue in Toronto. He struck and killed a pedestrian who was standing still in the centre of the left-turn lane in which Hutchings was travelling. The pedestrian had been looking away from the oncoming traffic. She was dressed in dark, non-reflective clothing with a hood over her head.

The traffic was light to moderate, the weather was cloudy, the road conditions were good, and the roads were dry. There was nothing obstructing Hutchings's view. Visibility was good, and the area was illuminated by the gradually rising sun, by streetlights, by lighting from the surrounding buildings in this densely populated area, and by the lights of other motor vehicles driving east and west along Dixon Road.

Hutchings was in good health; there was nothing wrong with his car, and his headlights were on. He had not consumed any alcohol or any non-prescription drugs. He had no physical or emotional problems that could have affected his driving, and he was familiar with the area. He did not see the victim at all prior to the accident, and therefore did not apply his brakes until the impact. Hutchings was extremely remorseful.

---

2   *R v Roy*, 2012 SCC 26, [2012] 2 SCR 60.

3   *R v Beatty*, 2008 SCC 5, [2008] 1 SCR 49.

At trial, Justice Kowarsky offered the following reasons for his decision to convict Hutchings of careless driving:

> On the totality of all the evidence before the Court, I am satisfied that the Crown has established a **prima facie** case of Careless Driving against the defendant. Mr. Hutchings has not provided a reasonable explanation as to why he did not see the victim prior to the collision so as to enable him to take action to avoid the collision. Consequently, the evidence does not raise a reasonable doubt that the defendant's manner of driving was careless in the circumstances.
>
> For these reasons I find that the Prosecution has proved its case beyond a reasonable doubt, and that the defendant's driving infringed Section 130 of the Highway Traffic Act in that he was driving without "due care and attention" as envisaged by the legislation. Accordingly, there will be a conviction registered against the defendant for Careless Driving.

(*R v Hutchings*, 2004 ONCJ 155)

prima facie
a fact presumed to be true unless it is disproved

Aggressive Driving and Road Rage

Although aggressive driving and road rage are not specifically mentioned in the HTA, they can lead to charges under the Act, including careless driving charges. The term "road rage" is often used when a driver threatens violence or assaults another driver, while acts of aggressive driving include tailgating, driving too closely to a pedestrian or object, passing on the shoulder of the road, cutting someone off, making rude gestures, pulling into a parking space that someone else is waiting for, and changing lanes without signalling.

Of particular interest here is speeding in excess of 50 km/h over the posted speed limit. Ministry of Transportation data indicates that the risk of death or injury is much higher at 50 km/h over the limit than it is at speeds closer to the speed limit, with those risks being greater on roads with lower posted speed limits than on roads with limits of 110 km/h. For this reason, the penalties for driving at more than 50 km/h over the limit are greatly increased, with fines ranging from $2,000 to $10,000 and lengthy driver suspensions for repeat offenders.[4]

Note that road rage and aggressive driving may go beyond a mere departure from the standards of a prudent driver that would constitute an HTA offence such as careless driving, and may be evidence of a reckless or wanton disregard for other road users, which would constitute a CC driving offence such as dangerous driving.

Rules of the Road: HTA, Part X

Direction of Traffic by Police Officer: HTA, Section 134

A police officer who is required to maintain orderly movement of traffic in order to prevent injury or damage to persons or property, or to deal with an emergency, may direct traffic and, in the event that his or her directions conflict with the rules of the road, the officer's exercise of discretion to direct traffic takes precedence over the rules of the road. As part of the power to direct traffic, an officer may also close a portion of a highway by posting signs or traffic-signalling devices, in which case no vehicle may be driven on the closed roadway except emergency vehicles and private vehicles driven by firefighters in the performance of their duties—a situation that is common in rural areas where volunteer firefighters often use their own vehicles when they are called out. Refer to the *Provincial Offences Act* (POA) wordings to gain a greater appreciation of all of the charges within this section.

---

4   O Reg 339/94. See also Ontario, Ministry of Transportation, *Dealing with Particular Situations* (2016), online: <http://www.mto.gov.on.ca/english/dandv/driver/handbook/section2.10.1.shtml>.

HELPFUL HINT

As you read through the sections describing the rules of the road, you should refer to the short-form wordings and set fines in Schedule 43 of Reg 950 to the POA, included in Appendix A to this text. These short forms assist police officers in writing the appropriate charge wordings.

In Schedule 43, the HTA section and subsection references are listed in the order in which they appear in the HTA (see Column 2 in Appendix A), and the description of the offence is listed beside them on the left (Column 1 in Appendix A). Each offence has a chronological item number (the left-most column) and a set fine, where applicable (the right-most column). For example, s 134 deals with direction of traffic by a police officer. In Schedule 43 you will see four items related to s 134—items 343 (disobey officer directing traffic), 343.1 (disobey officer directing traffic—community safety zone), 344 (drive on closed highway), and 344.1 (drive on closed highway—community safety zone).

Erection of and Effect of Signs: HTA, Section 182

Regulations may be made under the HTA to provide for or require road signs and markings on any highway in the province, and may prescribe the type of signs and markings to be used. Section 182(2) of the HTA makes obedience to the instructions given by signs or markings mandatory. This means that a sign may impose a duty in addition to that imposed by other rules of the road set out in the HTA. For example, s 143 sets out a number of circumstances where U-turns are prohibited. In addition, U-turns would also be prohibited where a sign indicates that to be the case, even if it would otherwise be permitted under s 143.

Right of Way—Uncontrolled Intersection: HTA, Section 135

Where two roads intersect and there is no traffic control sign or device, a driver approaching an intersection shall yield to a vehicle that has already entered the intersection from an adjacent highway. If both vehicles enter the intersection from adjacent highways at the same time, the vehicle on the right has the right of way over the vehicle on the left (see Figure 4.1). Note that this section uses a broad definition of "vehicle" and explicitly includes streetcars.

Stop-Sign—Controlled Intersections: HTA, Section 136

When approaching a stop sign at an intersection, a driver is required to come to a full stop

- at the stop line or, if none,
- at a crosswalk or, if there is neither a stop line nor a crosswalk, then
- immediately before entering the intersection.

If a driver stops on, or beyond, rather than at the stop line or crosswalk, he or she could be charged with "disobey stop sign—stop wrong place" (HTA, s 136(1)(a)). If a driver proceeds all the way into the intersection (past the extension of the edges of the adjoining roadway), he or she should be charged with "disobey stop sign—fail to stop" (s 136(1)(a)). The driver shall yield the right of way to traffic on the adjacent crossroad that is in the intersection or so close to the intersection that to proceed would create an immediate hazard (for example, if the driver pulled out from the stop line, causing a vehicle with the right of way to brake sharply).

FIGURE 4.1 Uncontrolled Intersection

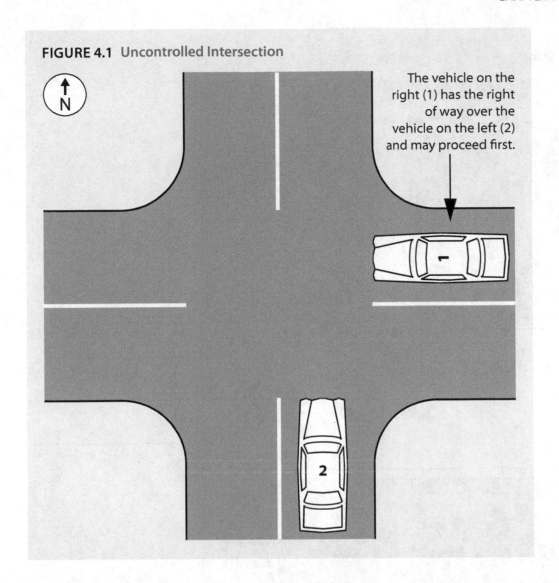

The vehicle on the right (1) has the right of way over the vehicle on the left (2) and may proceed first.

Yield-Sign-Controlled Intersections: HTA, Section 138

A driver approaching an intersection controlled by a yield right-of-way sign shall slow down or stop, if necessary, in order to yield the right of way to traffic already in the intersection or so close to the intersection that failure to yield would create an immediate hazard. When entering a highway from a private road, the driver is required to yield to highway traffic whether or not the private road is controlled by a yield sign (HTA, s 139).

Pedestrian Crossovers: HTA, Section 140

A driver shall yield to a pedestrian or person in a wheelchair if the person is proceeding in the crossover on the part of the roadway that the driver is approaching. If the person is proceeding on the other side of the roadway, the driver must still yield and wait until the pedestrian has safely crossed the roadway.

As of January 2016, when a pedestrian enters a pedestrian crossover or school crossing, traffic on both sides of the road must come to a stop, and remain stopped until the pedestrian has completely crossed the roadway. This means that even where the pedestrian has passed the lanes of traffic on one side of the road, vehicles must remain stationary until the pedestrian has cleared the entire crossover.

FIGURE 4.2 Overtaking Stopped Vehicle at Crossover

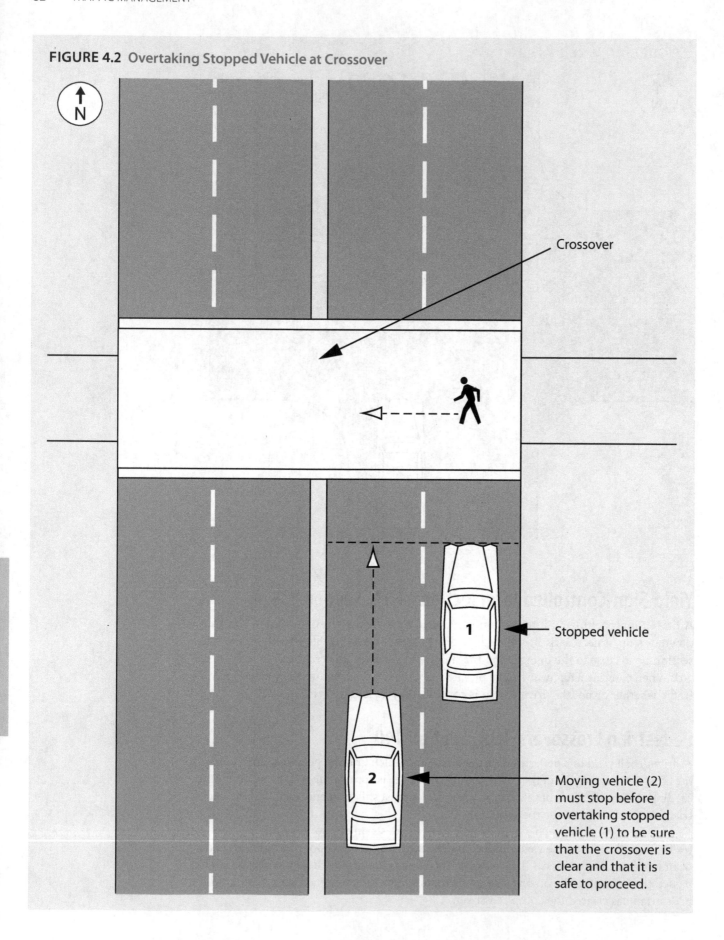

Crossover

Stopped vehicle

Moving vehicle (2) must stop before overtaking stopped vehicle (1) to be sure that the crossover is clear and that it is safe to proceed.

FIGURE 4.3 Overtaking Moving Vehicle Near Crossover

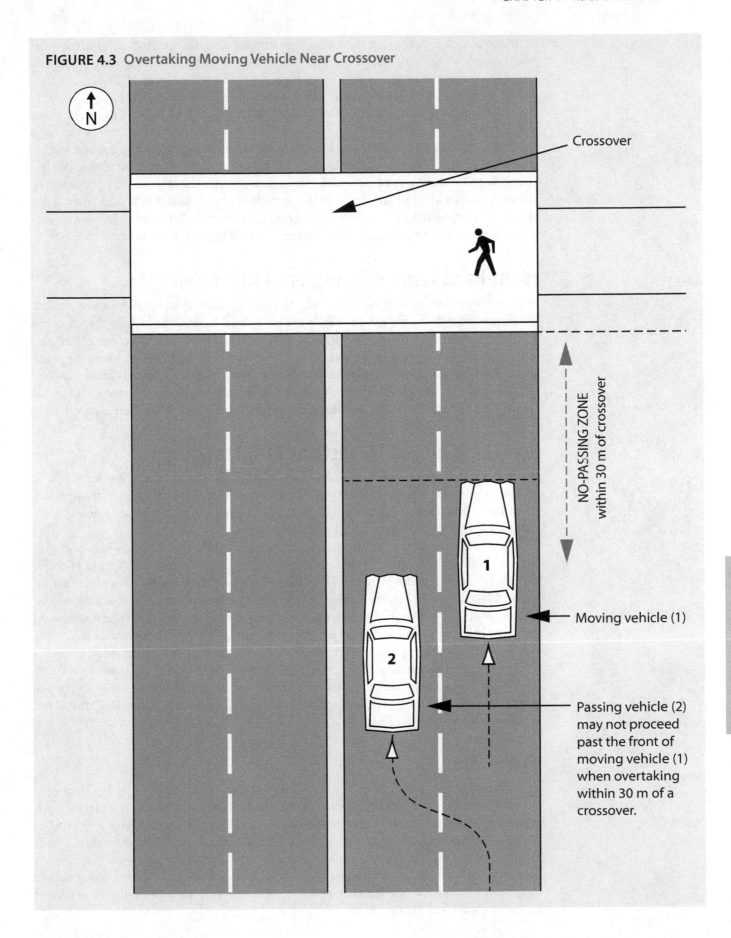

Crossover

NO-PASSING ZONE within 30 m of crossover

Moving vehicle (1)

Passing vehicle (2) may not proceed past the front of moving vehicle (1) when overtaking within 30 m of a crossover.

If one vehicle is overtaking another vehicle stopped at a crossover, the driver of the overtaking vehicle shall stop before entering the crossover and yield the right of way to any pedestrian until the pedestrian is no longer on the roadway (see Figure 4.2).

If a vehicle is overtaking another vehicle that is moving within 30 m of a crossover, the overtaking vehicle shall not allow the front of the vehicle to pass beyond the front of the vehicle that is being overtaken (see Figure 4.3). Because the overtaking driver's view of a pedestrian to his or her right would be obstructed both while approaching the intersection and while stopped, this rule is intended to prevent the overtaking driver from hitting a pedestrian whom he or she cannot see until it is too late to stop. On the other hand, a pedestrian or person in a wheelchair should not enter an intersection where a vehicle is so close that it is impractical or impossible for the driver to yield the right of way. Cyclists who wish to use a crossover must become pedestrians by dismounting and walking their bikes across the highway.

Right-Hand Turns: HTA, Sections 141(2) to (4)

A driver intending to turn right onto an intersecting highway must, if there are marked lanes, use the right-hand lane or, if there are no marked lanes, must keep to the left of the right curb or the edge of the roadway, and shall make the right turn by entering the right-hand lane of the intersecting highway, or, if there is no right-hand lane, by keeping to the left of the right-hand curb or edge of the roadway being entered. If there is more than one lane designated as a right-hand turn lane, a driver shall approach the intersection in one of the lanes, and turn from that lane into the corresponding adjacent lane (see Figure 4.4).

Left-Hand Turns: HTA, Sections 141(5) to (8)

A driver intending to turn left onto a roadway other than at an intersection—for example, to enter a private driveway—shall cross the path of vehicles approaching from the opposite direction only when it is safe to do so. It is safe as long as the driver does not cause an accident or cause drivers of approaching vehicles to panic.

Where a driver intends to turn left at an intersection, he or she shall, where there are marked lanes, approach the intersection in the left-hand lane provided for use of traffic travelling in the direction in which his or her vehicle is proceeding, or, where there are no marked lanes, then by keeping immediately to the right of the centre line of the highway or its extension. He or she shall then leave the intersection by turning onto the intersecting highway, entering it in the left-hand lane for traffic moving in the direction he or she is proceeding. Where there is no marked left-hand lane in the intersecting highway, he or she shall make the turn entering the intersecting roadway to the right of the centre line.

If there is more than one left-turn lane, the driver shall approach the intersection in one of the lanes, leave the intersection in that lane, and enter the corresponding lane of the intersecting highway (see Figure 4.5).

Exceptions

Exceptions to these rules can be made for long vehicles, such as tractor-trailers, that cannot make a right or left turn in the confines of the turn lanes provided (HTA, s 141(9)). Such vehicles are deemed to be in compliance with s 141 if they comply as closely as is practicable. In reality, a long vehicle may need to make a wide right turn, moving quite far out from the curb or the right-turn lane into an adjacent lane, or across the centre line, in order to complete the turn without running over the curb or the sidewalk. Similarly, a long vehicle may need to make a wide left turn in order to avoid side-swiping a centre-line road divider or traffic signal (see Figure 4.6).

FIGURE 4.4 Right-Hand Turn

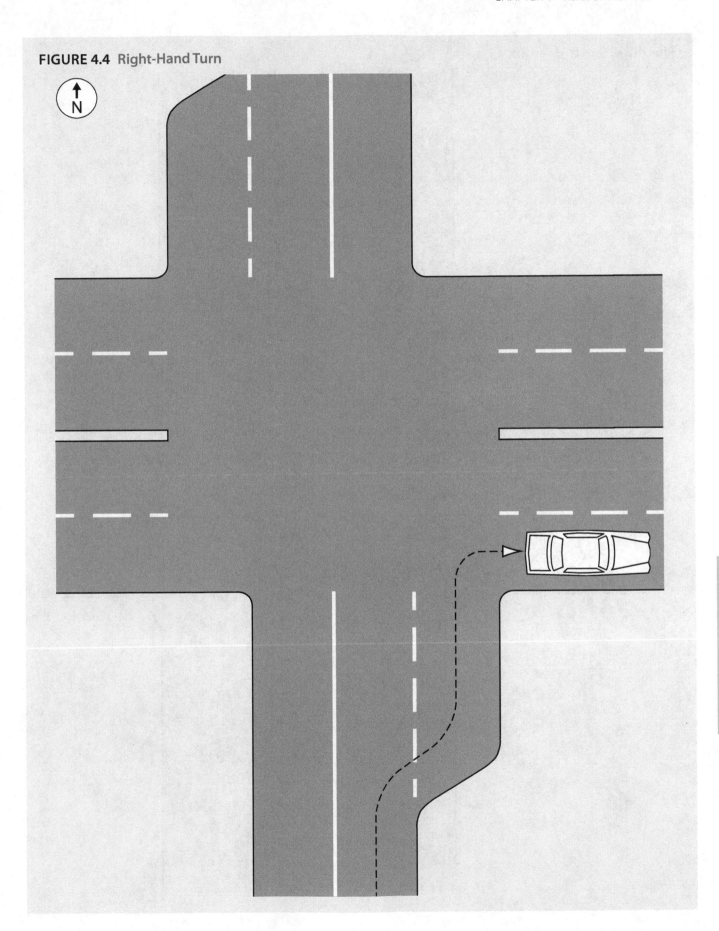

FIGURE 4.5 Left-Hand Turn

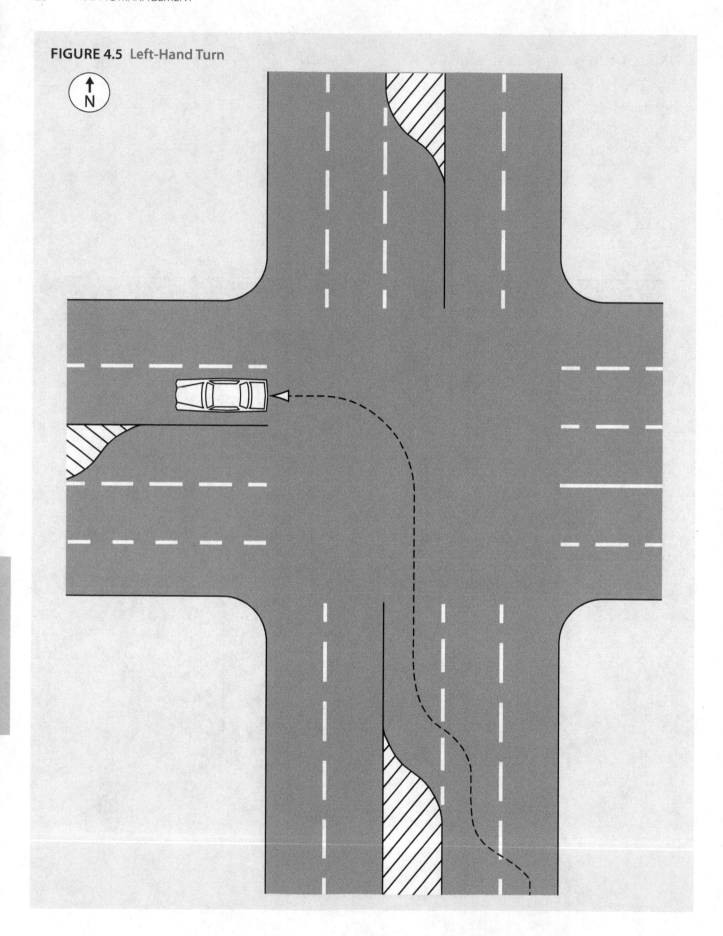

FIGURE 4.6 Wide Turns

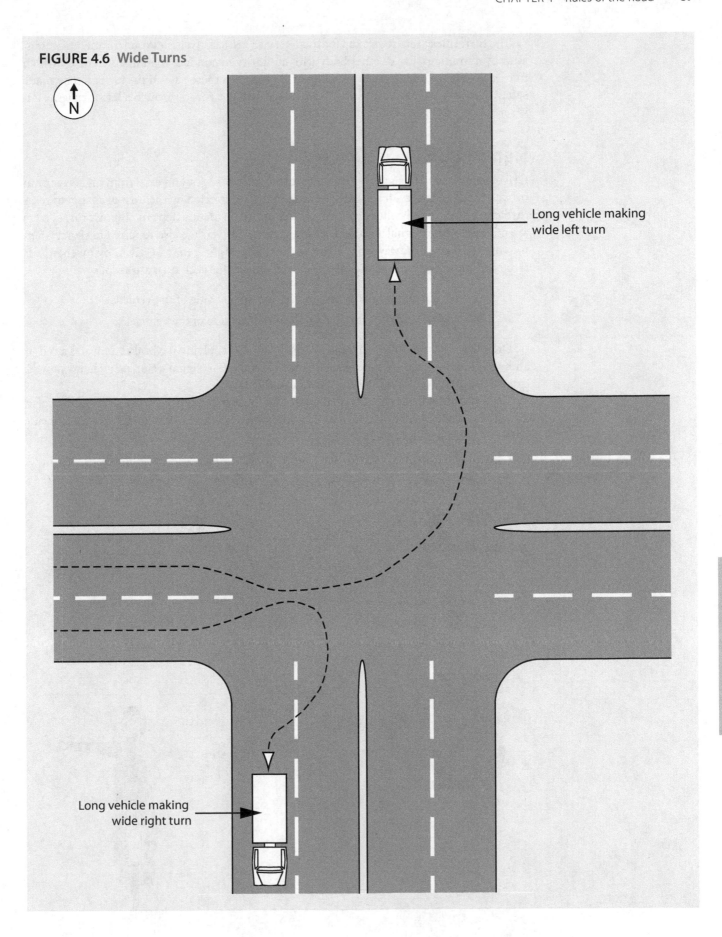

Long vehicle making wide left turn

Long vehicle making wide right turn

The turn rules are also relaxed for road-service vehicles (vehicles used for road maintenance by a municipality or other body with authority to conduct road maintenance), which may make right and left turns without complying with these rules if the turns can be made safely. A road-service vehicle may also proceed straight ahead through a left-turn lane, if it is safe to do so (HTA, ss 141(4) and (8)).

Signalling: HTA, Section 142

Drivers are obliged to signal right and left turns, lane changes, and exits from highways onto private roads or drives, if any other vehicle might be affected by the turn or manoeuvre. A turn can be made only after determining that it can be made safely. In other words, drivers are not required to signal if no vehicle is near them. Drivers are also required to signal when moving onto the roadway from a parked position. Signals may be given by mechanical/electrical means or by hand signals. The hand signals for each turn are as follows:

- Left turn: Extend the arm horizontally out the left side of the vehicle.
- Right turn: Extend the arm upward out the left side of the vehicle.

Drivers are also required to indicate stops. Usually, applying the brakes activates a red or amber light on the rear of the vehicle to indicate a stop. To signal a stop using hand signals, extend the arm downward out the left side of the vehicle.

The hand signals for cyclists are the same as those for motor vehicle drivers, although a cyclist may also signal a right turn by extending the right arm horizontally on the right side of the bicycle (see Figure 4.7).

FIGURE 4.7
Hand
Signals

Left-hand turn: Left arm straight

Stop: Left arm bent down

Right-hand turn: Left arm bent up

Right-hand turn
on bicycle:
Right arm
straight

Yielding to Buses in Bus Bays: HTA, Section 142.1, and O Reg 393/02

Drivers in a lane adjacent to a bus bay shall yield right of way to a bus leaving the bus bay and re-entering traffic when the driver of the bus has signalled his or her intention to do so. A bus driver shall not signal an intention to re-enter traffic until he or she is ready to do so, and the driver shall not re-enter the stream of traffic if a vehicle in the adjacent lane is so close that it is impractical for the driver of that vehicle to yield the right of way. O Reg 393/02 defines a "bus bay" as a part of the highway next to a bus stop from which passengers enter or exit the bus, and from which the bus exits and enters the adjacent stream of traffic. The bus bay may be inset, as indicated in Figure 4.8, or it may be the lane nearest the curb where the bus stop is located. The regulation also requires buses to have a bus bay yield sign attached to the back of the bus.

U-Turns: HTA, Section 143

In general, drivers may make U-turns provided that it is safe to do so and that they signal their intention to do so. However, U-turns are prohibited in the following circumstances:

- on a curve, where traffic approaching from either direction cannot be seen by the driver making the U-turn within a distance of 150 m;
- on or within 30 m of a railroad crossing (absolute prohibition);
- on an approach or near the crest of a grade, where the turning vehicle cannot be seen by a driver of another vehicle approaching from either direction within 150 m; or
- within 150 m of a bridge, viaduct, or tunnel, where the driver's view is obstructed within that distance.

Traffic Lights: HTA, Section 144

Where there is a traffic light at an intersection, a driver must stop at the stop line or, if there is no stop line, before entering a crosswalk or, if there is no sign or crosswalk, immediately before entering the intersection. If there is a traffic light that is not at an intersection, the same rules apply, except that if there is neither a sign or a crosswalk, the vehicle will stop at least 5 m back from the traffic light (see Figure 4.9).

When a driver is permitted to proceed but there is a pedestrian lawfully in a crosswalk, the driver shall yield to the pedestrian in the crosswalk. For example, where the driver wishes to make a right turn on a green light and pass through a crosswalk, he or she must yield to any pedestrian lawfully walking through a crosswalk on a green light. A driver who may turn right on a red light must also yield to oncoming traffic in the lane he or she seeks to enter because the traffic facing a green light has the right of way. This rule also applies to vehicles in private driveways and roadways controlled by a traffic light where the driver faces a red light and wishes to turn right.

Where there is a traffic light system with different light or arrow signals for different lanes, the driver shall obey the light or arrow signal for the lane he or she is in.

Green Lights: HTA, Section 144

A driver approaching a green circular light may proceed or turn left or right, unless otherwise indicated. A driver approaching a flashing green light or a solid or flashing green arrow together with a circular solid green light may proceed forward or turn left or right. If a driver is approaching a green arrow, or arrows in combination with a red or amber circular light, the driver may proceed only in the direction indicated by the green arrows.

FIGURE 4.8 Yielding to Bus

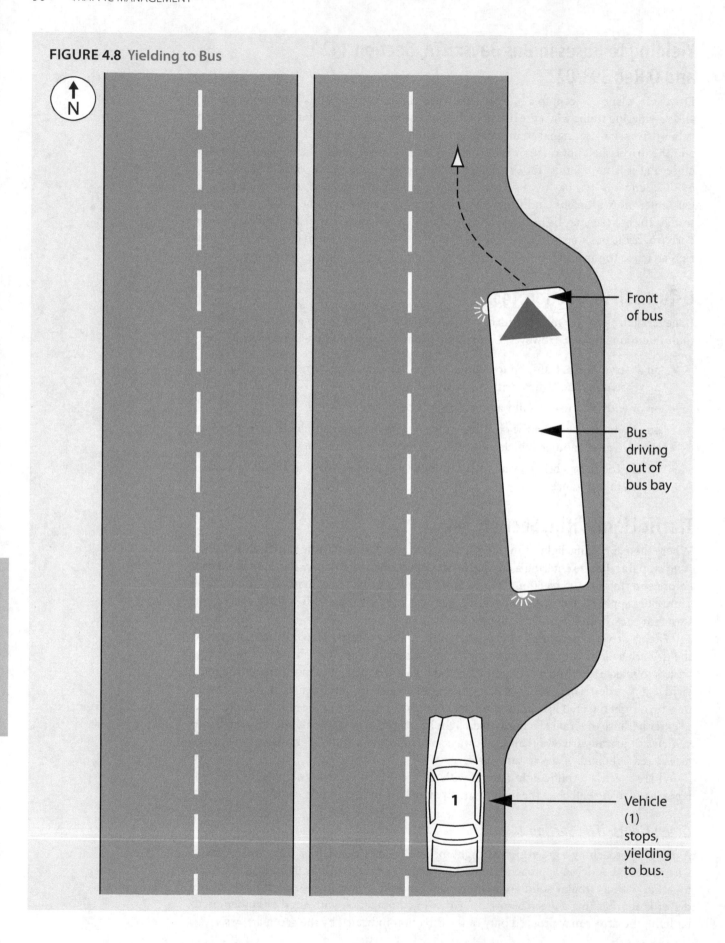

Front of bus

Bus driving out of bus bay

Vehicle (1) stops, yielding to bus.

FIGURE 4.9 Traffic Lights

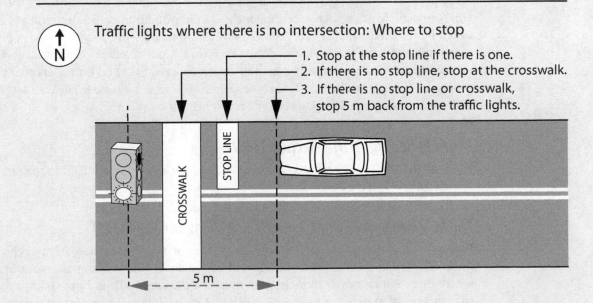

Traffic lights at intersection: Where to stop

1
Stop at
the stop line
if there is one.

STOP LINE

CROSSWALK

2
If there is no
stop line, stop at
the crosswalk.

2

CROSSWALK

3

3
If there is no stop line or
crosswalk, stop before
entering the intersection.

Traffic lights where there is no intersection: Where to stop

1. Stop at the stop line if there is one.
2. If there is no stop line, stop at the crosswalk.
3. If there is no stop line or crosswalk,
   stop 5 m back from the traffic lights.

CROSSWALK

STOP LINE

5 m

Amber Lights: HTA, Section 144

A driver approaching an amber light shall stop his or her vehicle if he or she can safely do so; otherwise, he or she may proceed through the light with caution. Similarly, if a driver is approaching an amber arrow, he or she shall stop if it is safe to do so; otherwise, he or she may proceed with caution in the direction indicated by the amber arrow. A driver approaching a flashing amber light may proceed with caution; this light functions much like a yield sign.

Red Lights: HTA, Section 144

A driver approaching a red light shall stop and not proceed until a green light is shown. Anyone who violates the rule with respect to a red light is guilty of an offence under s 144(31.2.1) of the HTA and is liable to a fine of not less than $200 and not more than $1,000. Anyone who violates the rule with respect to an amber light is guilty of an offence under s 144(31.2) and is liable to a fine not less than $150 and not more than $500. Sections 144(18.1) to (18.6) deal with a charge of running a red light where the evidence for the offence has been obtained by a red light camera. In this case, a charge is issued on the basis of the camera evidence and may be laid against the owner of the offending vehicle if the driver cannot be identified. The charge must be laid under s 144(18.1) if it is against the owner, or under s 144(18.2) if it is against the driver.

Right and Left Turns on Red Lights: HTA, Section 144(19)

Despite the stop-on-red rule, a driver facing a red light who stops and yields the right of way to approaching traffic may turn right on a red light or turn left on a red light from a one-way street into a one-way street (see Figure 4.10).

Right and Left Turns for Transit Authority Buses: HTA, Section 144(19.1)

A bus driver on a scheduled route approaching a traffic signal showing a white vertical bar may turn right or left with caution.

Emergency Vehicles: HTA, Section 144(20)

A driver of an emergency vehicle as defined in the HTA—that is, a vehicle being used in an emergency on which a siren is continuously sounding and from which intermittent flashes of red light or red and blue light are visible in all directions—*may, after stopping*, proceed through a red light *if it is safe to do so*. Therefore, a police officer driving a marked or unmarked cruiser, upon entering an intersection on a red light and hitting another vehicle proceeding on a green light, will likely be charged (for example, under HTA, s 144(18), red light—fail to stop, for failing to stop at a red light).

Flashing Red Light: HTA, Section 144(21)

A driver shall stop and proceed with caution, treating a flashing red light in the same way as a stop sign (HTA, s 144(21)).

Traffic Signals and Pedestrians: HTA, Sections 144(22) to (29)

Pedestrians are not free to step out on the roadway at any time or place of their choosing, even though they generally have the right of way when lawfully crossing the roadway. First, where there is a crosswalk, a pedestrian must use the crosswalk and not simply cross the road at a location of his or her own choosing. A pedestrian facing a circular green light, a

FIGURE 4.10 Right and Left Turns on Red Lights

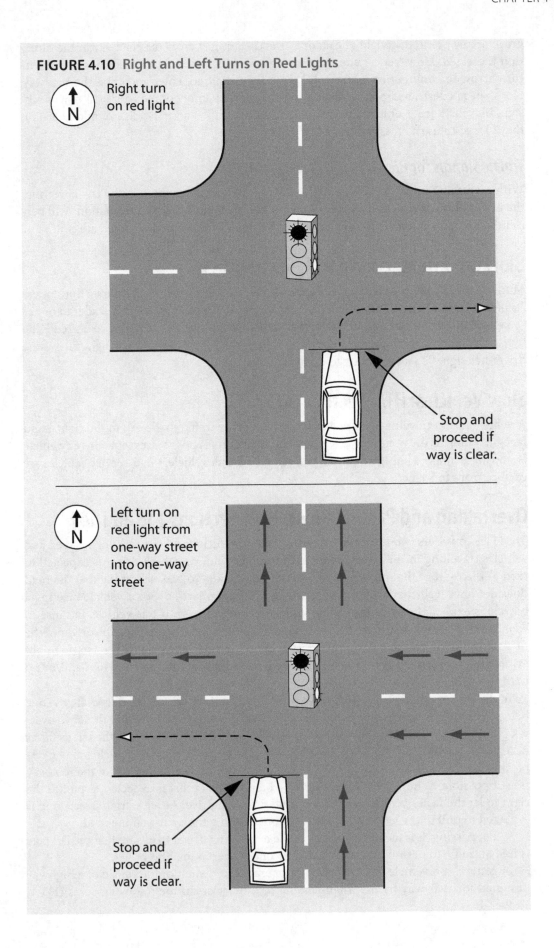

Right turn
on red light

Stop and
proceed if
way is clear.

Left turn on
red light from
one-way street
into one-way
street

Stop and
proceed if
way is clear.

green arrow pointed straight ahead, or a "walk" sign may cross the roadway in the direction indicated. However, a pedestrian facing a flashing green light or flashing green left-turn arrow in conjunction with a solid green light shall not enter and cross the roadway. Nor shall a pedestrian cross the roadway when facing an amber or red light or a "don't walk" sign. Bicyclists are prohibited from riding in a crosswalk, and must dismount and walk if they intend to use a crosswalk.

Traffic Signals for Bicycles: HTA, Section 144(32)

With increasing use of bicycles, particularly in urban areas, changes in the law governing the use of bicycles may be expected. For example, as of January 2017, regulations will permit the Ministry to create special bicycle traffic signals for use in designated areas.

Blocking Intersections: HTA, Section 145

Municipalities may pass bylaws prohibiting drivers from entering an intersection unless "traffic in front of him or her is moving in a manner that would reasonably lead him or her to believe he or she can clear the intersection before the signal … changes to … red." The bylaw does not apply to drivers entering an intersection to make a left or right turn if the driver has signalled an intention to do that.

Slow Vehicles: HTA, Section 147

A vehicle that is travelling at a slower speed than other traffic shall keep to the right-hand lane or, if there is only one lane, as close to the right curb as possible, except where a vehicle is slowing to make a left-hand turn or overtaking another vehicle. Road-service vehicles are exempt from this rule.

Overtaking and Passing Rules: HTA, Sections 148 and 149

The HTA considers two situations involving passing vehicles: vehicles meeting head on and vehicles travelling in the same direction. In the "head on" case, each driver is expected to turn to the right of the roadway to allow each other room to pass, assuming that the road does not have well-marked lanes of adequate width. Similarly, a motor vehicle meeting a bicycle is expected to give the cyclist sufficient room to pass. If one vehicle, because of weight or load, cannot turn to the right to make room for another to pass, the driver of the first vehicle shall stop and, if necessary, assist the other vehicle to pass. This scenario might arise with an oversized or long vehicle on a narrow highway with narrow lanes and/or no hard shoulder.

equestrian
a person riding a horse

In the case of a vehicle or **equestrian** overtaking another vehicle or equestrian, the one being overtaken is required to pull to the right in order to permit the other driver to overtake him or her. Similarly, the overtaking vehicle is obliged to pull out to the left as far as necessary to avoid collision with the other vehicle or equestrian. The vehicle being overtaken is not expected to pull off the road, but is expected to leave one-half of the roadway free, if possible. Where a vehicle is passing a bicycle, the cyclist is expected to pull to the right to let the faster vehicle pass; at the same time, the driver or equestrian overtaking is expected to pull to the left to pass safely without running the cyclist off the road.

When passing, it is the responsibility of the overtaking driver to ensure that the left lane is free of traffic to permit passing and that no one is overtaking him or her.

In general, no vehicle is to be driven or operated to the left of the centre of a highway designed for two-way traffic, when passing or otherwise, in the following cases (HTA, s 149(1)):

- when approaching the crest of a hill, where the driver's view is obstructed;
- on a curve in a roadway, where the driver's view is obstructed;
- within 30 m of a bridge, viaduct, or tunnel, where the driver's view is obstructed so that an approaching vehicle cannot be seen within that distance; or
- within 30 m of a railway crossing, whether or not the view is obstructed.

There are some exceptions: highways divided into lanes, where there are more lanes in one direction than another, and one-way roads. Road-service vehicles also may be driven to the left of the centre line, provided that appropriate precautions are taken (HTA, s 149(2)).

Passing on the Right and the Use of Shoulders: HTA, Sections 150 and 151

Although passing on the right is usually prohibited, there are some circumstances where it is permitted:

- where the vehicle being overtaken is about to make a left turn and has signalled a left turn, and the pavement of the lane is wide enough to safely permit the manoeuvre (only if the shoulder is paved); and
- where a highway is designated for the use of one-way traffic.

However, no vehicle shall pull off the roadway to pass another vehicle. Remember that the roadway includes the travelled part of the pavement, but not the shoulder. There are exceptions to this rule—if the shoulder is paved, and the vehicle being overtaken has signalled and is making a left turn, passing on the right is permitted. Tow trucks responding to a police request for assistance, road-service vehicles, and emergency vehicles may also pass on the right. There is also a provision that permits a person with authority, employed on a road-building machine or a road-service vehicle, to direct traffic to pass that vehicle on the right.

The Ministry of Transportation may also designate, through a regulation and appropriate signs, any paved shoulder on a King's Highway for the use of traffic (HTA, s 151).

One-Way Traffic: HTA, Section 153

A one-way traffic lane is created by designation and by the posting of official one-way signs.

Multi-Lane Highways: HTA, Section 154

A highway may be divided into several clearly marked lanes. A vehicle must be driven within a lane, and shall not change lanes until the driver determines that the lane change can be made safely. Where a highway is divided into three lanes, no vehicle shall be driven in the centre lane, unless the vehicle is overtaking, making a left turn, or the lane is designated and signed for the use of vehicles to travel in a particular direction. Before using the lane, a driver must be sure that the roadway is visible and clear of other traffic for a safe distance.

Any lane may be designated for a particular class of vehicles, for slow moving traffic, or for traffic travelling in a particular direction where the lane has official signs posted (HTA, ss 154 to 155).

Divided Highways: HTA, Sections 156 and 157

Traffic on a divided highway must stay on the roadway and move in the direction indicated. Vehicles may not drive on the median or cross the median to another roadway, unless a crossing has been provided. A road-service vehicle may operate off the roadway, but must stay on its side of the separation between roadways. Reversing is also prohibited on divided highways, on either the roadway or the shoulder, where the maximum speed is more than 80 km/h. Emergency vehicles, road-service vehicles, and drivers reversing to render assistance to another driver are exempt from this rule. Service vehicles and bicycles may travel on a paved shoulder.

Maintaining a Safe Distance: HTA, Sections 158 and 159

A driver of a vehicle following another vehicle is expected to maintain a safe and prudent distance between his or her vehicle and the vehicle in front. There is no specific rule setting out a distance in metres; rather, a driver shall have regard to speed, amount of traffic, and highway conditions. However, if the vehicle following is a commercial vehicle travelling more than 60 km/h, it must keep at least 60 m back from the vehicle in front. This rule should not be interpreted to mean that a following vehicle is prevented from drawing closer if it is overtaking and passing another vehicle.

When an emergency vehicle approaches a vehicle from any direction, with emergency signals on, the driver is obliged to pull to the right-hand curb and stop, provided that the vehicle does not stop in an intersection. Where there is more than one lane in the same direction, the vehicle may pull to the nearest curb or side of the road and stop; this means that traffic in the left lane of a one-way highway with two or more lanes in the same direction should pull to the left-hand curb (see Figure 4.11).

If a driver is following a fire truck that is responding to an alarm (with its emergency lights flashing), the driver must keep back 150 m.

If an emergency vehicle or tow truck is stopped on a highway with its flashers on, a driver on the same side of the highway must slow down and observe caution when passing (HTA, s 159). If there are two or more lanes on the same side of the highway as the emergency vehicle, a driver shall move into another lane to leave an empty lane between the lane the driver is travelling in and the stopped emergency vehicle, if it is practical to do so (see Figure 4.12). The fine for failing to slow down and use caution, or to leave a lane between the driver's vehicle and the emergency vehicle on a highway with more than two lanes in the direction of travel, is between $400 and $2,000 for the first offence, with increased penalties for subsequent convictions, including higher fines (between $1,000 and $4,000), imprisonment (not exceeding six months), and/or licence suspension (not more than two years).

Towing Other Vehicles: HTA, Sections 160 to 161 and 178

A vehicle may only tow one vehicle unless the towing vehicle is a commercial vehicle (HTA, s 161). This means that a sport utility vehicle, no matter how powerful, may not tow a camper trailer and a boat trailer at the same time. Nor shall any person ride as a passenger in any house or boat trailer in tow (s 188). Towing a person riding a skateboard, a bicycle, coaster, sled, toboggan, toy vehicle, or any other type of conveyance, or wearing roller skates, in-line skates, or skis is prohibited (s 160). Also, a person on a motor-assisted bicycle, bicycle, coaster, sled, toboggan, skateboard, toy vehicle, or any other type of conveyance, or wearing roller skates, in-line skates, or skis, may not attach themselves to, or cling to, a motor vehicle on a highway. A bicycle that is designed for one person shall not carry more than one person, and a motor-assisted bicycle, by definition, can carry only one person (s 178).

Crowding the Driver's Seat: HTA, Section 162

A driver shall not have persons or property in the front seat (if a bench seat) or driver's seat that impedes the management or control of the vehicle. Note that there is no precise or explicit list of prohibitions.

FIGURE 4.11 Giving Way to Emergency Vehicle on One-Way Highway

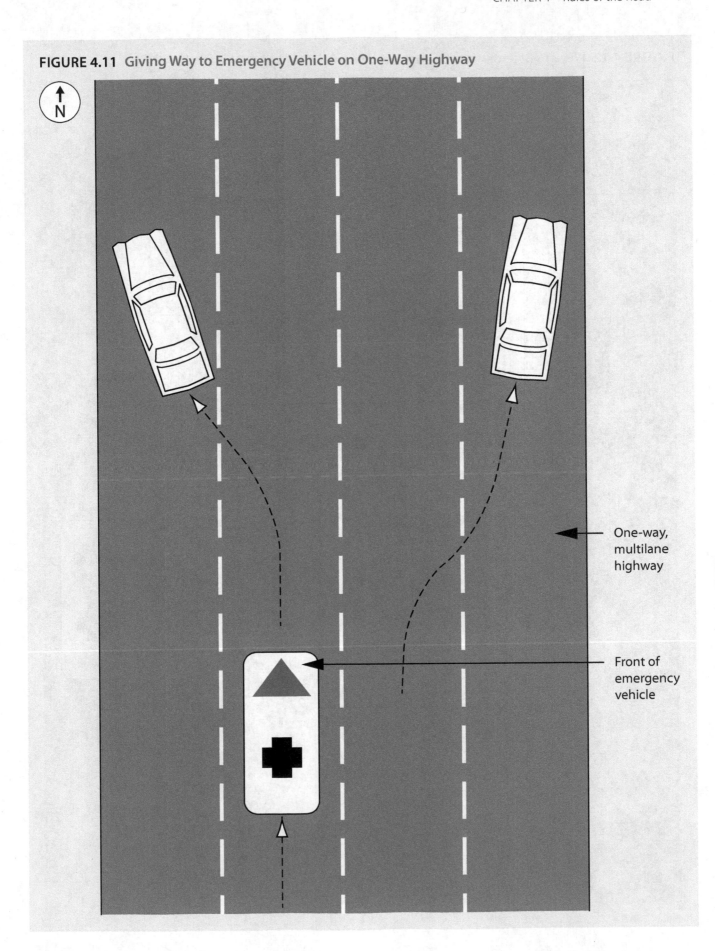

One-way, multilane highway

Front of emergency vehicle

FIGURE 4.12 Passing Stopped Emergency Vehicle on a Two-Lane Highway

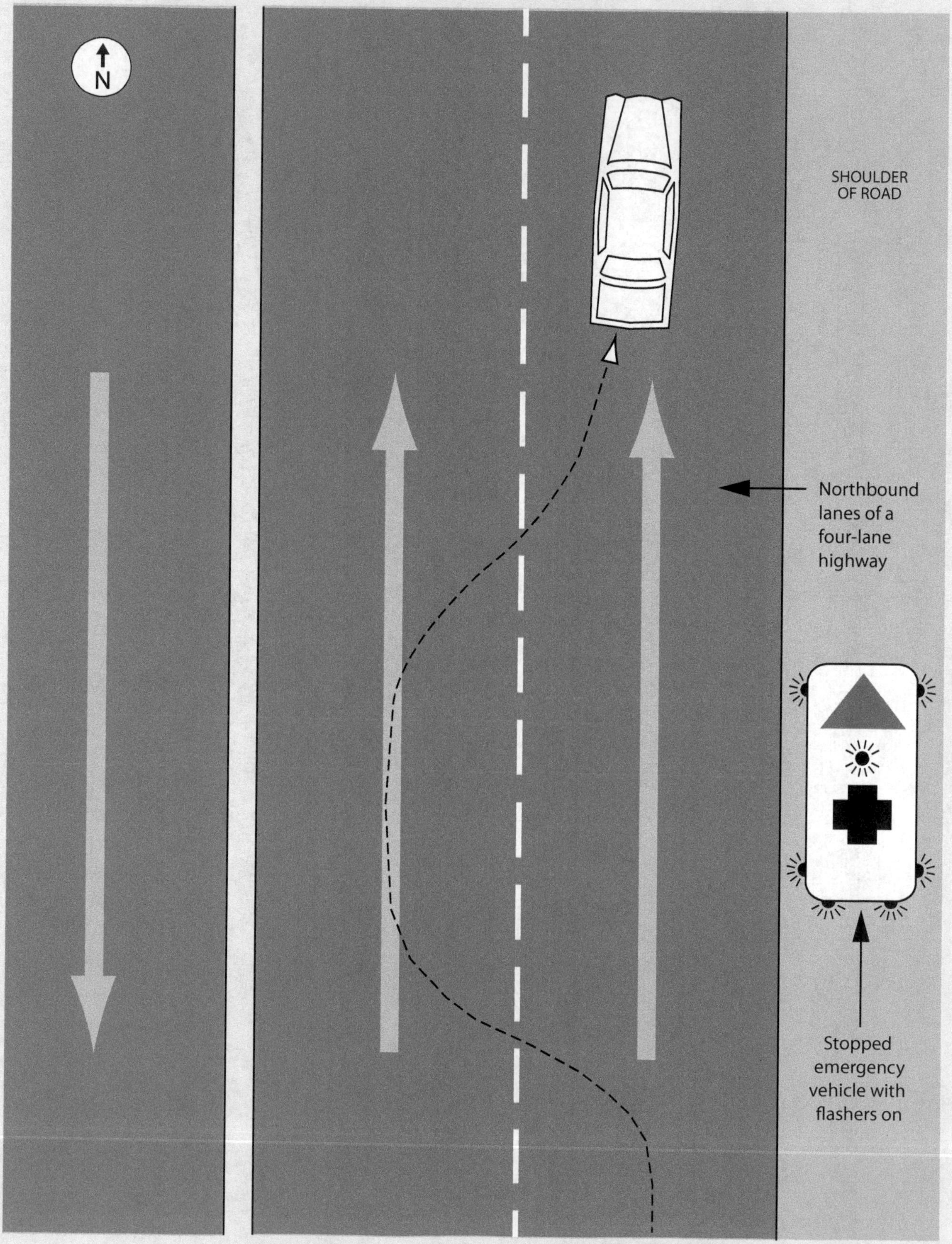

N

SHOULDER
OF ROAD

Northbound
lanes of a
four-lane
highway

Stopped
emergency
vehicle with
flashers on

Stopping at Railway Crossings: HTA, Sections 163 and 164

A driver approaching a railway crossing when a flag person or signal system is warning of an approaching train shall stop at least 5 m from the nearest rail and proceed only when it is safe to do so. If there is a crossing gate or other barrier, driving around or under it while it is closed or closing is prohibited. Remember that public buses and school buses are subject to special rules regarding precautions at railroad crossings. These are set out in s 174 of the HTA and discussed later in this chapter.

Opening Vehicle Doors on the Highway: HTA, Section 165

No one shall open a door on either side of a motor vehicle on the highway before ensuring that this will not interfere with the movement of any other person or vehicle. Similarly, no one shall leave a door open on the side of the vehicle available to moving traffic for longer than necessary to pick up or drop off passengers. In urban areas, it is the violation of this section that often leads to cyclists getting the "door prize."

Approaching and Passing Streetcars: HTA, Section 166

No vehicle or equestrian shall overtake a streetcar standing in the roadway for the purpose of taking on or discharging passengers. All vehicles must stop at least 2 m back from the front or rear entrance of the streetcar on the side on which passengers are disembarking, and may not resume until all passengers have boarded the streetcar or are clear of it. Where a safety zone for loading and disembarking passengers has been created by municipal bylaw, other vehicles are not required to stop. As well, no vehicle shall pass on the left any streetcar that is operating in the centre of the roadway, whether it is standing or moving, except where the streetcar is operating on a one-way street.[5] Municipal fire trucks may pass a streetcar on the left in the course of responding to an emergency.

Approaching Horses Ridden or Driven on the Highway: HTA, Section 167

The driver of a motor vehicle or motor-assisted bicycle is obliged to approach with caution an equestrian, a vehicle being drawn by a horse or other animal, or a horse being led, so as not to frighten the animal or cause injury to persons riding on the animal or in a vehicle drawn by the animal. This section is of little significance in urban areas, but is of some importance where members of some Mennonite and other Anabaptist religious communities use horses and horse-drawn wagons and carriages on highways.

Use of Headlights: HTA, Sections 168 and 169

When vehicle lamps are required to be lit, the driver shall use the lower beam when approaching within 150 m of an oncoming vehicle and when following within 60 m of another vehicle, except when in the act of overtaking that vehicle. Emergency vehicles and public utility emergency vehicles may be equipped with high-beam lamps that produce alternate flashes of white light to be used when responding to an emergency.

---

5   Section 166 also refers to electric railways. This reference is to a form of streetcar referred to as an interurban car or radial railway. These were relatively high-speed streetcars, often on their own rights of way, that provided service to suburban areas in the first two decades of the 20th century. The fact that the reference is still there long after the disappearance of these railways, and after many statutory revisions, indicates that the HTA is a relatively old statute that has not been thoroughly revised in terms of language and content. However, what goes around, comes around: under proposed public transit plans in major cities such as Toronto, light rapid transit vehicles with their own right of way are making a comeback.

Parking, Standing, or Stopping: HTA, Section 170

The general rule is that no vehicle shall park, stand, or stop on the roadway where it is possible to park off the roadway. If it is not possible to park off the roadway, there must be a clear view of the vehicle for 125 m in either direction. Exceptions to this rule are made for the following:

- roadways in a city, town, village, township, county, or police village that has bylaws regulating parking, standing, and stopping;
- road-service vehicles, if they have parked safely; and
- vehicles that are so disabled that it is impossible to avoid temporarily contravening these provisions.

On many highways, parking is controlled by regulations or, in built-up areas, by municipal bylaws, so that the basic rule often does not apply. If there is a conflict between a municipal bylaw and a Ministry of Transportation regulation governing a stretch of roadway, the regulation will prevail. If a police officer or municipal bylaw enforcement officer with duties under the HTA finds a vehicle on the highway contravening these provisions, he or she may move the vehicle or have it towed.

A vehicle parked or standing on the highway must be secured to prevent the vehicle from being set in motion. This means that the parking brake or hand brake should be set and, if on a grade, the wheels should be blocked.

There are special safety rules for parked or standing commercial vehicles. If the highway permits a speed in excess of 60 km/h during a time when lights are required, the vehicle shall have a sufficient number of flares, lamps, or lanterns, approved by the Ministry, that will display warning lights visible for 150 m for a period of eight hours. Alternatively, the vehicle may be equipped with Ministry-approved reflectors. If the commercial vehicle becomes disabled and is parked on the roadway where the speed is in excess of 60 km/h at a time when lights are required, the driver is required to light the lamps or lanterns or set out flares and reflectors, which shall be placed 30 m in advance of the vehicle and 30 m behind the vehicle.

In no case shall a vehicle be parked to interfere with the movement of traffic or the clearing of snow. A violation may result in a fine of between $20 and $100. However, if there is a municipal bylaw that deals with impeding traffic or clearing snow, it shall prevail over the rule in the HTA. In either case, a police officer or bylaw enforcement officer may remove the vehicle and store it in a suitable place, and the costs of doing this shall be a lien on the vehicle, enforceable like a civil debt. An unpaid lien may result in the vehicle being sold and the sale proceeds applied to pay off the debt.

Tow-Truck Services: HTA, Section 171

Because tow-truck operators can monitor police and emergency communications, several may arrive at the scene of a collision, sometimes before police and ambulances. It is not hard to imagine a collision scene where several competing tow-truck operators are attempting to sell their services. In order to make it easier for emergency crews and police to do their jobs at a collision scene, the HTA sets out some rules governing what tow-truck operators may and may not do at a collision scene on a King's Highway:

- No tow-truck operator may make or convey an offer of towing services while the operator is within 200 m of the scene of a collision or a vehicle involved in a collision.
- No tow truck may park or stop within 200 m of a collision scene or a vehicle involved in a collision if there are already enough tow trucks at the scene to tow vehicles damaged in the collision.

If the police, highway maintenance staff, a person involved in a collision, or another authorized person requests the services of a tow truck, the restrictions in s 171 of the HTA do not apply. Note that s 171 applies to King's Highways (numbered provincial highways), but not to other provincial roads or county or municipal roads. However, counties, regional governments, and municipalities may regulate the activities of tow-truck operators through licensing and bylaws. Contravention of s 171, where it does apply, may result in fines of between $200 and $1,000 for a first offence. A subsequent offence, within five years less a day of a previous conviction, may result in a fine of between $400 and $2,000, or in imprisonment for a term of not more than six months, or in both.

As of January 2017, the regulatory power governing tow-truck operations will be broadened to give the Ministry of Transportation more power to define what a tow truck is and how and where tow trucks may operate.

Racing and Stunts Prohibited on Highways: HTA, Sections 172 and 173

Drag racing and other types of motor vehicle racing or stunt driving—or betting or wagering on any of these activities—are all offences under the HTA, provided that the activities take place on a highway; stunt driving in a mall parking lot would *not* constitute an offence under the HTA. The activities that make up racing under the HTA are broadly defined, and in addition to a race would include stunts, such as "demolition derbies" (in which drivers attempt to bash each other's vehicles or force another vehicle off the road) and "chicken" (in which drivers drive headlong at each other to see which driver will "chicken out" first). However, the offence does not require a contest: cutting off other drivers, preventing someone from passing another vehicle, and driving too closely to another vehicle or to pedestrians have all been deemed to fall within the definitions in s 172 of the HTA. O Reg 455/07, which sets out the actions and conduct that qualify for a s 172 offence, is very detailed (see the "What Does the Law Say?" box).

WHAT DOES THE LAW SAY?

O Reg 455/07, Races, Contests and Stunts

1. Revoked: O. Reg. 406/08, s. 1.

Definition, "race" and "contest"

2.(1) For the purposes of section 172 of the Act, "race" and "contest" include any activity where one or more persons engage in any of the following driving behaviours:

1. Driving two or more motor vehicles at a rate of speed that is a marked departure from the lawful rate of speed and in a manner that indicates the drivers of the motor vehicles are engaged in a competition.

2. Driving a motor vehicle in a manner that indicates an intention to chase another motor vehicle.

3. Driving a motor vehicle without due care and attention, without reasonable consideration for other persons using the highway or in a manner that may endanger any person by,

i. driving a motor vehicle at a rate of speed that is a marked departure from the lawful rate of speed,

ii. outdistancing or attempting to outdistance one or more other motor vehicles while driving at a rate of speed that is a marked departure from the lawful rate of speed, or

iii. repeatedly changing lanes in close proximity to other vehicles so as to advance through the ordinary flow of traffic while driving at a rate of speed that is a marked departure from the lawful rate of speed.

(2) In this section,

"marked departure from the lawful rate of speed" means a rate of speed that may limit the ability of a driver of a motor vehicle to prudently adjust to changing circumstances on the highway.

Definition, "stunt"

3. For the purposes of section 172 of the Act, "stunt" includes any activity where one or more persons engage in any of the following driving behaviours:

1. Driving a motor vehicle in a manner that indicates an intention to lift some or all of its tires from the surface of the highway, including driving a motorcycle with only one wheel in contact with the ground, but not including the use of lift axles on commercial motor vehicles.

2. Driving a motor vehicle in a manner that indicates an intention to cause some or all of its tires to lose traction with the surface of the highway while turning.

3. Driving a motor vehicle in a manner that indicates an intention to spin it or cause it to circle, without maintaining control over it.

4. Driving two or more motor vehicles side by side or in proximity to each other, where one of the motor vehicles occupies a lane of traffic or other portion of the highway intended for use by oncoming traffic for a period of time that is longer than is reasonably required to pass another motor vehicle.

5. Driving a motor vehicle with a person in the trunk of the motor vehicle.

6. Driving a motor vehicle while the driver is not sitting in the driver's seat.

7. Driving a motor vehicle at a rate of speed that is 50 kilometres per hour or more over the speed limit.

8. Driving a motor vehicle without due care and attention, without reasonable consideration for other persons using the highway or in a manner that may endanger any person by,

    i. driving a motor vehicle in a manner that indicates an intention to prevent another vehicle from passing,

    ii. stopping or slowing down a motor vehicle in a manner that indicates the driver's sole intention in stopping or slowing down is to interfere with the movement of another vehicle by cutting off its passage on the highway or to cause another vehicle to stop or slow down in circumstances where the other vehicle would not ordinarily do so,

    iii. driving a motor vehicle in a manner that indicates an intention to drive, without justification, as close as possible to another vehicle, pedestrian or fixed object on or near the highway, or

    iv. making a left turn where,

        (A) the driver is stopped at an intersection controlled by a traffic control signal system in response to a circular red indication;

        (B) at least one vehicle facing the opposite direction is similarly stopped in response to a circular red indication; and

        (C) the driver executes the left turn immediately before or after the system shows only a circular green indication in both directions and in a manner that indicates an intention to complete or attempt to complete the left turn before the vehicle facing the opposite direction is able to proceed straight through the intersection in response to the circular green indication facing that vehicle.

Exceptions

4(1) Despite section 2, "race" and "contest" do not include,

(a) a rally, navigational rally or similar event that is conducted,

    (i) under the supervision of the Canadian Association of Rally Sport,

    (ii) under the supervision of a club or association approved in writing by the Ministry, or

    (iii) with the written approval of the road authority or road authorities having jurisdiction over the highway or highways used;

(b) motor vehicle owners engaged in a tour, scenic drive, treasure hunt or other similar motoring event in which the participants drive responsibly and in a manner that indicates an overall intention to comply with the provisions of the Act; or

(c) an event held on a closed course with the written approval of the road authority having jurisdiction over the highway, including any event lawfully using any of the trademarks "CART," "Formula One," "Indy," "IndyCar," "IRL" or "NASCAR."

(2) Despite sections 2 and 3, "race," "contest" and "stunt" do not include any activity required for the lawful operation of motor vehicles described in subsections 62(15.1) or 128(13) of the Act, or the lawful operation of an emergency vehicle as defined in subsection 144(1) of the Act.

5. Omitted (provides for coming into force of provisions of this Regulation).

Stunt driving under the HTA also includes driving at speeds in excess of 50 km/h over the posted speed limit, although there have been legal challenges. In *R v Raham*,[6] a woman attempted to pass a tractor trailer on a two-lane provincial highway with a speed limit of 80 km/h. When she realized the truck was speeding, to clear the lane quickly, she sped up

---

6   *R v Raham*, 2010 ONCA 206.

to 130 km/h to get back into the right-hand driving lane. She was charged with stunt driving. However, the Court of Appeal found that although this was a strict liability offence (where a conviction does not require criminal intent), as it can carry a prison sentence, it was contrary to s 7 of the *Canadian Charter of Rights and Freedoms*. The Charter guarantees the right to "life, liberty, and security of the person and the right not to be deprived thereof except in accordance with the principles of fundamental justice." This case also examined carefully the definitions of "stunt driving" and "racing," which seem to involve more than simply excessive speed, regardless of the circumstances that led the driver to drive at speeds well over the limit. Thus, the driver's intent may in fact be an important consideration.

A conviction for the offence of racing carries a fine of between $2,000 and $10,000, six demerit points, and/or imprisonment of up to six months. In addition, a driver's licence may be suspended for up to 2 years on a first offence, and for up to 10 years on a second offence committed within 10 years of the first offence. Further, where a police officer believes that the offence of racing has been committed, the officer shall require surrender of the driver's licence and shall detain the motor vehicle in order to enforce an immediate mandatory seven-day suspension of the licence and impoundment of the motor vehicle. There is no appeal of the seven-day suspension/impoundment, the purpose of which is to prevent repetition of the offences while current charges are pending.

Note that bicycle and in-line skate racing does not appear to be prohibited, because the more explicit term "motor vehicles" is used in defining the offence. However, racing or driving horses or other animals "furiously" on a highway *is* explicitly prohibited (HTA, s 173). Use of the term "furiously" in the HTA goes back to the beginning of the last century, but because a horse or another animal may very well not be capable of exceeding a posted speed limit, evidence of racing would consist of driving or riding the animal "furiously"—at or near its apparent top speed.

Street Racing Under the Criminal Code

The focus of the HTA racing offence is on the commission of *the offence itself*, whether or not any person or property is harmed. The HTA offence is broadly defined to include racing and other stunts, and wagering on the outcome of a stunt or race, any of which is enough to sustain a conviction under the HTA.

Racing is also a distinct offence under the CC, where it is called "street racing" and is defined differently. In s 2 of the CC, street racing is defined as "operating a motor vehicle in a race with at least one other vehicle on a street, road, highway or other public place." Thus, while the CC defines the activities that constitute street racing more narrowly, they can occur *anywhere* (that is, they are not restricted to highways). Therefore, before a decision can be made regarding whether to charge a person under the HTA or under the CC, it is necessary to consider (1) *where* the offence took place, and (2) *what* actually occurred. Racing in a private parking lot in a mall, for example, is not a racing offence under the HTA, but it could be the offence of street racing under the CC. And if stunt driving were involved, it might not be a street racing offence under the CC (because it arguably falls outside the CC definition of "street racing") *or* a racing offence under the HTA (because it did not occur on a highway). However, while the narrow offence of street racing may not apply to this scenario, the driver could possibly be charged with dangerous operation of a motor vehicle under s 249(1) of the CC (see the discussion of this provision in Chapter 6).

Section 249.2 of the CC creates the indictable offence of criminal negligence causing death while street racing, with a maximum penalty of life imprisonment. Section 249.3 of the CC creates the indictable offence of criminal negligence causing bodily harm while street racing, with a maximum penalty of 14 years. Section 249.4 of the CC creates a separate offence of dangerous operation of a motor vehicle while street racing, whether or not there is death or injury, with a specific penalty of up to 5 years, whether bodily harm or death ensues as a result. The net effect of these provisions is that an accused charged with dangerous operation of a motor vehicle while street racing faces higher penalties if bodily harm or death results than he or she would if charged merely with dangerous operation of a motor vehicle. In effect, Parliament has decreed that dangerous driving while street racing is a more serious offence than mere dangerous driving. The differences between the HTA approach to the offence of racing and the CC approach to the offence of street racing are illustrated in the chart below.

	HTA, ss 172 and 173	**CC ss 249.2, 249.3, and 249.4**
Definition of offence	Racing, stunt driving, betting, or wagering	Street racing and dangerous driving, where: • neither death nor bodily harm ensues • bodily harm ensues • death ensues
Where	On a highway	Anywhere
Penalty	• $2,000 to $10,000 fine and/or imprisonment of up to 6 months • Automatic 7-day licence suspension and vehicle impoundment	• Neither death nor bodily harm: 5 years' imprisonment or summary penalty • Bodily harm: up to 14 years • Death: up to life

Public Vehicles and School Buses at Railway Crossings: HTA, Section 174

A public vehicle is required to stop at a railway crossing that does not have gates, signals, or a flagman directing traffic. The driver must look both ways, open the door to listen for a train, put the vehicle in gear, and cross the tracks without changing gears. A driver of a school bus must do the same at a railway crossing, even if the crossing is equipped with gates and signal lights.

Safe Operation of a School Bus: HTA, Section 175

A school bus driver who is about to stop to drop off or pick up children or developmentally delayed adults must switch on the overhead red signal lights on the bus, and, as soon as the bus is stopped, the driver must activate the school bus stop arm. These devices must remain on until all passengers who have to cross the highway to the other side or to a median strip have done so.

However, the signalling system is *not* to be used by the driver

- at an intersection controlled by traffic signals or within 60 m of it; or
- where there is a traffic signal, other than at an intersection, at a sign or roadway marking, indicating where a bus should stop, just before a crosswalk, within 5 m of a traffic signal, or within 60 m of the locations identified here.

Where there is a school bus loading zone, a driver must pull the bus as close to the right-hand curb of the loading zone as possible. The school bus driver need not use the stop signalling system if loading or unloading in a school bus loading zone.

Where a driver of a vehicle approaches a stopped school bus from either direction (other than at a highway separated by a median strip) with its overhead red signal lights flashing, the driver must stop before reaching the bus until the overhead red signal lights have stopped flashing or the bus moves. If a driver approaches the rear of a stopped school bus, he or she must stop at least 20 m behind the school bus. Failure to stop when required can result in a fine of between $400 and $2,000. For a subsequent offence committed within five years less a day of a previous conviction, a fine of between $1,000 and $4,000 or imprisonment for a term of not more than six months, or both, may be imposed.

School Crossing Guards: HTA, Section 176

A school crossing guard about to direct children across a highway with a speed limit of not more than 60 km/h shall display a school crossing stop sign. Where a driver of a vehicle approaches a crossing guard displaying this sign, the driver must stop before reaching the crossing.

Hitchhiking: HTA, Section 177

Hitchhiking is prohibited on all roadways, as is stopping or attempting to stop vehicles to sell the drivers or occupants goods or services. However, if a vehicle is stopped, offering goods and services to the driver or occupants does not appear to be prohibited under the HTA, although it may be prohibited under a municipal bylaw or other legislation.

Pedestrians Walk on the Left: HTA, Section 179

Where there is no sidewalk, a pedestrian walking on the highway shall walk on the left, keeping as close to the curb as possible. This requirement does not apply to someone walking a bicycle, if crossing to the left side of the road is impracticable. Pedestrians may also be prohibited from walking on a highway, and a police officer may require a pedestrian in a prohibited area to accompany the officer to an intersection with the nearest highway where a pedestrian is permitted (HTA, s 185(3)).

Littering or Depositing Snow or Ice: HTA, Sections 180 and 181

Anyone who deposits any kind of rubbish on the highway is guilty of littering; "litter" is broadly defined by the HTA. Similarly, no one may deposit snow or ice on the roadway without the permission of the ministry or authority responsible for maintaining the road.

Logs to Be Kept by Drivers of Commercial Vehicles: HTA, Section 190

There is a blanket requirement that drivers of commercial vehicles maintain a daily log and carry it when in charge of a commercial vehicle. The log is used to record hours of work and other working-condition matters, as prescribed by the regulations as found in s 190(7) of the HTA. Similarly, the regulations may exempt various types of commercial vehicle drivers from keeping a log. A log must be surrendered to a police officer on request. Violation of s 190 or the regulations can lead to a fine of between $250 and $20,000 and/or to a term of imprisonment of up to six months. In 2015, new versions of s 191 governing log keeping and applications for exemptions were enacted but as of this writing, have not yet been proclaimed in force.

Vehicle Equipment Requirements: HTA, Part VI

Although many requirements with regard to the design and structure of a vehicle are the responsibility of manufacturers, some requirements are the responsibility of the owner or driver of a vehicle. Often, when a police officer stops a motor vehicle, it is apparent that the vehicle does not meet equipment requirements or standards. In such cases, a police officer has some broad powers under s 82 of the HTA to require the driver or owner of a motor vehicle, including a motor-assisted bicycle, to subject the vehicle to examination and tests as the officer sees fit (s 82(2)). If the vehicle is found to be unsafe, it can be ordered off the highway until it is fixed. A written notice to that effect must be issued by the police officer, who also has the power to remove the plates from the vehicle (ss 82(5) and (13)(a)). There are similar provisions for commercial vehicles (s 82.1). Some of the more frequently encountered equipment requirements are set out below.

Lighting Requirements: HTA, Section 62

The basic requirement is two white or amber lights in front, and one red lamp in back, to be switched on one half-hour before sunset to one half-hour after sunrise, or when fog or adverse weather reduces visibility. Lights must be visible at a distance of 150 m. In addition, front lights must be powerful enough for a driver to see a person clearly at a distance of 110 m. However, for those who would like to install banks of fog or flood lights on the front of a vehicle, the limit is four bright lights in total, including the headlights that are part of the vehicle. Again, the lights must be visible at a distance of 150 m and powerful enough for the driver to see a person clearly at a distance of 150 m. There are slightly different requirements for motorcycles, which must have two lamps: one white, in front, and one red, at the back. If the motorcycle has a side car, there must be two white or amber lights in front on either side of the vehicle and one red light at the rear. The rear light on motorcycles and other motor vehicles must illuminate the number plate.

For long and wide vehicles, there are further requirements of marker lights on the side of the vehicle.

Bicycles are required to have a white or amber front light and a red tail light, red flashing light or reflector, visible for 150 m. The headlight does not have to cast as powerful a light as motor vehicles do. Its primary purpose is to make the bicycle visible from the front to other road users, rather than to illuminate the roadway for the cyclist. As well, the front forks must have white reflector tape, and the rear must have red reflector tape.

Windshield Wipers and Mirrors: HTA, Sections 66 and 73

All motor vehicles, except motorcycles, are required to have windshield wipers. All motor vehicles must have mirrors that allow the driver to see vehicles behind him or her. Mirrors must allow a view through the rear of the vehicle, unless the driver can see behind his or her vehicle with side-view mirrors on either side of the vehicle. Windshields must be free of sight-line obstructions, such as stickers, and windshields and windows to the right or left of the driver may not be colour-coated in a manner that obstructs the view of the road or conceals a view of the interior of the vehicle.

Mufflers: HTA, Section 75

All motor vehicles, including motor-assisted bicycles with internal combustion engines, must have mufflers. The use of "cut-outs" and hollywood mufflers is expressly prohibited. Excessive noise from horns or bells on a vehicle is also prohibited.

Hand-Held Devices: HTA, Sections 78 and 78.1

According to studies, drivers using cellphones are significantly more likely to be involved in a crash than those who are focused on the road. In an effort to minimize distracted driving, a "distracted driving law" was added to the HTA in 2009. The law makes it illegal for drivers to use hand-held cellphones and other hand-held communications and entertainment devices to talk, text, type, dial, or email while driving. Hands-free use of these devices is permitted while driving. However, some evidence indicates that the use of the devices is a source of distraction regardless of whether the use is hands-free or not, so that limiting the restrictions to hand-held devices may not be the most effective way of preventing accidents caused by driver distraction. For the moment, the prohibition concerns hand-held devices, although the law also makes it illegal to view display screens that are not related to driving, such as those of laptop computers or DVD players. But if you talk on the phone without looking at a screen, you cannot be prosecuted.

Law enforcement and emergency personnel—including police, paramedics, and firefighters—may continue to use certain hand-held devices and view display screens in the normal performance of their duties, as may some commercial drivers and public service workers. All drivers may use hand-held devices to call 911. Drivers may also use hand-held devices when all of the following conditions are met: the vehicle is off the roadway or lawfully parked on the roadway, is not in motion, and is not impeding traffic.

The following devices are *not* prohibited under the ban:

- display screens used for collision avoidance systems (for example, devices that warn drivers when other vehicles may be travelling too close);
- display screens providing information on the immediate environment of the vehicle (for example, screens that allow drivers to see behind the vehicle when backing up);
- display screens of instruments, gauges, or systems that provide information to the driver about the status of systems in the motor vehicle (for example, dashboard displays that provide vehicle maintenance reminders, fuel mileage, and engine temperature information); and
- display screens that provide information on road and weather conditions.

Radar Warning Devices: HTA, Section 79

Radar warning devices (called "speed measuring warning devices" in the HTA) are illegal and may be seized from a vehicle and are **forfeited to the Crown** (HTA, ss 79(3) and (4)). No compensation is paid.

forfeit to the Crown the government's right to seize property held or used illegally; the right is usually set out in a statute or regulation

Commercial Vehicles—Wheels Becoming Detached: HTA, Section 84.1

In response to public concern about unsafe commercial vehicles on highways, it is now an offence if a wheel becomes detached from a commercial vehicle, or from a vehicle being towed by a commercial vehicle. This is an absolute liability offence; an occurrence will result in a conviction, no matter how careful or diligent the operator and/or owner was in checking and maintaining the wheels.

Helmets: HTA, Section 104, and O Reg 610

Motorcyclists and their passengers must wear approved helmets while driving on a public highway.

Per s 104(2.1) of the HTA, all persons are required to wear a helmet that complies with the regulations when riding a bicycle on a highway. However, as per O Reg 610(5), a person who is 18 years old or older is not required to comply with s 104(2.1) of the HTA.

Parents of children under 16 shall not knowingly permit or authorize a child to ride a bicycle without a helmet. Helmets, however, are not required by law for skateboarders or in-line skaters of any age.[7]

Bicycle helmets must meet prescribed standards, must be worn with a snug chin strap, and must be undamaged, as required by O Reg 610.

Religious Exemptions for Helmets?

In 2005, Mr. Baljinder Badesha received a $110 ticket for riding his motorcycle in Brampton without a helmet. Instead of a helmet, Badesha was wearing a turban in accordance with his Sikh faith. Badesha had previously resided in British Columbia, where Sikhs are exempt from wearing helmets; similar exemptions exist in Manitoba, the United Kingdom, Hong Kong, and India.

Badesha argued before the Ontario Court of Justice that the helmet law violates his religious rights under the Charter, saying that he understands the risks associated with not wearing a helmet but that he is willing to take them to observe the tenets of his religion. In his ruling in the case, Justice James Blacklock stated that allowing individuals to ride motorcycles without helmets would represent an "undue" hardship on Ontario, as it would force the province to abandon a "reasonable safety standard." The helmet law is justifiable because it is clear that helmets "meaningfully" reduce deaths and injuries experienced by motorcycle riders; without them, we all pay the price. Despite the Ontario Human Rights Commission's argument that the helmet requirement is discriminatory, Ontario's Attorney General indicated that the province has no plans to change the legislation at present.

(*R v Badesha*, 2011 ONCJ 284)

Seat Belts: HTA, Section 106, and O Reg 613

Motor vehicles in Canada are generally required to have seat belts for the driver and for each passenger seat in the vehicle. The technical requirements for motor vehicle seat belts are set out in the federal *Motor Vehicle Safety Act*, which makes seat belts mandatory equipment in vehicles manufactured after certain dates. In effect, nearly all motor vehicles on the road today have seat belts.

The requirements for child restraint systems and their use are discussed in the next section. For others, the use of seat belts is governed by s 106 of the HTA and O Reg 613.

The general rule is that the driver and all passengers must use the seat belts provided for them, subject to some exemptions spelled out in the HTA and O Reg 613. The general areas of exemption are as follows:

- those with certificates from a medical practitioner exempting them from seat belt use for medical reasons or where size, body build, or other physical characteristic renders them unable to use a seat belt;

- those engaged in work where they must frequently enter and leave a vehicle, and the motor vehicle does not travel at a speed exceeding 40 km/h; and

- those engaged in other kinds of work that makes the use of seat belts impractical or dangerous (guards transporting prisoners, ambulance attendants attending to patients and some other emergency workers, and taxi drivers).

---

7   Some municipalities, Ottawa among them, require skaters in public arenas to wear helmets. The *Highway Traffic Amendment Act, 2004* amended section 104 of the HTA to require those using muscular-powered devices, including in-line skates and Rollerblades, to wear a helmet. However, the amendment has yet to be proclaimed in force, although the Act passed in the provincial legislature.

A driver must ensure that passengers under the age of 16 are using seat belts as required (either child restraint systems or adult seat belts, depending on the age of the child). Other passengers are personally responsible for using seat belts and may be charged for not using them, unless they are exempt.

Failure to use a seat belt is an offence punishable by a fine of between $200 and $1,000.

Although there has been debate about requiring seat belts for passengers in school buses, no proposals have been made to require this by legislation. The reason is that safety studies do not indicate that school bus passengers would be safer in a collision if seat belts were required.

Child Restraint Systems: O Reg 613

Sections 8 and 8.1 of O Reg 613 govern child restraint systems. The regulation creates three categories of children under eight years of age based on size, with corresponding requirements for child restraint systems for each category:

- Infants: children weighing less than 9 kg.
- Toddlers: children weighing between 9 and 18 kg.
- Preschool to primary-grade children: children weighing between 18 and 36 kg who are less than 145 cm tall.

For each of these categories, there is a specific type of restraint system as approved under the *Motor Vehicle Safety Act*. The restraint system must be installed and anchored as required by the manufacturer and by the regulations. It must also be used as required by the manufacturer—that is, all harnesses, belts, and other parts must be properly connected.

Preschool to primary-grade children shall not be secured in a seat for which there is an operating front airbag. This requirement means that these children should not be sitting in the front seat of most vehicles because most vehicles on the road today have front airbags.

Short-term leased vehicles (60 days or less), taxicabs, and ambulances are exempt from these child restraint requirements. However, taxicabs and small buses under contract to transport children to and from school are not exempt. Passenger vehicles imported into or manufactured in Canada prior to January 1, 1974 are also exempt, because the restraint systems cannot be installed in them without substantial modification to the auto frame or body.

HTA Road Offence Penalties: Victim Surcharge

Any HTA fine, whether for speeding or any other HTA offence, will have added to it a victim surcharge. The victim surcharge is authorized under s 60.1 of the POA. The surcharge applies not only to fines under the HTA but also to any fine levied for any provincial offence. The surcharge was established as a mechanism to fund programs set up to assist victims of crime.

The surcharge is calculated on a sliding scale, rising with the amount of the fine levied, as set out in the table here. See O Reg 161/00.

FINE RANGE	SURCHARGE
$0-50	$10
$51-75	$15
$76-100	$20
$101-150	$25
$151-200	$35
$201-250	$50
$251-300	$60
$301-350	$75
$351-400	$85
$401-450	$95
$451-500	$110
$501-1,000	$125
Over $1,000	25 percent of the actual fine

HTA Driving Offences: The Demerit Point System

Under the HTA, the province does not tolerate without penalty those drivers who are constantly being charged with driving offences. Instead, it uses a demerit point system to track violations, assigning demerit points for each conviction of a driving offence or moving violation. The number of demerit points depends on the specific offence; some offences result in more points than others. Although demerit points are deleted from a driver's record after a period of time, once a driver has amassed a certain number of points, progressive corrective measures are taken, starting with a warning letter, followed by a mandatory interview by a Ministry of Transportation official, and ending with licence suspension. In theory, bad drivers who consistently commit driving offences, even minor ones, can eventually accumulate enough points to be taken off the road if they fail to correct their driving behaviour. Under the graduated licensing system, probationary and novice drivers are watched more carefully than those who are more experienced, and the threshold for intervention by the ministry is lower than it is for fully licensed drivers. For example, probationary drivers who accumulate demerit points during the probationary period may have their probationary period extended.

Table 4.1 sets out the demerit points that may be given for specific HTA offences. Note that for speeding, just as fines are on a sliding scale, rising with the number of kilometres per hour over the speed limit, so are demerit points: the higher the speed is over the speed limit, the greater the number of points assigned.

TABLE 4.1 Demerit Point System Under O Reg 339/94

	COLUMN 1	COLUMN 2	COLUMN 3
Item	*Provisions for Offences*	*Demerit Points*	*Short Description of Offences for Convenience of Reference Only*
1	Section 200 of the *Highway Traffic Act*	7	Failing to remain at scene of accident
1.1	Section 216 of the *Highway Traffic Act*, except where a suspension order is made under subsection 216(3)	7	Driver failing to stop when signalled or requested to stop by a police officer
2	Section 130 of the *Highway Traffic Act*	6	Careless driving
3	Section 172 of the *Highway Traffic Act*	6	Racing
4	Section 128 of the *Highway Traffic Act*; subsection 13(3) of Regulation 829 of the Revised Regulations of Ontario, 1990; any provision of the National Capital Commission Traffic and Property Regulations CRC 1978, c. 1044 made under the *National Capital Act* (Canada) fixing maximum rates of speed and any municipal bylaw fixing maximum rates of speed where the rate of speed is exceeded by,		
	(a) 50 km/h or more	6	Exceeding speed limit by 50 km/h or more
	(b) 30 km/h or more and less than 50 km/h	4	Exceeding speed limit by 30 to 49 km/h
	(c) more than 15 km/h and less than 30 km/h	3	Exceeding speed limit by 16 to 29 km/h
5	Subsections 174(1) and (2) of the *Highway Traffic Act*	5	Driver of public vehicle or school bus failing to stop at railway crossings
6	Section 164 of the *Highway Traffic Act*	3	Driving through, around or under railway crossing barrier
7	Subsections 135(2) and (3), clause 136(1)(b), subsection 136(2), subsection 138(1), subsection 139(1), subsection 141(5) and subsections 144(7), (8), and (21) of the *Highway Traffic Act*	3	Failing to yield right of way

	COLUMN 1	COLUMN 2	COLUMN 3
Item	*Provisions for Offences*	*Demerit Points*	*Short Description of Offences for Convenience of Reference Only*
8	Clause 136(1)(a), subsections 144(14), (15), (16), (17), (18), and (21), subsections 146(3) and (4) and section 163 of the *Highway Traffic Act*, any municipal bylaw requiring a driver to stop for a stop sign or signal light, and the National Capital Commission Traffic and Property Regulations CRC 1978, c. 1044 made under the *National Capital Act* (Canada) requiring a driver to stop for a stop sign	3	Failing to obey a stop sign, signal light or railway crossing signal
9	Subsection 134(1) of the *Highway Traffic Act*	3	Failing to obey directions of police constable
10	Subsection 134(3) of the *Highway Traffic Act*	3	Driving or operating a vehicle on a closed highway
11	Subsections 199(1) and (1.1) of the *Highway Traffic Act*	3	Failing to report an accident
12	Subsection 148(8), sections 149, 150 and 166 of the *Highway Traffic Act*	3	Improper passing
13	Section 154 of the *Highway Traffic Act*	3	Improper driving where highway divided into lanes
14	Subsections 175(11) and (12) of the *Highway Traffic Act*	6	Failing to stop for school bus
15	Section 158 of the *Highway Traffic Act*	4	Following too closely
16	Section 162 of the *Highway Traffic Act*	3	Crowding driver's seat
17	Clause 156(1)(a) of the *Highway Traffic Act*	3	Drive wrong way—divided highway
18	Clause 156(1)(b) of the *Highway Traffic Act*	3	Cross divided highway—no proper crossing provided
19	Section 153 of the *Highway Traffic Act*	3	Wrong way in one way street or highway
20	Subsection 157(1) of the *Highway Traffic Act*	2	Backing on highway
21	Subsections 140(1) and (3) of the *Highway Traffic Act*	3	Pedestrian crossover
22	Subsections 148(1), (2), (4), (5), (6), and (7) of the *Highway Traffic Act*	2	Failing to share road
23	Subsections 141(2) and (3) of the *Highway Traffic Act*	2	Improper right turn
24	Subsections 141(6) and (7) of the *Highway Traffic Act*	2	Improper left turn
25	Subsections 142(1), (2), and (8) of the *Highway Traffic Act*	2	Failing to signal
26	Section 132 of the *Highway Traffic Act*	2	Unnecessary slow driving
27	Section 168 of the *Highway Traffic Act*	2	Failing to lower headlamp beam
28	Section 165 of the *Highway Traffic Act*	2	Improper opening of vehicle door
29	Section 143 and subsection 144(9) of the *Highway Traffic Act* and any municipal bylaw prohibiting turns	2	Prohibited turns
30	Section 160 of the *Highway Traffic Act*	2	Towing of persons on toboggans, bicycles, skis, etc., prohibited
31	Subsection 182(2) of the *Highway Traffic Act*	2	Failing to obey signs prescribed by regulation under subsection 182(1)
32	Subsection 106(2) of the *Highway Traffic Act*	2	Driver failing to properly wear seat belt
33	Subclause 106(4)(a)(i) of the *Highway Traffic Act*	2	Driving while passenger under 16 fails to occupy position with seat belt
33.1	Subclause 106(4)(a)(ii) of the *Highway Traffic Act*	2	Driving while passenger under 16 fails to properly wear seat belt

	COLUMN 1	COLUMN 2	COLUMN 3
Item	Provisions for Offences	Demerit Points	Short Description of Offences for Convenience of Reference Only
33.2	Clause 106(4)(b) of the *Highway Traffic Act*	2	Driving while child passenger not properly secured
34	Subsection 8(2) of Regulation 613 of the Revised Regulations of Ontario, 1990	2	Driver failing to ensure infant passenger is secured as prescribed
34.1	Subsection 8(3) of Regulation 613 of the Revised Regulations of Ontario, 1990	2	Driver failing to ensure toddler passenger is secured as prescribed
34.2	Subsection 8(4) of Regulation 613 of the Revised Regulations of Ontario, 1990	2	Driver failing to ensure child passenger is secured as prescribed
35	Clause 159(1)(a) of the *Highway Traffic Act*	3	Failing to stop on right for emergency vehicle
36	Clause 159(1)(b) of the *Highway Traffic Act*	3	Failing to stop—nearest curb—for emergency vehicle
36.1	Clause 159(1)(b) of the *Highway Traffic Act*	3	Failing to stop—nearest edge of roadway—for emergency vehicle
36.2	Subsection 159(2) of the *Highway Traffic Act*	3	Failing to slow down and proceed with caution for emergency vehicle
36.3	Subsection 159(3) of the *Highway Traffic Act*	3	Failing to move into another lane for emergency vehicle—if safe to do so
36.4	Subsection 159(4) of the *Highway Traffic Act*	3	Following fire department vehicle too closely
37	Subsection 79(2) of the *Highway Traffic Act*	3	Motor vehicle equipped with or carrying a speed measuring warning device
38	Subsection 154.1(3) of the *Highway Traffic Act*	3	Improper use of high occupancy vehicle lane
39	Subsection 146.1(3) of the *Highway Traffic Act*	3	Failing to obey traffic control stop sign
40	Subsection 146.1(4) of the *Highway Traffic Act*	3	Failing to obey traffic control slow sign
41	Subsection 176(3) of the *Highway Traffic Act*	3	Failing to obey school crossing stop sign
42	Section 78 of the *Highway Traffic Act*	3	Driving with display screen visible to driver
43	Section 78.1 of the *Highway Traffic Act*	3	Driving while holding or using hand-held device
44	Subsection 148 (6.1) of the *Highway Traffic Act*	2	Failing to leave one metre while passing bicycle

Source: Demerit Point System, O Reg 339/94, table.

CHAPTER SUMMARY

Parts IX, X, and VI of the HTA set out, respectively, the rules governing the speed at which vehicles may travel, the rules of the road, and vehicle equipment requirements. Part IX also addresses the offence of careless driving, defined as driving "without due care and attention" or "without reasonable consideration for other persons using the highway."

When issuing a speeding ticket, officers must be sure to record all of the relevant facts in issue for court purposes. The facts in issue may be recorded on the back of the officer's copy of the PON or in the officer's notebook, with a cross-reference to the notebook number and page number recorded at the top of the officer's copy of the PON. The fines for speeding increase progressively depending on how much beyond the speed limit the driver is travelling, and they differ among different locations (community safety zones, construction zones, and so on). Special penalties apply to drivers guilty of the offence of racing or performing stunts, and/or found to be travelling at speeds in excess of 50 km/h over the speed limit. The short-form set wordings in Reg 950, Schedule 43 to the POA assist police officers with proper wording when they are writing out charges (see Appendix A).

Ontario uses a demerit point system to track violations, with demerit points assigned for each conviction of a driving offence or moving violation. The number of demerit points depends on the offence.

ON THE SCENE

Speeding Infraction

Scenario

On [use today's date: DD/MM/YYYY] at 3:00 p.m., Mary Elizabeth Brown, of 123 Orange Street, Kitchener, Ontario, L0G 5P0, home phone number: 519-555-4567, is in a hurry. It is a rainy, windy afternoon. Her son Anthony, age 15, is late for his drumming lesson. Brown, travelling southbound on Albert Street, glances at the speedometer and notices that she is travelling at 73 km/h, which is above the posted speed limit. For this time of the afternoon, Brown thinks that her speed is okay and that she can drive a bit faster since no other traffic is on Albert Street. She fails to notice, however, a marked police cruiser parked at a gas station and the police officer inside it who had been pointing a hand-held laser radar device at her as she drove past.

Moments later, Brown, driving a 2001 white Uplander van, Ontario licence plate# IJKL123, hears the sound of a siren and sees the cruiser's roof lights in her rear-view mirror. Brown promptly pulls over, and the cruiser stops behind her van. The uniformed officer identifies herself as Constable (Cst.) Erin Schwartz and indicates to Brown that she was stopped as a result of speeding at 73 km/h in a 50 km/h posted zone. Cst. Schwartz asks Brown for her documents. Brown, after giving the current and up-to-date documents, states, "Officer, please give me a break, I'm late for an appointment and there was no one else on the road."

Cst. Schwartz replies, "I will be charging you for 73 km/h in a posted 50 km/h zone. After I have written the Provincial Offence Notice, I will explain your three options." Cst. Schwartz, **after reviewing the PON carefully to make sure nothing was missed**, returns with the filled-out ticket (PON# 95090983), hands over all of Brown's documents to her, and explains the three options open to her. Brown indicates that she understands the three options. The Provincial Offence Notice (PON) is issued and Cst. Schwartz returns to her cruiser, deactivates the cruiser roof lights, and drives back to the gas station parking lot, where she carefully completes her notes on the back of the PON for possible court purposes.

What Actions Should the Officer Take?

1. What kind of computer check should Cst. Schwartz have undertaken? What other actions should she undertake?

2. What are some of the actions Cst. Schwartz can take to ensure her safety?

3. How should Cst. Schwartz approach the vehicle?

4. What documents should Cst. Schwartz request from Brown?

5. What equipment is essential when conducting traffic stops at night, as compared with traffic stops during the day?

6. What guidelines should Cst. Schwartz follow in communicating with Brown?

KEY TERMS

CASES AND WEBSITES

- *R v Raham*, 2010 ONCA 206
- *R v Badesha*, 2011 ONCJ 284
- Comment on *R v Raham* in Iain Marlow and Jason Miller, "'Stunt-Driving' Grandma Gets Reprieve from Judge," *Toronto Star* (10 September 2009), online: <http://www.thestar.com>
- Comment on *R v Badesha* in Terrance S Carter, "Motorcycle Helmets and Religion: A Case Comment on the Badesha Decision," *Church Law Bulletin* (23 January 2009), online: <http://www.carters.ca/pub/bulletin/church/2009/chchlb24.htm>
- Creed case law review <http://www.ohrc.on.ca/en/creed-case-law-review>
- Police radar unit testing with a tuning fork <http://www.pbelectronics.com/radar_tuning_fork.htm>
- Police radar tuning fork test <https://www.youtube.com/watch?v=e6idl6scNOQ>
- Marnie Luke & Lori Ward, "Inconsistent Radar Testing Casts Doubt on Validity of Millions of Speeding Tickets," *CBC News* (25 January 2016), online: <http://www.cbc.ca/news/canada/speeding-tickets-police-radar-testing-1.3415927>
- "Radar Testing Accurate, Say Calgary Police after CBC News Probe," *CBC News* (26 January 2016), online: <http://www.cbc.ca/news/canada/calgary/radar-speeding-tuning-forks-1.3420551>
- Satoshi Kanazawa, "Why the Ban on Hand-Held Devices in Cars May Not Reduce Accidents," *Psychology Today* (7 February 2010), online: <https://www.psychologytoday.com/blog/the-scientific-fundamentalist/201002/why-the-ban-hand-held-devices-in-cars-may-not-reduce>
- US Government website for distracted driving <http://www.distraction.gov>

REVIEW QUESTIONS

Short Answer

Briefly answer the following questions.

1. A police officer may direct traffic when he or she considers it reasonably necessary to do so.

   a. Describe three situations in which a police officer would consider it necessary to direct traffic.

   b. Could a pedestrian be prosecuted for disobeying a police officer's manual signal for traffic direction? Explain your answer.

   c. May a police officer legally direct a motorist through an intersection against a red traffic light? Explain your answer.

   d. Give the statutory reference for a, b, and c.

2. a. Under what section of the HTA do the police have the authority to close a highway?

   b. What procedure should a police officer follow to close a highway lawfully?

   c. Identify the person or persons who are exempt from the prohibition of operating a vehicle on a closed highway.

3. a. Certain rules govern traffic at uncontrolled intersections (where there are no signs or traffic lights). Describe the two rules that have to do with right of way that are imposed on drivers of vehicles approaching uncontrolled intersections.

    b. Give the statutory reference.

4. a. The driver of any vehicle or streetcar, on approaching a stop sign at an intersection, is required to stop in one of three places. Identify these places and list them in the proper order.

    b. Give the statutory reference.

5. After a driver has lawfully stopped at a stop sign, there is a lawful requirement for both the stopped driver and the traffic on the through highway.

    a. Describe the requirements for the stopped driver.

    b. Describe the requirements for traffic on the through highway.

    c. Give the statutory reference.

6. Section 144 of the HTA describes the rules regarding traffic control signals.

    a. Where must a driver of a vehicle stop when approaching an intersection, facing a red light?

b. Where must the driver of a vehicle stop when approaching a red traffic light at a location other than at an intersection?

c. Section 144 describes the rules with regard to traffic control signals other than red lights. List these other traffic control signals and what they require or permit a driver to do.

7. a. What responsibility is placed on the driver of a vehicle who is approaching an intersection and facing a yield sign?

    b. Give the statutory reference.

8. a. What responsibility is placed on the driver of a vehicle intending to enter a highway from a private road or driveway?

    b. Give the statutory reference.

9. a. List and describe the three duties imposed on the driver of a vehicle at a pedestrian crossover.

    b. Give the statutory reference.

10. Section 141 sets out the correct method for making turns at an intersection.

    a. Describe the term "centre line" as it is used in this section.

b. Describe the lawful requirements with regard to the position of a vehicle making a right turn at an intersection, including multi-lane situations.

c. Describe the lawful requirements with regard to the position of a vehicle making a left turn at an intersection, including multi-lane situations.

11. a. Two duties are imposed on the driver of a vehicle on a highway before turning left or right at an intersection, private drive, or from one lane to another. What are those two duties?

b. Give the statutory reference.

c. Is the driver of a vehicle that is parked or stopped on the highway always required to signal before setting the vehicle in motion? Explain.

d. How may a driver commit an offence with regard to the use of directional signals for an improper purpose?

12. a. Under certain conditions, the driver of a vehicle on a highway is prohibited from turning his or her vehicle so that it proceeds in the opposite direction—that is, making a U-turn. List the conditions that prohibit U-turns.

b. Under what conditions is a driver prohibited from making a U-turn, regardless of the view?

c. Give the statutory references for a and b.

13. a. Driving to the left of the centre of a roadway is prohibited under certain conditions. List these conditions.

b. When is a driver prohibited from driving left of the centre of a roadway, regardless of the driver's view?

c. Name the exceptions listed when it is not an offence to drive left of the centre of a roadway.

d. Give the statutory references for a, b, and c.

14. Certain duties are imposed on persons driving vehicles on highways when being met or overtaken by other vehicles.

a. What must a driver do when meeting an oncoming vehicle?

b. What two duties are imposed on the driver of a vehicle intending to overtake and pass another vehicle going in the same direction?

c. Give the statutory reference for a and b.

15. a. What duty is imposed on the driver of a vehicle that is being overtaken by a faster vehicle?

b. Give the statutory reference.

16. a. The driver of a motor vehicle on a highway may overtake and pass to the right of another vehicle only where the movement can be made in safety and under certain circumstances. What are these circumstances?

b. Give the statutory reference.

c. Name two circumstances where it is permissible to pass on the right while going off the roadway.

17. a. Certain duties are imposed on drivers of vehicles using highways that have been divided into clearly marked lanes. This means a highway with three or more clearly marked lanes, not a highway divided only by a centre line. What must the driver do before moving from one clearly marked lane to another? On multi-lane highways, a vehicle must be driven within a lane and shall not change lanes until the driver determines that the lane change can be made safely.

b. Give the statutory reference.

c. Is it permissible to drive straddling the lane markings? Explain.

d. Give two examples of how lanes may be designated for use of certain traffic by erecting official signs for a particular movement of traffic.

e. When may the driver of a vehicle lawfully use the centre lane of a highway divided into three lanes?

18. There are six instances in the HTA where the driver of a vehicle must stay on the right-hand side of the road, having regard to the direction in which the vehicle is being driven. Identify these six instances.

19. a. What are the duties imposed on the driver of a vehicle on the approach of an emergency vehicle that is sounding a bell or siren or has a flashing red light on the roof?

b. Give the statutory reference.

c. Under law, what is the minimum distance that a vehicle must remain behind a fire department vehicle responding to an alarm?

20. What sections of the HTA prohibit a person from clinging to a vehicle or from being towed on a bicycle, sled, or toboggan or from attaching himself or herself to the outside of a vehicle while riding a bicycle, sled, or toboggan?

21. a. Crowding the driver's seat so as to interfere with the proper management or control of a vehicle is prohibited. Give two examples of how this offence could be committed.

b. Give the statutory reference.

22. a. The driver of a vehicle approaching a railway crossing must stop when an electrical or mechanical signal device or a flag person is giving warning of an approaching train. Give the statutory reference.

b. Where must the driver stop?

c. When may the driver proceed?

23. a. Two duties are imposed on a person who opens the door of a motor vehicle on a highway. What are these two duties?

b. Give the statutory reference.

24. Under certain circumstances, the driver of a motor vehicle on a highway must use the lower beam of multiple-beam headlamps when lighted lamps are required. At what distance must a driver use the lower beam in the following circumstances?

a. When approaching an oncoming vehicle.

b. When following another vehicle.

c. Give the statutory references for a and b.

25. a. Three duties are imposed on the driver of a school bus when picking up or dropping off children or developmentally disabled adults. What are these duties?

b. In what two locations on a roadway should the driver of a school bus not activate the flashing red lights when picking up or dropping off children or adults with developmental disabilities?

c. Describe where the driver of a vehicle or streetcar must stop in relation to a school bus when encountering a school bus that is stopped for the purpose of picking up or discharging children or adults with developmental disabilities in the following instances.

i. When facing the bus.

ii. When following the bus.

d. Give the statutory references for a, b, and c.

26. a. What are the minimum exterior lamp requirements for passenger motor vehicles other than motorcycles?

b. What rules apply to the tinting of a vehicle's windows?

c. Must all passengers on motorcycles wear helmets? Explain.

d. Give the statutory references for a, b, and c.

27. Create a chart that lists distances (30 m, 150 m, and so on) set out in sections of the HTA that you have studied in this chapter. For each distance listed, summarize the various statutory requirements. (For example, under 30 m, you could describe various requirements governing U-turns and passing other vehicles.)

28. In *R v Raham*, a 62-year-old woman was charged with stunt driving under s 172 of the HTA. She was attempting to pass a truck on a two-lane provincial highway and, because the truck was speeding, in order to clear the passing lane quickly, she accelerated to 130 km/h or 50 km/h over the posted limit of 80 km/h. Review s 172 of the HTA and O Reg 455/07, and answer the following question: What is the rationale for charging Ms. Raham with stunt driving on these facts?

29. The HTA creates the offence of racing, while the CC creates the offence of street racing. Describe three differences between these offences as they are defined in their respective acts.

Discussion Questions

1. Anna is driving on a highway where the posted speed is 80 km/h. The roadway is clear, dry, and level. Anna hears a grinding sound whenever she puts her car into fourth gear, so she decides to leave it in third gear, which allows her to travel at about 55 km/h and no faster. Traffic is beginning to build up behind her, and some drivers are growing impatient, passing in relatively risky places (on curves and hills with limited visibility). Can Anna be charged with any offence? Should she be, in these circumstances? Discuss the pros and cons of charging her.

2. Describe how red light camera systems and photo-radar systems work. What are the arguments in favour of using these kinds of systems, and what are the arguments against using them? Is there any evidence to show how effective these kinds of systems are? (These questions may require some research. You may wish to undertake an online search for "photo radar" and "red light camera.")

3. You have been asked to write a code of road rules for cyclists and users of motor-assisted bicycles. Use the rules of the road as the basis for providing practical guidelines for bicycle and motor-assisted bicycle riders, noting where the rules require drivers of these vehicles to act in certain ways and where these drivers need to adapt to some of the rules of the road that cannot easily be applied to bicycles (making left turns at a multi-lane intersection, for example).

4. You are assigned the job of writing a guide for the drivers of certain classes of vehicles, alerting them to the exemptions and exceptions to the rules of the road that apply to them and their vehicles. Examining the rules of the road, prepare a guide for drivers of the following vehicles:

a. road-service vehicles, including self-propelled road-building machinery;

b. school buses;

c. ambulances; and

d. fire trucks.

Highway Traffic Act Offences

5

LEARNING OUTCOMES

After completing this chapter, you should be able to:

- Understand how to interact with motorists in traffic stop situations where there is no apparent risk to the officer.

- Explain the duties of police officers under O Reg 266/10, *Suspect Apprehension Pursuits*, and understand what police officers should do before, during, and after a suspect pursuit.

- Distinguish between a charge and an arrest, and know the circumstances in which a police officer should either arrest and charge or simply charge an offender.

- Understand and be able to apply the ticketing procedure in the *Provincial Offences Act*.

- Identify arrestable offences under the *Highway Traffic Act* (HTA).

- Recognize that a number of driving offences are covered in the *Criminal Code*.

Introduction

This chapter introduces the reader to safe stop and safe pursuit procedures in more detail, and to some of the more common offences under the *Highway Traffic Act* (HTA). Particular attention is paid to identifying the essential elements of offences and the circumstances required to proceed with a charge or an arrest. In reading this chapter, you may wish to refer to a copy of the HTA for the specific language used in creating an offence and as a reference to defences, procedures, and penalties.

Motor Vehicle Stops

Motor vehicle stops are a common way in which members of the general public come into contact with police officers. Public support for the police can be greatly enhanced if this contact is conducted professionally. Make all your vehicle stops **GREAT** stops.

The procedure outlined here is a guide on how to handle the verbal interaction between an officer and a motorist in situations where there is no risk to the officer.

G *Greeting*	• Indicate location of stop for dispatch. • Upon approaching the vehicle, touch the left rear corner of the vehicle with your right hand to indicate that you were present. • Stand behind the driver. • Greet the driver courteously; "Good morning, sir/ma'am" is sufficient. • Do not make this greeting in the form of a question. "How are you this morning?" invites a sarcastic response. • Do not ask the driver whether he or she knows why he or she was stopped—this is asking the driver to incriminate himself or herself, and you should already have the evidence needed for the moving violation or you would not have stopped the vehicle. This is not an investigative situation where you have no suspect.
R *Reason for the stop*	• Immediately after the greeting, inform the driver of the reason for the stop: "The reason I stopped you is _____." Be specific. Do not "ramble on." • The driver is going to ask you what the problem is anyway, so tell him or her promptly.
E *Explanation*	• Pause briefly after telling the driver why you have stopped him or her. The pause permits the driver to offer an explanation, if there is one. • Note verbatim what the driver's explanation is. • Sometimes the driver has a valid explanation and a police officer will look foolish in court if the officer showed no interest in an explanation that could have saved everyone concerned a lot of time and effort.
A *Accreditation*	• After pausing briefly for an explanation, ask the driver to produce his or her driver's licence, vehicle permit, and evidence of insurance. • If the driver takes the pause as an opportunity for verbal abuse, cut him or her off with a demand for the accreditation that he or she must lawfully provide. • If the driver continues the verbal abuse, sternly repeat your demand for the documents. Do not engage in an argument. You could be recorded.
T *Tell the driver what you are going to do and what he or she must do*	• Tell the driver whether you are going to give him or her a ticket. • If you do not tell the driver what you are going to do, he or she is likely to get out of the car and walk back to the cruiser to ask whether he or she is going to be given a ticket—this makes the stop much more dangerous. • Tell the driver to stay in his or her car and that you will speak to him or her as soon as the ticket is complete. • Always review the ticket after you complete it. • When you return to the driver's window, courteously explain the driver's responsibilities with regard to the ticket.

If you follow the above procedure, motorists may respond with "thank you." The motorist is obviously not thanking you for the ticket, but for the courteous and professional way that you treated him or her. This positive experience is much more beneficial than a stressful experience in which the officer is verbally abused. Remember, it is important to pause for an explanation, but cut the driver off quickly with a demand for his or her driver's licence, vehicle permit, and insurance if he or she becomes verbally abusive.

Remember the Risks

In the majority of cases, enforcing the HTA poses little risk of serious injury to police officers: an officer observes an offence being committed, pulls the vehicle over, gives a warning or, in most cases, issues a ticket, and everyone continues on their way. However, as mentioned, there is no such thing as a "routine" traffic stop, and although the majority of people will comply with an officer's directives, the potential exists that a traffic stop may end in tragedy. It is not always possible to prevent loss of life or to foresee certain events that may unfold, and officers are putting their lives on the line during *any* tour of duty. Consider the following case.

On the morning of March 8, 2010 at 1012 hours, 37-year-old Ontario Provincial Police (OPP) Constable Vu Pham, a 15-year veteran, pulled over a white pickup on a country road in Huron County. Constable Pham radioed his position, requested his partner to respond, and signalled the driver, Fred Preston, 70, to stop. Preston quickly got out of the pickup carrying a Browning 30-60 rifle (used for hunting deer or moose) with .270 calibre ammunition and opened fire, immediately and critically wounding Constable Pham. A second OPP officer, Constable Dell Wilfred Mercey, quickly arrived on the scene, advised dispatch of the shooting, and began to exchange fire with Preston, who was shot six times in the exchange and later died in hospital when he was taken off life support. It was later learned that Preston's 52-year marriage was crumbling and that he had broken into the home of his sister-in-law, near the shooting scene, and called his daughter. The conversation led her to call police, because she thought he was going to do something "radical." Sometime after that, Preston was pulled over.

Constable Pham, who was married and had three young sons, became the 104th OPP officer to die in the line of duty since 1909. More than 5,000 police officers from across Canada and the United States attended Constable Pham's funeral in Wingham, Ontario.

Recognizing Driver Behaviour

If a police officer is subjected to verbal abuse by a driver, then it is valuable to be able to recognize the driver's pattern of behaviour. Recognition of driver behaviour enables the officer to understand the interaction and not *personalize* abusive comments. The cumulative effect of personalizing verbal attacks can be devastating for an officer's mental health. Remember that in the majority of cases, the driver is frustrated, angry, and generally upset, and is attacking what the officer *represents*, not the officer personally.

Negative driver responses can be grouped into seven categories.

1. **Indignant Response**

   "Is this all you've got to do?"

   "Why aren't you catching the rapists and murderers instead of stopping me for _____?"

2. **Influencing Response**

   "I'm a good friend of the chief."

   "Is _____ working today?"

3. **Denial of Responsibility**

   "You're absolutely wrong!"

   "I did no such thing!"

4. Assertion of Discrimination

"You stopped me just because I'm _____!"

5. Insulting Response

"You're just a _____!"

"All you cops are the same!"

6. Emotional Response

"Officer, I can't afford a ticket, I have to feed my kids."

"Officer, my husband will kill me if I get a ticket!"

Other emotional responses include excessive crying and attempts at flirtation with the police officer.

7. Bribery Response

Although bribery is not a common response, you may occasionally find cash located between the driver's licence, registration, and insurance. If this happens, *immediately* return the money. The driver will likely respond by saying something such as, "Gee, I'm sorry, officer—I wasn't aware that that was in my documents." It is wise in a situation such as this to forward a message to your supervisor about what transpired. In addition, it is important to make a note of what happened, and of what your response was, either in your notebook or on the back of the ticket.

Code of Conduct for Police Officers

The Code of Conduct schedule to O Reg 268/10 under the *Police Services Act* (PSA) governs the behaviour of police officers in Ontario. Under the PSA, all officers—including everyone from constable to the rank of chief—are held to a higher level of accountability and responsibility than "ordinary citizens." The PSA acts as a "check and balance" on officers, ensuring that they do not abuse their power.

The Code of Conduct, which is reproduced in Appendix D of this text, outlines actions that constitute misconduct; these include discreditable conduct, insubordination, neglect of duty, deceit, breach of confidence, corrupt practice, unlawful or unnecessary exercise of authority, damage to clothing or equipment, and consuming drugs or alcohol in a manner prejudicial to duty. When carrying out their duties in *all* areas, including traffic management, officers must consider their actions and potential actions in light of the requirements of the Code of Conduct. They must remember that while carrying out their duties they will be constantly evaluated, whether by the public or by their fellow officers and their superiors.

DISCUSSION POINT

An officer stops a driver for speeding—driving 110 km/h in an 80 km/h zone. When the officer approaches and asks the driver for his particulars, the driver produces a police badge from another jurisdiction and smiles. What are the police officer's options in this situation? How should he or she respond, and why?

PROFESSIONAL PRACTICE

Bribes

The Code of Conduct schedule to O Reg 268/10 outlines actions that constitute misconduct. These include the category of "corrupt practice," which includes accepting bribes (s 2(1)(f)(i)).

Suspect Apprehension Pursuits

Rather than totally banning police pursuits or allowing pursuits for any infraction, the government of Ontario allows pursuits when specific criteria are met. Suspect pursuits are governed by O Reg 266/10, *Suspect Apprehension Pursuits*, under the PSA.

Highlights of the Suspect Apprehension Pursuits Regulation

- A pursuit may be carried out if an officer believes a *criminal offence* has been committed or is about to be committed, or if it is necessary to identify a vehicle or a person in it.
- Before launching a pursuit, the officer must determine that there is no alternative method available to prevent an offence or identify a vehicle or person in it.
- An officer must determine that to protect public safety it is necessary to launch a pursuit and that this necessity outweighs risk to the public from the pursuit itself.
- This risk assessment is ongoing and continuous, and if in reassessing the situation the officer decides that the risk to the public from continuing the pursuit outweighs the benefit of apprehending a person or vehicle, he or she is obliged to discontinue the pursuit.
- No pursuit should be continued for a non-criminal offence if the identity of the person is known and, once the motor vehicle or the fleeing person has been identified, the pursuit should cease.
- An officer is obliged to notify a dispatcher once a pursuit starts.
- The dispatcher is obliged to notify the communications supervisor and road supervisor, if there is one; either supervisor will carry out further risk assessment to determine when and whether to break off a pursuit. If ordered to break off pursuit, the officer must discontinue the pursuit.
- Every police service has its own established pursuit rules that are consistent with this regulation, and these rules must be in writing and describe the duties of the officers, dispatchers, and road and communications supervisors, and specify the equipment to be used in pursuits.
- Firearms should not be used for the sole purpose of stopping a fleeing vehicle.
- Where possible, pursuit in unmarked police vehicles should be avoided.
- A police vehicle may be used to physically stop a fleeing vehicle if the fleeing vehicle has lost control or collided and come to a stop, and then tries to escape.
- A police officer may intentionally cause a police vehicle to come into physical contact with a fleeing motor vehicle for the purposes of stopping it only if the officer believes on reasonable grounds that to do so is necessary to immediately protect against loss of life or serious bodily harm. Every officer should be familiar with the policies and procedures of his or her police service regarding the use of police vehicles.
- Police officers must undergo training in the techniques of using police vehicles to physically stop fleeing vehicles.
- If more than one jurisdiction is involved, the supervisor where the pursuit took place has responsibility and control, but may hand over control to a supervisor in another jurisdiction.
- Every police force must establish written procedures on the management of suspect apprehension pursuits.

- An officer who decides not to initiate a pursuit, or who breaks one off, will not be deemed to have violated the Code of Conduct if he or she has reason to believe that the risk to public safety that may result from the pursuit outweighs the risk to public safety if the fleeing motor vehicle is not immediately apprehended or identified.

- All officers, dispatchers, and supervisors must receive pursuit training that is approved by the solicitor general, and all pursuits must be recorded on forms approved by the solicitor general.

The *Suspect Apprehension Pursuits* regulation is set out in Appendix C.

PROFESSIONAL PRACTICE

Before, During, and After a Suspect Pursuit

Before pursuing a suspect, officers should ask themselves the following questions:

- What kind of offence has been committed?
- Am I responsible for a "civilian" in the cruiser (for example, a student on a "ride along" or someone who is being taken into custody)?
- Was information received indicating that there are weapons in the vehicle, and if so, that they were used in the commission of a criminal offence?
- What is the age of the suspect(s) in the suspect vehicle?
- What time of day is it and what are traffic conditions (for example, rush hour)?
- How is the suspect driving? Am I (and are my backup officers) familiar with termination methods (for example, roadblocks or pins)?
- Do I know the driver? Can the driver be physically identified?

The answers to the above questions will help the officer decide whether to pursue the suspect vehicle, and there is always the option of proceeding via a warrant instead if the suspect driver is identified. Remember that officers who decide not to pursue because doing so would place unreasonable risk on public safety are *not* breaching the Code of Conduct and will *not* be disciplined for terminating or deciding not to engage in a pursuit (O Reg 266/10, s 12).

When an officer decides to engage in a pursuit, he or she should follow these steps:

- Ensure that the supervisor is advised, and maintain consistent contact with dispatch.
- Make a request to "clear the air" or use another channel while the pursuit is in progress (alternatively, the communications sergeant may advise the officer to go to a specific channel while the pursuit is in progress).
- Ensure that the adjacent police jurisdiction is informed of the pursuit.

- Note the mileage of the cruiser and the location at the beginning and end of the pursuit and report this information to dispatch.
- Advise dispatch of the make and colour of the suspect vehicle; the number of occupants (if known); the direction of travel; the road and overall weather conditions; the speed of the pursuit (constant/fluctuating); the driving behaviour of the suspect; the area (residential/commercial); information regarding the number of pedestrians/traffic conditions; whether items (drugs, weapons, etc.) appear to have been thrown out of the vehicle and, if so, their location; and whether any hydro poles, bus stops, parked vehicles, etc. were struck.
- Advise dispatch of any HTA offences that are committed (for example, not stopping for stop signs, proceeding through red traffic lights). If any vehicles or pedestrians are struck during the pursuit, the individual circumstances of the pursuit will determine the most appropriate officer response. (For example, where an officer who is a sole pursuer observes a pedestrian being struck by the fleeing driver, the officer should stop and attend to the pedestrian, because the officer has a fundamental duty to preserve life.)

During a pursuit, police officers must constantly re-evaluate the situation and ask whether, in light of the circumstances, attempting to apprehend the suspect(s) via a pursuit is worth the risk the pursuit poses to the safety both of members of the public and the officer(s) involved. An officer who is ordered by a supervisor to terminate a pursuit must immediately do so. Note that where a pursuit goes into the territory of another police service, the order to end a pursuit may come from a supervisor from the other police service. Following a pursuit, the officer(s) involved should make all the necessary notes and submit a report as required by the pursuit policy of his or her police service.

When Is a Suspect Apprehension Pursuit Justified?

Suspect apprehension pursuits can result in devastating outcomes for the officer and suspect involved, for bystanders, and for their families. The consequences may include death, serious injury, Special Investigations Unit (SIU) charges against the officer(s) involved, civil litigation, property damage, and emotional and psychological trauma.

On June 2, 2007 at about 0200 hours, 15-year-old Chevon Josephs sped by two marked police cruisers that were parked outside a west Toronto residence. When the officers ran the licence plate, they determined that the car was stolen and initiated pursuit. Within about 90 seconds of speeding past the cruisers, Josephs ran a red light before hitting two cabs. The cruisers had been following at about 100 km/h. As a result of the collision, two teenage passengers in one of the cabs, Monique McKnight, 16, and Aleisha Ashley, 17, died, as did Josephs.

A number of individuals commented on the events that unfolded and raised arguments for and against police pursuit in this case and in general:

Arguments in support of pursuit

- "[Police] have a duty to investigate and apprehend those who are suspected of breaking the law."*

    (Bill Blair, former Toronto Police Chief)

- The officers "acted in accordance with their duties, and the theft of an automobile is a significant criminal event and has been decreed so by Parliament and the public."*

    (Gary Clewley, lawyer for the involved officers)

- "Public safety is the 'paramount consideration' when a decision is made to start a pursuit, and then only as 'a last resort.'" It is important to keep the context in mind: in 2006, 245 pursuits took place in Toronto, with most over "in a matter of seconds" and none of which went "wrong."*

    (Alok Mukerjee, former Toronto Police Services Board chair)

- "[Limiting pursuits] to catching criminals suspected of committing serious offences ... could be very restrictive ... [b]ecause there may be conditions or circumstances in which pursuits may be necessary and may be justified."*

    (Alok Mukerjee)

- "In many cases a stolen car has someone in it who is carrying a gun, or has guns. ... They [police] can't pick and choose and say, 'That's a stolen car, let's let it go.' That's the law, and their duty is to uphold the law."*

    (Monte Kwinter, former Minister of Community Safety and Correctional Services)

Arguments against pursuit

- "I don't understand why three lives have to be lost because the police are chasing after a 15-year-old."*

    (Jannett Scott-Jones, mother of Aleisha)

- A stolen car "isn't worth risking the lives of anyone." The myth that "everyone who flees has what we call 'a dead body in the trunk'" is simply not true. Rather, "[m]ost people who flee are just young kids making really stupid decisions." A second myth is that "everyone's going to run from you" if police call off chases except in cases where a violent offender is being sought. "Most people don't run. The downside is you may lose a few criminals, but you save a lot of lives."†

    (Geoffrey Alpert, University of South Carolina criminologist)

In the Josephs' case, the SIU cleared both officers and concluded that the pursuit "balanced the interest of apprehending the suspect" and the "interest of public safety."

* Chris Sorenson & Tamara Cherry, "Grieving Families Demand Answers," *Toronto Star* (4 June 2007), online: <http://www.thestar.com>.

† Betsy Powell, "Car Crashed at 150 km/h: Lawyer," *Toronto Star* (5 June 2007), online: <http://www.thestar.com>.

HTA Offences

Two separate actions may be taken against a person who is guilty of an offence under the HTA: a charge and an arrest. A charge occurs when an accused is issued a document that accuses the named person of committing an offence and sets out the offence, the location and time of the offence, and the requirement that the accused attend court at a named place and time to answer the charge. An **arrest** occurs when a person is taken into custody and is not released until certain conditions have been satisfied.

Under the HTA, a person can be charged with an offence without being arrested. Usually, offenders are charged and given a Provincial Offence Notice (PON). Because most HTA offences are committed in the presence of an officer, it is usually sufficient to simply use a ticket to charge the offender where proper identification and a vehicle permit are produced; in this case, there is no need to arrest a person in order to establish his or her identity. In the event that a person *is* arrested under the HTA, he or she is also likely to then be charged. Usually, where a person is arrested for an HTA offence, he or she will be released once the offence has ceased and proper identification has been obtained so that the offender can be ticketed. Provincial policy is to avoid the costlier and time-consuming arrest procedure where possible, and it is for this reason that the right to arrest is restricted to situations where there is uncertainty about the identity of a driver or vehicle, where there is the risk of the offence being repeated or continuing, or where further investigation may be required prior to a charge being laid. *Who* may arrest and the offences for which a person may be arrested are discussed in the section "Arrest Authorities: HTA, Sections 217(2) and (3.1)," later in this chapter.

To sum up, the distinguishing features of a charge and an arrest are as follows:

arrest
results when a person's physical liberty is inhibited by conveying an intention to restrict the person's liberty; the actual restraint may involve physical force, although an arrest may occur without the use of force

Charge	• court date to answer charge
Arrest	• custody
	• release on condition and on being charged
	• court date to answer charge

Provincial Offences Act Ticketing Procedure

The procedure for ticketing is described in the *Provincial Offences Act* (POA). Figure 5.1 reproduces the five pages of a multi-layered PON. The complete ticket is reproduced in Appendix B at the back of this text. You can photocopy it and practise completing a ticket with the appropriate information and wording for the charge for any scenario you create.

Personal Service of Notice on Date of Offence

Several pages make up what is collectively called the PON. The top page is the Certificate of Offence, which is the copy that is filed with the Provincial Offences Court. Printing firmly on this top page will mark all subsequent pages. The second page is the Offence Notice, which is served on the defendant. Note that the original signature of the issuing officer must appear on both the page that is filed with the court and the page that is served on the defendant.

- Complete the Certificate of Offence (top page) down to and including the certification area. This is the box about halfway down the ticket where the issuing officer signs to certify that he or she served the Offence Notice (second page) on the person charged. *Do not* sign the certification area yet.

FIGURE 5.1 Provincial Offence Notice (Top Page), front (white)

ICON Location Code *Code d'emplacement du RIII*	Offence number *Numéro d'infraction*

Form 1, *Provincial Offences Act,* Ontario Court of Justice, O. Reg. 108/11
Formulaire 1, Loi sur les infractions provinciales, *Cour de justice de l'Ontario, Règl. de l'Ont. 108/11*

Certificate of Offence
Procès-verbal d'infraction

I, _____,
Je soussigné(e)   (print name / nom en lettres moulées)

believe and certify that on the day of   Y / A   M / M   D / J   Time / heure
crois et atteste que le   2 0 ___ ___ ___ ___ ___ ___ M

Name _____
Nom   (family / nom de famille)

_____
(given / prénom)   (initials / initiales)

Address _____
Adresse   (number and street / numéro et nom de la rue)

_____
(municipality / municipalité)   (P.O. / C.P.)   (province)   (postal code / code postal)

Driver's licence no. / *N° de permis de conduire*   Juris / Aut. Lég.
| | | | | | | | | | | | | | | | |

Birth date / *Date de naissance*	Sex / Sexe	Motor vehicle involved / *Véhicule impliqué*	Collision involved / *Collision*	Witnesses / *Témoins*
Y / A M / M D / J		☐ N / N	☐ Y / O	☐ Y / O

At _____
À   (municipality / municipalité)

Did commit the offence of _____
A commis l'infraction de

contrary to _____ sect. _____
contrairement à   *l'art.*

Plate no. *N° de la plaque d'immatriculation*	Juris *Aut. Lég.*	Commercial *Utilitaire*	CVOR *IUVU*	NSC *CNS*	Code
		☐ Y / O	☐ Y / O	☐ Y / O	

CVOR No. - NSC No. / *N° de l'IUVU - N° du CNS*

And I further certify that I served an offence notice   ☐ Or other service date of:
personally upon the person charged on the offence date.   *Autre date de signification, le :*
J'atteste également qu'à la date de l'infraction, j'ai signifié, en
mains propres, un avis d'infraction à la personne accusée.

Signature of issuing Provincial Offences Officer *Signature de l'agent des infractions provinciale*	Officer No. *N° de l'agent*	Platoon *Peloton*	Unit *Unité*

Set fine of *Amende fixée de* $ $	Total payable ***Montant total exigible*** $ $	Total payable includes set fine, applicable victim fine surcharge and costs. / *Le montant total exigible comprend l'amende fixée, la suramende compensatoire applicable et les frais.*

Summons issued. You are   Y / A   M / M   D / J   Time / heure
required to appear in court on   2 0 ___ ___ ___ ___ ___ ___ M
Assignation. *Vous êtes*   Ct. room / Salle   at the Ontario Court of Justice POA Office at / *à la Cour*
tenu(e) de comparaître devant   d'audience   *de justice de l'Ontario, Bureau des infractions provinciales au*
le tribunal le

Deemed not to dispute charge under s. 9(1)(a) of the *Provincial Offences Act.* Set fine imposed. / *Réputé ne pas*
contester l'accusation aux termes de l'alinéa 9 (1) (a) de la Loi sur les infractions provinciales. Amende fixée imposée.

                                        Y / A   M / M   D / J
_____   2 0 ___ ___ ___ ___
               Justice / *Juge*

POA 0847 (November 2, 2011 / 2 novembre 2011) CSD

FIGURE 5.1 Provincial Offence Notice (Top Page), back (white)

Affidavit of service upon defendant

I, _____ , make oath and

say that on the _____ day of _____ yr 20 _____ , I personally

served the offence notice/summons* issued with the attached certificate of offence upon the defendant named in the attached certificate of offence.

*(strike out inapplicable term)

The Corporate defendant named in the attached certificate of offence by leaving it with
_____
Person Served
_____ , at _____
Position   Address

_____
Signature of Provincial Offences Officer

_____   _____
Badge number   Unit

Sworn before me at _____

This _____ day of _____ yr 20 _____

_____
A Justice of the Peace/Commissioner for Taking Affidavits

Court Record

Date	Adjourned to	Requested by	on Consent

Date	Pleads:	
	☐ Guilty	☐ Failed to appear
	☐ Not Guilty	☐ Charge Withdrawn
	☐ Guilty to a substituted offence	

Finding of Court

☐ Guilty / Convicted   ☐ Suspended sentence

☐ Dismissed   ☐ Fine Imposed _____

☐ S.9.1 Conviction   Costs [s.60(2)] _____

☐ Quashed

Time to pay

Reasons: _____

The POA provides that the victim fine surcharge (s.60.1) and certain costs (s.60(1)) are added administratively upon conviction.

For Prosecutor	For Defendant
Reporter	Clerk

_____
Justice

Defaulted fine enforcement

_____
Justice

FIGURE 5.1 Provincial Offence Notice (Second Page), front (yellow)

ICON Location Code *Code d'emplacement du RIII*	Offence number *Numéro d'infraction*

Form 3, *Provincial Offences Act,* Ontario Court of Justice, O. Reg. 108/11
Formulaire 3, Loi sur les infractions provinciales, *Cour de justice de l'Ontario, Règl. de l'Ont. 108/11*

Offence Notice
Avis d'infraction

(print name / *nom en lettres moulées*)   ,

believes and certifies that on the day of   Y / A   M / M   D / J   Time / *heure*
croit et atteste que le   2   0   M

Name
Nom   (family / *nom de famille*)

(given / *prénom*)   (initials / *initiales*)

Address
Adresse   (number and street / *numéro et nom de la rue*)

(municipality / *municipalité*)   (P.O. / C.P.)   (province)   (postal code / *code postal*)

Driver's licence no. / *N° de permis de conduire*   Juris / *Aut. lég.*

Birth date / *Date de naissance* Y / A M / M D / J	Sex / *Sexe*	Motor vehicle involved / *Véhicule impliqué* ☐ N / N	Collision involved / *Collision* ☐ Y / O	Witnesses / *Témoins* ☐ Y / O

At
À   (municipality / *municipalité*)

Did commit the offence of
A commis l'infraction de

contrary to _____ sect. _____
contrairement à _____ , *art.*

Plate no. *N° de la plaque d'immatriculation*	Juris *Aut. lég.*	Commercial *Utilitaire* ☐ Y / O	CVOR *IUVU* ☐ Y / O	NSC *CNS* ☐ Y / O	Code
CVOR No. - NSC No. / *N° de l'IUVU - N° du CNS*					

And I further certify that I served an offence notice   ☐ Or other service date of:
personally upon the person charged on the offence date.   *Autre date de signification, le :*
J'atteste également qu'à la date de l'infraction, j'ai signifié, en
mains propres, un avis d'infraction à la personne accusée.

Signature of issuing Provincial Offences Officer *Signature de l'agent des infractions provinciales*	Officer No. *N° de l'agent*	Platoon Peloton	Unit Unité

Set fine of *Amende fixée de* $ $	Total payable *Montant total exigible* $ $	Total payable includes set fine, applicable victim fine surcharge and costs. / *Le montant total exigible comprend l'amende fixée, la suramende compensatoire pour l'aide aux victimes applicable et les frais.*

Important:
You have 15 days from the day you receive this notice to choose one of the options on the back of the notice.

Important :
À compter de la réception du présent avis, vous avez 15 jours pour choisir une des options décrites au verso de l'avis.

POA 0848 (March 15, 2014 / *15 mars 2014*) CSD

FIGURE 5.1 Provincial Offence Notice (Second Page), back (yellow)

Important – If you do not exercise one of the following options within 15 days of receiving this notice, you will be deemed not to dispute the charge and a justice may enter a conviction against you. Upon conviction, additional costs will be added to the total payable. If the fine goes into default, an administrative fee will be added and steps will be taken to enforce your defaulted fine. For example, information may be provided to a consumer reporting agency and for certain offences, including speeding, your driver's licence may be suspended.

Important – Si vous n'exercez pas l'une des options suivantes dans un délai de 15 jours à compter de la réception du présent avis, vous serez réputé(e) ne pas contester l'accusation et un juge pourra inscrire une déclaration de culpabilité contre vous. Sur déclaration de culpabilité, des frais additionnels s'ajouteront au montant total exigible. En cas de défaut de paiement de l'amende, des frais d'administration s'ajouteront et des mesures seront prises pour faire exécuter le paiement de votre amende. Par exemple, l'information pourra être transmise à une agence de renseignements sur le consommateur et dans le cas de certaines infractions, dont l'excès de vitesse, votre permis de conduire pourra être suspendu.

OPTION 1
Plea of Guilty – Voluntary Payment of **Plaidoyer de culpabilité – paiement**
Total Payable: I plead guilty and payment **volontaire du montant total exigible :** *Je* of the total payable is enclosed (follow the *plaide coupable et le montant total exigible est* instructions on the "payment notice"). *joint au présent avis (suivre les instructions* *figurant sur « l'avis de paiement »).*

OPTION 2
Plea of guilty – Submissions as to **Plaidoyer de culpabilité – observations** **Penalty:** I want to appear before a justice *au sujet de la peine : Je désire comparaître* to enter a plea of guilty and make *devant un juge pour inscrire un plaidoyer de* submissions as to penalty (amount of fine *culpabilité et présenter des observations au* or time to pay). **Note: You must attend** *sujet de la peine (montant de l'amende ou* **the court office** shown below within the *délai de paiement). Remarque : Vous* times and days shown. Bring this notice *devez vous présenter au greffe du* with you. *tribunal indiqué ci-après aux dates et* *heures indiquées. Apportez le présent avis*

Ontario Court of Justice, Provincial Offences Office

Cour de justice de l'Ontario, Bureau des infractions provinciales

OPTION 3
Trial Option, Ontario Court of Justice, ***Procès,** Cour de justice de l'Ontario,* Provincial Offences Office *Bureau des infractions provinciales*

Notice of intention to appear in court: ***Avis d'intention de comparaître devant*** ***le tribunal :***

☐ I intend to appear in court to enter a ☐ *J'ai l'intention de comparaître devant le* plea of not guilty **at the time and** *tribunal pour inscrire un plaidoyer de* **place set for the trial** and I wish to *non-culpabilité **à l'heure et au lieu*** have the trial conducted in the English ***prévus pour le procès** et je désire* language. *que le procès se déroule en français.*

I request a *Je demande l'aide d'un interprète en langue* language interpreter for the trial. (Leave _____ *pour le procès.* blank if inapplicable.)

(À remplir, s'il y a lieu.)

Note: If you **fail to notify** the court office ***Remarque :** Si vous **omettez de prévenir*** of address changes, you may not receive *le greffe du tribunal de tout changement* important notices, e.g.: your Notice of *d'adresse, vous pourriez ne pas recevoir* Trial. You may be convicted in your *d'importants avis (p. ex., votre avis de* absence if you do not attend the trial. *procès). Si vous n'assistez pas au procès,* *vous pourriez être déclaré(e) coupable en* *votre absence.*

_____ _____
Signature *Signature*

Changes to your address (if *Changement d'adresse (le cas échéant) :* **applicable):**

_____

_____

Telephone Number: *Numéro de téléphone :*

_____

FOR INFORMATION ON ACCESS TO ONTARIO COURTS FOR PERSONS WITH DISABILITIES: [Court to insert information]
POUR OBTENIR DES RENSEIGNEMENTS SUR L'ACCÈS DES PERSONNES HANDICAPÉES AUX TRIBUNAUX DE L'ONTARIO : [ajouter l'information]

POA-0848 (March 15, 2014 / 15 mars 2014) CSD

FIGURE 5.1 Provincial Offence Notice (Third Page), front (back is blank)

FIGURE 5.1 Provincial Offence Notice (Fourth Page), front

FIGURE 5.1 Provincial Offence Notice (Fourth Page), back

Enforcement Agency notes/*Notes de l'agence d'exécution*

FIGURE 5.1 Provincial Offence Notice (Fifth Page), front

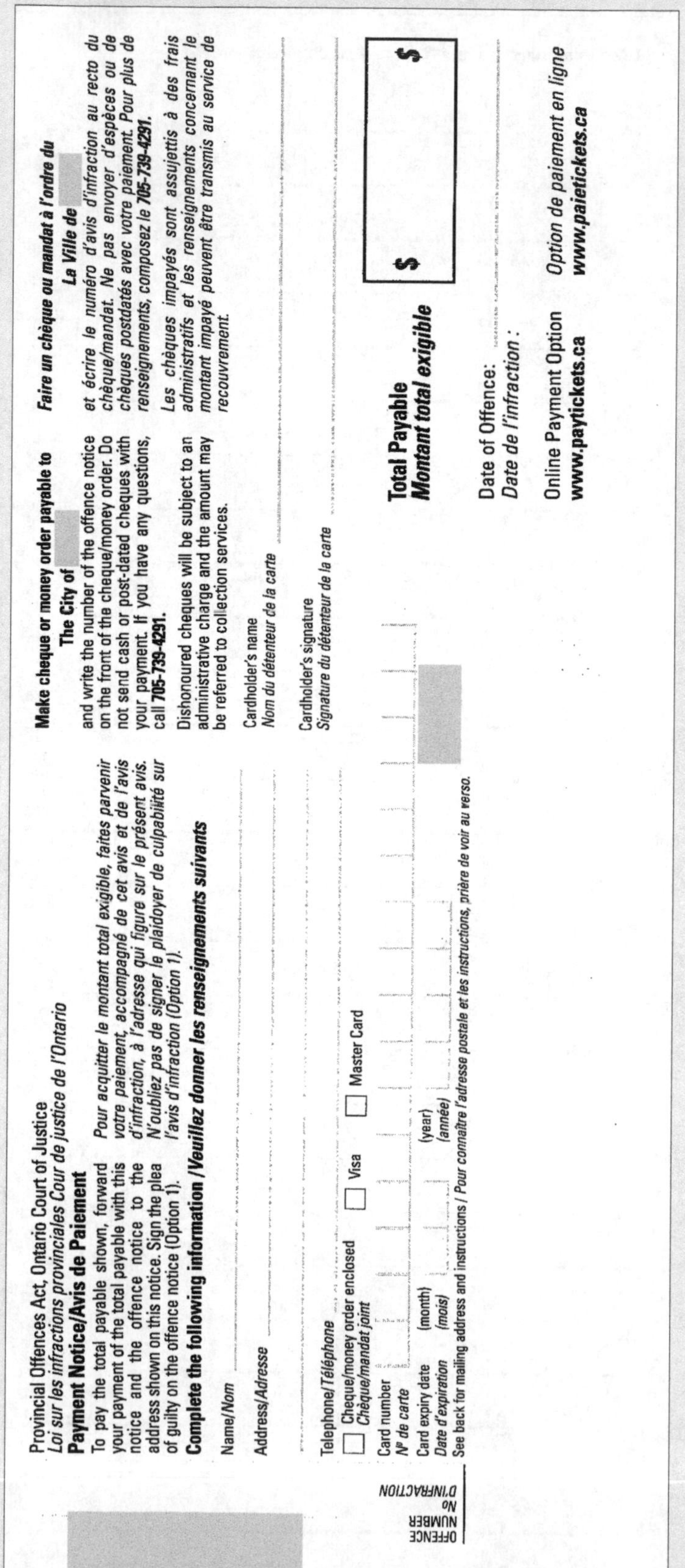

OFFENCE NUMBER *No D'INFRACTION*

Provincial Offences Act, Ontario Court of Justice
Loi sur les infractions provinciales Cour de justice de l'Ontario

Payment Notice/Avis de Paiement

To pay the total payable shown, forward your payment of the total payable with this notice and the offence notice to the address shown on this notice. Sign the plea of guilty on the offence notice (Option 1).

Pour acquitter le montant total exigible, faites parvenir votre paiement, accompagné de cet avis et de l'avis d'infraction, à l'adresse qui figure sur le présent avis. N'oubliez pas de signer le plaidoyer de culpabilité sur l'avis d'infraction (Option 1).

Complete the following information /*Veuillez donner les renseignements suivants*

Name/*Nom*

Address/*Adresse*

Telephone/*Téléphone*

☐ Cheque/money order enclosed *Chèque/mandat joint* ☐ Visa ☐ Master Card

Card number *Nº de carte*

Card expiry date *Date d'expiration* (month) *(mois)* (year) *(année)*

See back for mailing address and instructions / *Pour connaître l'adresse postale et les instructions, prière de voir au verso.*

Make cheque or money order payable to The City of

and write the number of the offence notice on the front of the cheque/money order. Do not send cash or post-dated cheques with your payment. If you have any questions, call **705-739-4291.**

Dishonoured cheques will be subject to an administrative charge and the amount may be referred to collection services.

Faire un chèque ou mandat à l'ordre du La Ville de

et écrire le numéro d'avis d'infraction au recto du chèque/mandat. Ne pas envoyer d'espèces ou de chèques postdatés avec votre paiement. Pour plus de renseignements, composez le ***705-739-4291.***

Les chèques impayés sont assujettis à des frais administratifs et les renseignements concernant le montant impayé peuvent être transmis au service de recouvrement.

Cardholder's name
Nom du détenteur de la carte

Cardholder's signature
Signature du détenteur de la carte

Total Payable
Montant total exigible $ $

Date of Offence:
Date de l'infraction :

Online Payment Option
www.paytickets.ca

Option de paiement en ligne
www.paietickets.ca

FIGURE 5.1 Provincial Offence Notice (Fifth Page), back

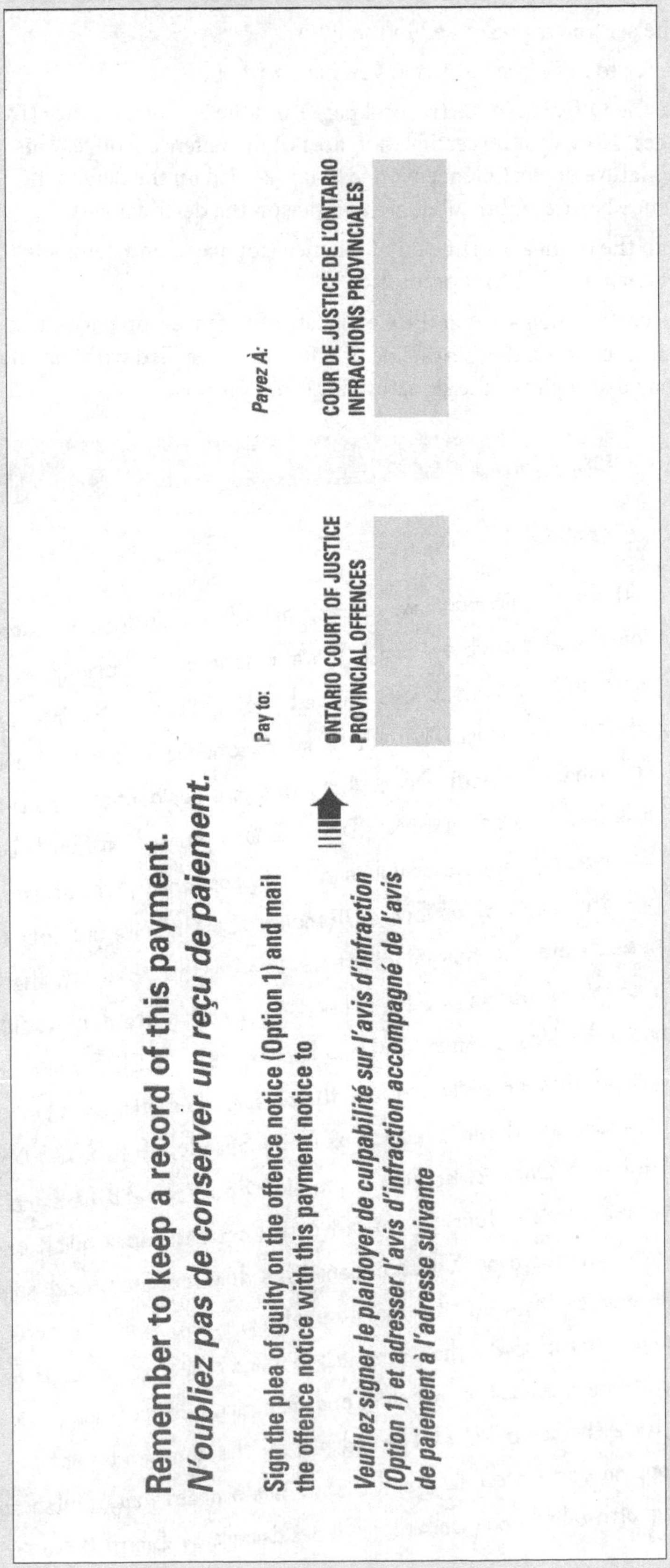

Remember to keep a record of this payment.
N'oubliez pas de conserver un reçu de paiement.

Pay to:

Sign the plea of guilty on the offence notice (Option 1) and mail the offence notice with this payment notice to

Veuillez signer le plaidoyer de culpabilité sur l'avis d'infraction (Option 1) et adresser l'avis d'infraction accompagné de l'avis de paiement à l'adresse suivante

ONTARIO COURT OF JUSTICE PROVINCIAL OFFENCES

Payez À:

COUR DE JUSTICE DE L'ONTARIO INFRACTIONS PROVINCIALES

- When writing the description of the offence, make sure to use the short-form wordings for the offence as prescribed in the POA and reproduced in Appendix A.

- Enter the set fine as prescribed in the POA.

- Remember to *always* review what you have written.

- Remove the Offence Notice (second page) and the Payment Notice (front of the fifth page). Now sign the certification area of the Offence Notice. This places an original signature on the Offence Notice that is served on the defendant. Serve both the Offence Notice and the Payment Notice on the defendant.

- Return to the original Certificate of Offence (top page) and complete the Code Box (top left corner), if it is not preprinted.

- Sign the certification area on the Certificate of Offence (top page). Now an original signature appears on the Certificate of Offence that is filed with the court, and the court may use copies of the signature for other purposes.

PROFESSIONAL PRACTICE

Effective Note-Taking

For court purposes, it is imperative that *all* of the facts in issue are noted, whether on the lined back of the Enforcement Agency Record (fourth page) or in the officer's notebook, with a cross-reference to the book/ticket number. The way in which an officer writes his or her notes has an important bearing on the officer's credibility in court. The two examples here describe the same situation. Residents in the area of Smith Drive and Brown Avenue, in Kitchener, Ontario, have contacted the police because many drivers are disregarding a stop sign located on Brown Avenue at Smith Drive. An officer was asked by his sergeant to respond to the intersection and enforce s 136(1)(a) of the HTA, disobey stop sign—fail to stop.

Example 1 shows how *not* to write out the facts in issue; it is

EXAMPLE 1

At 9:15 in the morning, I was parked in a northbound direction on the east curb of Smith Drive, Kitchener, Ontario in my blue and white cruiser. I was parked pretty close to the intersection of Brown Avenue. This is a T intersection with Brown Avenue "running" into Smith Drive. Also, this is a residential area with a school located on Brown Drive. I was parked on Smith Drive because people have complained that people are just not stopping for the stop sign on Brown Avenue at Smith Drive and lots of pedestrians use this intersection. The weather is great, there are a couple of people walking around. The roads are dry. At 9:17 I noticed a blue Camaro, Ontario licence plate ABC123 being driven in a southbound direction and the driver, later identified with a valid Ontario driver's licence as John Speedo, of 125 Jail Drive, Kitchener, Ontario. He didn't even slow down, nor did he signal when he made a right turn. I got out of my cruiser really quick and waved Speedo over. Speedo opened his drive car door and said to me, and by the way, this really upset me, "Shit, don't you cops have better things to do than stop law-abiding citizens?" Speedo gave his driver's licence, ownership, and insurance without any problems. I gave the guy a ticket, warned him of the dangers of not stopping for a stop sign, and wished him a great day. I also saw a lady with a little boy walking on the sidewalk of Smith Drive.

EXAMPLE 2

W—snny, clr sky; Rds—dry—lvl; Vis.—clr; Loc—res/school on Brown
0915—Parked E/B on S/S of Smith Dr., Kit., in marked cruiser
#123, 20 m W of Brown Ave., in front of 17 Brown Ave. T int
Brown (N/S bound) and "runs" into Smith (E/W bound). S/Sign 5
m N of Smith and 1 m W off Brown. Ped. walkway 1 m N of Smith
on Brown. S/Line 5 m N of Smith on Brown. No obstruction of
stop sign 4 me. 0917—Blue Camaro, Lic#ABC123 S/B on Brown
and dr made r/turn—clearly coasted past s/sign; did not signal.
Noted 1 a/female with m/child walking E/B on N/S of Smith about
30 m W of Brown. Stopped dr N/S across from cruiser. Dr, id
as Speedo (only occ.), opened dr door and stated "Shit, don't you
cops have better things to do than stop law—abiding citizens?" A/F
DLic/Ins/O—in order. Explained options as C/W said offence. T/A
rights and confirmed understanding, dr stated "yes."

long and opinionated. Example 2 illustrates how to note the facts in a concise manner, using short forms and objective statements, which will enhance the credibility of the officer before a justice of the peace.

When making notes, remember the following:

- Always use the 24-hour clock.
- Take the time to include rough measures of distances (for example, location of the stop sign, pedestrian walkway, and stop line).
- Use short forms (see examples, right) where possible to reduce the overall length of notes.
- Do not personalize interactions; you will have to answer for *all* written comments in court.
- Make note of whether pedestrians were in the area and, if so, how many, as public safety is paramount.
- Ensure that the notes are made *during or immediately after the offence*, as the defence lawyer will always ask when the notes were made. Notes that are made "contemporaneously with the event" are deemed to be more believable and credible by a judge than notes made much later.

Include a diagram with measurements in your notebook (cross-referenced to the ticket number), as this will enhance the professionalism of your notes.

SHORT-FORM EXAMPLES		
lvl	=	level
dr	=	driver
E/B	=	eastbound
S/Line	=	stop line
A/F	=	asked for
DLic	=	driver's licence
Ins/O	=	insurance/ownership
C/W	=	charged with
T/A	=	talked about

Personal Service of Summons on Date of Offence

When an offence has no set fine prescribed in the POA, an Offence Notice with an out-of-court settlement cannot be used. Instead, the defendant must be summoned to Provincial Offences Court, and a justice of the peace will determine the fine at the conclusion of the trial.

In this case, the Provincial Offence summons (see Figure 5.2) would be used and served on the defendant when the maximum fine is under the prescribed *Provincial Offences Act* (POA) Part I maximum fine (currently $1,000) or a Part III summons if it exceeds the POA Part I maximum (see Part III Summons and Information). If the Provincial Offence summons is used, a summons can be found at the back of the ticket book that is issued to police officers. There are only three summonses per book of 25 tickets because they are not used as often as tickets.

- Insert the Summons behind the Certificate of Offence (top page).
- Complete the Certificate of Offence down to and including the certification area. *Do not* sign the certification area yet.
- Enter the next applicable court date as determined by the court office and local police service (this list is available to all officers).
- Remember to *always* review what you have written.
- Remove the Summons copy. Enter the Certificate of Offence number in the top right corner of the Summons. Enter the location code in the Code Box in the upper left corner, if applicable.
- Sign the Summons and serve it on the defendant.
- Sign the certification area on the Certificate of Offence. Now an original signature appears on the Certificate of Offence that is filed with the court, and the court may use copies of the signature for other purposes.
- Discard the Offence Notice at the police detachment.

In this case, the Payment Notice (front of the fifth page) is not served on the defendant, because there is no set fine for an out-of-court settlement.

Part III Summons and Information

Section 22 of the POA states:

> Where a provincial offences officer believes, on reasonable and probable grounds, that an offence has been committed by a person whom the officer finds at or near the place where the offence was committed, he or she may, before an information is laid, serve the person with a summons in the prescribed form.

This prescribed form is a Part III summons (summons to defendant) and is used for more serious offences where an increased fine is expected, or where the statute provides for a minimum fine that exceeds the *Provincial Offences Act* Part I maximum, such as driving without insurance. Figure 5.3 presents the first page of a Part III summons (a complete Part III summons is included in Appendix B.)

Following the serving of a Part III summons, a Part III information must be sworn to by the officer in the presence of a commissioner. Section 23(1) of the POA states:

> Any person who, on reasonable and probable grounds, believes that one or more persons have committed an offence, may lay an information in the prescribed form and under oath before a justice alleging the offence and the justice shall receive the information.

Note that an information may be sworn to by any person, whereas the Part III summons must be served by a provincial offences officer. An information may be laid anywhere in Ontario.

FIGURE 5.2 Provincial Offence Summons, front (pink)

ICON Location Code
Code d'emplacement du RIII

Form 7, *Provincial Offences Act*, Ontario Court of Justice
Formulaire 7, Loi sur les infractions provinciales, Cour de justice de l'Ontario

Summons
Assignation

(print name / *nom en lettres moulées*)

believes and certifies that on the day of
croit et atteste que le

Y / A	M / M	D / J	Time / *heure*
2 0			M

Name
Nom

(family / *nom de famille*)

(given / *prénom*)   (initials / *initiales*)

Address
Adresse

(number and street / *numéro et nom de la rue*)

(municipality / *municipalité*)   (P.O. / C.P.)   (province)   (postal code / *code postal*)

Driver's licence no. / *N° de permis de conduire*   Juris / *Aut. Lég.*

Birth date / *Date de naissance*			Sex / Sexe	Motor vehicle involved / *Véhicule impliqué*	Collision involved / *Collision*	Witnesses / *Témoins*
Y / A	M / M	D / J		☐ N / N	☐ Y / O	☐ Y / O

At
À

(municipality / *municipalité*)

Did commit the offence of
A commis l'infraction de

contrary to _____   sect.
contrairement à   *l'art.*

Plate no. *N° de la plaque d'immatriculation*	Juris *Aut. Lég.*	Commercial *Utilitaire*	CVOR *IUVU*	NSC *CNS*	Code
		☐ Y / O	☐ Y / O	☐ Y / O	

CVOR No. - NSC No. / *N° de l'IUVU - N° du CNS*

This is therefore to command you in Her Majesty's name to appear before the Ontario Court of Justice. / *Pour ces motifs, il vous est enjoint, au nom de Sa Majesté, de comparaître devant la Cour de justice de l'Ontario.*

Officer No. *N° de l'agent*	Platoon *Peloton*	Unit *Unité*

	Y / A	M / M	D / J	Time / *heure*
	2 0			M

Ct. room / *Salle d'audience*	at the Ontario Court of Justice POA Office at / *à la Cour de justice de l'Ontario, Bureau des infractions provinciales au*

And to attend thereafter as required by the court in order to be dealt with according to law, this summons is served under Part I of the *Provincial Offences Act*.
Et d'être présent(e) par la suite selon les exigences du tribunal, afin d'être traité(e) selon la loi. La présente assignation vous est signifiée conformément à la Partie I de la Loi sur les infractions provinciales.

_____
Signature of Provincial Offences Officer / *Signature de l'agent des infractions provinciales*

POA 0861 (March 17, 2011 / *17 mars 2011*) CSD

FIGURE 5.2 Provincial Offence Summons, back

Note to defendant

You are required to appear in court. You may appear personally or by representative.

When you appear you may:
- (A) Plead guilty to the offence
  or
- (B) Set a date for trial
  or
- (C) The trial may proceed.

If you do not appear:
- (A) The court may issue a warrant for your arrest
  or
- (B) The trial may proceed in your absence.

Remarque à l'intention du défendeur/de la défenderesse

Vous êtes tenu(e) de comparaître devant le tribunal. Vous pouvez comparaître en personne ou par représentant.

Lors de votre comparution :
- *(A) soit vous pouvez plaider coupable à l'infraction;*
- *(B) soit vous pouvez fixer une date de procès;*
- *(C) soit le procès peut avoir lieu.*

Si vous ne comparaissez pas :
- *(A) soit le tribunal peut décerner un mandat d'arrestation contre vous;*
- *(B) soit le procès peut avoir lieu en votre absence.*

For information on access to Ontario Courts

for persons with disabilities, call **705-739-4291**

Pour plus de renseignements sur l'accès des personnes handicapées

*aux tribunaux de l'Ontario, composez le **705-739-4291***

FIGURE 5.3 Part III Summons (yellow) (First Page)

Form 104 — Courts of Justice Act R.R.O. 1990 Reg. 200
Formule 104 — Loi sur les tribunaux judiciaires L.R.O. 1990, Régl. 200

SUMMONS TO DEFENDANT
SOMMATION ADRESSÉE AU DÉFENDEUR
Under Section 22 of the Provincial Offences Act
Aux termes de l'article 22 de la Loi sur les infractions provinciales

Ontario Court of Justice Province of Ontario
Cour de Justice de l'Ontario Province de l'Ontario

You are charged with the following offence
Vous êtes accusé(e) de l'infraction suivant

On the / *Le* .... day of .... yr / *an* 20 ...... at / *à* .... [M]

Name / *Nom* ....
Last/*Nom de famille* — First/*Prénom* — Middle/*Initiale*

Address / *Adresse* ....
Number and Street/*N° et rue*

At / *À*
Municipality/*Municipalité* — P.O./*C.P.* — Province — Postal Code/*Code postal*

Did commit the offence of
Vous avez commis l'infraction suivante ....
Municipality/*Municipalité*

Contrary to
Par dérogation à ....
Section
Article ....

Therefore you are commanded in Her Majesty's name to appear before the Ontario Court of Justice	À ces causes, au nom de Sa Majesté, vous êtes sommé(e) de comparaître devant la Cour de Justice de l'Ontario
At / *À*	On the / *Le* .... day of ....
yr / *an* 20 ...... at / *à* ...... [M]	Courtroom/*Salle d'audience*
and to appear thereafter as required by the court in order to be dealt with according to law.	et de comparaître par la suite chaque fois que le tribunal l'exigera de façon à ce que vous soyez jugé(e) selon la Loi.

Issued this day - *Délivré ce jour* .... yr / *an* 20 ......

Signature of Provincial Offences Officer
Signature de l'agent d'infractions provinciales

Summons confirmed / *Sommation confirmée* ☐   Summons cancelled / *Sommation annulée* ☐

this / *le* .... day of .... yr / *an* 20 ...... by / *par* ....
A Judge or Justice of the Peace
Juge ou juge de paix

Driver's Licence No. / *N° du permis de conduire* .... Juris / *Juri* — Class/*Catégorie* — Cond/*Restriction*

Sex / *Sexe* ...... Birthdate / *Date de naissance* D/J — M — Y/A ...... Plate No. / *N° de plaque d'immatriculation* ...... Juris / *Juri* — Commercial ☐ Y/O

CVOR / *CECVU* ☐ Y/O   NSC / *CNS* ☐ Y/O   CVOR No. - NSC No. / *N° du CECVU - N° du CNS*

Officer No. / *Matricule de l'agent de police* — Unit / *Groupe* — Code — Witnesses / *Témoins* ☐ Y/O — P.I. — P.D. — D ☐ R ☐ P ☐

Note: This summons is issued under Part III of the Provincial Offences Act.
Cette sommation est émise aux termes de la partie III de la Loi sur les infractions provinciales.

POA 0516 (rev. 08/07)

Arrest Authorities: HTA, Sections 217(2) and (3.1)

According to ss 217(1), (2), and (3) of the HTA, the power to arrest a person for violation of specific offences is granted to the following people under certain conditions:

- Any person finding someone committing an offence listed under s 217(2) may, under s 217(3.1), arrest that person without a warrant.
- Under s 217(2), a police officer *may arrest without a warrant* a person whom the officer, on reasonable grounds, believes has committed an offence listed in s 217(2).

WHAT DOES THE LAW SAY?

HTA, Section 217(3.1)
Arrest without warrant for contravention of subs. 177(2)

(3.1) A police officer who believes on reasonable and probable grounds that a person has contravened subsection 177(2) may arrest the person without warrant if,

(a) before the alleged contravention of subsection 177(2), the police officer directed the person not to engage in activity that contravenes that subsection; or

(b) the police officer believes on reasonable and probable grounds that it is necessary to arrest the person without warrant in order to establish the identity of the person or to prevent the person from continuing or repeating the contravention.

See Table 5.1 for s 217(2) offences for which an offender may be arrested.

TABLE 5.1 Arrestable Offences Under Section 217(2)

SECTIONS	DESCRIPTION OF OFFENCE	A = Anywhere H = Highway
s 9(1)	Making a false statement.	A
s 12(1)(a)	Defacing or altering a permit, number plate, or evidence of validation.	A
s 12(1)(b)	Using or permitting the use of a defaced or altered permit, number plate, or evidence of validation.	A
s 12(1)(c)	Removing a number plate without the authority of the owner.	A
s 12(1)(d)	Using or permitting the use of a number plate on a vehicle other than the number plate authorized for use on that vehicle.	A
s 12(1)(e)	Using or permitting the use of evidence of validation on a number plate other than the evidence of validation furnished by the Ministry of Transportation for that vehicle.	A
s 12(1)(f)	Using or permitting the use of a number plate or evidence of validation other than in accordance with the HTA or its regulations.	A
s 13(1)	Exposing a number other than that furnished by the ministry on a part of a motor vehicle or trailer in a position or manner that would confuse the identity of a number plate.	A

SECTIONS	DESCRIPTION OF OFFENCE	A = Anywhere H = Highway
s 33(3)	Failing to identify self or failing to surrender driver's licence.	H
s 47(5)	Applying for, procuring, or having in his or her possession the plate portion of a permit issued to him or her while his or her permit is suspended or cancelled or while he or she is prohibited from owning a motor vehicle.	A
s 47(6)	Applying for, procuring, or having in his or her possession a driver's licence while he or she is suspended or he or she is prohibited from operating a motor vehicle.	A
s 47(7)	Applying for or procuring a Commercial Vehicle Operator's Registration Certificate (**CVOR certificate**) while his or her CVOR certificate is suspended.	A
s 47(8)(a)	Operating a commercial motor vehicle where fleet limitation certificate no carried when fleet limitation imposed.	H
s 47(8)(b)	Operating a commercial motor vehicle when his or her permit or certificate is under suspension.	H
s 51	Operating a motor vehicle for which the permit has been suspended or cancelled.	H
s 53	Driving a motor vehicle while his or her driver's licence is suspended.	H
s 106(8.2)	Passenger failing to identify himself or herself when a police officer asks him or her to do so.	H
s 130	Careless driving.	H
s 172	Drive a motor vehicle in a race or on a bet or wager.	H
s 184	Removing, defacing, or interfering with any notice or obstruction lawfully placed on a highway.	H
s 185(3)	Being a pedestrian on a highway where prohibited.	H
s 200(1)(a)	Failing to remain at the scene of a collision.	H
s 216(1)	Failing to stop when signalled or requested by a police officer.	H
s 217(3.1)	Officer on reasonable grounds believes that a person has contravened subsection 177(2) (stopping or approaching vehicle on roadway) if the officer directed the person not to engage in the activity or on reasonable grounds believes arrest necessary to establish identity.	H
s 218(4)	Cyclist failing to identify self.	A

CVOR certificate
the Commercial Vehicle Operator's Registration Certificate, which must be held by the operator of a commercial vehicle unless he or she is excluded or exempted under the HTA; requires commercial vehicle operators to comply with safety requirements under the HTA and other legislation

Seizure Authorities Under the HTA

The HTA authorizes the seizure of permits, validation tags (valtags), number plates, motor vehicles, driver's licences, and radar warning devices in circumstances set out in the HTA.

Permits, Valtags, and Number Plates

Under s 14(1) of the HTA , a police officer who has reason to believe that a permit, valtag, or number plate was obtained under false pretenses, is not authorized for use on a particular vehicle or furnished for a particular vehicle, or is defaced or altered may seize the permit, valtag, or number plate (or all of them, if the facts warrant) and retain it until the facts as to the issue of improper use have been determined.

Other sections of the HTA also authorize a police officer to seize permits, plates, and motor vehicles. For example:

- Section 20(2) authorizes a police officer to detain a commercial motor vehicle and seize its plates and permits.
- Section 82(13) authorizes a police officer to seize plates when the vehicle in question is deemed unsafe.
- Section 217(4) authorizes a police officer to seize a motor vehicle with which an offence was committed until the HTA and/or *Criminal Code* (CC) charges involved are dealt with in court. The motor vehicle may be released on security by a provincial judge or justice of the peace.
- Section 221(1) authorizes a police officer to remove a vehicle without proper plates on or near a highway.

WHAT DOES THE LAW SAY?

HTA, Section 14(1)

Improper number plate

14(1) Where a police officer or an officer appointed under this Act has reason to believe that,
- (a) a number plate attached to a motor vehicle or trailer,
  - (i) has not been authorized under this Act for use on that vehicle,
  - (ii) was obtained by false pretences, or
  - (iii) has been defaced or altered;
- (b) evidence of validation of a permit displayed on a motor vehicle,
  - (i) was not furnished under this Act in respect of that motor vehicle,
  - (ii) was obtained by false pretences, or
  - (iii) has been defaced or altered; or
- (c) a permit carried by a driver of a motor vehicle,
  - (i) was not authorized under this Act in respect of that motor vehicle,
  - (ii) was obtained by false pretences, or
  - (iii) has been defaced or altered,

the officer may take possession of the number plate, evidence of validation or permit and retain it until the facts have been determined.

Radar Warning Device

Under s 79(3) of the HTA, a police officer who has reasonable grounds to believe that a motor vehicle is equipped with or carries a radar warning device may stop the vehicle, enter it, and search it without a warrant. If he or she finds a radar warning device, it may be seized. If the person accused of having such a device is convicted, the seized radar warning device is forfeited to the Crown (s 79(4)). Note that the warrantless search under s 79(3) does not extend to a search of the body of the driver or other occupants of the vehicle, unless the device is in plain sight of the officer or the search is incidental to an arrest. Searches of vehicles and drivers are discussed in general in Chapter 6.

WHAT DOES THE LAW SAY?

HTA, Section 79(3)

Powers of police officer

(3) A police officer may at any time, without a warrant, stop, enter and search a motor vehicle that he or she has reasonable grounds to believe is equipped with or carries or contains a speed measuring warning device contrary to subsection (2) and may seize and take away any speed measuring warning device found in or upon the motor vehicle.

Driver's Licences

Under s 48(5) of the HTA, a police officer may take possession of a person's driver's licence when he or she is given a 3, 7, or 30-day suspension under s 48(14), or a 24-hour suspension under s 48.1.[1] If the person fails to produce the licence or is unable to produce it, the licence is considered suspended and invalid. As well, if a court suspends a person's driver's licence (on conviction for an offence where suspension is a possible penalty), s 212 authorizes a police officer to seize the licence. A police officer may also seize the licence under s 212 when the licensee is notified of suspension by a police officer.

Motor Vehicles

A motor vehicle may be seized under s 48(14) on a 3-, 7-, or 30-day suspension under s 221(1) when it has been abandoned on or near a highway, and under s 217(4), when the driver is arrested. The costs of the tow and subsequent storage charges are incurred by the owner of the vehicle. Police officers may also impound for seven days a vehicle involved in street racing under ss 172(5), (7), and (8), and as of December 1, 2010, under the *Road Safety Act, 2009*, for seven days in the following circumstances:

- where a driver has already had his or her driver's licence suspended under a specific section of the HTA (this includes suspension for failure to pay family support but not suspension for a medical condition or defaulted fines);

- where a driver is required to have a vehicle ignition interlock but is caught driving without one; and

- where a driver is caught with a blood alcohol concentration over 0.08, or when a driver refuses or fails to provide a breath sample.

Criminal Code Driving Offences

In addition to the driving offences in the HTA, a number of driving offences exist in the CC. Impaired driving, criminal negligence in the operation of a motor vehicle, and other CC driving offences have complex procedural requirements and are discussed in Chapter 6, as is CC procedure, which differs significantly from HTA procedure (particularly with respect to apprehension).

---

1 Under s 48(4) of the HTA, a driver who registers "warn" or "alert" or otherwise registers a blood alcohol concentration of 50 milligrams or more of alcohol in 100 millilitres of blood on a roadside screening device may have his or her licence immediately suspended under s 48(14) for 3 days on the first suspension, 7 days on a second suspension, and 30 days on a third or subsequent suspension. Further, under s 48.1(5.1), a novice driver may have his or her licence suspended for 24 hours when a mere presence of alcohol is registered on a roadside screening device.

CHAPTER SUMMARY

Motor vehicle stops are one of the many ways that members of the public come into contact with police officers. For this reason, officers should take steps to ensure that their exchanges with all motorists are courteous and professional wherever possible. Of course, not all exchanges will be positive, and officers must be familiar with categories of negative driver behaviour and appropriate officer responses to them.

Suspect apprehension pursuits are governed by O Reg 266/10, which sets out, among other things, the circumstances under which officers may initiate and continue to engage in a pursuit, the obligations of officers in a pursuit, and the circumstances under which officers must terminate a pursuit. The *Suspect Apprehension Pursuits* regulation is reproduced in Appendix C. It is important to note that under s 2 of O Reg 268/10, officers who decide for reasons of public safety not to initiate a pursuit, or who break off a pursuit, will not be deemed to have violated the Code of Conduct schedule to O Reg 268/10 under the PSA. The Code of Conduct is reproduced in Appendix D.

Once a decision has been made to charge a person with an HTA offence, the person may simply be charged, or charged and arrested. Usually, individuals are arrested under the HTA to determine their identity when they have not produced proper identification. If a decision is made to charge a person with an HTA offence, the officer will issue a PON or, for more serious offences where an increased fine is expected, a Part III summons. Officers must ensure that they follow the correct ticketing procedure and take notes in such a way as to enhance their credibility in court. Sections 217(2) and (3.1) of the HTA outline arrest authorities under the Act. The HTA also outlines the circumstances under which permits, valtags, number plates, motor vehicles, driver's licences, and radar warning devices may be seized by police officers.

ON THE SCENE

Driving a Motor Vehicle with No Insurance

Scenario

On [use today's date, DD/MM/YYYY], Constable (Cst.) Fahima El-Amin is on routine patrol. At 2:00 a.m. she observes a slow-moving vehicle, a brown Chevrolet Impala, with Ontario licence plate QRST123, being driven northbound on Winnipeg Road, which is located in an industrial area in the city of Hamilton. Cst. El-Amin is aware that during the past two weeks, three commercial break-and-enters occurred in the immediate area.

Cst. El-Amin notes that the vehicle is being driven at about 20 km/h in a posted 50 km/h zone. Cst. El-Amin inputs her traffic stop location on the computer, activates roof lights and high beams, and observes that the driver does not stop immediately, but continues on for about 150 metres before stopping fully. Cst. El-Amin takes out her flashlight and approaches the vehicle with caution. She notes that only one occupant is in the vehicle. Cst. El-Amin advises the driver that he has been stopped because he was driving well below the posted 50 km/h. The driver replies that he is lost. The driver, upon Cst. El-Amin's request, promptly provides a current Ontario driver's licence, ownership, and expired insurance card. The driver's licence indicates that the driver is Harold James Bradwell, date of birth 1 November, 1995, of 1 Aspen Crescent, Hamilton, N0G 1Z4, home phone: 413-555-1234, driver's licence number B4569-51109-51101. Bradwell stutters when asked why the insurance is outdated and, after several more questions by the officer, states, "You've got me, I've got no insurance on the Impala."

What Actions Should the Officer Take?

1. Should Cst. El-Amin have called for backup to respond?

2. Cst. El-Amin put the traffic stop location on the computer. Should she have advised dispatch of her location verbally?

3. Should Cst. El-Amin document the stop? If she does, would she be guilty of "carding/racial profiling" an innocent citizen, since Bradwell is black?

4. If Cst. El-Amin were to treat white and non-white drivers differently, why would that be a problem?

5. Should Cst. El-Amin issue a PON or a Part III summons?

6. Should Cst. El-Amin search the interior of the car based on the knowledge that the driver has no insurance on the vehicle?

KEY TERMS

arrest, 128

CVOR certificate, 145

REVIEW QUESTIONS

True or False?

In the space provided next to each statement, place a "T" if the statement is true or an "F" if the statement is false.

1. A Summons is used when an offence has *no set fine* prescribed in the POA, because a justice of the peace will determine the fine. _____

2. There is no difference between a charge and an arrest under the HTA. _____

3. Defacing or altering a permit, number plate, or evidence of validation (s 12(1)(a)) is not an arrestable offence under the HTA. _____

4. If you suspect that a person's number plate has been altered, you can seize it under s 14(1) of the HTA. _____

5. A person whose driver's licence is suspended for demerit points in Ontario is guilty of a provincial offence if he or she drives his or her car on a highway in Ontario. _____

6. A police officer may use his or her own judgment when deciding to undertake a suspect apprehension pursuit. _____

Short Answer

Briefly answer the following questions.

1. List five rules from the *Suspect Apprehension Pursuits* regulation.

2. List five offences under the HTA for which an offender may be arrested.

3. List the five steps an officer should use when communicating with a driver during a vehicle stop.

Discussion Questions

1. Why is it important for an officer to recognize abusive driver behaviour and not personalize it?

2. What are the possible driver responses to a vehicle stop?

Impaired Driving and Other Criminal Code and Highway Traffic Act Offences

6

LEARNING OUTCOMES

After completing this chapter, you should be able to:

- Understand the role of case law in lower courts involving provincial offences, and in courts involving *Criminal Code* (CC) offences.

- Explain the essential elements of some of the more common motor vehicle offences in the CC.

- Identify and understand the essential elements of the offences of being impaired and being "over 80" that must be proved to obtain a conviction.

- Understand and appreciate the kind of evidence needed to support "reasonable suspicion" and "reasonable grounds to believe" that a driver is either impaired or "over 80."

- On assessing evidence, determine whether an impaired or "over 80" charge can be laid.

- Understand the essential elements of the offence of driving while disqualified and be able to apply that understanding to determine the various circumstances in which that charge can be laid.

- Decide when a search warrant is required under the CC to search a vehicle, and when a search may be conducted without a warrant.

Overview of Jurisdiction over Motor Vehicle Law

General: Provincial Law and Criminal Law

Laws governing regulations and offences involving motor vehicles are contained in the Ontario *Highway Traffic Act* (HTA) and in regulations made under that Act, as well as in some other provincial legislation, as noted in earlier chapters. Some of the more serious operating offences are contained in the federal *Criminal Code* (CC).

Laws governing the rights of citizens to sue for personal injury and property damage arising from a motor vehicle collision are governed by provincial negligence law and motor vehicle insurance law. Although negligence and insurance law are not concerns of this text, a police officer, like any other citizen, can be summonsed to give evidence at a trial in a civil action for negligence, and his or her oral evidence, the contents of the officer's notebook, and the contents of an accident report prepared by the officer may all be relevant to the issues in a civil trial. An officer who is served with a summons issued under the Ontario *Rules of Civil Procedure* should notify his or her superiors and follow department procedures for responding to a civil summons.

The Importance of Case Law in Interpreting Criminal Law Statutes

Leaving aside negligence law, you should always be aware of whether the motor vehicle law you are dealing with is federal or provincial, because the prosecution procedures are different. Another distinction has to do with how case law may change the interpretation of the HTA or the CC. Most HTA cases are heard by justices of the peace (JPs). While a JP makes a decision, the JP rarely provides written reasons for that decision. This point is important because, in many cases, judges must follow the interpretations that previous judges have made in their written reasons. Consequently, a good deal of variation may exist in how a section of the HTA is interpreted from one JP's court to another. This problem is compounded by the fact that there are few appeals of JPs' decisions, which might result in written reasons being given, because an appeal is too expensive to be worth the bother in most cases. Given the absence of HTA case law as a guide to interpretation of the HTA, in some cases there is a risk of inconsistent decisions—one JP may be quite unaware of how another is ruling, particularly where there is little case law to serve as an interpretive aid.

Cases under the CC are another matter. Cases involving impaired driving or other criminal offences under the CC are usually heard by a judge of the Ontario Court of Justice, or, depending on the nature of the CC offence, by an Ontario Superior Court judge, with or without a jury. At this level, the court procedures are much more formal, and judges often give written reasons for judgment that other judges and lawyers read. Written reasons for judgment are important because

- they may become precedents (that is, court decisions made for the first time on new points of law) for interpreting the CC or other laws;
- they are treated as persuasive by other judges at the same court level—that is, the reasoning in the written reasons for judgment is likely to be followed by other judges in future cases in the same court; and
- if a decision is appealed at trial to an appellate court, the appellate court's decision and its reasons for judgment become not just persuasive but binding on lower trial courts hearing similar cases (this means that lower courts must follow the decision in an appellate court).

What all of this means is that CC cases are more likely to involve situations where the meaning and interpretation of a section of the CC has been changed or affected by written reasons interpreting that section. Therefore, the meaning of a section of the CC is not static, but changes as new case law interprets the meaning of the section. As a result, you must be aware that a case decision may affect how you deal with impaired drivers or other offenders. It is not your responsibility as an officer to research or interpret case law, but it is your responsibility to be aware of the effect that case law changes can have on what you need to do to secure convictions.

Impaired driving offences in particular have provided judges and lawyers with a fertile field in which to develop case law that interprets the various applicable CC sections. One reason for this is that CC driving offences are common in the courts, and involve a broader cross-section of the population than is the case for most criminal offences. Many of those charged with a CC driving offence have the resources to hire good lawyers and mount technical defences. The result is a tremendous amount of case law on impaired driving offences, much of which comes from provincial appellate courts and the Supreme Court of Canada. We will refer to some of the more important cases in the course of our discussion of CC impaired driving offences.

Criminal Code Procedure: An Overview

Offences under the CC, such as offences involving impaired driving, are not provincial offences; they are criminal offences. CC offences are dealt with through procedures and courts that are different from those used for HTA offences. Most CC offences, including impaired driving offences, are dual procedure offences (also called *mixed offences* or *hybrid offences*). This means that the Crown initially has the right to decide to try the offence as a summary conviction offence or as an indictable offence. If the Crown chooses to proceed summarily, as it usually does, the trial is held before a judge of the Ontario Court of Justice.

If the Crown elects to try the offence as an indictable offence, the procedural route depends on whether the offence falls under s 553, 536, or 469 of the CC. The following list describes the procedure for a "553" offence, a "536" offence, and a "469" offence:

- If the offence is listed as a "553" offence, the trial procedure is the same as if the Crown had elected to proceed summarily, but the Crown can ask for a longer sentence than it could have asked for if it had proceeded summarily.

- If the offence is a "536" offence, the accused has the right to elect to be tried by an Ontario Court judge alone, or by a Superior Court judge alone, or by a Superior Court judge and jury.

- If the offence is a "469" offence—most of which are very serious, such as murder— the trial goes before a Superior Court judge and jury.

The procedural routes for CC offences are illustrated in Figure 6.1.

Criminal Code Motor Vehicle Offences

As we have noted, laws about driving motor vehicles are within the jurisdiction of the province, under the division of powers set out in ss 91 and 92 of the *Constitution Act, 1867*. All driving offences are provincial offences.

However, criminal offences involving drinking and driving or negligence causing serious injury or death using motor vehicles, vessels, and aircraft have been held to be constitutionally valid criminal law under the exercise of the federal power over criminal law and

FIGURE 6.1 Procedural Routes for HTA and CC Offences

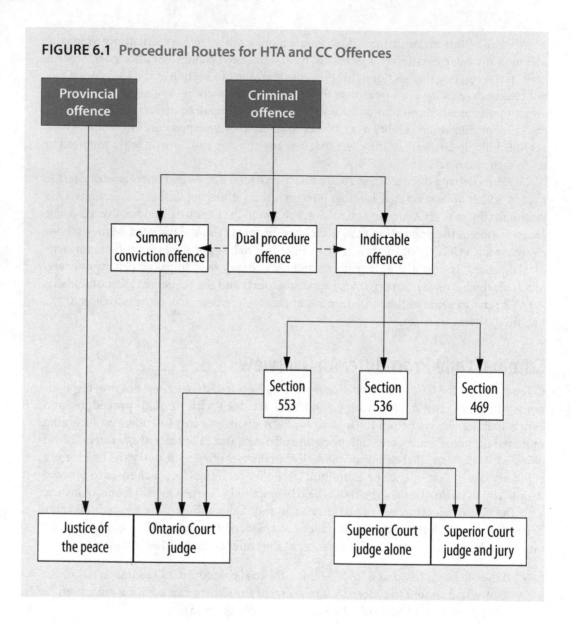

procedure as set out in s 91(27) of the *Constitution Act, 1867*. This is because these offences are not merely about driving, but about behaviour deemed to be criminal. Furthermore, the offences in the CC are different from and generally broader than the offences in the HTA.

The definition of "motor vehicle" in these "operation" and "care or control" offences (s 253 CC) is found in s 2 of the CC. It is much broader than and quite different from the definition in the HTA. The CC definition includes any land vehicle "that is drawn, propelled, or driven by any means other than muscular power, but does not include railway equipment." The CC definition therefore includes snowmobiles, farm tractors, self-propelled implements of husbandry (that is, reapers and combines), road-building machines, and traction engines, whether operated on a highway or not.

Based on the CC definition of "motor vehicle," a person can be convicted of impaired operation of a farm tractor in his or her own back field, although such a charge would be unusual in the absence of a complaint related to danger to other persons or property. Another way of putting this is that CC offences are "anywhere" offences—that is, they can be committed anywhere.

Definitions of "Motor Vehicle"

LAW	"MOTOR VEHICLE"	
	INCLUDES	EXCLUDES
Criminal Code	• Any vehicle that is drawn, propelled, or driven by any means other than muscular power but does not include railway equipment (s 2)	
Highway Traffic Act	• Automobiles • Motorcycles • Motor-assisted bicycles (unless otherwise indicated) • Any other vehicle propelled or driven by power other than muscular power (s 1)	• Motorized snow vehicles • Farm tractors • Self-propelled implements of husbandry • Road-building machines • Streetcars or motor vehicles on rails • Traction engines • Power-assisted bicycles

Criminal Negligence, Dangerous Driving, and Other Criminal Code Offences Involving Motor Vehicles

As you will see later in this chapter, offences concerned with impaired driving involve especially complex procedures for investigating, apprehending, and charging someone. For that reason, impaired driving offences are discussed separately from other CC driving offences. Some of the other CC offences involving motor vehicles are the following:

- criminal negligence causing bodily harm and criminal negligence causing death (ss 220 and 221);
- dangerous operation of a motor vehicle (s 249);
- flight from a pursuing peace officer causing death or bodily harm (s 249.1);
- failure to stop at the scene of an accident (s 252); and
- street racing (ss 249.2 to 249.4).

These offences are discussed in the following sections.

Criminal Negligence Causing Bodily Harm and Criminal Negligence Causing Death: CC, Sections 220 and 221

Criminal negligence is defined in s 219 of the CC as an act, or omission to perform a duty imposed by law, that shows reckless disregard for the lives or safety of other persons. Section 220 sets out the penalty for causing death by criminal negligence, and s 221 sets out the penalty for causing bodily harm. Both criminal negligence offences are indictable and can carry lengthy prison sentences, including life imprisonment for criminal negligence causing death. It is clear that the breach of a provincially imposed duty is not itself sufficient to support a charge of criminal negligence. Nor is mere civil negligence—the failure to meet the standard of care expected of a reasonably prudent person. Instead, indifference is the standard for criminal negligence: the accused knew or ought to have known that the act or omission could threaten the life or safety of another person, but acted without regard for the consequences. It is not necessary to prove that the act was wilful or deliberate; *indifference* is sufficient. However, it is not clear from the cases whether indifference is an objective standard (determining whether a reasonable person would assume that the accused acted wilfully in light of all the circumstances) or a subjective one (proving that the accused was in fact indifferent in deciding to act or failing to act).[1]

Clearly, if there is evidence of what the accused actually thought and evidence that he or she was indifferent to the consequences, that subjective evidence of criminal negligence will support a conviction. While the Supreme Court of Canada has not been as clear as it could be about reliance on an objective test to determine the basis for criminal negligence, the Ontario Court of Appeal has ruled that until the Supreme Court of Canada holds otherwise, it is still open to the court to apply an objective test, which usually involves an inference drawn from the type of driving engaged in by the accused—that is, the accused's behaviour shows a marked departure from the norm.[2] That may be enough to objectively infer criminal negligence. There is no need to advance evidence of what the accused actually thought.[3]

> **NOTE** The finding on the conduct of the accused to prove criminal negligence requires that the accused's conduct represent a marked departure from the norm, and whether the objective or subjective test of intention is used makes very little difference in making that finding (*R v Anderson*, [1990] 1 SCR 265, 53 CCC (3d) 481, 75 CR (3d) 50).

Although these two offences often arise in cases involving the operation of a motor vehicle, they do not require the accused to be driving a motor vehicle or have a motor vehicle in his or her care or control. The offence is much broader than that, encompassing all kinds of situations.

CASE ILLUSTRATION

Determining Criminal Negligence

In the case of *R v Waite*,* the accused had been drinking and, while driving his car, struck and killed four young people taking part in a hayride, and injured a fifth. The hayride involved several tractors pulling wagons loaded with hay on a public highway. Some of the young people had been running alongside the wagons when the accused came up to the hayride. He drove behind it for a short while, then passed it, turned his vehicle around and deliberately sped toward the hayride at high speed and on the wrong side of the road.

At trial, the accused was found not guilty of criminal negligence causing death and injury, but was found guilty of the included offence of dangerous driving. The Crown appealed the acquittals on the charges of criminal negligence.

The Crown appeal was granted. The Supreme Court of Canada ruled that criminal negligence requires conduct assessed objectively: the conduct must be a marked departure from the norm, that goes beyond mere negligence. There is also a subjective mental element, which is the minimal intent of awareness of the prohibited risk or wilful blindness to the risk. Some of the justices noted that the mental element of intention can be found in the conduct of the accused—a marked departure from the standard observed by a reasonably prudent person, which is an objective test, without resort to a subjective test on what the accused actually thought regarding the risks he undertook. In the circumstances, the court issued an order for a new trial on the criminal negligence charges. Note that this

---

1   *R v Waite*, [1989] 1 SCR 1436 and *R v Tutton*, [1989] 1 SCR 1392 continue to be the leading Supreme Court of Canada cases defining the standards for determining criminal negligence. See *R v Krzyzanowski*, 2014 ONCJ 479 and *R v McWatters*, 2016 ONSC 1477.

2   See *R v Nelson* (1990), 54 CCC (3d) 285, 75 CR (3d) 70 (Ont CA); and *R v Cabral* (1990), 54 CCC 317 (Ont CA).

3   The objective test is used in *R v Sharp* (1984), 12 CCC (3d) 428, 39 CR (3d) 367 (Ont CA).

case did not resolve the issue of whether the marked departure is to be measured subjectively or objectively.

The Supreme Court of Canada's Interpretation of Criminal Negligence

The Supreme Court of Canada has attempted to clarify both the act and the mental element required to prove criminal negligence.

The Supreme Court has decided that if an imaginary "ordinary person" were to observe the accused's conduct and consider it to be extremely reckless or risky (a marked departure from reasonable behaviour), that would be sufficient to prove that the accused's conduct constitutes criminal negligence.

The Supreme Court has also held that intent is required to prove criminal negligence. The prosecution must prove that the accused was aware that his or her conduct was high risk and that he or she went ahead and engaged in that conduct knowingly. However, the Supreme Court has been less clear on whether intent should be inferred from an objective assessment of an accused's act or a subjective assessment of his or her thoughts or intentions.

It is much easier to obtain a conviction when intent can be inferred from an act that is a marked departure from prudent conduct. The standards for prudent driving are known, and there is usually physical evidence of the act committed by the accused that would allow objective and precise determination of whether it is a marked departure from what an ordinarily prudent person would do. If the conduct is a marked departure from prudent behaviour, then the accused must have intended to be criminally negligent. However, it is much more difficult to prove intent based on what was going on in the mind of the accused at the time of the act. One would have to provide clear and hard evidence of someone's mental processes, which would require subjective interpretation.

Until the Supreme Court provides clear guidelines on how intent is to be proved, the Ontario Court of Appeal has ruled that criminal intent may be inferred from the nature of the conduct itself.

---

* *R v Waite*, [1989] 1 SCR 1436.

Dangerous Operation of a Motor Vehicle: CC, Section 249(1)(a)

An accused commits the offence of dangerous operation of a motor vehicle, or dangerous driving, when he or she operates a motor vehicle in a manner that is dangerous to the public who were present or who might have been present. Determining whether the operation of the vehicle is dangerous to the public requires consideration of the surrounding circumstances:

- the nature, condition, and use of the place at which the motor vehicle is being operated; and
- the amount of traffic that at the time is, or might reasonably be expected to be, at that place.

Dangerous driving is a mixed or hybrid offence if no one is injured, but, if the accused causes bodily harm or death, the offence is deemed to be indictable and carries correspondingly greater penalties. Dangerous driving is deemed to be a lesser and included offence in charges of criminal negligence causing death (CC, s 220), bodily harm (CC, s 221), or manslaughter (CC, s 236). There is a specific and related offence for impaired driving causing death or bodily harm (CC, s 255).

To obtain a conviction for dangerous driving, there is no need to prove that anyone was harmed. It is sufficient to show that someone *might have been* harmed.[4] The Supreme Court of Canada, in *R v Beatty*,[5] has fully considered the required acts and mental element required to sustain a conviction for dangerous driving. The modified objective test to be used requires a marked departure from the standard of the prudent driver, which appears

---

4 See *R v Edland* (1990), 23 MVR (2d) 37.

5 *R v Beatty*, 2008 SCC 5, [2008] 1 SCR 49 continues to be the leading Supreme Court of Canada case relied on in applying the law with respect to dangerous driving. See *R v Schubert*, 2016 SKQB 137; and *R v Hazelton*, 2016 ONSC 2734.

actus reus
the act or omission that is required to sustain a conviction

mens rea
the mental element or intention that is required to sustain a conviction

to be the same standard required for criminal negligence. A mere departure from the standard may support a finding of civil negligence, but it will not be sufficient to obtain a criminal conviction. The difference between a *mere* departure and *marked* departure is a matter of degree. The **actus reus** of the offence is the act of driving dangerously, and it is the manner in which the vehicle was driven that is in issue. If someone is injured or killed, that fact may assist in assessing the amount of risk undertaken by the accused, but it does not by itself determine whether the vehicle was driven dangerously or not. The **mens rea** of the offence can be satisfied by an objective test: Was the conduct a marked departure from the conduct of a reasonably prudent person? This test is based on the premise that a reasonable person would have appreciated the risk arising from the manner of driving and taken steps to minimize the risk.

Driving at an excessive rate of speed, given the condition of the highway, or passing other vehicles on a two-lane highway where there is heavy traffic in both directions are examples of acts from which, objectively, the departure from the ordinary standard may be determined. But each act is subject to any legally recognized excuse or defence. For example, subjective evidence of intent may demonstrate a lack of the required intent for a particular act. It has been held that if a driver is suffering from automatism or drowsiness, he cannot be convicted of dangerous driving, unless he knew or ought to have known that there was a real risk he would fall asleep or become drowsy while at the wheel.[6]

CASE ILLUSTRATION

Dangerous Driving

In the case of *R v Richards*,* the accused had two passengers in his car and was driving on a four-lane divided highway when he veered off onto the shoulder, continued onto the grass divider, and hit a bridge pillar, where his car burst into flames. His two passengers were killed. There was evidence that he was probably travelling at 120 km/h in a 100 km/h zone. Police evidence indicated that vehicle speeds in the left lane, on passing, commonly reached 130 km/h, and right-lane speed ranged from 80 to 110 km/h. The accused could not explain why the car left the road, although there was evidence that he applied the brakes. The evidence was that he was not driving erratically prior to the collision. The only evidence of a marked departure from the norm was speed in excess of the limit. The accused was acquitted. On appeal, the Ontario Court of Appeal ordered a new trial holding that excessive speed alone could be the basis for a dangerous driving charge, and as the evidence of actual speed was not all that clear, a new trial was appropriate.

---

*   *R v Richards* (2003), 174 CCC (3d) 154, 169 OAC 339 (Ont CA).

Flight from a Pursuing Peace Officer Causing Bodily Harm or Death: CC, Section 249.1

An accused commits this offence when he or she operates a motor vehicle while being pursued by a peace officer in a motor vehicle. If the accused, in order to escape the pursuit, fails to stop as soon as practicable, then the offence is complete. It does not matter whether the accused stopped at a later point if he or she failed to stop at the first reasonable opportunity. The offence is a mixed or hybrid offence, unless the accused has caused bodily harm or death, in which case the offence is indictable and carries increased penalties. A driving prohibition order may also be imposed. It is a lesser and included offence for criminal negligence causing bodily harm or death, and also for manslaughter.

---

6   See *R v Jiang*, 2007 BCCA 270, 220 CCC (3d) 55, 48 CR (6th) 49.

Failure to Stop at the Scene of an Accident: CC, Section 252

An accused commits the offence of failing to stop at the scene of an accident if he or she has the care or control of or is in charge of a motor vehicle that is involved in an accident with a person, vehicle, aircraft, vessel, or cattle in the charge of someone. If the accused fails to stop, provide identification, and, where any person has been injured or appears to require assistance, offer assistance, the offence is complete. See Table 6.1. For this offence, if the accused knows that a person has been injured or appears to require assistance, the offence is a hybrid offence. The offence is indictable if the accused knows that bodily harm has occurred; or knows that someone involved in the accident is dead; or knows that bodily harm has occurred and the accused is reckless as to whether death might occur and it, in fact, does occur. The accused can be convicted once it is shown that he or she failed to perform the duties described above (stop, identify himself or herself, and offer assistance when necessary). However, in the case of an indictable offence, a conviction will not follow if the prosecution proves only that the accused should have known that someone suffered bodily harm or death. To obtain a conviction, the prosecution must show that the accused knew that someone had suffered bodily harm or death. Some cases also indicate that the accused will not be convicted of failing to stop if the act causing the collision was deliberate rather than accidental; in such cases, other charges, including assault or manslaughter, could be laid.[7]

> **NOTE** The offence of "failure to stop at scene of accident" occurs when it is established that the defendant failed to perform any one of the three statutory duties that comprise the offence: fails to stop, fails to identify himself or herself, or fails to render assistance. See *R v Steere* (1972), 6 CCC (2d) 403, 19 CRNS 115 (BCCA).

TABLE 6.1 Hit and Run Offences

SECTION NUMBER	LOCATION	TYPE OF VEHICLE	TYPE OF DAMAGE	DUTIES	PERSON CHARGED	TIME LIMIT TO ISSUE CHARGE	ARREST WITHOUT WARRANT
Fail to remain HTA, s 200(1)	Highway	Vehicle or streetcar	• Any accident *Note: By those directly or indirectly involved*	(a) Remain at or immediately return to scene, (b) Render all possible assistance, and (c) Upon request, give in writing: • Driver's name and address, • Registered owner's name and address, and • Permit number of vehicle to • anyone sustaining loss • any witness • police	Driver	6 months	Yes, for clause (a) only

---

7   See *R v O'Brien* (1987), 39 CCC (3d) 528 (Nfld SC (TD)).

SECTION NUMBER	LOCATION	TYPE OF VEHICLE	TYPE OF DAMAGE	DUTIES	PERSON CHARGED	TIME LIMIT TO ISSUE CHARGE	ARREST WITHOUT WARRANT
Fail to stop CC, s 252(1)	Anywhere	Vehicle	• Vehicle • Person • Cattle in the charge of a person *Note: Does not include a vehicle striking a house, building, or other fixed object*	(a) Stop, (b) Offer assistance to injured person, and (c) Give a name and address (whether requested or not)	Must identify driver	Dual	Yes
Fail to report HTA, s 199(1)	Anywhere	Motor vehicle or streetcar	• Damage apparently exceeding $2,000 • Personal injuries *Note: By those directly or indirectly involved*	• Report forthwith to nearest police (if driver is physically incapable, the passenger—if there is one—makes the report) • Attend location as directed by police and report • Furnish information to registrar	Person in charge	6 months	No
Fail to report (highway property) HTA, s 201	Highway	Vehicle or animal	• Property on highways, shrubs, signs, poles, fence, etc. *Note: By any accident or otherwise*	Report forthwith to police	Driver/ Owner	6 months	No
Fail to report MSVA, s 13(1)	Anywhere	Motorized snow vehicle	• Damage apparently exceeding $400 • Personal injuries *Note: By those directly or indirectly involved*	Report forthwith to nearest police these particulars: (a) Name and address, (b) Date and location of incident, and (c) Circumstances	Driver/ Owner	6 months	No
Fail to disclose particulars CAIA, s 4(1)	Highway	Motorized vehicle	• Any accident *Note: By those directly or indirectly involved*	On request, disclose particulars of contract of automobile insurance— CAIA, s 4(2)	Operator	6 months	No

Note: CC, s 252(2): "In proceedings under subsection (1), evidence that an accused failed to stop his vehicle, ... offer assistance where any person has been injured ... and give his name and address is, in the absence of any evidence to the contrary, proof of an intent to escape civil and criminal liability." Also in this regard, an earlier version of the CC was referred to in *R v Roche*, [1983] 1 SCR 491 at 493.

HTA = *Highway Traffic Act*; CC = *Criminal Code*; MSVA = *Motorized Snow Vehicles Act*; CAIA = *Compulsory Automobile Insurance Act*.

Source: Provincial Offences Wordings and Fines (St. Catharines, Ont: MacBeth, 2015) at 19.

Street Racing: CC, Sections 249.2 to 249.4

The CC offence of street racing, discussed in Chapter 4, carries greater penalties if it includes convictions for dangerous driving, criminal negligence causing death, or criminal negligence causing bodily harm. The penalties also increase for repeat offenders. Driving prohibition orders can also be imposed on repeat offenders, up to and including a lifetime ban. You will recall that racing is also an HTA offence (s 172).

Impaired Driving

We now turn to those sections of the CC that address the issue of impaired driving. The offence of being impaired refers to impairment by alcohol or drugs. However, a lawful demand for a breath sample for an approved screening device or breathalyzer can only be made if alcohol is involved, not drugs. To arrest a person for operating a motor vehicle while impaired by drugs, the police officer must obtain an admission from the person as to the reason for the "impaired behaviour" or obtain a voluntary urine sample for analysis.

Some Costs of Impaired Driving

MADD Canada reports the following statistics on the magnitude of the alcohol and drug-related crash problem in Canada:

- *Fatalities* In 2010, an estimated 2,541 individuals were killed in motor vehicle crashes in Canada. Of these fatalities, MADD Canada estimates that 1,082 were impairment-related. MADD Canada considers this estimate to be conservative and limited by a number of factors, including the underreporting that results from the inability to conduct alcohol tests on surviving impaired drivers, and from the need to rely on police reports. Also, the figure underestimates the percentage of crash deaths that involve drugs. The rate of accidents involving drivers impaired by drug use has seen recent dramatic increases.

   The 1,082 figure also leaves out individuals killed in impaired crashes on water. An average of 135 boating deaths occurred per year from 2006 to 2008, and more than 50 percent are believed to have involved alcohol and/or drugs. The figure also excludes deaths arising from aircraft, trains, and industrial vehicles such as forklifts. As a result, MADD Canada estimates that between 1,250 and 1,500 impairment-related crash deaths occur in Canada each year (3.4 to 4.1 deaths per day).
- *Injuries* In 2010, of the 299,838 individuals who were injured in motor vehicle crashes, MADD Canada estimates that approximately 63,821 were injured in impairment-related crashes (about 175 per day).
- *Property damage* In 2010, an estimated 1,651,650 motor vehicles were involved in property-damage-only crashes in Canada. Of these, MADD Canada estimates that approximately 210,932 were impairment-related damage crashes (about 578 per day).
- *Estimated monetary costs* Based on a social cost model (which takes into account fatalities, injuries, property damage, traffic delays, out-of-pocket expenses, hospital and health costs, and police, fire, and ambulance costs), impairment-related driving deaths, injuries, and property-damage-only crashes in Canada are estimated to have cost $20.62 billion in 2010. This model is recent, is based on extensive analysis, and was prepared for the federal Ministry of Transportation. This figure is also limited to motor vehicle crashes.[*]

Statistics Canada reports the following impaired driving statistics (for 2011) in Canada:

- Demographically, impaired driving is highest for 20- to 24-year-olds.
- Impaired driving rates are increasing for women.
- Impaired driving incidents peak shortly after bar closings.[†]

---

[*] Adapted from MADD Canada, "The Magnitude of the Alcohol/Drug-Related Crash Problem in Canada: Overview," *MADD Canada* (April 2013), online: <http://madd.ca/pages/impaired-driving/overview/statistics>.

[†] Adapted from Statistics Canada, "Impaired Driving in Canada, 2011," by Samuel Perrault, in *Juristat*, Catalogue No 85-002-X (Ottawa: Statistics Canada, 2013) at 11, online: <http://www.publicsafety.gc.ca/lbrr/archives/jrst11739-eng.pdf>.

Impaired Driving: Current Trends

The following excerpt from Statistics Canada's "Police-Reported Crime Statistics in Canada, 2014"* outlines some recent trends in impaired driving.

Police-reported impaired driving down for third consecutive year

Police reported about 74,800 alcohol or drug impaired driving incidents in 2014, about 3,000 fewer than the year before. The rate of impaired driving decreased by 5% in 2014 to 210 impaired driving incidents per 100,000 population, representing the third consecutive decline [see Chart 14].

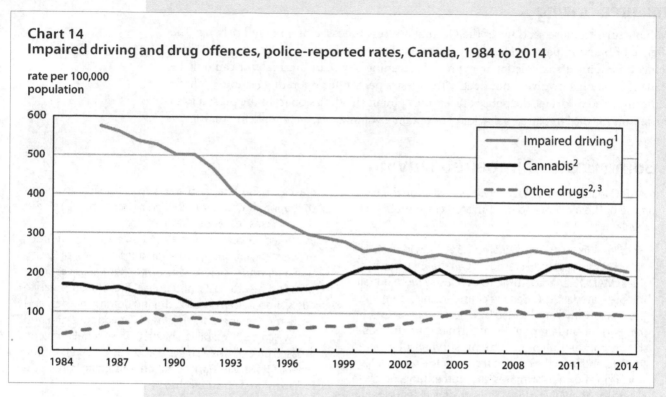

Chart 14
Impaired driving and drug offences, police-reported rates, Canada, 1984 to 2014

rate per 100,000
population

Legend:
— Impaired driving[1]
— Cannabis[2]
--- Other drugs[2, 3]

1. Data not available prior to 1986. Includes alcohol and/or drug impaired operation of a vehicle, alcohol and/or drug impaired operation of a vehicle causing death or bodily harm, failure or refusal to comply with testing for the presence of alcohol or drugs and failure or refusal to provide a breath or blood sample. In some jurisdictions, including British Columbia, impaired driving incidents that meet the elements of the Criminal Code may be handled using a provincial statute. Collection of these incidents is within the scope of the Uniform Crime Reporting Survey.

2. Includes possession, trafficking, production or distribution.

3. Includes cocaine, heroin, methamphetamines (e.g., crystal meth), methylenedioxyamphetamine (e.g., ecstasy) and other controlled drugs and substances, as well as possession of precursors and equipment.

Source: Statistics Canada, Canadian Centre for Justice Statistics, Uniform Crime Reporting Survey.

Since July 2008, under the *Criminal Code*, police can perform compulsory roadside checks and assessments if they suspect a driver is under the influence of drugs . . . . Almost all police-reported impaired driving incidents continued to involve alcohol in 2014 (97%), while a small proportion (3%) involved drugs.

Unlike the overall decline in impaired driving between 2013 and 2014, the number and rate for almost all drug impaired driving violations increased over the same period. In total, there were 2,500 drug impaired driving violations in 2014, just over 500 more than the previous year. Despite this increase, the rate of drug impaired driving (7 per 100,000 population) remained low compared with alcohol impaired driving (203 per 100,000 population). The low rate for drug impaired driving may be partly explained by the fact that determining and measuring the level of drug impairment can be more difficult and less reliable than the measures used to detect alcohol impaired driving . . . .

Impaired driving rates declined in every province except Nova Scotia, where the rate remained stable between 2013 and 2014. Nunavut was the only territory to record a decrease in its impaired driving rate between 2013 and 2014, as both the Northwest Territories (+30%) and Yukon (+22%) recorded increases.

It is important to note that the number of impaired driving offences reported by police can be influenced by a number of factors, including changes in legislation, varying law enforcement practices across jurisdictions (e.g., R.I.D.E. programs), and changing societal attitudes toward drinking and driving . . . .

We must also take into consideration the impact on impaired driving that may flow from the Liberal government's promised legalization of cannabis. Will greater accessibility and legalization result in a further increase in driving while under the influence of drugs? Will effective drug impairment detection and screening procedures be developed to perform similar functions to a breathalyzer? Will changes in the law regarding impaired driving be required? It is too early to tell what the trends will be for drugs and driving or what techniques and strategies will be developed to detect and apprehend drug-impaired drivers.

---

* Statistics Canada, "Police Reported Crime Statistics in Canada, 2014," by Jillian Boyce, in *Juristat* 35:1, Catalogue No 85-002-X (Ottawa: Statistics Canada, 2015) at 21-22, online: <http://www.statcan.gc .ca/pub/85-002-x/2015001/article/14211-eng.pdf>.

Basic Terms and Concepts

Before we examine the law associated with the impaired operation of a motor vehicle, it is necessary to understand the following concepts.

Ability Impaired

Proof of impairment is established through a *description of a person's condition* as a result of the consumption of alcohol or a drug. The description must convince the court that the person so described does not have the ability to operate a motor vehicle safely because he or she has been drinking or because he or she ingested a drug. The degree of impairment depends on a person's tolerance. Some people are impaired after consuming just a couple of drinks or a small amount of a drug, while others require many drinks or larger amounts of a drug before they become impaired.

NOTE There is a crucial distinction between impairment generally and impairment of a person's ability to operate a motor vehicle. When a person has a drink, his or her ability to drive is not necessarily impaired. The alcohol might impair his or her ability to, say, thread a needle, but not impair his or her ability to drive. See *R v Andrews*, 1996 ABCA 23, 104 CCC (3d) 192.

Over 80 Milligrams

Under the CC, it is unlawful to operate a motor vehicle with more than 80 mg of alcohol per 100 ml of blood. (Recall that under the HTA, there are consequences for having a blood alcohol concentration [BAC] between 0.05 and 0.08.) This measurement simply proves whether you are over the legal limit, and should not be confused with proof of impairment. It is possible to be "over 80" and not be impaired, or be impaired and not be "over 80."

NOTE It is not necessary to prove that the accused knew or ought to have known that he or she was or might be "over 80." Criminal intent is proved if it is shown that the accused voluntarily consumed alcohol. See *R v Murray* (1985), 22 CCC (3d) 502 (Ont CA).

Operating

Operating means that the person is *driving* a motor vehicle, steering a boat, or piloting an aircraft—that is, the vehicle is under way with the person directing its movement.

Care or Control

"Care or control" means that the person is not operating the motor vehicle, vessel, or aircraft, but is *using* the vehicle or its equipment, or is involved in some activity that risks putting the vehicle in motion. For example, a person who gets into the driver's seat of a car, puts the key in the ignition, and turns the engine on, but does not drive it, would be considered to have the care or control of the vehicle.

> **NOTE** The mere fact that a person has custody of a vehicle is not sufficient to convict the accused. There must be some risk that the vehicle could be set in motion. See *R v Decker*, 2002 NFCA 9, 162 CCC (3d) 503.

Reasonable Suspicion

Reasonable suspicion refers to a hunch or suspicion for which there is some rational basis to suspect that someone has been consuming alcohol. The odour of an alcoholic beverage on someone's breath is sufficient evidence to form reasonable suspicion.

> **NOTE** Reasonable suspicion applies only to the issue of whether the accused has alcohol in his or her body, and not to operation or control of a vehicle; the latter element must be proved as a fact. See *R v Swietorzecki* (1995), 97 CCC (3d) 285 (Ont CA).

Reasonable Grounds to Believe

"Reasonable grounds to believe" refers to a set of circumstances that would satisfy an ordinary, cautious, and prudent person that there is reason to believe that certain facts are true—it goes *beyond mere suspicion*. In other words, establishing reasonable *grounds* to believe requires much more evidence than the evidence that would establish reasonable *suspicion*. For example, in addition to smelling alcohol on a driver's breath, an officer would need to make other observations, such as the driver's difficulty keeping his or her balance when getting out of the car, in order to have reasonable grounds to believe that the driver is impaired. Observation of more than one of these behaviours or acts is usually required.

DISCUSSION POINT   As a patrol officer you stop a motor vehicle. The driver is your best friend, and you have reasonable grounds to believe that she is impaired by alcohol. What do you do?

> **NOTE** Reasonable grounds to believe need not be based on the accused's operation of a vehicle. They may be based on the officer's observance of the accused's condition, or on information supplied by third parties. See *R v Strongquill* (1978), 43 CCC (2d) 232 (Sask CA).

In Court: "Reasonable Grounds" Versus "Reasonable Suspicion"

A police officer will often be challenged in court about his or her "reasonable grounds to believe." The challenge will usually be about whether the officer had enough evidence to have "reasonable grounds for believing" or whether there was only enough evidence to support a "reasonable suspicion."

Reasonable suspicion is not usually enough to provide a lawful authority for police officers to take action. Reasonable suspicion is limited to the authority to demand a breath sample using an approved screening device. Police officers cannot arrest someone on reasonable suspicion that he or she committed an indictable offence.

Recall that reasonable grounds to believe refers to a set of facts or circumstances that would satisfy an ordinary, cautious, and prudent person that there is reason to believe those facts are true, and which goes beyond mere suspicion. This definition indicates that belief is more than suspicion and should be based on information. Defence counsel will always question whether the police officer had enough evidence to convince an average person, other than himself or herself.

Defence counsel will also challenge the officer on the truthfulness of the evidence that supports reasonable grounds to believe. This evidence often consists of a police officer's subjective impressions (odour of alcohol or slurred speech) and is easier to attack.* The officer's testimony needs to include very specific and detailed examples of how the accused exhibited those characteristics. However, the more objective evidence gathered from the approved screening device, breathalyzer, or blood test will corroborate the officer's subjective impressions.

---

* Counsel will also focus on whether the police were scrupulous in affording the right to counsel and whether the testing procedures were carried out properly. Because impaired driving is an offence that crosses class and income divisions, there are more offenders who have the money and resources to support an aggressive and imaginative defence than is the case for most criminal charges. For this reason, a disproportionately large number of reported criminal cases in the published law reports are "drunk driving" cases.

Approved Screening Device: CC, Section 254

An approved screening device is an instrument that indicates whether there are reasonable grounds to believe that a person is "over 80." In order to demand a breath sample for the screening device, a police officer must have a reasonable suspicion that a person has been consuming alcohol. If the person fails the screening device test, the officer can turn reasonable suspicion that a person has been drinking into reasonable grounds to believe that the person is "over 80." This instrument does not indicate the exact amount of alcohol in the blood, but it does place the person in a "pass," "warn," or "fail" category. Section 254(1) of the CC defines "breathalyzer" and "screening device" differently. A breathalyzer is defined as an "approved instrument" and is subject to specifications set out in the CC and the regulations. A screening device is defined as an "approved screening device" and is subject to its own, distinct specifications. These devices test to different standards, the breathalyzer being the more precise instrument.

NOTE It is not necessary to lead expert evidence on the capabilities of an approved screening device. It is sufficient for a certified technician to explain what the device does and testify that it was in good working order at the time of use. See *R v Delorey*, 2004 NSCA 95, 188 CCC (3d) 372.

Breathalyzer: CC, Section 258

The breathalyzer (defined in CC, s 254(1)) is a more sophisticated instrument than the screening device. The breathalyzer accurately measures the amount of alcohol in a person's blood, whereas the screening device merely identifies drivers who *may* be "over 80." In order for a police officer to demand breath samples for a breathalyzer, he or she must have reasonable grounds to believe either that a person is "over 80" or that a person's ability is impaired. See Table 6.2 for the stages of alcoholic influence and intoxication.

TABLE 6.2 Stages of Alcoholic Influence and Intoxication

BLOOD ALCOHOL CONCENTRATION (MG PER 100 ML)	STAGE OF ALCOHOLIC INFLUENCE	CLINICAL SIGNS AND SYMPTOMS
10-50	Sobriety	• Influence/effects usually not apparent or obvious • Behaviour nearly normal by ordinary observation
30-120	Euphoria	• Mild euphoria, sociability, talkativeness • Increased self-confidence; decreased inhibitions • Diminished attention, judgment, and control • Some sensory-motor impairment • Slowed information processing
90-250	Excitement	• Emotional instability; loss of critical judgment • Impairment of perception, memory, and comprehension • Decreased sensory response; slower reaction time • Reduced visual acuity and peripheral vision; slow glare recovery • Sensory-motor incoordination; impaired balance; slurred speech; vomiting; drowsiness
180-300	Confusion	• Disorientation, mental confusion; vertigo; dysphoria • Exaggerated emotional states (fear, rage, grief, etc.) • Disturbances of vision (double vision, etc.) and of perception of colour, form, motion, dimensions • Increased pain threshold • Increased muscular incoordination; staggering gait; loss of full control over body movements • Apathy, lethargy
250-400	Stupor	• General inertia; approaching loss of motor functions • Markedly decreased response to stimuli • Marked muscular incoordination; inability to stand or walk • Vomiting; incontinence of urine and feces • Impaired consciousness; sleep or stupor
350-500	Coma	• Complete unconsciousness; coma; anesthesia • Depressed or abolished reflexes • Subnormal temperature • Impairment of circulation and respiration • Possible death
450+	Death	• Death from respiratory arrest

Source: Based on Kurt M. Dubowski, University of Oklahoma, Stages of Acute Alcoholic Influence/Intoxication (table). Copyright © 2006 by Dr. Kurt M. Dubowski. All rights reserved. Reprinted by permission.

The Supreme Court of Canada has made it clear that a person detained to provide a breath sample must be advised of the reason for his or her detention and of the right to counsel without delay under s 10(b) of the *Canadian Charter of Rights and Freedoms*. The driver must be able to *understand* that he or she has a right to counsel, which may be difficult if the detainee is so impaired that he or she cannot process the information. Proceeding with a breathalyzer in this situation may result in a court finding that the accused's rights have been infringed, and the breathalyzer evidence rendered inadmissible. There is no burden on the Crown, however, to show that the accused was advised of his or her rights—the onus is on the accused to prove that his or her rights have been infringed.

Driver Evaluation

When a police officer approaches the driver of a motor vehicle that he or she has just stopped, there are three possible scenarios:

1. The officer quickly appreciates that the driver has not been drinking and continues with the procedure for the driving offence for which the driver was stopped.

2. The officer forms *reasonable suspicion* that the driver has alcohol in his or her system. The officer can now lawfully make a demand that the driver provides a breath sample for an approved screening device.

3. The officer forms *reasonable grounds* to believe that the driver's ability to operate a motor vehicle is impaired by alcohol. The officer can now arrest the driver because he or she has reasonable grounds to believe that the driver has committed an indictable offence (see Figure 6.2). The officer will advise the suspect of the right to counsel and make the breathalyzer demand. The suspect is usually taken to the police station for the breathalyzer test.

Sample wordings for the various demands discussed in this section appear in the "Professional Practice: Sample Wordings for Demands" box later in this chapter.

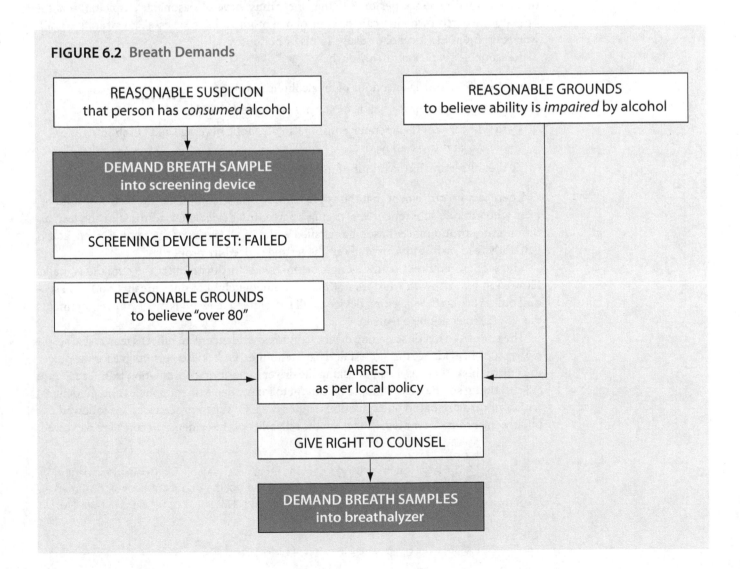

FIGURE 6.2 Breath Demands

DISCUSSION POINT

During a night shift in a small town, an officer is following a car whose driver is proceeding in an erratic and dangerous manner on the roadway. Suddenly, the driver pulls over and stops, leaving the officer no time to check the rear licence plate number or the driver on the on-board computer. The driver quickly gets out of her vehicle and, slurring her words, begins speaking in an aggressive manner. The officer calls for backup, and, after getting out of her cruiser, stands at its left front corner. Without warning, the driver rushes the officer, rips off her portable radio and throws it onto the ground, screaming, "You're not f … … talking into your g … … radio!" The driver knees the officer in the stomach and attempts to remove the officer's handgun from its holster. During this sudden assault, the officer notes a strong odour of alcohol coming from the driver. What should the officer have done before, during, and after the altercation? What can the driver be charged with?

Grounds for a Lawful Demand for an Approved Screening Device or Coordination Test: CC, Sections 254(2)(a) and (b)

Before a police officer[8] can demand that a breath sample be blown into a screening device, or a coordination test be performed, the officer must have a "reasonable suspicion" that the operator or person who has care or control of a motor vehicle, a vessel, an aircraft, or railway equipment has alcohol or drugs in his or her body.

Reasonable suspicion can arise when

- the officer smells the odour of an alcoholic beverage on the person's breath;
- the operator admits that he or she has consumed alcohol;
- the officer sees the operator consume an alcoholic beverage and climb into his or her car and drive away; or
- the officer smells the odour of marijuana coming from inside the car.

There is no requirement that the apprehending officer administer the test. A second officer who attends subsequently, bringing a screening device, may administer the test, although the second officer has to be satisfied with the adequacy of the sample given, and is generally responsible for carrying out the testing procedure properly.

The section requires that the sample be provided "forthwith" after the demand is made. How soon is "forthwith"? It does not mean "immediately," but does mean "soon." If a second officer brings the screening device a half hour after a demand is made, the requirements of s 254(2) may not be satisfied.

The use of a roadside screening device to buttress evidence of an officer's reasonable suspicion results in evidence that is clear and hard to refute. But it is also permissible for the officer to confirm his or her suspicion by asking the driver to perform coordination tests (see Figure 6.3). In doing so, the officer should be careful to follow department policies and guidelines, which in turn are based on regulations under the CC. When procedures are followed explicitly, the grounds for a legal attack on the reliability of the evidence in court are narrowed.

NOTE The legal test for making a demand for a breath sample for a roadside screening device is the consumption of alcohol alone, not the amount of alcohol consumed or the behaviour that flows from it. See *R v Gilroy* (1987), 3 MVR (2d) 123, 79 AR 318 (Alta CA).

---

8 The CC uses the more encompassing term "peace officer."

FIGURE 6.3 Officer Observation and Coordination Tests

Most police services have a form with check boxes for officers to use to record their observation of the driver's condition and the results of coordination tests. The following is a sample form that includes information officers may be required to observe and record.

OBSERVATION OF DRIVER'S CONDITION

BREATH (odour of alcohol)
- ☐ absent
- ☐ present

FACE COLOUR
- ☐ appears normal
- ☐ tanned
- ☐ pale
- ☐ flushed
- ☐ red

EYES (condition)
- ☐ watery
- ☐ normal
- ☐ glassy
- ☐ bloodshot

**VISIBLE SCARS/INJURIES
(note as observed)**
_____
_____
_____
_____

CLOTHES
TYPE:
_____
_____
_____
_____

CONDITION:
- ☐ orderly
- ☐ disarranged
- ☐ soiled

FOOTWEAR
TYPE:
_____
_____
_____

CONDITION:
_____
_____
_____

SPEECH
- ☐ good
- ☐ fair
- ☐ slurred
- ☐ stuttering
- ☐ incoherent
- ☐ accented

ATTITUDE
- ☐ polite
- ☐ cooperative
- ☐ talkative
- ☐ carefree
- ☐ abusive
- ☐ other

UNUSUAL ACTIONS
- ☐ hiccuping
- ☐ belching
- ☐ vomiting
- ☐ fighting
- ☐ crying
- ☐ other

COORDINATION TESTS

BALANCE
- ☐ sure
- ☐ fair
- ☐ swaying
- ☐ unsure
- ☐ unsteady
- ☐ falling
- ☐ in a circle
- ☐ side to side
- ☐ back and forth

FINGER TO NOSE
- ☐ Right:
- ☐ sure
- ☐ hesitated
- ☐ missed
- ☐ Left:
- ☐ sure
- ☐ hesitated
- ☐ missed

WALKING
- ☐ (heel to toe)
- ☐ sure
- ☐ swaying
- ☐ unsteady
- ☐ stumbling
- ☐ lost balance

TURNING
- ☐ sure
- ☐ swaying
- ☐ unsteady
- ☐ staggering
- ☐ stumbling
- ☐ falling

Demand for a Screening Device Test

In the case of *R v Padavattan*,* the accused was at a fast food restaurant just before midnight; a witness suspected that he had been drinking, and called the police. The officer arrived within minutes and approached the accused's vehicle. The officer spoke to the accused, who was sitting in the driver's seat with the engine running, waiting for his food. The officer noted the odour of an alcoholic beverage on the accused's breath. The officer asked the accused if he had consumed any alcohol that evening. The accused initially denied having done so, but then conceded that he had had "a beer." At this point, the officer formed a reasonable suspicion that the respondent had alcohol in his body and at 12:04 a.m., he made a demand for a sample of the respondent's breath. Prior to his arrival at the scene, the officer, who did not have a screening device with him, had radioed for one to be brought to the location by another police officer. The second officer arrived with the device within approximately three minutes and administered the test to the respondent in the presence of the first responding officer. A "fail" result was obtained at 12:10 a.m.

The first officer arrested the accused for "care and control, over 80" and, at 12:16 a.m., made a demand for a breathalyzer test. The test was administered at the station shortly thereafter by a qualified technician, who took two samples, 15 minutes apart, both of which were over 80. The accused was convicted.

---

* *R v Padavattan* (2007), 233 CCC (3d) 221, 45 CR (6th) 405 (Ont Sup Ct J).

Grounds for a Lawful Demand for a Breathalyzer Test: CC, Section 254(3)(a)

Before a police officer can lawfully demand that breath samples (two samples, taken at least 15 minutes apart) be provided by having the accused breathe into a breathalyzer instrument, the officer must have reasonable grounds to believe that the operator or person with care or control of a motor vehicle, a vessel, an aircraft, or railway equipment is "over 80" or that, within three hours preceding the demand being made, his or her ability was impaired by alcohol. When an officer demands a breath sample for the approved screening device or a coordination test and the person fails the screening device or coordination test, the officer has "reasonable grounds to believe" that the person is "over 80." Failure of the screening device or coordination test is the only way for an officer to obtain the reasonable grounds to believe that the person is "over 80"; it is unacceptable to the court that an officer could look at a person and reasonably determine with accuracy that the person is "over 80," because the officer does not know the person's tolerance for alcohol.

Reasonable grounds arise under either of the following conditions:

- when, on an officer's reasonable suspicion, a person breathes into an approved screening device and fails the test; or
- when a person's behaviour and demeanour provide the officer with reasonable grounds to believe, beyond reasonable suspicion, that the person's ability is impaired by alcohol.

The grounds do not have to include a belief based on the actual operation of the vehicle, because observation of the driver's condition may be enough. Further, the officer may rely on information from third parties. An officer may only make the demand in the territorial jurisdiction in which his appointment is effective. There is no particular form for the demand, but it must be made clearly and unequivocally: "I require you to give a breath sample"; not "I would like you to give a breath sample."

CASE ILLUSTRATION

Demand for a Breathalyzer Test

In the case of *R v Bush*,* the accused was charged with impaired driving and being "over 80." The arresting officer had received a report from the dispatcher that an individual had called 911 and described the accused as driving erratically. The witness also said the accused was intoxicated. With this information, the officer responded and came upon the accused just after the accused had collided with a parked vehicle. The officer detected alcohol on the accused's breath, noted that his eyes were glassy, and observed that he was unsteady on his feet. Without questioning the accused, and relying on these observations and the dispatcher's report, the officer made a breathalyzer demand.

The accused argued that in these circumstances, the officer did not have reasonable and probable grounds to make a breathalyzer demand. The Ontario Court of Appeal held that the officer was entitled to rely on his observations, together with the hearsay statements of the witness who reported his observations to the dispatcher, who relayed this information to the officer.

_____
* *R v Bush*, 2010 ONCA 554, 101 OR (3d) 641.

Grounds for a Lawful Demand for Blood: CC, Sections 254(3)(a)(ii), (b), and (4)

In a situation where a lawful breathalyzer demand could be made but the person is incapable of providing breath samples or it is impractical to obtain breath samples, a police officer can demand blood samples. A person may be *incapable* of providing breath samples because he or she has sustained an injury to the face, mouth, or lungs. It might be *impractical* to take breath samples because the person has been injured and needs immediate medical attention; the safety of the person is more important than performing a breathalyzer test. However, before determining incapacity or impracticability, the officer must have reasonable grounds to believe that a person is either "over 80" or impaired, or has been so within the preceding three hours from when the officer formed the suspicion. The driver's consent is required.

NOTE The blood samples must be taken by or under the supervision of a qualified medical practitioner who must be satisfied that it will not endanger the life and health of the person. Failure to ensure this constitutes a violation of the security of the person under s 7 of the Charter and an unlawful search under s 8 of the Charter. See *R v Green*, [1992] 1 SCR 614.

PROFESSIONAL PRACTICE

Sample Wordings for Demands

The following wordings are used by police services for the demands discussed in this chapter; if at any time an individual asks for a right or a demand to be repeated by the officer, the officer must do so, and must make notes regarding the request. To ensure that the rights are delivered in a consistent manner to *all* individuals, officers are advised to read directly from the rights and demands in his or her own notebook, rather than memorize them and attempt to deliver them in the same way to each person. Delivering rights from memory may have implications if the case goes to trial—for example, if the officer cannot remember exactly how he or she delivered the rights in a particular case, a "reasonable doubt" will have been raised, and it is possible that the Crown will withdraw the case.

WHAT IS BEING DEMANDED	SAMPLE WORDING
Approved screening device	"I demand that you provide forthwith a suitable sample of your breath directly into an approved screening device, to enable a proper analysis of your breath to be made, and that you accompany me for the purpose of enabling these samples to be taken."
Standard field sobriety tests	"I demand that you perform standard field sobriety tests to determine whether your ability to operate a motor vehicle is impaired by alcohol, a drug or a combination of both, and to accompany me for the purpose of performing such tests. Do you understand?"
Drug recognition expert	"I demand that you submit to an evaluation conducted by an evaluating officer to determine whether your ability to operate a motor vehicle is impaired by a drug or a combination of a drug and alcohol, and that you accompany me for this purpose. Do you understand?"
Breathalyzer test or blood sample	"I demand that you provide suitable samples of your [*breath directly into an approved instrument*]/[*blood*] to enable an analysis to be made to determine the concentration, if any, of alcohol in your blood, and that you accompany me for the purpose of enabling these samples to be taken."

Grounds for a Blood Warrant: CC, Section 256

In some circumstances, instead of demanding breath samples or blood samples, the police officer may apply to a JP for a warrant to obtain blood samples, whether or not the person consents. Before a blood warrant can be sought, the following prerequisites must be met:

- there was a collision resulting in the death of another person or bodily harm to another person or to the alleged offender; and
- the police officer has lawful grounds for a blood demand, but the person is unable to consent to the blood demand because of a mental or physical condition arising from the consumption of alcohol or from the collision.

An example of a mental condition that could prevent a person from consenting to a blood demand is shock. A person in shock would probably not hear the blood demand or understand it, and therefore could not properly consent to or refuse the demand. An example of a physical condition that could prevent a person from consenting to a blood demand is unconsciousness. Note that in charging a person with impaired operation causing bodily harm, the harm must be to a person other than the driver, although injury to the driver qualifies as a ground for a blood warrant. The person must be conscious and able to understand the blood demand made by a police officer. If the person refuses, he or she can be charged with "refusal" under s 254(5) of the CC. If the person consents, blood samples can be taken.

If the subject is unconscious or unable to understand the blood demand, the police officer must go before a JP to get permission to seize blood samples from the person. The JP acts as an independent adjudicator to determine whether the police have sufficient grounds to justify issuing a warrant to seize blood from a person who cannot respond to a lawfully made blood demand. The JP's function is to protect the rights of the person, so that the police do not proceed at will to seize blood samples without the subject's knowledge or consent. The officer has four hours from the time of the offence to obtain the warrant. However, even though the officer has four hours to obtain the warrant, if the samples are not taken within two hours of the offence, the BAC presumption is lost (see the discussion in the section "Time Limits on Breath and Blood Samples: CC, Sections 254 and 258" below). In this case, whatever the blood alcohol reading, expert evidence will have to be given to show the rate at which the BAC was decreasing, and to give some idea of what the BAC was likely to have been at the time of the offence. If the officer is not sure when the person was driving the vehicle, he or she can always proceed with the arrest on the basis that the person had care or control of the vehicle, because this can usually be established.

The reason for a blood warrant is often incorrectly presumed to be for situations where a person refuses a blood demand. This is not the case. If a person refuses a blood demand, he or she will simply be charged with refusal to supply a blood sample. The penalty is the same as for a conviction for being impaired or being "over 80."

As mentioned above, when a collision results in an injury, rather than simply making a blood demand, the situation provides the police officer with the obligation to obtain a blood warrant.

NOTE Information about blood alcohol content from a blood sample taken for medical purposes other than determining blood alcohol content may not be used in evidence without obtaining a warrant for the blood sample. See *R v Dersch*, [1993] 3 SCR 768.

CASE ILLUSTRATION

Blood Demand

In the case of *R v Kay*,* the accused was charged with being impaired. The accused's car swerved across two lanes of traffic coming in the opposite direction, hitting the curb on the wrong side of the road and then striking another vehicle. An officer arrived within 15 minutes of the collision, by which time medical help had arrived. The accused was taken by ambulance to hospital and admitted.

Prior to speaking to the accused, the officer spoke to two people in the car that the accused struck, and to the physician in charge of the accused's treatment. The accused was immobile with a neck brace; the officer asked the accused if he had had any alcohol, and the accused said he had. The officer then made a demand for a blood sample. The accused indicated that he understood the demand, but said he was in no position to call a lawyer. The officer, who had advised the accused of his right to call a lawyer, indicated that the accused's wife, who was present, could call. The wife did not call, and the accused indicated that he would provide the blood sample.

The trial judge found that there was a reasonable basis for making the demand, that the accused had been advised of his right to counsel, and had waived the right to counsel, and that, in the circumstances, the accused consented to having a blood sample taken. The evidence of impairment based on the blood sample was admissible and the accused was convicted.

* *R v Kay* (1990), 53 CCC (3d) 500 (BCCA).

Time Limits on Breath and Blood Samples: CC, Sections 254 and 258

Once a police officer believes that he or she has reasonable grounds to believe that a person has committed the indictable offences of operating or having care or control of a motor vehicle while impaired or while being "over 80," the police officer can arrest the person immediately. The officer should then advise the person of his or her right to counsel and make a breathalyzer or blood sample demand.

To be lawful, the demand for the first of the breathalyzer or blood samples must be made within two hours of the commission of the offence of being impaired while operating or having the care or control of a motor vehicle, or being "over 80." In any case, the demand should be made immediately, or as soon as is practicable, once the officer has concluded

legal presumption
the proof of one fact by the Crown means that a second fact is presumed to be true without the Crown having to adduce evidence to prove the second fact; however, the accused may present evidence to disprove the second fact, thereby rebutting the presumption

that he or she has reasonable grounds to believe that the person's ability is impaired by alcohol or that the person has over 80 mg of alcohol per 100 ml of blood.

An important **legal presumption** exists with regard to breath and blood samples. Where breath samples are taken, if the first of the two breath samples for breathalyzer analysis is taken within two hours of the offence, the breathalyzer analysis is presumed to indicate the BAC at the time of the offence. Unlike the first breath sample, the second does *not* have to be taken within the two-hour limit for the presumption to hold; it must be taken at least 15 minutes after the first, although 20 minutes is the usual practice (to make sure that it is more than 15 minutes after the first sample was taken). There is no specific maximum time for taking the second sample, although it should be taken within two hours for the presumption to hold. The breathalyzer technician reports the lower of the two readings to the court. Blood samples must be taken within two hours of the commission of the offence or the presumption is lost.

If the demand for breathalyzer or blood samples has been made within two hours of the offence, but the first of the two breath samples, or both blood samples, cannot be obtained within two hours of the offence, the person still has to provide the samples. However, the presumption that the BAC at the time of the offence is the same as at the time of the test is lost. If a lawful demand for breathalyzer samples is made at 3 hours and 30 minutes after the offence, for example, the subject is still lawfully required to provide the samples, but the presumption is lost. The Crown attorney must now decide whether he or she wishes to subpoena an expert from the Centre of Forensic Sciences to provide evidence of the BAC at the time of the offence.

PROFESSIONAL PRACTICE

Obtaining Samples

Failure to justify to the court's satisfaction any delay in taking breath or blood samples can lead to their exclusion as evidence. The court does not consider an inconvenience to police procedure to be a justifiable excuse.

For a Breathalyzer or Blood Demand to Be Lawful

- The officer must have reasonable grounds to believe that the subject's ability is impaired by alcohol, or
- the officer must have reasonable grounds to believe that the subject has over 80 mg of alcohol per 100 ml of blood in his or her system, and
- the demand must be made within **three hours** of the offence (not the arrest).

For the BAC* Presumption to Apply

- The police officer must have had lawful grounds for a breathalyzer or blood demand,
- the breathalyzer or blood demand must have been made within **three hours** of the offence, and
- the first of two breathalyzer tests must have been made within **three hours** of the offence, or both blood tests must have been made within **three hours** of the offence.

---

* BAC at time of test = BAC at time of offence

Criminal Charges and Other Consequences

Impaired and "Over 80" Charges Under the CC

When a person fails the approved screening device test and is arrested on the basis that there are reasonable grounds to believe that he or she has committed the offence of being "over 80," he or she can be charged only with being "over 80."

As stated previously, when a person's ability is assessed as being impaired by alcohol, the person may be arrested because there are reasonable grounds to believe that the person has committed the offence of driving while impaired. If the subsequent breathalyzer tests prove that the person is "over 80," he or she can be charged with being both impaired and "over 80" under the CC. Charging with both offences is only possible when the person is both impaired and "over 80." Remember that someone can be "over 80" and not show any signs of being impaired.

3-Day, 7-Day, and 30-Day Suspensions: HTA, Section 48

An immediate roadside suspension of a driver's licence is a useful tool for a police officer who encounters a driver who has enough alcohol in his or her system to cause concern (a BAC between 0.05 and 0.08, placing the driver in the "warn" range), but not enough to charge the driver with being impaired or "over 80." It can also be used with a driver who refuses to provide a breath sample. As a result of legislative reaction to public concerns about impaired driving, what used to be a 12-hour suspension is now 3 days for the first suspension, 7 days for the second suspension, and 30 days for the third and subsequent suspensions. The province issues driver's licences under the HTA and authorizes their suspension. Because driving is a privilege and otherwise within the jurisdiction of the province, no court hearing is required when a licence is suspended. When a suspension is in effect, the person may not drive a motor vehicle. A suspension may be imposed when

- a driver blows "warn" on an approved screening device,
- a driver blows 50 mg or more on a breathalyzer, or
- a driver refuses:
  - an approved screening device breath sample demand,
  - a breathalyzer breath sample demand, or
  - a blood sample demand.

When the results of a breathalyzer test indicate a BAC of *less* than 50 mg, no HTA licence suspension can be imposed lawfully, even if the person is charged with being impaired solely on the strength of the officer's subjective observations of the driver. The driver may also demand a second test on the screening device.

A police officer can have the motor vehicle seized and towed away at the expense of the owner if the officer believes that the car should be removed and that the owner cannot arrange for its removal. Further, as of December 1, 2010, under the *Road Safety Act, 2009*, police officers may impound a vehicle for seven days where a driver is caught with a BAC over 0.08 percent or where a driver refuses or fails to provide a breath sample.

Ninety-Day Suspensions: HTA, Section 48.3

If a person blows "over 80" on both breathalyzer tests, or refuses to supply a breath sample for the breathalyzer, or a blood, urine, or oral fluid sample, or fails to perform physical co-ordination tests or submit to an evaluation, the police can immediately send a fax or use other means of telecommunication to contact the Ontario Ministry of Transportation licensing office, which will fax or otherwise transmit back a 90-day suspension order. The driver must hand over his or her licence to the officer, who must forward the licence and other documents as required under the regulations to the registrar of motor vehicles. The officer will forward the documents surrendered by the driver after the arrest but before trial, and this surrender is in addition to any penalty that the court might impose if the person is found guilty. If the person is found not guilty, there is no compensation for the suspension. As with the licence suspension, where a driver's BAC registers between 0.05 and 0.08 on a roadside screening device, the officer can have the vehicle towed away at the owner's expense, unless the owner can arrange for its removal.

The 90-day suspension has been strongly criticized because a person is punished before he or she is found guilty. And the punishment is severe; it can cause real hardship for an accused, who may lose his or her job because he or she is unable to get to work. A similar provision has withstood a court challenge in Manitoba, in part because the suspension is seen as protection for the public, not punishment for the accused (per s 48.3(10) of the HTA). For an overview of impaired driving offence procedures, see Figure 6.4.

WHAT DOES THE LAW SAY?

HTA, Section 48.3(4)

Duties of officer

(4) Every police officer who asks for the surrender of a licence under this section shall,

(a) notify the Registrar of that fact, or cause the Registrar to be so notified, in the form and manner and within the time required by the Registrar;

(b) keep a record of the licence received with the name and address of the person and the date and time of the suspension;

(c) provide the licensee with a written statement of the time from which the suspension takes effect, the period of time for which the licence is suspended and the place where the licence may be recovered; and

(d) forward to the Registrar such other material or information as may be prescribed by the regulations.

Impaired Drivers in Court

According to the results of a national survey of over 1,000 Crown prosecutors and defence lawyers that was released in 2009 and funded by the Canadian Council of Motor Transport Administrators and Transport Canada, a combination of factors—including harsher penalties for a conviction—have resulted in an increase in the number of accused impaired drivers who take their cases to court. The increase in trials as well as other factors, including overworked prosecutors, has in turn resulted in an increased number of acquittals.

The survey found that, across Canada, 40 percent of people charged with impaired driving choose to go to trial and plead not guilty, with figures highest in Ontario, at 52 percent. And while in the 1990s, 90 percent of Canadians who pled not guilty were *convicted* of the charges against them, figures today show that in Ontario only 52 percent of individuals who plead not guilty are convicted.

Despite the fact that breathalyzer readings are now considered conclusive proof of a defendant's BAC—meaning that defence challenges of such readings are limited—the problems within the system that have led to more acquittals are increasing, and having a "significant impact" on the judicial system; compared with a decade ago, not only have conviction rates decreased, but resolving cases takes longer. According to the survey, action is necessary to address factors in the criminal justice system that impede the processing of impaired driving cases. More importantly, actions are necessary "to reinforce the deterrent effect of laws to ensure that persons convicted of impaired driving do not continue to offend."*

---

*   Based on Ian MacLeod, "Drunk Drivers Increasingly Winning Court Cases: Survey," *The Province* (Vancouver) (11 July, 2009).

Ignition Interlock Programs: CC, Section 259, and HTA, Section 41.2

There were 15,149 impaired driving convictions in Ontario in 2014, a decrease of 5 percent from 2013, and the third year in which the number of convictions continued to decline. While the vast majority of these convictions were for first offenders, it was long recognized that approximately 20 percent of these convictions involved repeat offenders. Repeat offenders have been the focus of intense efforts to deter the repetition of this offence. Efforts include increased suspension periods, mandatory assessment for alcohol abuse, education and treatment, increased fines, and impoundment of vehicles.[9]

In 2001, Ontario introduced its Ignition Interlock Program. Sections 41.2 to 41.4 of the HTA provides the authority for the establishment and operation of an ignition interlock

---

9   Statistics Canada, "Police Reported Crime Statistics in Canada, 2014," by Jillian Boyce, in *Juristat*, Catalogue No 85-002-X (Ottawa: Statistics Canada, 2015) at 21, online: <http://www.statcan.gc.ca/pub/85-002-x/2015001/article/14211-eng.pdf>.

FIGURE 6.4 Impaired Driving Offence Procedures at a Glance

NOTE: Drivers 21 years of age and under, and drivers who hold a G1 or G2 licence, must have a zero BAC while driving.

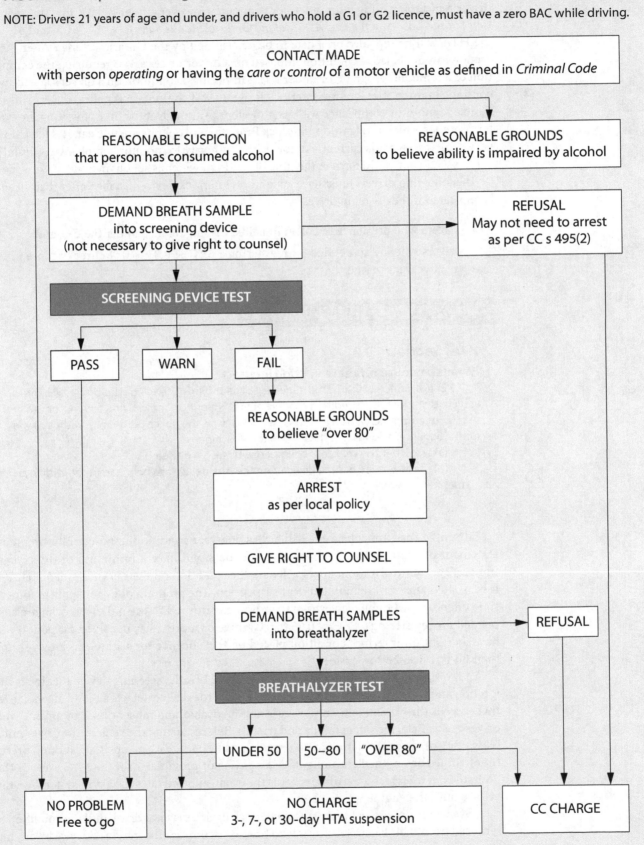

program in Ontario. Likewise, s 259 of the CC authorizes a court to allow an offender to drive during a period in which driving would be otherwise prohibited, provided that the driver registers in an ignition interlock program. However, under Bill 31, the *Transportation Statute Law Amendment Act (Making Ontario's Roads Safer)*, ss 41.1, 41.2, and 41.3 of the HTA will be repealed on a date to be determined by the Ontario cabinet. After those sections are repealed, a condition imposed on a driver under s 41.1 requiring the completion of a remedial program, or under s 41.2 imposing a condition on a driver's licence will continue in force. The Ignition Interlock Program will continue and police officers will still be able to monitor compliance with its provisions. Although at the time of writing the exact terms under which the Ignition Interlock Program will operate are unclear, it is likely to be very similar to what is currently in force. The authority to monitor compliance is found in HTA, s 79.2 (not yet in force at the time of writing), which is set out below.

The following drivers must have an ignition interlock device installed after their licence is reinstated if they want to drive:

- drivers who are convicted of an impaired driving offence under the CC, and
- drivers who are suspended for registering a BAC of 0.05 to 0.08 three or more times in a five-year period.

WHAT DOES THE LAW SAY?

HTA, Section 79.2

Powers of police officer re ignition interlock

79.2 If a police officer determines that the driver's licence of the driver of a motor vehicle is subject to a condition that prohibits him or her from driving any motor vehicle that is not equipped with an ignition interlock device, the police officer may, without a warrant, stop, enter and inspect the vehicle to determine,

(a) whether the vehicle is equipped with such a device; and

(b) if the vehicle has the device, whether the device has been tampered with in any manner.

Currently, first-time offenders will have a one-year condition imposed following reinstatement of their licence, second-time offenders will have a minimum of three years imposed, and third-time offenders will have the condition on their licence indefinitely if it is reinstated after a minimum ten-year suspension. The program does not apply to fourth-time offenders, who will never have their licence returned to them. Drivers who are suspended for registering a BAC of 0.05 to 0.08 three or more times in a five-year period will have an ignition interlock condition placed on their licence for six months after serving their 30-day licence suspension.

An ignition interlock device is an in-car alcohol breath screening device that locks the ignition and prevents a driver from starting a car if the device detects a blood alcohol level that exceeds the preset limit. The device is not removable, and must be used by anyone who drives the vehicle, including family and friends. Before starting the vehicle, the driver must blow into the device, and must also provide additional breath samples at random, preset times while the engine is running. If a sample is not provided, or if the BAC exceeds the limit, the device issues a warning, records the event, and activates the alarm systems on the vehicle until the engine is turned off.

Drivers who choose not to install an interlock device may not drive until the condition is removed from their licence. A driver who tries to circumvent the interlock device by driving a vehicle that is not equipped with an interlock device, or who tampers with the device, will face fines of up to $20,000 in the case of a commercial vehicle, and $1,000 in the case of other motor vehicles. In addition, if a driver is apprehended while driving a vehicle that is not equipped with a device, or if tampering is reported by the interlock device service provider, the interlock condition on the licence will be extended for a further period. Finally, as of December 1, 2010, under the *Road Safety Act, 2009*, the police may impound the vehicle of a driver who is required to have a vehicle ignition interlock but is caught driving without one. If a vehicle owner knowingly allows a driver with an interlock condition on his or her licence to drive the vehicle owner's car, the vehicle owner may be subject to penalties under the HTA. Note that the police may impound a vehicle where the driver is not the owner. In such case, under s 41.4 of the *Road Safety Act, 2009*, notice must be given personally or by mail to the owner that the car has been impounded.

Once the period of the ignition interlock condition has expired, the driver must apply for removal of the condition; otherwise, it remains on his or her licence.

An officer doing a traffic stop will readily discover on a licence check whether there is a condition. If there is, the officer should check to see that the vehicle has an operating ignition interlock device. Effective December 1, 2010, drivers required to have a vehicle ignition interlock device and who are caught driving without such a device will face a seven-day vehicle impoundment.

Operating a Motor Vehicle While Disqualified (CC) and Suspended (HTA)

These provisions provide a penalty in some, but not all, cases where a person operates a motor vehicle while disqualified from doing so. The disqualification may be either a prohibition from driving or a licence suspension that arose from

- a conviction for being impaired,
- a conviction for being "over 80," or
- an absolute or conditional discharge for being impaired or being "over 80" (the person is discharged, but the court still imposes the penalty of a prohibition from driving for a specified period of time).

"Disqualified" means that either a judge has made a prohibition order or the province has suspended the licence.

A driver's licence suspension under the HTA, or a suspension for unpaid parking tickets, cannot be the basis for a charge of driving while disqualified. For these HTA violations, the s 53(1) HTA offence of driving while suspended is applicable.

A **prohibition order** prohibits the operation of a motor vehicle as defined in the CC on a street, road, highway, or other area where the public is permitted to operate a motor vehicle (for example, in a private parking lot). A prohibition order is imposed by a judge for a driving offence under s 259(4) of the CC.

A **suspension** of a driver's licence is undertaken by the authority of a province under its traffic laws. For example, in Ontario the suspended driver cannot drive a motor vehicle (as defined in the HTA) on a highway (as defined in the HTA). The driver can be suspended for a CC conviction or for an HTA offence.

A prohibition order is more extensive than a suspension because it covers all kinds of motor vehicles, except railway equipment. The HTA definition excludes several types of motor vehicles that would be included by the CC. The prohibition order also covers practically any place that a motor vehicle could physically operate in or on. A suspension under the HTA only affects highways, which is a narrower definition.

It is possible for a person to be both "prohibited" and "suspended" at the same time. When this situation arises, the prohibition order is more significant because it is broader and more inclusive.

prohibition order
made on conviction for a CC driving offence and disqualifies a person from driving a motor vehicle as defined in the CC

suspension
may be made under the authority of the HTA for either a CC offence or an HTA offence; disqualifies a driver from driving a motor vehicle as defined in the HTA on a highway as defined in the HTA

See Table 6.3 for further details on disqualified and suspended drivers.

TABLE 6.3 Disqualified Versus Suspended Drivers

Statute Reference	Conditions	Cannot drive motor vehicle as defined ...	Location	Charge
Prohibited Drive Conviction (CC)	Prohibited by a judge anywhere in Canada for a CC conviction	in criminal law	Street, road, highway, other public place (Canada)	Disqualified Operation Section 259(4), CC
Suspended Drive Conviction (CC)	Licence suspended for conviction of offence listed in 259(1) or (2) CC	in HTA	Highway as defined in HTA (Canada)	
Suspended Drive Reason (HTA)	Licence suspended by Province of Ontario for other than CC	in HTA (includes streetcar)	Highway as defined in HTA (Canada)	Drive while under suspension Section 53, HTA

Suspended Drivers—Documentary Evidence	
Prohibited Operation (CC)	• Document from MTO certifying the conviction and suspension • If above cannot be obtained, then certified copy of prohibition order from convicting court and certified copy of suspension from MTO • Notice of Intention to produce a certificate • Driving record for use upon conviction
Suspend Drive (CC)	• Certified copy of the disqualification from MTO • Notice of intention to use a certificate • Driving record for use upon conviction • Certified copy of court conviction, should accused's knowledge of suspension arise
Driving Under Suspension (HTA)	• Certified copy of suspension from MTO • Copy of registered letter notifying accused of suspension • Driving record for use upon conviction

CC = Criminal Code; HTA = Highway Traffic Act; MTO = Ministry of Transportation of Ontario.

Source: *Provincial Offences Wordings and Fines* (St Catharines, Ont: MacBeth Publishing, 2015) at 20.

Vehicle Searches

The case law on vehicle searches falls into two categories: search incidental to arrest and search of a vehicle as a place.

Search Incidental to Arrest

The courts have long held that when an individual is arrested, an officer may search the suspect's body on arrest without first obtaining a search warrant. The courts have also held that where the suspect is arrested in a vehicle, or emerges from one at the time of or shortly after his or her arrest, the vehicle may also be searched without a warrant. Some cases have gone further, and stated that if a vehicle was in the vicinity of the arrest, there is no reason not to include the vehicle in the accused's vicinity as part of a search incidental to arrest. Some cases indicate that the warrantless search may be conducted hours after the arrest if there is a reasonable explanation for the delay. The search may extend to the vehicle's interior, including the trunk, and possibly under the hood. However, if parts of the car have to be taken apart as part of the search, a warrant may be required.

PROFESSIONAL PRACTICE

Conducting an Effective Vehicle Search

When conducting a vehicle search, it is important to be systematic and thorough, and to refrain from hurrying. Patience is needed in such situations, and there is no room for complacency. In addition, remember the hidden dangers that may be presented by the drivers and occupants of the vehicle, or by arrested individuals.

When searching a vehicle, police officers search the following areas in the ways described below:

- *Exterior of the vehicle* Use your flashlight to do a lot of tapping—for example, on doors and fenders. Check all of the lights, and check for screws that are missing, new, or that appear to have been tampered with. Check behind the front and rear licence plate areas. Check the tires, and release some air from the valves, as this may reveal drugs hidden in the tires. Check for contraband by looking behind the side-view mirrors and making sure that the chrome has not been tampered with.

- *Hood* Check the battery, hood cover, hoses, front fender wells, air cleaner, and heater for modifications. Check for new clamps. Be on the lookout for clean spots in areas under the hood that would otherwise be greasy and/or dirty.

- *Trunk* Check for fresh glue, duct tape, and tar that may hide a false bottom. Check under the trunk lid for contraband. Search and shake the spare tire, check under it, and tap the exterior; again, release air from valve stem.

- *Underneath* Tap the gas tank and check for any clean areas that would normally be greasy or dirty. Check whether the second exhaust really functions, or whether it has been used to store contraband.

- *Inside the motor vehicle* Check the gauges, air inlets, door frames, seats, heater, armrests, floor, glove compartment, roof, rocker panels, ashtray compartments, and console area. Check for screws that are missing or new, or that appear to have been tampered with. Move the windows up and down. Remove the back seat.

While conducting a search as described above, be aware that some individuals go to extreme lengths to modify motor vehicles and motorcycles, and to modify various objects to serve as weapons when needed. Many such weapons are difficult to detect—for example, a tire pressure gauge gun is a tire gauge modified to fire when the pin on the side of the gauge is cocked and released; a gas cap knife is a knife welded to the inside of the gas tank cap, which can be as long as the gas tank is deep.

Search of a Vehicle as a Place

In some circumstances, a vehicle may be considered a place, like a house or an office. In this case, a warrant must be obtained under s 487(1) of the CC. To obtain a warrant, an officer must, at the time that the warrant is sworn, have reasonable grounds to believe that an identified tangible thing that is evidence of an offence will be found in the vehicle. If a vehicle is found in a place for which a search warrant has been issued, then it may be searched, in the same way that a room or a container in the place may be searched. However, the situation is different if the vehicle is on the same property as the place named in the warrant but not contained within it. For example, if the warrant clearly describes a house that may be searched, the search will not include a vehicle that is parked on the property on which the house is located, but not contained within the house. If the vehicle were parked in a garage that forms part of the house, then it could be searched because the warrant indicates that the house is the place to be searched and the garage is part of the house. The proper approach here is to obtain a separate warrant to search the vehicle.

Because a vehicle, unlike a house, has wheels and can be moved beyond the reach of law enforcement officials, there are some circumstances where a warrantless search may be conducted. In such circumstances, there must be grounds to obtain a search warrant, but, due

exigent
requiring immediate
aid or action

to **exigent** circumstances, it is impractical to obtain a warrant. A warrantless search may be conducted if it can be shown that

- the vehicle was lawfully stopped or the occupants were lawfully detained (although not necessarily arrested);
- the officer conducting the search had reasonable grounds to believe that an offence had been, was being, or was about to be committed, and a search would disclose evidence relevant to that offence; and
- exigent circumstances existed, such as imminent loss, removal, or destruction of the evidence, so that it was not feasible to obtain a search warrant.

CHAPTER SUMMARY

All driving offences are provincial offences. However, certain offences involving motor vehicles—such as those involving drinking and driving or negligence causing serious injury or death using land vehicles, whether operated on a highway or not—are considered criminal, and thus federal, offences, because these offences are not only concerned with driving but with behaviour deemed to be criminal.

When a police officer approaches the driver of a motor vehicle that he or she has just stopped, the officer may form a *reasonable suspicion* that the driver has alcohol in his or her system; in this case, the officer can lawfully demand that the driver provide a breath sample for an approved screening device or perform coordination tests. Where the officer instead forms *reasonable grounds* to believe that the driver's ability to operate a motor vehicle is impaired by alcohol, the officer may arrest the driver on reasonable grounds to believe that he or she has committed an indictable offence. In this case, the officer must advise the suspect of the right to counsel and make a breathalyzer demand or, where a person is incapable of providing a breath sample or it is impractical to obtain breath samples, the officer may demand blood samples. In situations where a collision has resulted in the death of another person or bodily harm to another person or to the alleged offender, and where the officer has lawful grounds for a blood demand but the person is unable to consent to the blood demand because of a mental or physical condition arising from the consumption of alcohol or from the collision, the officer may apply to a JP for a warrant to obtain blood samples instead of demanding breath or blood samples.

Police officers must request and ensure that they obtain breath and blood samples within the time limits prescribed. To be lawful, the demand for the first of the breathalyzer or blood samples must be made within three hours of the commission of the offence of being impaired while operating or having the care or control of a motor vehicle, or being "over 80." For the courts to accept the BAC results as conclusive proof of the BAC of the accused at the time of the offence without requiring an expert to testify, the first of two breathalyzer tests must have been made within two hours of the offence, or both blood tests must have been made within two hours of the offence.

A driver who refuses to provide a breath sample or who blows a "warn" (a BAC between 0.05 and 0.08 percent) on an approved screening device faces immediate roadside suspension of his or her licence. Offenders will receive a 3-day suspension for their first offence, a 7-day suspension for their second offence, and a 30-day suspension for their third offence. A driver who blows "over 80" on both breathalyzer tests, or refuses to supply a breath sample for the breathalyzer, or a blood, urine, or oral fluid sample, or fails to perform physical coordination tests or submit to an evaluation may receive a 90-day suspension. Another consequence of operating a vehicle while impaired or "over 80" is the requirement for an ignition interlock device to be installed and used correctly in order to operate a vehicle. If a driver who is required to have an interlock device is found driving without one, the vehicle can be impounded. Under the CC, it is an offence to operate a motor vehicle while disqualified. The disqualification may be either a prohibition imposed by a judge for a driving offence under s 259(4) of the CC or a licence suspension imposed by the province under the HTA. Where a suspect is arrested in a vehicle, or emerges from one at the time of or shortly after his or her arrest, the police may search the vehicle without a warrant. Where a vehicle is considered a "place" for purposes of a search, a warrant must be obtained prior to the police executing a search.

ON THE SCENE

Reduce Impaired Driving Everywhere (R.I.D.E.) and an "Over 80" Example

Scenario

On [use today's date, DD/MMM/YYYY], Aaron Brown (date of birth, 15 July 1995) attended a birthday party with friends and is driving home at about 1:00 a.m. He is driving a yellow 2013 Nissan Altima, Ontario licence plate ZQMN509, in a southbound direction on Wellesley Road, approaching Metro Street, in Hamilton, Ontario. As Brown approaches the intersection, he notices red flashing lights and a uniformed officer waving him to pull over to the curb of the roadway. The officer, Constable (Cst.) Roger Knight, Badge #789, approaches the driver's door and advises Brown that the reason for the stop is that a R.I.D.E. program is being conducted. Cst. Knight asks whether Brown has consumed any alcoholic beverages during the evening. Brown indicates that he was at a birthday for the previous six hours and states, "Yes, I had a couple." Cst. Knight asks Brown to clarify what he means by "a couple," to which Brown responds, "Do I have to spell it out for you? I had, I think, two beers and that is all I remember drinking." The officer writes, subsequently, in his notes, that when the driver's window was rolled down he noticed a smell that seemed like an alcoholic beverage coming from within the vehicle. Brown is taken to the cruiser, where he provides a .130 breath sample.

What Actions Should the Officer Take?

1. On what grounds can Cst. Knight stop the vehicle?

2. What is the importance of writing down verbatim (word for word) the statement that Brown gave Cst. Knight if Brown decides to plead "not guilty" and elects to go to trial?

3. Should Cst. Knight search the interior and trunk of the vehicle if Brown has now committed a criminal offence?

4. Should Cst. Knight tow the vehicle?

KEY TERMS

actus reus, 158

exigent, 182

legal presumption, 174

mens rea, 158

prohibition order, 179

suspension, 179

WEBSITES

Trends in Impaired Driving

- Canadian Press, "OPP See Surge in Impaired Driving Charges," *Global News* (11 May 2015), online: <http://globalnews.ca/news/1990822/opp-see-surge-in-impaired-driving-charges/ >.

- Greg Neinstein, "Don't Drive While Impaired This Holiday Season," *Neinstein Personal Injury Lawyers* (23 December 2014), online: <http://www.neinstein.com/tag/drinking-and-driving/>.

- "OPP Disappointed by Impaired Driving Rates over Holidays," *CBC News* (3 January 2013), online: <http://www.cbc.ca/news/canada/ottawa/opp-disappointed-by-impaired-driving-rates-over-holidays-1.1399436>.

- Chart 14: Impaired Driving and Drug Offences, Police-Reported Rates, Canada, 1984-2014 in Statistics Canada, "Police Reported Crime Statistics in Canada, 2014," by Jillian Boyce, in *Juristat* 35:1, Catalogue No 85-002-X (Ottawa: Statistics Canada, 2015) at 21, online: <http://www.statcan.gc.ca/pub/85-002-x/2015001/article/14211-eng.pdf>.

REVIEW QUESTIONS

Short Answer

Briefly answer the following questions.

1. a. What is the difference between the definitions of "motor vehicle" in the HTA and the CC?

   b. Why is this difference important?

2. How could a person be "over 80" but not be impaired?

3. What is the difference between "reasonable suspicion" and "reasonable grounds to believe"?

4. Explain what the differences are between a breathalyzer and an approved screening device in terms of function and purpose.

5. What are the grounds for a lawful demand for the following?

   a. A breath sample for an approved screening device.

   b. A breath sample for a breathalyzer.

   c. A blood sample.

6. Explain the significance of the two-hour and three-hour limits with regard to attempting to determine an individual's BAC.

7. May a police officer make a breathalyzer demand of someone he or she has grounds to believe is impaired by drugs? Explain your answer.

8. Cite the statute and section number that authorize the following:

   a. A demand for a breath sample for an approved screening device.

   b. A demand for a breath sample for a breathalyzer.

   c. A demand for a blood sample.

   d. An application for a warrant to obtain a blood sample.

   e. Suspension of a driver's licence for 3, 7, or 30 days.

   f. Suspension of a driver's licence for 90 days.

9. Explain what events must occur or what factors must be present before the police may lawfully take the steps described in question 8.

   a. A demand for a breath sample for an approved screening device.

b. A demand for a breath sample for a breathalyzer.

c. A demand for a blood sample.

d. An application for a warrant to obtain a blood sample.

e. Suspension of a driver's licence for 3, 7, or 30 days.

f. Suspension of a driver's licence for 90 days.

Discussion Questions

1. Rank the following four topics in the order in which they would occur sequentially and describe the basis for your ordering.

   a. blood warrant

   b. blood demand

   c. breathalyzer demand

   d. approved screening device demand

2. "In impaired driving cases, timing is everything." Discuss this statement in terms of the nature of the offences, the requirements of the law, and any other relevant matter.

3. Discuss the following statements:

   a. Breathalyzer evidence is only corroborative evidence for a charge of operating a motor vehicle while ability is impaired by alcohol, but is essential evidence for a charge of operating a motor vehicle with over 80 mg of alcohol per 100 ml of blood.

   b. Failing an approved screening test is not sufficient evidence by itself for a charge of operating a motor vehicle with over 80 mg of alcohol per 100 ml of blood.

   c. If a peace officer has the lawful grounds to make a breathalyzer demand, he or she also has the lawful grounds to make an arrest.

   d. If a driver is arrested on the basis that there are reasonable grounds to believe that he or she is "over 80," an additional charge of being impaired is not possible. However, if the driver is arrested on reasonable grounds to believe that he or she is impaired, an additional charge of "over 80" is possible.

4. Oscar is clearly impaired. He goes to his car, unlocks it, climbs into the back seat, lies down on it, puts his jacket under his head, and falls asleep. This is where Officer Singh finds him. Discuss whether Oscar could be said to have "care or control of a motor vehicle."

Collision Investigation

7

LEARNING OUTCOMES

After completing this chapter, you should be able to:

- Describe the steps in investigating a collision.
- Explain how to prioritize emergencies (for example, injuries, downed hydro lines, the presence of dangerous goods) at a collision scene.
- Recognize and understand the significance of the signs and symbols for dangerous goods.
- Understand your duty with respect to assisting injured persons.
- Explain when and how to close off and safeguard a collision scene.
- Manage people at the collision scene.

Introduction

This chapter introduces basic collision investigation practices and techniques. The focus here is on arriving safely at the scene, surveying it, and prioritizing emergencies so as to be able to secure and manage the collision scene. Managing the scene includes dealing with injuries, dangerous goods, fires, and other hazards. The officer also must effectively interview persons at the scene to attempt to determine what happened, using various interview techniques.

Collision Investigation and Reconstruction

The police are required to investigate or receive a report of a collision from drivers involved in every motor vehicle collision in Ontario where a personal injury occurs or there is property damage valued at more than $2,000 (RRO 1990, Reg 596, s 11). Because even minor damage to motor vehicles is expensive to repair, the $2,000 reporting threshold is easily reached in most cases and, as a result, the police investigate virtually every motor vehicle collision in Ontario.

Some collisions will receive additional attention. Besides an investigation, a serious collision may also require a collision reconstruction if it appears that criminal or provincial charges may be laid, civil litigation is likely, or a coroner's inquest may be called.

Police officers attend motor vehicle collisions for many reasons. They must record the identification of all persons involved, the types of injuries sustained, the registration of the vehicles involved, the insurance particulars of the vehicle owners, the type and amount of damage to vehicles and property, and the location and time of the collision. This information, recorded and saved by the police, is necessary to prevent incorrect or fraudulent claims, to provide a basis for statistical analysis by the Ontario Ministry of Transportation, and to provide evidence for prosecutions and inquests.

Note that although police officers must investigate any violations of the law and collect evidence relevant to a prosecution, this is not necessarily the same as finding fault. A driver may be "at fault" for the purposes of a civil suit for negligence, but the conduct of the driver may fall far short of what is required for a prosecution under provincial legislation or under the *Criminal Code* (CC). "Fault" is a term of interest to insurance companies dealing with civil liability for negligence; it is not a term of interest to the police.

PROFESSIONAL PRACTICE

Arrest Without Warrant

At times, drivers will fail to remain at the scene of an accident. Both the *Highway Traffic Act* (HTA) (s 200(1)(a), s 217(2)) and the CC (s 252) provide police officers with the authority to arrest without a warrant in such cases.

Steps in a Collision Investigation

The steps described here are general in nature and do not apply to all situations. The steps that make up this approach to collision investigation should be considered a good starting framework that you can develop further as you become more experienced.

Approach the Scene

Obtain as Much Information as Possible

An officer, while responding to any accident, should review in his or her mind what documents and equipment may be required to expedite an efficient and effective handling of the collision scene.

Find out the exact location of the collision, and determine the lane and lane direction, if it is a divided highway.

Ascertain whether there are any injuries and, if there are, ask whether medical personnel have been dispatched. Ask whether any other emergency services are needed and, if they are, ask whether they have been dispatched. These could include hydro personnel (if there are downed wires), the fire department, officers for traffic control, or environmental protection personnel.

Mental Role Playing

Psychologists have determined that in some circumstances the mind cannot tell the difference between an imagined experience and a real one. Russian sports psychologists have exploited this idea by having their figure skaters and gymnasts visualize their routines repeatedly so that the pattern becomes imprinted in their minds; thus, the athletes act more instinctively when performing their routines. This visualization technique also allows the athletes to practise much more in their minds than their bodies could manage physically.

A police officer can employ this mental role-playing technique to condition himself or herself to act more instinctively when confronting a collision scene. During quiet times on his or her shift, a police officer can imagine a collision scenario and then think of the correct response to the scene. The brain becomes accustomed to the pattern of response and the officer will then act instinctively under the pressure of a collision situation.

Officers can further improve their response over time if they "debrief" themselves. After each collision, officers must ask themselves how they could improve their performance. Debriefing is an important way to reinforce and refine the skills used in carrying out a procedure.

DISCUSSION POINT   En route to a daytime collision, you are advised by dispatch that a car, as the result of hitting another car, is submerged in water. The car contains one adult male, one adult female, and one infant. How will you prepare mentally? When you arrive, you find that you are the first officer on the scene. It is estimated that ambulance and fire personnel will not arrive for at least ten minutes. What should you do?

Guarantee Your Arrival

At the Ontario Police College, new police recruits were given the task of driving a given route to a collision scene as fast as possible. Each recruit was timed with a stopwatch, and his or her time was recorded. The recruits invariably turned this exercise into a competition with other students. The recruits drove at excessive speeds and hit many of the pylons along the route and also had to brake and slow down suddenly and frequently. They were then asked to drive the same route again, using a car that could not exceed a predetermined speed limit. Each recruit was again timed with a stopwatch and his or her time recorded. The recruits were surprised to discover that the second controlled run was always faster. The moral of this story: *If you slow down and drive at a more controlled speed, you will actually get there faster and more safely.*

Section 128 of the HTA deals with rate of speed and exempts police officers in the lawful performance of their duties from the speed limits imposed in the HTA or any speed bylaw. Responding to a motor vehicle collision is within the lawful performance of a police officer's duty (HTA, s 128(13), so police officers may exceed the speed limit when en route to a collision scene (HTA, s 128(13)(b)). Police officers would be wise to remember that driving excessively over the speed limit is inefficient and unnecessarily risky. Higher speeds pose additional dangers for drivers, including police officers.

The HTA also authorizes the driver of an emergency vehicle, after stopping the vehicle at a red light, to proceed through the red light, if it is safe to do so (HTA, s 144(20)). Emergency vehicles do not, however, have blanket authority to run through red lights. If the driver of an emergency vehicle is involved in a collision while proceeding through a red light, the presumption is that it was not safe to run the light. The burden of proving that it was safe is always on the driver of the emergency vehicle.

The HTA defines an "emergency vehicle" as a vehicle used by a police officer in the lawful performance of his or her duties on which a siren is continuously sounding, and from which intermittent flashes of red light or red and blue light are visible from all directions (in addition to definitions provided for other emergency vehicles, such as fire trucks and ambulances) (HTA, s 144(1)). This definition means that a police officer cannot lawfully proceed through a red light in an emergency situation unless the flashing red lights are on and the siren is continuously sounding. In the event that an officer is involved in a collision while proceeding through a red light, civil liability issues could arise for the officer and the police service.

The HTA also permits a police department vehicle to drive off the roadway to overtake another vehicle (HTA, s 150(1)). Passing on the shoulder is sometimes necessary when traffic is stopped on the roadway and no other lane is open. If the shoulder is unpaved and is found to be "soft," care should be taken in order to prevent a possible rollover.

In the event that a motorist fails to pull over to permit an emergency vehicle to pass, not much can be done at the time by the police officer responding to a collision. However, all other officers can enforce the law when they see such an obstruction of other emergency vehicles. The HTA states that, on the approach of an ambulance, a fire department vehicle, a police department vehicle, or a public utility emergency vehicle that is sounding its bell or siren or producing intermittent flashes of red light or red and blue light, the driver of a vehicle shall immediately bring such vehicle to a standstill as close as is practicable to the right-hand curb or edge of the roadway, parallel to it, and clear of any intersection. If the vehicle is on a roadway that has more than two lanes for traffic and is designated for the use of one-way traffic, the driver shall stop as close as is practicable to the nearest curb or edge of the roadway, parallel to it, and clear of any intersection (HTA, s 159(1)).

PROFESSIONAL PRACTICE

SIU Investigations

If a police officer is in a hurry in responding to an accident and drives carelessly, and if as a result the officer is involved in an accident where serious injury or death results, the Special Investigations Unit (SIU) will be contacted and will investigate. While an SIU investigation can exonerate a police officer, it can also lead to internal discipline from the police service, criminal charges, or a civil suit.

The "BE SAFE" acronym

B (Before)

E (Entering)

S (Stop)

A (And)

F (First)

E (Evaluate)

Prioritize Emergencies

When officers arrive at a collision scene, they must stop to evaluate what they are confronting. If there is more than one emergency, officers need time to determine which emergency, if left unattended, would result in the most serious consequences. You can remember this important step by using the mnemonic device "BE SAFE" acronym, set out here.

When considering what action to take, the officer should be mindful of the priorities at all collision scenes: YOU, THE PUBLIC, IT. Your first priority should be your own safety. If you rush into a collision scene where there is a spill of dangerous goods or downed hydro lines, you may become another casualty. In order for you to be effective, you cannot become one of the injured. You may need to close the road to protect yourself as you enter the scene and to prevent the situation from becoming worse. Second, if there are injured persons, attend to them. Last, concern yourself with property damage.

Situations that could result in the most serious consequences if left unattended are as follows:

- the presence of dangerous goods
- injuries
- an unprotected collision scene and unprotected evidence
- downed hydro lines
- vehicle fires
- dangerous road conditions
- property at risk of being stolen
- altercations among drivers and/or passengers.

DISCUSSION POINT   Why is it important for the first officer arriving at the scene of a collision to be assertive and display leadership skills? What particular traits and skills are required?

Identify Dangerous Goods

Transport Canada has developed a system of dangerous-goods placards that are to be placed on all vehicles transporting dangerous goods, and a similar system of dangerous-goods labels that are to be placed on containers of dangerous goods. The purpose of these placards and labels is to alert emergency response crews, who can quickly identify the dangerous goods in question, so that appropriate action can be taken. Prompt and appropriate action minimizes damage and saves lives when these goods are loaded on vehicles that are involved in collisions.

If emergency personnel are unsure of the dangers at a collision scene, they can call emergency phone numbers at both the federal and provincial levels of government to obtain information on the appropriate response to a particular situation. Police officers should record these numbers for quick access.

The dangerous-goods placards and labels use a three-part system to identify the goods:

- colour,
- symbols, and
- class numbers.

The first officer at a collision scene, when evaluating the situation from a distance, may first recognize the category of dangerous goods by colour. Colour is easily recognizable from a distance. For example, the colour of the placard can warn the officer whether he or she is dealing with a toxic substance, explosives, or radioactive materials. Symbols on the placards assist in interpreting the meaning of the colour of the placard. For example, a red placard enhanced with the symbol of a flame conveys the message that the goods are flammable. Be aware that in poor light conditions, it is harder to recognize and to distinguish one colour from another. A strong flashlight and a closer look may be necessary.

Reduce the Risks

When arriving on the scene of an accident involving dangerous goods, police officers should take the following measures to enhance their own safety and that of the public:

- Expand the collision scene, ensuring that people who are just standing or parked nearby the accident are evacuated and do not remain in proximity to the dangerous goods.
- Be aware of the dangers of shifting winds, which can present additional risks for both the officer and the public.
- Identify the type of cargo or dangerous goods involved, and notify dispatch immediately.
- Fight the tendency toward "tunnel" vision—that is, do not look only at the accident scene, but, in-

stead, continually be aware of the "big picture" in terms of personal and public safety.

Unlike firefighters and certain other emergency personnel, police officers do have equipment that is designed to protect them from the hazards associated with dangerous goods, and they will be vulnerable. Officers who have not received training on how to use oxygen equipment should submit a memo to the police training branch requesting training in this area in conjunction with the fire department. In the event that a particular situation warrants the use of oxygen, officers should be comfortable using the tank and breathing through the apparatus.

Remember: exposure to dangerous goods can entail long-term—even fatal—health problems.

bill of lading
a receipt for merchandise that accompanies the merchandise when it is being transported from one place to another; it should provide detailed information about the cargo carried by a commercial vehicle

oxidizer
a substance that combines with oxygen, which may be quite volatile, flammable, or otherwise chemically active and therefore dangerous

Binoculars may be required to identify the class number printed on the bottom of the dangerous-goods placard. For example, a number "2" at the bottom of the placard tells emergency personnel that the goods involve a gas. This information, along with the condition of the vehicle or the containers, needs to be immediately relayed to the communications centre, which in turn should notify the appropriate authorities. If a tanker truck is ruptured and the gas is toxic, only emergency personnel with protective clothing and a breathing apparatus may approach the scene. They may be able to obtain the **bill of lading** from the cab of the vehicle to identify the specific cargo. Their job will also be to neutralize any danger and to enable safe and effective investigation and cleanup. The police are responsible for securing the scene and evacuating the area downwind of the collision to minimize injury and damage.

Obviously, police officers need to know the meaning of the colour symbols and class numbers used on dangerous-goods placards and labels in order to prevent injury to themselves and others and to prevent further damage to property.

As stated above, dangerous-goods placards can be initially identified from afar by colour. The table below provides a list of these colours and the types of dangerous goods they identify.

COLOUR	TYPE OF DANGEROUS GOODS
Orange	Explosives
Red	Anything flammable
Green	Non-flammable gases
Blue	Substances that are dangerous when wet

COLOUR	TYPE OF DANGEROUS GOODS
Yellow	**Oxidizers**
White	Toxic and infectious substances
Yellow over white	Radioactive materials
White over black	Corrosives

Dangerous-goods placards and labels employ the use of nine symbols that assist in the interpretation of the colour. See Figure 7.1 for a breakdown.

Dangerous goods are divided into nine classes. The class number is printed at the bottom of the placard or label. Transport Canada's chart of dangerous goods ("The Marks of Safety") is reproduced in colour on the inside front and back covers of this text. The nine classes of dangerous goods are listed in the table below, together with their corresponding colours and descriptions of their symbols.

CLASS		COLOUR	SYMBOL
Class 1	Explosives	Orange	Exploding bomb
Class 2	Gases	Red	Flame
		Green	Gas cylinder
		White	Skull
Class 3	Flammable liquids	Red	Flame
Class 4	Flammable solids	Red and white stripes	Flame
		White over red	Flame
		Blue	Flame

CLASS		COLOUR	SYMBOL
Class 5	Oxidizers	Yellow	Burning "O"
Class 6	Toxic and infectious substances	White	Skull
		White	Biomedical symbol
Class 7	Radioactive materials	Yellow over white	Trefoil
Class	Corrosives	White over black	Acid on hand or metal
Class 9	Miscellaneous	Black stripes over white	

FIGURE 7.1 Dangerous Goods Symbols

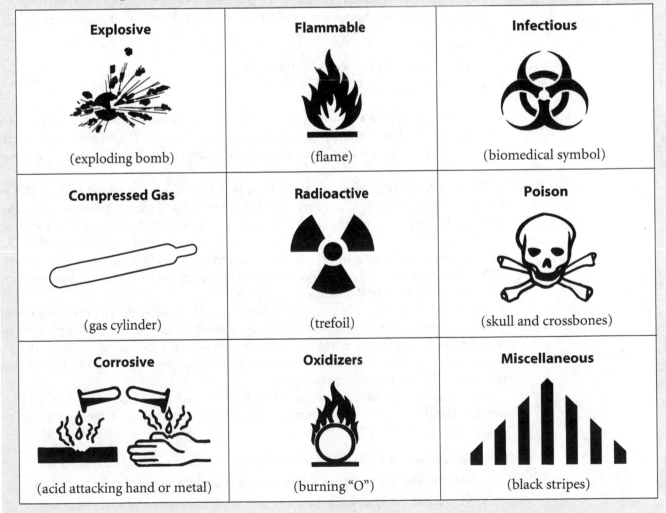

Explosive (exploding bomb)

Flammable (flame)

Infectious (biomedical symbol)

Compressed Gas (gas cylinder)

Radioactive (trefoil)

Poison (skull and crossbones)

Corrosive (acid attacking hand or metal)

Oxidizers (burning "O")

Miscellaneous (black stripes)

Note that the flammable gas placard and the flammable liquid placard are both red and carry the flame symbol; they differ only in their class number.

HELPFUL **HINT**

To remember the class number for class 2, 3, and 4 of dangerous goods, use the following mnemonic device: the higher the class number, the denser the substance.

- **Class 2** Gases
- **Class 3** Liquids (more dense than gas)
- **Class 4** Solids (most dense)

Deal with Injuries

Injured persons should not be moved if there is a risk of aggravating the injury; however, they may have to be moved if leaving them where they are poses a risk to their safety.

If a live victim needs to be removed from a vehicle, stabilization is required. Stabilization of the scene, the vehicle, and the victim must all be considered before a victim is moved. Ambulance and fire personnel are best equipped to treat and move injured persons, so it is imperative to get these experts to the scene as soon as possible.

Only medical practitioners (doctors) can pronounce someone dead. Police officers, however, can presume that a person at a collision scene is dead in these circumstances:

- decapitation,
- transection (cutting in half) of the body, or
- decomposition of the body.

According to the Ontario *Coroners Act*, no person, including a police officer, shall interfere with or move a dead body until directed by the coroner. When a police officer can assume death, he or she should cover the body and its parts with a blanket until the coroner arrives.

There will be times when police officers will not be able to assume that death has occurred. Because police officers are qualified in first aid and cardiopulmonary resuscitation (CPR), they are obligated (if emergency medical personnel are not on the scene) to render first aid to every victim whom they cannot assume is dead. Failure to provide first aid can lead to a charge of neglect of duty under the Ontario *Police Services Act* and possibly a charge of criminal negligence causing death under the CC. There is also the possibility of a civil action by the victim or his or her family.

Officers should make sure that each victim is identified before the victims are removed from a collision scene. Obviously, discretion is required to make sure that attempts to identify victims do not interfere with the services of emergency medical personnel. Officers should also make sure that they know the name of the hospital where each victim is being taken and who is transporting the victims.

In a collision with multiple victims where there is a lack of emergency medical personnel, a police officer will have to prioritize who needs treatment first. Officers will have to group victims into three categories:

1. Victims whose injuries are life threatening and require immediate treatment.
2. Victims whose injuries are not life threatening and who can wait for treatment.
3. Victims whose injuries are so severe that death is imminent, and survival is unlikely.

Note that category 1 victims are the officer's top priority.

Hopefully, an officer will never have to make these kinds of decisions, but by clarifying the decision-making process, and using the mental role-playing technique described earlier, an officer can prepare himself or herself for such a situation.

If the collision involves only property damage, a police officer should not trivialize the collision. The collision may be routine for the police officer, but it is a dramatic life event for the victim. A little sympathy can go a long way to enhancing the image of the police service. Remember, the officer's report is important, but it is not more important than public support.

DISCUSSION POINT   As a police officer, how would you respond to a home and inform the family that a family member has died as the result of a serious collision?

Protect the Scene

The HTA authorizes a police officer to close a highway or any part thereof to ensure the orderly movement of traffic, to prevent injury or damage to persons or property, or to permit proper action in an emergency. Every person shall obey the officer's directions (HTA, s 134). Emergency and service vehicles are exempt from road-closure rules. For the purposes of closing a highway or any part of it, a police officer may post or cause to be posted signs to that effect, or may place or cause to be placed traffic control devices as prescribed by the regulations.

The regulations prescribe the use of a "Do Not Enter" sign and not fewer than three orange cones, or not fewer than two rectangular shapes with horizontal orange and black stripes mounted on posts, or not fewer than two barricades that are orange or orange with black bars. See Figure 7.2.

The HTA also authorizes police officers to direct traffic to ensure the orderly movement of traffic, to prevent injury or damage to persons or property, or to permit proper action in an emergency.

With these powers comes the responsibility to ensure that no further injury or damage occurs at a collision scene. This responsibility means that officers attending a collision scene must warn other traffic approaching the scene so that the traffic has time to slow down and stop, if necessary. Flares are usually used for this purpose and must be placed far enough ahead of the collision scene, according to the circumstances, to give fair warning to oncoming traffic. On a long, straight road with no view obstructions, only the speed limit is a factor in determining how far from the collision to place the flares. On a road with curves, hills, bridges, or other view obstructions of the collision scene, the flares may have to be placed much farther ahead.

Until the proper road or lane closure devices are in place, or if none are available, officers will have to direct traffic manually. Doing so may require several police officers. If other officers are not available, a police cruiser, with the red lights activated, may be used to close a lane. Especially at night, officers directing traffic should ensure that they are wearing the appropriate reflective vests in order to avoid personal injury.

Identify Downed Hydro Lines

If hydro lines are down at a collision scene, hydro distribution companies recommend that police officers stay in their police cruiser until the power can be shut off. If the road is wet, stepping onto the road could result in death by electrocution. The investigating officer should also take steps to keep other persons away from the collision scene and tell those involved in the collision to stay in their cars until the power has been shut off. Once the

FIGURE 7.2 Barricades

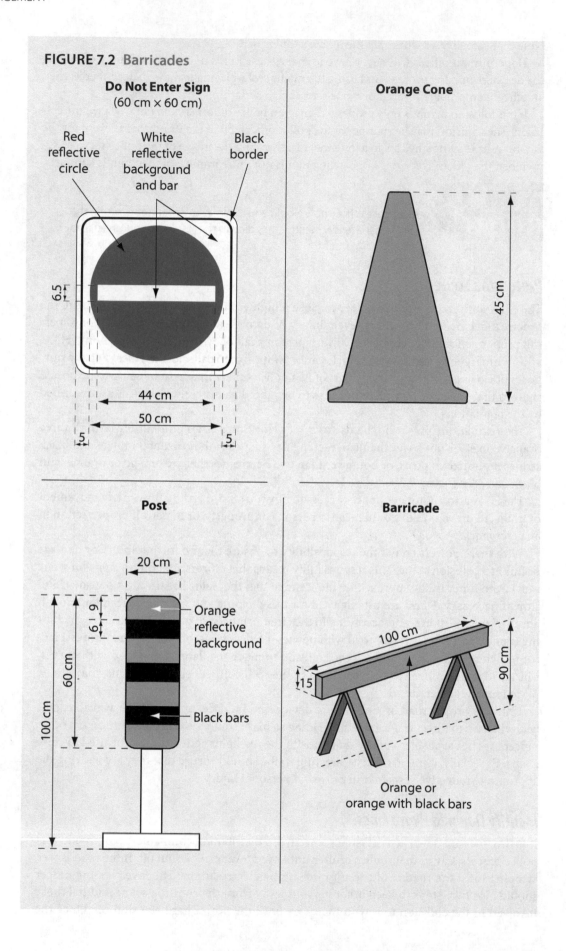

Do Not Enter Sign
(60 cm × 60 cm)

Red reflective circle

White reflective background and bar

Black border

6.5

44 cm

50 cm

5

5

Orange Cone

45 cm

Post

20 cm

9

6

60 cm

100 cm

Orange reflective background

Black bars

Barricade

100 cm

15

90 cm

Orange or orange with black bars

power has been shut off, the officer can continue to deal with other emergencies arising from the collision.

Deal with Vehicle Fires

If there are no dangerous goods involved, and a vehicle is on fire, the ignition should be turned off, if possible, and all people kept away until the fire department arrives. If the fire is small and can be extinguished, a dry-chemical extinguisher should be used, if available; this extinguisher is usually located in the trunk of a cruiser. If no extinguisher is available, the fire should be smothered with dirt or a blanket—*not* water. The officer should remember when trying to save a car that is on fire that the officer's personal safety has priority over property. If occupants are still in the vehicle, rescue the occupants, if possible.

Take Care of Road Conditions

Often after an ice storm road conditions may cause a serious collision if left unattended. When investigating a serious collision due to icy roads, notify the communications centre to dispatch road-sanding and road-salting equipment to the scene to reduce the likelihood of further collisions. Failure to do so may result in a charge of neglect of duty and exposure to civil liability.

Prevent Theft

Sometimes valuable cargo is spilled on the road, and looting ensues. If looting happens, the investigating officer should immediately call for assistance to help secure the scene. If the first officer on the scene runs after someone who has stolen some cargo, the scene is left unprotected. At least one officer must protect the cargo while the investigating officer attends to other aspects of the incident.

If the road must be closed to prevent other accidents or injuries, or if the present accident has resulted in injuries, protecting the cargo is obviously secondary to attending to the injured. It would be unjustifiable, not to mention extremely unprofessional, for an officer to chase someone who has stolen a laptop or a case of beer from spilled cargo if the driver is unconscious from injuries. Remember the motto "YOU, THE PUBLIC, IT"; property is the last priority. An officer's first instinct may be to chase someone who is running from the scene with some cargo, but the officer must first be concerned with the safety of the accident victims.

Stop Drivers from Fighting

The first officer on the scene must immediately call for backup if drivers are fighting. After doing so, the officer must attempt to stop the fight and keep the drivers apart. When backup arrives, it may be necessary to place each driver in the back of separate police cruisers until the officer finds out what happened. Criminal charges may need to be laid, and neither driver should be allowed to leave until the incident is fully understood by the officer on the scene. This temporary incarceration will allow each driver time to cool down. The authority to arrest in this case is granted to prevent a continuing breach of the peace. If there are no other charges pending, each driver may be released when he or she has calmed down.

Manage People at the Scene

Collision investigations are one of the most common situations during which members of the public come into contact with the police. Police officers must ensure that *all* of their dealings with the public are done in a manner that upholds and enhances the professionalism of the police service. This includes being seen to be courteous, sympathetic, and fair.

Officers must always remember that a motor vehicle collision, even a minor one, is a major event for any citizen. It is not uncommon for citizens to submit verbal or written comments to the police service about an officer with whom they have dealt, either commending the officer's empathy and interest in the crash or reproaching the officer's total lack of interest.

PROFESSIONAL PRACTICE

Questioning a Witness

1. Use open-ended question techniques such as "What can you tell me about what you saw here?" or "Is there anything more that you think I need to know?" These questions do not box witnesses in—they encourage witnesses to tell the story in their own way to convey information that is important to them.

2. If the witness goes off onto matters that are irrelevant, redirect the witness back to the issues you are concerned with by using short, clarifying questions to help him or her focus. A question that starts with "So what you are saying is ... " may be enough to get the witness back on track.

3. Once the witness has told his or her story, you can ask questions that tend to narrow the issues and focus on matters that require more elaboration.

4. Use narrow questions to get at specific points not covered in the witness's original account. "How soon did the driver speak to you after the collision?" is an example of a narrow question.

5. Listen actively. Nodding affirmatively or saying "uh-huh" may encourage the witness to continue, and will show that you are listening. When taking notes, try to do so unobtrusively.

6. If the witness is emotional, acknowledge the emotion. Saying "I understand that you are angry" is an example of how you might do this, depending on the emotion you are dealing with.

7. Try to avoid the following:
   - jumping in to add comments when a witness is giving his or her version of events;
   - fidgeting with paper and equipment, or tapping pens in notebooks, etc.;
   - answering a question with a question;
   - pretending to understand a situation when you do not; and
   - using clichés, such as "I hear you."

Source: Adapted from Laurence M Olivo & Mary Ann Kelly, *Civil Litigation*, 3rd ed (Toronto: Emond Montgomery, 2014) ch 3.

Four Questions to Ask at a Collision Scene

1. "Is anyone hurt?"

When approaching people at a collision scene, the police officer should first ask whether anyone is hurt. This initial question shows concern for people first, and demonstrates that the police are not just there to lay charges or assign blame. This question also has investigative merit because the investigating officer may be challenged by an insurance company at a later date about why the officer did not initiate medical treatment for an injured person. If a person later claims that he or she sustained neck or back problems, the investigating officer can truthfully state that no one reported any injuries when questioned at the outset of the investigation. The question also has the indirect value of helping to sort out the crowd that may have gathered. The crowd will usually direct the officer to the injured person(s) and react in other ways that give the officer clues about who is involved in the collision and who is just a spectator. Officers must ensure that *everyone* is accounted for.

Police officers must make note of *any* and *all* injuries. For example, if a driver states, "I've got a bit of a sore neck, but it's nothing, really," the officer must record this complaint. The next day, the sore neck may be found to be symptomatic of a major head, neck, or back injury, or another medical issue. *Always* encourage any individual who complains of "minor" physical injuries or issues to *not* drive until he or she has been examined by a doctor. Remember to record everything in your notebook.

2. "Who is the driver of this vehicle?"

If there are no injuries, the police officer should walk over and touch one of the vehicles, and ask, "Who is the driver of this vehicle?" The voluntary answer to this investigative question is admissible in court because there will have been no mention of any charges at this stage. The question is also of such a nature that there is no dispute that the response is voluntary and not forced or coerced. The admission is important because it may be the only evidence of who was driving the vehicle. Once the driver is identified, the officer should ask the driver for his or her driver's licence, registration, and evidence of insurance. The officer should develop the habit of placing these documents together in a predetermined place, such as a right-hand pocket. This will save the officer the embarrassment of not being able to find the documents when he or she is ready to return them to the driver.

The officer could then ask the driver whether he or she was wearing a seat belt. Again, the confession is admissible in court if there is no dispute that the response is voluntary. The officer should then direct the driver to stay with his or her vehicle, or in another location if that would be safer, until the officer returns.

If another vehicle is involved in the collision, the officer should walk over and touch that vehicle and ask, "Who is the driver of this vehicle?" Again, a voluntary answer is admissible in court because there will have been no mention of any charges at this stage. The officer should ask this driver for his or her licence, registration, and evidence of insurance, and place these documents in a predetermined place, such as a left-hand pocket (to avoid mixing them up with the other driver's documents). Always check drivers in the Canadian Police Information Centre (CPIC). The officer should ask whether the driver was wearing his or her seat belt and direct the driver to stay with his or her vehicle, or at another location if that would be safer, preferably away from the other driver, to avoid a confrontation. The officer now has all documents for both drivers, which reduces the likelihood that either driver will leave the scene. The documents also provide the officer with basic information for accident reports and charges, if charges are necessary.

3. "Did anyone witness the collision?"

It is important to speak to any witnesses before they leave. The testimony of independent witnesses in court carries a lot of weight. The officer should approach the crowd and ask whether anyone witnessed the collision. If witnesses come forth, the officer should thank them for their assistance and speak to each witness separately. If one witness says that he or she must leave immediately because of a scheduled meeting or for some other urgent reason, record his or her name and a number where he or she can be reached by phone. Insisting that he or she stay will only produce a hostile witness, who is likely to give a poor-quality statement and be less helpful.

It is very important for the officer to listen to what each witness has to say before he or she asks for personal data. If the officer starts by asking for the witness's name, date of birth, address, phone number, place of employment, work phone number, and so on, the witness will likely fall into a question-and-answer mode, and may not offer information until he or she is asked for it. A better technique is for the officer to ask where the witness was in relation to the collision scene, and then ask the witness to recount, chronologically, what he or she saw. The officer should refrain from interrupting the witness with too many questions during the narrative, because it will disrupt the spontaneous flow of the witness's account and put the witness back into question-and-answer mode.

One technique to avoid interruptions, yet impose a logical order to the witness statement, is for the officer to hand the witness a card, and then ask the witness to please explain what he or she saw, following the order of the items on the card:

- Description of the vehicle.
- Direction of travel.
- Name of street.
- Lane of travel.
- Approximate speed.
- What happened?

If a card is used, copies of the card must be included in the witness statement for disclosure purposes.

It is always best to appear attentive when listening to a person who is speaking. People feel encouraged to talk when they see that you are listening. This point is very important to remember when taking any statement. The officer's interest and facial expressions will encourage a more detailed answer than would otherwise be obtained.

Listening means making continual eye contact and responding with facial expressions—not staring at your notebook and writing madly. If the investigating officer is looking only at his or her notebook, racing to record the witness's statement, and not paying attention to the witness, the witness becomes focused on the officer's writing and in some cases will actually begin to speak at the pace of the officer's handwriting speed. If the witness begins to concentrate on what the officer is doing, the witness may become distracted, which often results in the omission of details from the statement. To avoid this problem, the officer should listen to the statement first, and then ask the witness to repeat the statement as the officer writes it down. Then the officer knows what to expect and can record the statement more effectively. Although this two-step procedure may appear to take more time, in reality it does not; the number of interruptions required by the officer to obtain the required details is greatly reduced. There are other advantages to this approach: the statement is in the witness's own words, and in telling the story twice, the witness has the opportunity to consider the accuracy of his or her statement more carefully.

"will say" statements
a brief description or summary from an officer's notebook of what the witness will say in court; its primary audience is the Crown attorney and defence counsel, who will likely see the statement under evidentiary disclosure rules

These statements can be handled as formal statements or as **"will say" statements**, depending on the policy of the police service and the severity of the collision. The witness should be invited to read the statement, to make any changes that he or she wishes, and to sign the statement. Because the Crown and defence counsel are likely to see the document, and it may be questioned in court, attention must be paid to grammar, spelling, and clarity of language.

PROFESSIONAL PRACTICE

Written Statements and Record-Keeping

Make sure that, in any written statement, mistakes are noted and initialled by both the interviewee and the officer. The mistake(s) should have only *one* line through them, and correction fluid should *never* be used. In addition, make sure that any corrections and the bottoms of all pages are initialled by the interviewee as well as by the officer. When the statement is complete, the officer, after a brief pause, will conclude the written interview by asking: "Is there anything else you wish to add?" It is important to ask this question because the interviewee has by now had time to reflect on the incident, may feel more at ease, and as a result may come up with additional—sometimes critical—information. The officer must also note the time at which the interview started and the time at which it was completed. If a completed witness statement finishes three-quarters of the way down the page, the officer should draw a "Z" from under the last line of the statement to the bottom of the page to guard against material being added to a completed statement. The interviewee and the officer should then both initial beside the line.

Officers should make a habit of creating a file for each investigation where all documents, copies of charges, drawings, and other related items may be kept. On the front of the file, the following information should be highlighted: occurrence number, date of event, name of accused, and notebook page numbers for easy reference.

4. "Was anyone else involved in the collision?"

It is not usually necessary to take statements from passengers in the vehicles involved in the collision. These statements do not carry much weight because they are considered to be biased. In most cases, the officer requires only information about a passenger's identity, position in the vehicle, seat belt use, and injury. If a person admits that he or she was not wearing a seat belt, because the answer was voluntary, it is admissible in court. However, the question must have been asked in a manner that ensures there is no dispute that the response was voluntary.

Caution Statements

If the physical evidence is overwhelming or if independent witnesses supplied statements, the investigating officer may know beyond a reasonable degree of certainty that a violation of the HTA or CC has occurred. The officer should interview the non-offending driver first. The procedure for taking a statement from this driver is the same as for other witnesses. Get the driver's story first, and record the information from the driver's licence, registration, and insurance card last. With this approach, the non-offending driver and passengers will be able to leave the scene of the accident and the officer will be free to concentrate on the offending driver.

Before questioning a driver suspected of committing an offence, the officer should read the driver a police caution. The caution informs the suspect of the charges against him or her, and of his or her basic rights; in order for a suspect's statement to be admissible in court, the suspect must have been cautioned prior to giving the statement. The following is a sample wording for a police caution:

> You will be charged with _____. Do you wish to say anything in answer to the charge? You are not obliged to say anything unless you wish to do so, but anything you say may be given in evidence.

Be sure that any time you read anything of a formal nature to an accused that you do so in a clear and slow manner and that you note the location where you undertook the reading.

If, in response to the reading of the caution, the suspect driver does make a statement—known as a "caution statement"—it may be tendered as evidence at the trial. Prior to giving the contents of the statement as evidence, there will usually be a ***voir dire*** to ensure that the statement was voluntary and made without any inducements. The caution will go a long way to demonstrating that any subsequent statement was given voluntarily. Having the suspect driver read his or her statement over and make corrections before signing it also supports the case that the statement was given voluntarily.

If the driver refuses to make a statement after being cautioned, the officer may still charge the driver on the strength of physical evidence, on the evidence of the other driver,

voir dire
a "trial within a trial" conducted by a trial judge to determine whether evidence to be tendered is admissible in the main proceeding; an officer may have to give evidence on whether the accused was given a warning and whether his or her statement was voluntary and not compelled or coerced

and on the evidence of independent witnesses. If there are no independent witnesses, the statement of the driver may be more important. Extra care should be exercised in taking this caution statement because its admission in court may be vital to the case.

Statements Required by Statute

If the suspect driver does not wish to make a caution statement when asked to do so, he or she should be informed of the statutory requirement in the HTA (ss 199 and 200) to supply evidence necessary for the completion of the accident report. Failure to supply this information could result in a charge of failing to report a collision. However, care should be taken to explain to the driver that the statutory requirement invalidates the statement for use in court as evidence against the driver because it is a forced statement, not a voluntary one. Anything the driver says in providing information to complete the accident report cannot be used in court against the driver, but is required by the Ontario Ministry of Transportation for the planning of public safety. However, although the statement itself is not admissible in evidence against the driver, the information may provide useful insights that will assist the officer in gathering evidence that is admissible.

If the collision occurred at an intersection controlled by traffic lights and there is not enough physical evidence or statements from any independent witnesses, a statement given by statutory requirement will at least help determine the truth. In a case like this, no charges are feasible. Remember that the investigating officer should be more concerned with determining what happened than with laying charges.

Dealing with Unruly Spectators

If spectators become unruly, it is necessary to dispatch other police officers to the scene to assist. If spectators obstruct the officer in the lawful execution of his or her duty, a criminal charge of obstructing the police (CC, s 129) is possible, although this detracts from the primary purpose of the investigation and is best handled by other officers.

> **DISCUSSION POINT**
>
> You are investigating an accident involving the "head-on" collision of a motorcyclist and van. The motorcyclist was dragged under the van and sustained fatal injuries. Out of respect, you have covered the body. The coroner has been notified and is responding. You observe an adult male walking by the scene. He ignores the "Police—Do Not Enter" yellow tape, enters the scene area, crouches down, and picks up a piece of the accident debris. Can you arrest him?

Moving spectators back onto the sidewalk can be accomplished with an authoritative command. If people do not instantly obey the officer, an explanation of the consequences, given in a professional manner, is required. People who do not comply with this order are not necessarily "obstructing a peace officer"; there must be more evidence of interference with the collection of evidence or with other duties related to the collision investigation. Officers must not be overzealous in their wish to have everyone jump to their commands and should not immediately arrest those who do not comply. These kinds of arrests diminish the professionalism of the police service and give the public the impression that the police are capricious and abuse their power.

CHAPTER SUMMARY

In Ontario, the police are required to investigate or receive a report of a collision from drivers involved in any motor vehicle collision where a personal injury occurs or there is property damage valued at more than $2,000; in reality, this includes almost all collisions. Collision investigations are one of the most common situations during which members of the public come into contact with the police, and officers must ensure that *all* of their dealings with the public are done in a manner that upholds and enhances the professionalism of the police service.

The duty of police officers in investigating a collision is to investigate a violation of the law and collect evidence relevant to a prosecution—it is *not* to find fault. Police officers have a variety of responsibilities in such a situation, including recording the identification of all persons involved, the type of injuries sustained, the registration of the vehicles involved, the insurance particulars of the vehicle owners, the type and amount of damage to vehicles and property, and the location and time of the collision.

In investigating a collision, it is important that officers follow certain steps, although not all steps apply to all situations. Typically, once an officer is dispatched to a collision, he or she must obtain as much advance information as possible, and then take steps to arrive quickly but safely at the scene. On arrival at the scene, the officer prioritizes emergencies, if there is more than one. The officer may have to deal with the presence of dangerous goods, injuries, downed hydro lines, fighting drivers, and vehicle fires. The officer also needs to take steps to ensure the protection of the collision scene, preserve evidence, and safeguard goods.

One of the officer's most important tasks is "people management." The officer must determine whether anyone is hurt, who the drivers are, who the witnesses are, and, if necessary, obtain caution statements and witness statements using various interview techniques designed to elicit accurate information efficiently and effectively.

ON THE SCENE

Motor Vehicle Collision Report

Scenario

A motor vehicle accident occurred on [use today's date DD/MM/YYYY] at 2:45 p.m. The accident involved two vehicles that were stopped in an intersection.

Location: Queens Boulevard (Number of lanes: two) at Brant Street (Number of lanes: two), Kitchener, Ontario.

Responding officer: Constable (Cst.) Michael Sean Andrews, Badge #1125, Platoon #1, Traffic Division, Waterloo Regional Police Service. Cst. Andrews arrives on scene at 1500 hrs and speaks to the two drivers. There are no other occupants in either car. Cst. Andrews obtains the particulars of both drivers.

Driver #1

Woodward, John Richard

- 15 Smith Street, Waterloo, Ontario, N0G 4K2, home phone: 519-555-1968
- Date of birth: 1990 January 15
- Ontario driver's licence #W8241-25639-00115 (proper licence, not suspended, class G licence)
- Driver only occupant in vehicle
- Speed of driver was approximately 30 km/h
- Driver sustained no injuries; he did wear a lap and shoulder belt and was not ejected from vehicle

Statement of Woodward

On [use today's date DD/MM/YYYY] at 3:10 p.m., in back seat of cruiser #777:

Woodward: It happened so fast, officer. I was heading toward Brant on Queens. I saw the stop sign at the last second, slammed on the brakes, and hit the other car. Are you gonna charge me?

Cst. Andrews: Why did you see the stop sign at the last second?

Woodward: I haven't a clue.

[Statement signed by Woodward and Cst. Andrews. Indicate start and finish of statement.]

Vehicle #1

- 2008 Dodge Ram pickup, blue, Ontario licence #KRY123; no airbrakes and was not loaded
- Insurance company: All State Insurance; policy #8-8921731-1-04
- Driver #1 is the registered owner of the vehicle

Driver #2

Lance, April Monica

- 32 Middle Avenue, Kitchener, Ontario, A1R 5T3, home phone: 519-555-5101
- Date of birth: 1995 March 15
- Ontario driver's licence #L9527-48599-55315 (proper licence, not suspended, class G licence)
- Driver only occupant in vehicle
- Speed of driver was approximately 50 km/h
- Driver sustained no injuries; she did wear lap and shoulder belt and was not ejected from vehicle

Statement of Lance

On [use today's date DD/MM/YYYY] at 3:30 p.m., in back seat of cruiser #777:

Lance: I was driving the speed limit, about 50, eastbound on Brant, when, bam, the guy came from my right side and hit my car. I just bought this car last week. What a bummer!

Cst. Andrews: Are you hurt?

Lance: No.

[Statement signed by Lance and Cst. Andrews. Indicate start and finish of statement.]

Vehicle #2

- 2011 two-door Ford Escort, red, Ontario licence #ZAC982; no airbrakes and was not loaded
- Insurance Company: Co-operators; policy #K312642387264-01
- Driver #2 is the registered owner of the vehicle

Cst. Andrews Notes the Following on His Motor Vehicle Collision Report

The accident was intersection-related on a through lane. Visibility was clear and it was daylight. There is traffic control in the form of posted stop signs on Queens Avenue at Brant Street. Both streets are undivided in design with two-way traffic. Both streets are covered by asphalt, and the roads are in good condition; they are straight and level. There are no pavement markings. The road surfaces were dry at the time of the accident. Both vehicles, prior to the accident, had no apparent defects. John Woodward, while driving on Queens Ave-nue, had failed to stop for the stop sign at Brant Street. Both drivers indicated they were not hurt, had not consumed any alcoholic beverages, and appeared normal.

Neither vehicle, due to the moderate damage, could be driven away. Vehicle #1 sustained damage to the complete front end and vehicle #2 sustained damage to the right front. Woodward asked for Andy's Towing to respond and tow his vehicle to Waterloo Motors. Lance wanted her vehicle towed by K&K's Towing to Stu's Auto Body.

The measured skid marks of Vehicle #1 were 12.4 m; the point of impact (POI) was measured from the southeast curb: 2.7 m north of south curb and 2.4 m west of east curb. The width of the roads were measured as well: Queens Avenue is 8.3 m, and Brant Street is 8.5 m.

Provincial Offence Notice (PON) #95090983 was issued.

What Actions Should the Officer Take?

1. As the investigating officer, what evidence would Cst. Andrews look for to determine the truthfulness of what happened?

2. What safety equipment should Cst. Andrews be wearing while investigating the accident?

3. What charge, if any, should Cst. Andrews issue?

Filling out the MVC Report

Cst. Andrews should fill out a Motor Vehicle Collision Report. A blank report appears on the following page.

Ver 1
Use Template
Ver. 1 with
this report

Ontario

Motor Vehicle Collision Report

Ver 1

| Report Type | ☐ Original | ☐ Amended | ☐ Failed To Remain |

Collision Number

Page Of

Collision Date — Y — M — D — Day of the Week — Time :

Time Officer Arrived or Police Service Reported to:

Emergency Equipment in Attendance

Service Performed

Prod. Ident. No. (P.I.N.)

Dangerous Goods Involvement

Name of Investigating Officer

Badge No.

Div/Stat./Det.

Plat/Squad

Name of Submitting Police Service

MTO Use Only — Highway — Distance — Unit — Dir.

Location

R1 Trafficway

Distance ☐ M. ☐ Km. — Check as applicable ☐ N. ☐ S. ☐ E. ☐ W.

M T O — District — Keypoint/Geocode — Offset — Ramp No.

R2 Reference Point

Municipality

County, District, Reg. Municipality

Driver 1

Driver (Last Name First) — Code

Address

Telephone No.

Postal Code

Driver's Licence No. — Prov. — Class — Cond.

Sex — D.O.B. (Y/M/D) — Proper Licence to Drive Class of Vehicle ☐ Y ☐ N — Suspended Driver ☐ Y ☐ N — Breathalyzer, Blood Test, Admin. ☐ Y ☐ N

Vehicle (Indirectly Involved)

Make — Year — Model — Colour — Body Style

Air Brake ☐ Y ☐ N — Plate No. — Prov. — Number of Occupants in Vehicle

Owner (Last Name First) ☐ As above

Address — Telephone No.

Postal Code

Insurance Company and Policy No. ☐ None

Trailer

CVOR No. — Lic. Class Required — ☐ Loaded ☐ Unloaded — Approx. Speed Km/hr.

Make — Plate No. — Prov.

Owner (Last Name First) ☐ As vehicle above

Address — Telephone No.

Postal Code

Insurance Company and Policy No. ☐ As Vehicle Above

Driver 2

Driver (Last Name First) — Code

Address

Telephone No.

Postal Code

Driver's Licence No. — Prov. — Class — Cond.

Sex — D.O.B. (Y/M/D) — Proper Licence to Drive Class of Vehicle ☐ Y ☐ N — Suspended Driver ☐ Y ☐ N — Breathalyzer, Blood Test, Admin. ☐ Y ☐ N

Vehicle (Indirectly Involved)

Make — Year — Model — Colour — Body Style

Air Brake ☐ Y ☐ N — Plate No. — Prov. — Number of Occupants in Vehicle

Owner (Last Name First) ☐ As above

Address — Telephone No.

Postal Code

Insurance Company and Policy No. ☐ None

Trailer

CVOR No. — Lic. Class Required — ☐ Loaded ☐ Unloaded — Approx. Speed Km/hr.

Make — Plate No. — Prov.

Owner (Last Name First) ☐ As vehicle above

Address — Telephone No.

Postal Code

Insurance Company and Policy No. ☐ As Vehicle Above

Investigating Officer's Description of Collision & Diagram

Lanes/Speed

	Number of Lanes	Posted Speed Max.	Advisory
R1			
R2			

Descriptions of Code(s) 97, 98, 99

Describe Damage to Other Property

Person and/or Agency Advised — Y — M — D — Time :

| No. | Involved Persons - Injured Taken To/By | Independent Witnesses - Name | Error Entry |

Vehicle Taken To/By
V1
V2

Persons Charged - Section and Act & P.O.T. No.

Name of Coroner — Telephone No.

If School Age Child Involved, Indicate School Name

Signature of Investigating Officer — Report completed ☐ on — Y — M — D

Signature of Supervisor — Badge No. — Y — M — D

Involved Persons

| | Veh. No. | Ped. No. | | |

Press firmly you are making 5 copies

All boxes must be completed by officers submitting Report.
Specify all codes 97, 98, 99 on this Report

SR-LD-401 2012/05

UNIT 1

1 2 3 4 5 6 7 8 9 10 11 12 13 14 15 16 17 18 19 20 21 22 23 24 25 26 27 28 29 30 31 32 33 34 35 36 37 38 39 40

41 42 43 44 45 46 47 48 49 50 51 52 53 54 55 56 57 58 59 60 61 62 63 64 65 66 67 68 69 70 71 72 73 74 75 76 77 78

KEY TERMS

bill of lading, 194

oxidizer, 194

voir dire, 203

"will say" statements, 202

REVIEW QUESTIONS

Short Answer

Briefly answer the following questions.

1. What would you do if you arrived at a collision scene and discovered

    a. that hydro lines were down?

    b. that a damaged tanker truck has a placard coloured red, with a flame and a number 3 on it?

    c. that two drivers are punching each other in the middle of the road?

    d. that an injured person is badly cut, has bled profusely, and has no pulse, and a second person is sitting dazed on the side of the road, and appears to be in shock?

2. Explain what the following colours represent on dangerous-goods placards:

    a. yellow

    b. white

    c. yellow over white

    d. green

    e. blue

    f. white over black.

3. Briefly describe the nine classes of dangerous goods.

4. In what circumstances can an officer presume that a person at a collision scene is dead?

5. If an officer cannot presume that an injured person is dead, what must he or she do?

6. Suppose that the collision scene is on a two-lane road, with one lane in each direction. Both lanes are blocked by the collision. Describe what you would do to close the road, and indicate the tools or devices you would use to do it.

7. What are the four questions you should ask at most collision scenes?

8. If a driver refuses to answer your questions after being cautioned, is there any way to get information from that driver? Can that information be used in court?

9. Describe four things you should do when questioning a witness to a collision to encourage them to tell you what they know.

DISCUSSION QUESTION

Given the following facts, what steps you would take as the first officer on the scene, in order?

The Scene

You arrive at the scene of a collision at the intersection of two provincial highways in cottage country on a Friday at 10 p.m. in summer. It is dark and beginning to rain. The intersection is controlled by traffic signals and is lit by two overhead street lights. There appear to be three vehicles involved. On the shoulder is a 48-passenger public commercial bus, with the front end demolished. The engine is still running, and a number of passengers appear to be injured. About 15 people are gathered around the bus, some bleeding and dishevelled, and others that appear to be unhurt. A person you assume to be the driver is still in his seat, but he appears to be unconscious, and his clothing is covered with blood.

The second vehicle is a transport truck. It is in the intersection, lying on its side. It has completely blocked the roadway of both highways. Some of its cargo of red canisters has spilled. On the side of the truck you can see a red placard with a flame and the number 2 on it.

Lastly, there is a van behind the truck. Its front end is badly damaged. A man, woman, and two small children are standing next to the van. None of them appear to be injured.

The summer weekend traffic is snarled because vehicles cannot get through the intersection. Some vehicles are pulling onto the shoulder to try to inch past, others are trying to turn around to find an alternative route, and still others are pulling onto the grass to stop, either to help or merely to watch.

Appendixes

Short-Form Wordings and Set Fines from the Provincial Offences Act

This appendix sets out Schedules 43, A, B, C, D, E, and F of Regulation 950 under the *Provincial Offences Act*. The short-form wordings of charges set out in Schedule 43 may be used as an aid in locating topics in the *Highway Traffic Act* (HTA). Police officers who use the schedule for this purpose must remember that only charges are listed here. When using the short-form wordings to determine an appropriate charge, be aware that the wordings do not adequately reflect all of the facts in issue for an offence. The actual section, subsection, and clause in the HTA (which are noted in Column 2) should be referred to in order to determine whether a particular charge is appropriate. As long as you understand the limitations of the tables below, the short-form wordings are invaluable as an overview of all of the charges in the Act.

Note that an "N.S.F." entry in the Set Fine column means there is no set fine for the offence. In some cases, this column refers to Schedule A, B, C, D, E, or F where the relevant fines are set out depending on the particular details of the offence.

PROVINCIAL OFFENCES ACT
RRO 1990, Regulation 950
Proceedings Commenced by Certificate Of Offence
Schedule 43
The Highway Traffic Act

Sections without an item number may not be in the Regulations but are included for convenience.

Item	Column 1	Column 2 Section	Set Fine
1.	Drive motor vehicle, no permit	7(1)(a)	$85.00
2.	Drive motor vehicle, no currently validated permit	7(1)(a)	$85.00
3.	Drive motor vehicle, no plates	7(1)(b)(i)	$85.00
4.	Drive motor vehicle, fail to display two plates	7(1)(b)(i)	$85.00
5.	Drive motor vehicle, plate improperly displayed	7(1)(b)(i)	$85.00
6.	Drive motor vehicle, no validation on plate	7(1)(c)(i)	$85.00
7.	Drive motor vehicle, validation improperly affixed	7(1)(c)(i)	$85.00
8.	Draw trailer, no permit	7(4)(a)	$85.00
9.	Draw trailer, no plate	7(4)(b)	$85.00
10.	Draw trailer, plate improperly displayed	7(4)(b)	$85.00
11.	Fail to surrender permit for motor vehicle	7(5)(a)	$85.00
12.	Fail to surrender permit for trailer	7(5)(b)	$85.00
13.	Have more than one permit	7(15)	$85.00
14.	Drive motor vehicle, not in accordance with permit limitations	8	$140.00
15.	Permit driving of motor vehicle, not in accordance with permit limitations	8	$140.00
16.	REVOKED		
17.	Fail to notify change of address	9(2)	$85.00
18.	Fail to notify change of name	9(2)	$85.00
19.	Fail to notify change of address—lessee	9(3)	$85.00
20.	Fail to notify change of name—lessee	9(3)	$85.00
21.	Drive motor vehicle, no vehicle identification number	10(1)	$85.00
22.	Permit driving of motor vehicle, no vehicle identification number	10(1)	$85.00
23.	Draw trailer, no identification number	10(2)(a)	$85.00
24.	Permit drawing of trailer, no identification number	10(2)(a)	$85.00
25.	Draw conversion unit, no identification number	10(2)(b)	$85.00
26.	Permit drawing of conversion unit, no identification number	10(2)(b)	$85.00

Item	Column 1	Column 2 Section	Set Fine
27.	Draw converter dolly, no identification number	10(2)(c)	$85.00
28.	Permit drawing of converter dolly, no identification number	10(2)(c)	$85.00
29.	Fail to remove plates on ceasing to be owner	11(1)(a)	$85.00
30.	Fail to remove plates on ceasing to be lessee	11(1)(a)	$85.00
31.	Fail to retain plate portion of permit	11(1)(b)	$85.00
32.	Fail to give vehicle portion of permit to new owner	11(1)(c)(i)	$85.00
33.	Fail to give vehicle portion of permit to lessor	11(1)(c)(ii)	$85.00
34.	Fail to apply for permit on becoming owner	11(2)	$85.00
34.1	Fail to provide valid information package for inspection	11.1(1)	$140.00
34.2	Fail to deliver valid information package at time vehicle transfer	11.1(1)	$140.00
35.	Deface plate	12(1)(a)	N.S.F.
36.	Deface validation	12(1)(a)	N.S.F.
37.	Alter plate	12(1)(a)	N.S.F.
38.	Alter validation	12(1)(a)	N.S.F.
39.	Deface permit	12(1)(a)	N.S.F.
40.	Alter permit	12(1)(a)	N.S.F.
41.	Use defaced plate	12(1)(b)	N.S.F.
42.	Use defaced validation	12(1)(b)	N.S.F.
43.	Use altered plate	12(1)(b)	N.S.F.
44.	Use altered validation	12(1)(b)	N.S.F.
45.	Permit use of defaced plate	12(1)(b)	N.S.F.
46.	Permit use of defaced validation	12(1)(b)	N.S.F.
47.	Permit use of altered plate	12(1)(b)	N.S.F.
48.	Permit use of altered validation	12(1)(b)	N.S.F.
49.	Use defaced permit	12(1)(b)	N.S.F.
50.	Permit use of defaced permit	12(1)(b)	N.S.F.
51.	Remove plate without authority	12(1)(c)	N.S.F.
52.	Use plate not authorized for vehicle	12(1)(d)	$140.00
53.	Permit use of plate not authorized for vehicle	12(1)(d)	$140.00
54.	Use validation not furnished by Ministry	12(1)(e)	$140.00
55.	Use validation not furnished for vehicle	12(1)(e)	$140.00
56.	Permit use of validation not furnished by Ministry	12(1)(e)	$140.00
57.	Permit use of validation not furnished for vehicle	12(1)(e)	$140.00
58.	Use plate not in accordance with Act	12(1)(f)	$140.00

Item	Column 1	Column 2 Section	Set Fine
59.	Use plate not in accordance with regulations	12(1)(f)	$140.00
60.	Use validation not in accordance with Act	12(1)(f)	$140.00
61.	Use validation not in accordance with regulations	12(1)(f)	$140.00
62.	Permit use of plate not in accordance with Act	12(1)(f)	$140.00
63.	Permit use of plate not in accordance with regulations	12(1)(f)	$140.00
64.	Permit use of validation not in accordance with Act	12(1)(f)	$140.00
65.	Permit use of validation not in accordance with regulations	12(1)(f)	$140.00
66.	Confuse identity of plate	13(1)	$85.00
67.	Obstruct plate	13(2)	$85.00
68.	Dirty plate	13(2)	$85.00
69.	Entire plate not plainly visible	13(2)	$85.00
69.0.1	Obstruct plate, preventing accurate photograph by red light camera system	13(3.0.1)	$85.00
69.1	Obstruct plate preventing accurate photograph	13(3)	$85.00
69.2	Obstruct plate preventing identification by toll system	13(3.1)	$85.00
70.	Operate commercial motor vehicle—no valid CVOR certificate	16(2)	$260.00
71.	Drive commercial motor vehicle—no valid CVOR certificate	16(2)	$175.00
72.	Fail to carry fleet limitation certificate	16(3)	$175.00
73.	Fail to carry CVOR certificate	16(3)(a)	$85.00
74.	Fail to carry vehicle lease	16(3)(b)	$85.00
75.	REVOKED		
76.	Fail to surrender CVOR certificate	16(4)	$85.00
77.	Fail to surrender vehicle lease	16(4)	$85.00
78.	REVOKED		
79.	Fail to surrender fleet limitation certificate	16(4)	$175.00
80.	Fail to notify change of officer's name	18	$175.00
81.	Fail to notify change of officer's address	18	$175.00
82.	Fail to notify change of officers	18	$175.00
83.	Fail to retain copy of lease	20(1)	$175.00
83.0.1	Provide fictitious, altered or fraudulently obtained CVOR certificate	21(4)	$400.00
83.0.2	Use fictitious, altered or fraudulently obtained CVOR certificate	21(4)	$400.00
83.0.3	Permit the use of fictitious, altered or fraudulently obtained CVOR certificate	21(4)	$400.00
83.0.4	Improperly use CVOR certificate	21(4)	$400.00
83.1	Operate commercial motor vehicle—improper insurance	23(1)	N.S.F.
83.2	Driver of commercial motor vehicle—fail to carry proof of insurance	23(3)	$175.00

Item	Column 1	Column 2 Section	Set Fine
83.3	Driver of commercial motor vehicle—fail to surrender proof of insurance	23(3)	$175.00
83.4	Inadequate cargo insurance	23.1	$85.00
83.5	No evidence of cargo insurance in vehicle	23.1	$85.00
84.	Drive motor vehicle—no licence	32(1)	$260.00
	Possess illegally obtained disabled parking permit	27(1)(a)	N.S.F.
	Fail to surrender disabled parking permit	27(1)(b)	N.S.F.
	Refuse to surrender disabled parking permit	27(1)(c)	N.S.F.
	Improperly use disabled parking permit on Crown land	27(1)(d)	N.S.F.
84.1	Drive commercial motor vehicle—no licence	32(1)	$310.00
85.	Drive motor vehicle—improper licence	32(1)	$260.00
85.1	Drive commercial motor vehicle—improper licence	32(1)	$310.00
86.	Drive street car—no licence	32(2)	$260.00
87.	Drive vehicle with air brakes—no endorsement	32(3)	$200.00
87.1	Drive commercial motor vehicle with air brake —no endorsement	32(3)	$310.00
88.	Drive motor vehicle in contravention of conditions	32(9)	$85.00
88.1	Drive commercial motor vehicle in contravention of conditions	32(9)	$310.00
89.	Permit unlicensed person to drive motor vehicle	32(10)	$200.00
89.1	Permit unlicensed person to drive commercial motor vehicle	32(10)	$310.00
90.	Permit person with improper licence to drive motor vehicle	32(10)	$200.00
90.1	Permit person with improper licence to drive commercial motor vehicle	32(10)	$310.00
91.	Permit person to drive motor vehicle in contravention of condition	32(10.1)	$200.00
91.0.1	Permit person to drive commercial motor vehicle in contravention of condition	32(10.1)	$310.00
91.1	Permit operation of vehicles with air brakes—no endorsement on licence	32(11)	$200.00
91.2	Permit novice driver to drive in contravention of condition or restriction	32(11.1)	$200.00
92.	Driver fail to surrender licence	33(1)	$85.00
92.1	Accompanying driver fail to surrender licence	33(2)	$85.00
93.	Driver fail to give identification	33(3)	$85.00
93.1	Accompanying driver fail to give identification	33(3)	$85.00
94.	Possess illegal licence	35(1)(a)	N.S.F.
	Display cancelled, revoked or suspended licence	35(1)(b)	N.S.F.
	Cause or permit to be displayed a cancelled, revoked or suspended licence	35(1)(b)	N.S.F.
	Possess cancelled, revoked or suspended licence	35(1)(b)	N.S.F.
95.	Use illegal licence	35(1)(a)	N.S.F.
96.	Possess non–Photo Card portion of cancelled, revoked or suspended licence	35(1)(b)	N.S.F.

Item	Column 1	Column 2 Section	Set Fine
97.	Use non–Photo Card portion of cancelled, revoked or suspended licence	35(1)	N.S.F.
98.	Permit another person to use all or part of licence	35(1)(c)	N.S.F.
98.1	Use other person's licence	35(1)(d)	N.S.F.
98.2	Apply for more than one licence	35(1)(e)	N.S.F.
98.3	Secure more than one licence	35(1)(e)	N.S.F.
98.4	Possess more than one licence	35(1)(e)	N.S.F.
98.5	Fail to surrender suspended, revoked or cancelled licence	35(1)(f)	N.S.F.
99.	Driving under licence of other jurisdiction while suspended in Ontario	36	N.S.F.
100.	Employ person under 16 to drive	37(2)	N.S.F.
101.	Permit person under 16 to drive	37(2)	N.S.F.
101.1	Permit person under 16 on motor-assisted bicycle	38(2)	N.S.F.
101.2	Permit person under 16 on power-assisted bicycle	38(2)	N.S.F.
102.	Let unlicensed driver hire vehicle	39(1)	N.S.F.
103.	Fail to produce licence when hiring vehicle	39(3)	$85.00
103.1	Pick up passenger for compensation without authority	39.1(1)	$300.00
103.2	Owner—allow use of vehicle to pick up passenger for compensation without authority	39.1(2)	$300.00
103.3	Arrange for passenger pick-up for compensation without authority	39.1(3)	$300.00
103.4	Offer to arrange for passenger pick-up for compensation without authority	39.1(3)	$300.00
103.5	Fail to carry authority to pick up passengers for compensation	39.1(4)(a)	$300.00
103.6	Fail to surrender authority to pick up passengers for compensation	39.1(4)(b)	$300.00
103.7	Fail to identify self	39.1(6)	N.S.F.
103.8	Novice driver—B.A.C. above zero	44.1(3)	$85.00
103.9	Young driver—B.A.C. above zero	44.1(5)	$85.00
104.	Apply for permit while prohibited	47(5)	N.S.F.
105.	Procure permit while prohibited	47(5)	N.S.F.
106.	Possess permit while prohibited	47(5)	N.S.F.
107.	Apply for licence while prohibited	47(6)	N.S.F.
108.	Procure licence while prohibited	47(6)	N.S.F.
109.	Possess licence while prohibited	47(6)	N.S.F.
110.	Procure CVOR certificate while suspended or cancelled	47(7)	$260.00
111.	Apply for CVOR certificate while suspended or cancelled	47(7)	$260.00
112.	Operate commercial motor vehicle—fleet limitation certificate not carried	47(8)(a)	N.S.F.
113.	Operate commercial motor vehicle—CVOR certificate suspended	47(8)(b)	N.S.F.
113.1	Novice driver fail to provide breath sample	48.1(3)	$85.00

Item	Column 1	Column 2 Section	Set Fine
113.2	Novice driver refuse to provide breath sample	48.1(4)	$85.00
113.3	Novice driver fail to provide breath sample	48.1(4)	$85.00
113.4	Novice driver refuse to provide breath sample	48.1(4)	$85.00
113.5	Novice driver fail to surrender licence	48.1(5)	$85.00
113.6	Accompanying driver fail to provide breath sample	48.2(2)	$85.00
113.7	Accompanying driver refuse to provide breath sample	48.2(2)	$85.00
114.	Operate vehicle for which permit suspended	51	N.S.F.
115.	Operate vehicle for which permit cancelled	51	N.S.F.
116.	Driving while under suspension	53(1)	N.S.F.
116.1	Passenger fail to identify self	57.1.1(1)	$85.00
116.2	Passenger fail to give required information	57.1.1(2)	$85.00
117.	No licence to operate vehicle business	59(1)	N.S.F.
118.	Interfere with officer inspecting vehicle business	59(6)	N.S.F.
119.	Fail to keep records	60(1)	N.S.F.
120.	Deal with vehicle identification number altered	60(2)	N.S.F.
121.	Deface vehicle identification number	60(3)	N.S.F.
122.	Remove vehicle identification number	60(3)	N.S.F.
123.	Fail to notify re vehicle stored more than 2 weeks	60(4)	$60.00
124.	Fail to report damaged vehicle	60(5)	$140.00
124.1	Give false report	60(6)	N.S.F.
125.	Drive without proper headlights—motor vehicle	62(1)	$85.00
125.1	Drive without proper headlights—commercial motor vehicle	62(1)	$200.00
126.	Drive without proper rear light—motor vehicle	62(1)	$85.00
126.1	Drive without proper rear light—commercial motor vehicle	62(1)	$200.00
127.	Drive without proper headlight—motorcycle	62(2)	$85.00
128.	Drive without proper rear light—motorcycle	62(2)	$85.00
129.	Drive without proper headlights—motorcycle with sidecar	62(3)	$85.00
130.	Drive without proper rear light—motorcycle with side car	62(3)	$85.00
131.	Drive with improper headlights	62(6)	$85.00
131.1	Drive with improper headlights—commercial motor vehicle	62(6)	$200.00
132.	Drive with headlamp coated	62(7)	$85.00
132.1	Drive with headlight coated—commercial motor vehicle	62(7)	$200.00
133.	Drive with headlamp covered	62(7)	$85.00
133.1	Drive with headlamp covered—commercial motor vehicle	62(7)	$200.00

Item	Column 1	Column 2 Section	Set Fine
134.	Drive with headlamp modified	62(7)	$85.00
134.1	Drive with headlamp modified—commercial motor vehicle	62(7)	$200.00
135.	More than 4 lighted headlights	62(9)	$85.00
135.1	More than 4 lighted headlights—commercial motor vehicle	62(9)	$200.00
136.	Improper clearance lights	62(10)	$85.00
136.1	Improper clearance lights—commercial motor vehicle	62(10)	$200.00
137.	Fail to have proper identification lamps	62(11)	$85.00
137.1	Fail to have proper identification lamps—commercial motor vehicle	62(11)	$200.00
138.	Fail to have proper side marker lamps	62(13)	$85.00
138.1	Fail to have proper side marker lamps—commercial motor vehicle	62(13)	$200.00
139.	Use lamp producing intermittent flashes of red light	62(14)	$85.00
139.1	Use lamp producing intermittent flashes of red light—commercial motor vehicle	62(14)	$200.00
139.2	Unauthorized red and blue lights at front	62(14.1)	$85.00
139.3	Unauthorized red and blue lights at front—commercial motor vehicle	62(14.1)	$200.00
140	Red light at front	62(15)	$85.00
140.1	Red light at front—commercial motor vehicle	62(15)	$200.00
141.	Improper use of green flashing lights	62(16.1)	$85.00
141.1	Improper use of green flashing lights—commercial motor vehicle	62(16.1)	$200.00
142.	Improper bicycle lighting	62(17)	$85.00
143.	Improper lighting on motor assisted bicycle	62(17)	$85.00
144.	Improper number plate light	62(19)	$85.00
145.	Use parking light while vehicle in motion	62(20)	$85.00
146.	Have more than one spotlamp	62(22)	$85.00
146.1	Have more than one spotlamp—commercial motor vehicle	62(22)	$200.00
147.	Improper use of spotlamp	62(22)	$85.00
147.1	Improper use of spotlamp—commercial motor vehicle	62(22)	$200.00
148.	Improper lights on traction engine	62(23)	$85.00
149.	No red light on rear of trailer	62(24)	$85.00
149.1	No red light on rear of trailer—commercial motor vehicle	62(24)	$200.00
150.	No red light on rear of object	62(24)	$85.00
150.1	No red light on rear of object—commercial motor vehicle	62(24)	$200.00
151.	No proper red lights—object over 2.6 metres	62(25)	$85.00
151.1	No proper red light—object over 2.6 m—commercial motor vehicle	62(25)	$200.00
152.	No lamp on left side	62(26)	$85.00

Item	Column 1	Column 2 Section	Set Fine
152.1	No lamp on left side—commercial motor vehicle	62(26)	$200.00
153.	Improper lights on farm vehicle	62(27)	$85.00
154.	No directional signals	62(29)	$85.00
154.1	No directional signals—commercial motor vehicle	62(29)	$200.00
155.	No brake lights	62(29)	$85.00
155.1	No brake lights—commercial motor vehicle	62(29)	$200.00
156.	No blue flashing light on snow removal vehicle	62(31)	$85.00
157.	Improper use of blue flashing light	62(32)	$85.00
157.1	Improper use of red and blue flashing lights	62(32)(b)	$85.00
157.2	Improper use of red and blue flashing lights—commercial motor vehicle	62(32)(b)	$200.00
158.	No sign—"right hand drive vehicle"	63	$85.00
159.	Improper braking system	64(1)	$85.00
159.1	Improper braking system—commercial motor vehicle	64(1)	$400.00
160.	Improper brakes on motorcycle	64(2)	$85.00
161.	Improper brakes on motor-assisted bicycle	64(2)	$85.00
161.0.1	Improper brakes on power-assisted bicycle	64(2)	$85.00
161.1	Improper brakes on bicycle	64(3)	$85.00
162.1	Improper brakes on trailer—commercial motor vehicle	64(5)	$400.00
162.	Improper brakes on trailer	64(5)	$85.00
163.	Defective brakes	64(7)	$85.00
163.1	Defective brakes—commercial motor vehicle	64(7)	$400.00
164.	Defective braking system	64(7)	$85.00
164.1	Defective braking system—commercial motor vehicle	64(7)	$400.00
165.	Sell improper brake fluid	65(1)(a)	N.S.F.
166.	Offer to sell improper brake fluid	65(1)(a)	N.S.F.
167.	Install improper brake fluid	65(1)(a)	N.S.F.
168.	Sell improper hydraulic oil	65(1)(b)	N.S.F.
169.	Offer to sell improper hydraulic oil	65(1)(b)	N.S.F.
170.	Install improper hydraulic oil	65(1)(b)	N.S.F.
171.	Improper windshield wiper	66(1)(a)	$85.00
171.1	Improper windshield wiper—commercial motor vehicle	66(1)(a)	$200.00
172.	No windshield wiper	66(1)(a)	$85.00
172.1	No windshield wiper—commercial motor vehicle	66(1)(a)	$200.00
173.	Improper mirror	66(1)(b)	$85.00

Item	Column 1	Column 2 Section	Set Fine
173.1	Improper mirror—commercial motor vehicle	66(1)(b)	$200.00
174.	No mirror	66(1)(b)	$85.00
174.1	No mirror—commercial motor vehicle	66(1)(b)	$200.00
175.	Improper mudguards	66(3)	$85.00
175.1	Improper mudguards—commercial motor vehicle	66(3)	$200.00
176.	No mudguards	66(3)	$85.00
176.1	No mudguards—commercial motor vehicle	66(3)	$200.00
177.	No odometer	66(5)	$85.00
177.1	No odometer—commercial motor vehicle	66(5)	$200.00
178.	Defective odometer	66(5)	$85.00
178.1	Defective odometer—commercial motor vehicle	66(5)	$200.00
179.	Operate motor vehicle—mirrors more than 305 mm	67	$85.00
180.	No speedometer on bus	68	$85.00
181.	Defective speedometer on bus	68	$85.00
181.1	Drive commercial motor vehicle not equipped with working speed-limiting system	68.1(1)	$310.00
181.2	Permit operation of commercial motor vehicle not equipped with working speed-limiting system	68.1(1)	$310.00
181.3	Deactivate speed-limiting system	68.1(2)(a)	$310.00
181.4	Permit person to deactivate speed-limiting system	68.1(2)(a)	$310.00
181.5	Modify speed-limiting system	68.1(2)(b)	$310.00
181.6	Permit person to modify speed-limiting system	68.1(2)(b)	$310.00
181.7	Drive commercial motor vehicle with speed-limiting system tampering device	68.1(3)	$310.00
181.8	Permit operation of commercial motor vehicle with speed-limiting system tampering device	68.1(3)	$310.00
181.9	Fail to comply with officer's direction re speed-limiting system	68.1(5)	$310.00
181.10	Sell, offer or advertise speed-limiting system tampering device	68.1(7)	$310.00
182.	Improper tire—damage to highway	69(1)	$85.00
183.	Device on wheels—injure highway	69(2)	$85.00
184.	No lock shoe—animal drawn vehicle	69(3)	$85.00
185.	Improper tires	70(3)(a)	$85.00
185.1	Improper tires—commercial motor vehicle	70(3)(a)	$200.00
186.	Improper tires—drawn vehicle	70(3)(a)	$85.00
186.1	Improper tires—drawn vehicle—commercial motor vehicle	70(3)(a)	$200.00
187.	Improperly installed tires	70(3)(b)	$85.00
187.1	Improperly installed tires—commercial motor vehicle	70(3)(b)	$200.00
188.	Improperly installed tires—drawn vehicle	70(3)(b)	$85.00

Item	Column 1	Column 2 Section	Set Fine
188.1	Improperly installed tires—drawn vehicle—commercial motor vehicle	70(3)(b)	$200.00
189.	Fail to mark rebuilt tire	71(2)	N.S.F.
190.	Sell unmarked rebuilt tire	71(3)	N.S.F.
191.	Offer to sell unmarked rebuilt tire	71(3)	N.S.F.
192.	Sell new vehicle—no safety glass	72(2)	N.S.F.
193.	Register new vehicle—no safety glass	72(2)	N.S.F.
194.	Install non-safety glass	72(3)	N.S.F.
195.	Window obstructed	73(1)(a)	$85.00
196.	Windshield obstructed	73(1)(a)	$85.00
197.	Have object obstructing view	73(1)(b)	$85.00
198.	Drive with window coated—view obstructed	73(2)	$85.00
199.	Drive with windshield coated—view obstructed	73(2)	$85.00
200.	Colour coating obscuring interior	73(3)	$85.00
201.	No clear view to front	74(1)(a)	$85.00
202.	No clear view to sides	74(1)(a)	$85.00
203.	No clear view to rear	74(1)(b)	$85.00
204.	No muffler—motor vehicle	75(1)	$85.00
205.	No muffler—motor assisted bicycle	75(1)	$85.00
206.	Improper muffler—motor vehicle	75(1)	$85.00
207.	Improper muffler—motor assisted bicycle	75(1)	$85.00
208.	Excessive fumes	75(3)	$85.00
209.	Unreasonable noise—signalling device	75(4)	$85.00
210.	Unreasonable smoke	75(4)	$85.00
211.	Unnecessary noise	75(4)	$85.00
212.	No horn—motor vehicle	75(5)	$85.00
213.	No horn—motor assisted bicycle	75(5)	$85.00
214.	No horn—bicycle	75(5)	$85.00
215.	Defective horn—motor vehicle	75(5)	$85.00
216.	Defective horn—motor assisted bicycle	75(5)	$85.00
217.	Defective horn—bicycle	75(5)	$85.00
218.	Have a siren	75(6)	$85.00
219.	No slow moving vehicle sign	76(1)	$85.00
219.1	Slow moving vehicle sign not attached to rear of vehicle or trailer	76(1)	$85.00
219.2	Slow moving vehicle sign not attached in accordance with regulations	76(1)	$85.00

Item	Column 1	Column 2 Section	Set Fine
219.3	Slow moving vehicle sign placed on fixed object	76(4)	$85.00
219.4	Prohibited use of slow moving vehicle sign	76(6)	$85.00
219.5	Operate slow moving vehicle over 40 km/h	76(6.1)	$85.00
220.	No sleigh bells	77(1)	$5.00
221.	Drive—display screen visible to driver	78(1)	$400.00
222.	Drive—hand-held communication device	78.1(1)	$400.00
223.	Drive—hand-held entertainment device	78.1(2)	$400.00
224.	REVOKED		
225.	Drive motor vehicle with speed measuring warning device	79(2)	$140.00
225.1	Drive motor vehicle with pre-empting traffic control signal device	79.1(1)	$140.00
226.	Improper means of attachment	80	$85.00
226.1	Improper means of attachment—commercial motor vehicle	80	$200.00
227.	Refuse or fail to stop and move vehicle to a safe location	82(9)	$140.00
227.1	Refuse or fail to submit vehicle to examinations and tests	82(9)	$140.00
227.2	Refuse or fail to have vehicle repaired and submitted to further examinations and tests	82(9)	$140.00
227.3	Refuse or fail to have vehicle repaired and submit evidence of compliance	82(9)	$140.00
227.4	Refuse or fail to assist with examinations and tests of vehicle	82(9)	$140.00
227.5	Refuse or fail to place vehicle in safe condition	82(9)	$140.00
227.6	Refuse or fail to remove unsafe vehicle from highway	82(9)	$140.00
227.7	Operate unsafe vehicle on highway contrary to officer's prohibition	82(9)	$140.00
227.8	Permit operation of unsafe vehicle on highway contrary to officer's prohibition	82(9)	$140.00
227.9	Refuse or fail to stop and move vehicle to a safe location—commercial motor vehicle	82(10)	$400.00
227.10	Refuse or fail to submit vehicle to examinations and tests—commercial motor vehicle	82(10)	$400.00
227.11	Refuse or fail to have vehicle repaired and submitted to further examinations and tests —commercial motor vehicle	82(10)	$400.00
227.12	Refuse or fail to have vehicle repaired and submit evidence of compliance —commercial motor vehicle	82(10)	$400.00
227.13	Refuse or fail to assist with examinations and tests of vehicle—commercial motor vehicle	82(10)	$400.00
227.14	Refuse or fail to place vehicle in safe condition—commercial motor vehicle	82(10)	$400.00
227.15	Refuse or fail to remove unsafe vehicle from highway—commercial motor vehicle	82(10)	$400.00
227.16	Operate unsafe vehicle on highway contrary to officer's prohibition—commercial motor vehicle	82(10)	$400.00
227.17	Permit operation of unsafe vehicle on highway contrary to officer's prohibition —commercial motor vehicle	82(10)	$400.00
228.	Operate unsafe vehicle	84	N.S.F.
228.1	Operate unsafe vehicle—commercial motor vehicle	84	N.S.F.

Item	Column 1	Column 2 Section	Set Fine
229.	Operate unsafe street car	84	N.S.F.
230.	Operate unsafe combination of vehicles	84	N.S.F.
230.1	Operate unsafe combination of vehicles—commercial motor vehicle	84	N.S.F.
231.	Permit operation of unsafe vehicle	84	N.S.F.
231.1	Permit operation of unsafe vehicle—commercial motor vehicle	84	N.S.F.
232.	Permit operation of unsafe street car	84	N.S.F.
233.	Permit operation of unsafe combination of vehicles	84	N.S.F.
233.1	Permit operation of unsafe combination of vehicles—commercial motor vehicle	84	N.S.F
234.	Operate vehicle—fail to display device	85(1)	$200.00
235.	Permit operation of vehicle fail to display device	85(1)	$200.00
236.	Issue SSC not provided by Ministry	86	N.S.F.
237.	Affix vehicle inspection sticker not provided by Ministry	86	N.S.F.
238.	Unauthorized person issue SSC	90(1)	N.S.F.
239.	Unauthorized person affix vehicle inspection sticker	90(2)	$200.00
240.	Issue SSC without proper inspection	90(3)(a)	N.S.F.
241.	Affix vehicle inspection certificate without proper inspection	90(3)(a)	N.S.F.
242.	Issue SSC—vehicle not complying	90(3)(a)	N.S.F.
243.	Affix vehicle inspection sticker—vehicle not complying	90(3)(a)	N.S.F.
244.	SSC not made by inspection mechanic	90(3)(b)(i)	N.S.F.
245.	Vehicle inspection record not made by inspection mechanic	90(3)(b)(i)	N.S.F.
246.	SSC not countersigned	90(3)(b)(ii)	N.S.F.
247.	Unlicensed inspection station	91(1)	$400.00
248.	Corporation fail to notify change of officer or director	91(7)	N.S.F.
249.	Unregistered mechanic certify SSC	92(1)	N.S.F.
250.	Unregistered mechanic sign vehicle inspection record	92(1)	N.S.F.
251.	Obstruct inspector	98(6)	N.S.F.
252.	False statement in SSC	99(2)	N.S.F.
253.	Sell new vehicle not complying with standards	102(3)	N.S.F.
254.	Offer for sale new vehicle not complying with standards	102(3)	N.S.F.
255.	Expose for sale new vehicle not complying with standards	102(3)	N.S.F.
256.	Sell new vehicle not marked or identified	102(3)	N.S.F.
257.	Offer for sale new vehicle not marked or identified	102(3)	N.S.F.
258.	Expose for sale new vehicle not marked or identified	102(3)	N.S.F.
259.	No name on commercial vehicle	103(1)	$85.00

Item	Column 1	Column 2 Section	Set Fine
260.	Less than two reflectors—commercial vehicle	103(2)	$85.00
261.	Less than two reflectors—trailer	103(2)	$85.00
262.	Sell new commercial vehicle without two red rear lights	103(3)(a)	N.S.F.
263.	Offer to sell new commercial vehicle without two red rear lights	103(3)(a)	N.S.F.
264.	Sell trailer without two red rear lights	103(3)(a)	N.S.F.
265.	Offer to sell trailer without two red rear lights	103(3)(a)	N.S.F.
266.	Sell new commercial vehicle without two rear red reflectors	103(3)(b)	N.S.F.
267.	Offer to sell new commercial vehicle without two rear red reflectors	103(3)(b)	N.S.F.
268.	Sell trailer without two rear red reflectors	103(3)(b)	N.S.F.
269.	Offer to sell trailer without two rear red reflectors	103(3)(b)	N.S.F.
270.	No name and address on road-building machine	103(4)	$85.00
270.1	Fail to wear proper helmet on power-assisted bicycle	103.1(2)	$85.00
271.	Fail to wear proper helmet on motorcycle	104(1)	$85.00
272.	Fail to wear proper helmet on motor assisted bicycle	104(1)	$85.00
273.	Carry passenger under 16 not wearing proper helmet	104(2)	$85.00
273.1	Fail to wear proper helmet on bicycle	104(2.1)	$60.00
273.2	Permit person under 16 not wearing proper helmet on bicycle	104(2.2)	$60.00
273.3	Equestrian rider—fail to use proper equipment	104.1(1)	$60.00
273.4	Authorize or permit equestrian rider under 16 to ride without proper equipment	104.1(3)	$60.00
274.	Dealing with vehicle not conforming to standard	105(1)	N.S.F.
275.	Dealing with motor assisted bicycle—no document of compliance	105(2)	N.S.F.
276.	Drive with seat belt removed	106(1)	$200.00
277.	Drive with seat belt inoperative	106(1)	$200.00
278	Drive with seat belt modified	106(1)	$200.00
279.	Driver—fail to properly wear seat belt	106(2)	$200.00
280.	Passenger—fail to occupy position with seat belt	106(3)(a)	$200.00
281.	Passenger—fail to properly wear seat belt	106(3)(b)	$200.00
282.	Drive while passenger under 16 fails to occupy position with seat belt	106(4)(a)(i)	$200.00
283.	Drive while passenger under 16 fails to properly wear seat belt	106(4)(a)(ii)	$200.00
284.	Drive while child passenger not properly secured	106(4)(b)	$200.00
285.	REVOKED		
286.	REVOKED		
287.	REVOKED		
287.1	REVOKED		

Item	Column 1	Column 2 Section	Set Fine
288.	Fail to establish system to periodically inspect and maintain commercial motor vehicles and drawn vehicles	107(1)	$310.00
289.	Fail to keep written record of system to periodically inspect and maintain commercial motor vehicles and drawn vehicles	107(1)	$310.00
290.	Fail to ensure periodic inspections and maintenance are carried out	107(2)	$310.00
291.	Fail to ensure performance standards are met	107(3)	$310.00
292.	Fail to supply driver with daily inspection schedule	107(4)(a)	$310.00
293.	Fail to ensure daily inspection is conducted properly	107(4)(b)	$310.00
294.	Fail to ensure under-vehicle inspection is conducted properly	107(4)(c)	$310.00
295.	Fail to ensure daily inspection report is accurately completed	107(4)(d)	$310.00
296.	Fail to ensure under-vehicle inspection report is accurately completed	107(4)(d)	$310.00
297.	Fail to complete daily inspection report forthwith after inspection	107(5)	$200.00
298.	Fail to accurately complete daily inspection report	107(5)	$200.00
299.	Fail to complete under-vehicle inspection report forthwith after inspection	107(5)	$200.00
300.	Fail to accurately complete under-vehicle inspection report	107(5)	$200.00
301.	Fail to carry inspection schedule	107(6)	$85.00
302.	Fail to carry completed daily inspection report	107(6)	$85.00
303.	Fail to carry completed under-vehicle inspection report	107(6)	$85.00
303.1	Fail to surrender inspection schedule	107(7)	$85.00
303.2	Fail to surrender completed daily inspection report	107(7)	$85.00
303.3	Fail to surrender completed under-vehicle inspection report	107(7)	$85.00
303.4	Fail to enter defect in daily inspection report	107(8)(a)	$85.00
303.5	Fail to report defect to operator	107(8)(b)	$200.00
303.6	Fail to submit completed daily inspection report to operator	107(8)(c)	$85.00
303.7	Fail to submit completed under-vehicle inspection report to operator	107(8)(c)	$85.00
303.8	Drive commercial motor vehicle without required inspection	107(9)	$200.00
303.9	Drive commercial motor vehicle with a major defect in it or in drawn vehicle	107(11)	$310.00
303.10	Improperly drive commercial motor vehicle with a minor defect in it or in drawn vehicle	107(12)	$200.00
303.11	Fail to maintain books and records	107(13)	$310.00
303.12	Fail to produce books and records	107(13)	$310.00
304.	Overwidth vehicle	109(1)	$310.00
305.	Overwidth load	109(2)	$310.00
306.	Overlength vehicle	109(6)	$310.00
307.	Overlength combination of vehicles	109(7)	$310.00
307.1	Operate overlength combination of vehicles	109(8)	$310.00

Item	Column 1	Column 2 Section	Set Fine
308.	Overlength semi-trailer	109(10)	$310.00
309.	Overlength bus	109(11)	$310.00
310.	Overheight vehicle	109(14)	$310.00
311.	Fail to carry permit in vehicle	110(6)	$310.00
312.	Fail to produce permit	110(6)	$310.00
313.	Oversize vehicle—violate permit	110(7)	$310.00
314.	Overweight vehicle—violate permit	110(7)	$200.00 + Schedule A
314.1	Fail to comply with condition of permit	110(7)	$310.00
314.2	Violate non-weight condition of special permit	110.2(3)(a)	$310.00
314.3	Violate weight condition of special permit	110.2(3)(b)	Schedule A
314.4	Violate weight condition of special permit—liftable axle lifted	110.2(3)(b)	$200.00 + Schedule A
314.5	Violate weight condition of special permit—liftable axle deployed improperly	110.2(3)(b)	$200.00 + Schedule A
314.6	Violate more than one condition, including a weight condition, of special permit	110.2(3)(c)	$200.00 + Schedule A
314.7	Violate more than one condition, including a weight condition, of special permit—liftable axle lifted	110.2(3)(c)	$400.00 + Schedule A
314.8	Violate more than one condition, including a weight condition, of special permit—liftable axle deployed improperly	110.2(3)(c)	$400.00 + Schedule A
315.	Fail to mark overhanging load	111(1)	$130.00
315.1	Fail to mark overhanging load—commercial motor vehicle	111(1)	$200.00
316.	Insecure load	111(2)	$130.00
316.1	Insecure load—commercial motor vehicle	111(2)	$310.00
316.2	Operate vehicle with load not secured as prescribed	111(2.1)	$130.00
316.3	Operate commercial motor vehicle with load not secured as prescribed	111(2.1)	$310.00
316.4	Permit operation of vehicle with load not secured as prescribed	111(2.1)	$130.00
316.5	Permit operation of commercial motor vehicle with load not secured as prescribed	111(2.1)	$310.00
316.6	Drive commercial motor vehicle without conducting inspections	111(2.2)	$310.00
317.	Overweight on tires ...kg. ... less than 150 mm	115(1)(a)	Schedule A
317.1	Overweight on tires ...kg. liftable axle lifted	115(1)(a)	$200.00 + Schedule A
317.2	Overweight on tires ...kg.—liftable axle deployed improperly	115(1)(a)	$200.00 + Schedule A
318.	Overweight on tires ...kg. ... 150 mm or over	115(1)(b)	Schedule A
318.1	Overweight on tires ...kg.—liftable axle lifted	115(1)(b)	$200.00 + Schedule A
318.2	Overweight on tires ...kg.—liftable axle deployed improperly	115(1)(b)	$200.00 + Schedule A
319.	Overweight single axle (single tires) ...kg. Class A Highway	116(1)(a)	Schedule A
319.1	Overweight single axle (single tires) ...kg. Class A Highway—liftable axle lifted	116(1)(a)	$200.00 + Schedule A
319.2	Overweight single axle (single tires) ...kg. Class A Highway—liftable axle deployed improperly	116(1)(a)	$200.00 + Schedule A

Item	Column 1	Column 2 Section	Set Fine
320.	Overweight single axle (dual tires) . . . kg. Class A Highway	116(1)(a)	Schedule A
320.1	Overweight single axle (dual tires) . . . kg. Class A Highway—liftable axle lifted	116(1)(b)	$200.00 + Schedule A
320.2	Overweight single axle (dual tires) . . . kg. Class A Highway—liftable axle deployed improperly	116(1)(b)	$200.00 + Schedule A
321.	Overweight dual axle . . . kg. Class A Highway	116(1)(c)	Schedule A
321.1	Overweight dual axle . . . kg. Class A Highway —liftable axle lifted	116(1)(c)	$200.00 + Schedule A
321.2	Overweight dual axle . . . kg. Class A Highway —liftable axle deployed improperly	116(1)(c)	$200.00 + Schedule A
322.	Overweight triple axle . . . kg. Class A Highway	116(1)(d)	Schedule A
322.1	Overweight triple axle . . . kg. Class A Highway —liftable axle lifted	116(1)(d)	$200.00 + Schedule A
322.2	Overweight triple axle . . . kg. Class A Highway—liftable axle deployed improperly	116(1)(d)	$200.00 + Schedule A
323.	Overweight dual axle (single tires) . . . kg. Class A Highway	116(2)	Schedule A
323.1	Overweight dual axle (single tires) . . . kg. Class A Highway—liftable axle lifted	116(2)	$200.00 + Schedule A
323.2	Overweight dual axle (single tires) . . . kg. Class A Highway—liftable axle deployed improperly	116(2)	$200.00 + Schedule A
324.	Overweight triple axle (single tires) . . . kg. Class A Highway	116(3)	Schedule A
324.1	Overweight triple axle (single tires) . . . kg. Class A Highway—liftable axle lifted	116(3)	$200.00 + Schedule A
324.2	Overweight triple axle (single tires) . . . kg. Class A Highway—liftable axle deployed improperly	116(3)	$200.00 + Schedule A
325.	Overweight single front axle . . . kg. No verification. Class A Highway	116(4)	Schedule A
325.1	Overweight single front axle . . . kg. No verification. Class A Highway —liftable axle lifted	116(4)	$200.00 + Schedule A
325.2	Overweight single front axle . . . kg. No verification. Class A Highway —liftable axle deployed improperly	116(4)	$200.00 + Schedule A
326.	Overweight single front axle . . . kg. Exceed rating. Class A Highway	116(4)	Schedule A
326.1	Overweight single front axle . . . kg. Exceed rating. Class A Highway—liftable axle lifted	116(6)	$200.00 + Schedule A
326.2	Overweight single front axle . . . kg. Exceed rating. Class A Highway —liftable axle deployed improperly	116(6)	$200.00 + Schedule A
327.	Overweight two axle group . . . kg. Class A Highway	117(a)	Schedule A
327.1	Overweight two axle group . . . kg. Class A Highway—liftable axle lifted	117(1)(a)	$200.00 + Schedule A
327.2	Overweight two axle group . . . kg. Class A Highway—liftable axle deployed improperly	117(1)(a)	$200.00 + Schedule A
328.	Overweight three axle group . . . kg. Class A Highway	117(1)(b)	Schedule A
328.1	Overweight three axle group . . . kg. Class A Highway—liftable axle lifted	117(1)(b)	$200.00 + Schedule A
328.2	Overweight three axle group . . . kg. Class A Highway—liftable axle deployed improperly	117(1)(b)	$200.00 + Schedule A
329.	Overweight four axle group . . . kg. Class A Highway	117(1)(c)	Schedule A
329.1	Overweight four axle group . . . kg. Class A Highway—liftable axle lifted	117(1)(c)	$200.00 + Schedule A
329.2	Overweight four axle group . . . kg. Class A Highway—liftable axle deployed improperly	117(1)(c)	$200.00 + Schedule A
330.	Overweight vehicle . . . kg. Class A Highway	118	Schedule A
330.1	Overweight vehicle . . . kg. Class A Highway—liftable axle lifted	118	$200.00 + Schedule A
330.2	Overweight vehicle . . . kg. Class A Highway—liftable axle deployed improperly	118	$200.00 + Schedule A

Item	Column 1	Column 2 Section	Set Fine
331.	Overweight during freeze-up …kg.	119(4)	Schedule A
331.1	Overweight vehicle during freeze-up …kg.—liftable axle lifted	119(4)	$200.00 + Schedule A
331.2	Overweight vehicle during freeze-up …kg.—liftable axle deployed improperly	119(4)	$200.00 + Schedule A
332.	Overweight on axle …kg. Class B Highway	120	Schedule A
332.1	Overweight on axle …kg. Class B Highway —liftable axle lifted	120	$200.00 + Schedule A
332.2	Overweight on axle …kg. Class B Highway—liftable axle deployed improperly	120	$200.00 + Schedule A
333.	Overweight vehicle—violate permit …kg.	121(1)	Schedule A
334.	Fail to have receipt in vehicle	121(3)	$75.00
335.	Fail to produce receipt	121(3)	$75.00
335.1	Overweight on axle …kg.—reduced load period	122(1)	Schedule A
335.2	Overweight on axle …kg.—reduced load period—liftable axle lifted	122(1)	$200.00 + Schedule A
335.3	Overweight on axle …kg.—reduced load period—liftable axle deployed improperly	122(1)	$200.00 + Schedule A
335.4	Overweight on tire …kg.—reduced load period	122(3)	Schedule A
335.5	Overweight on tire …kg.—reduced load period—liftable axle lifted	122(3)	$200.00 + Schedule A
335.6	Overweight on tire …kg.—reduced load period—liftable axle deployed improperly	122(3)	$200.00 + Schedule A
336.	Fail or refuse to stop	124(3)	$200.00
337.	Fail or refuse to drive vehicle to scale	124(3)	$200.00
338.	Fail or refuse to redistribute or remove load	124(4)(a)	$100.00
338.1	Fail or refuse to stop—commercial motor vehicle	124(5)	$310.00
338.2	Fail or refuse to drive vehicle to scale—commercial motor vehicle subsection 124(5)	124(5)	$310.00
338.3	Fail or refuse to redistribute or remove load—commercial motor vehicle	124(6)(a)	$310.00
339.	Cause vehicle to be overloaded	126	Schedule A
340.	Speeding	128	Schedule B
340.1	Speeding—liability of owner where evidence obtained through photo-radar	128	Schedule C
340.2	Speeding—community safety zone	128	Schedule D
340.3	Owner—speeding pursuant to section 207 community safety zone	128	Schedule D
340.4	Speeding—construction zone	128	Schedule E
340.5	Speeding—construction zone—worker present	128	Schedule F
341.	Careless driving	130	$400.00
341.1	REVOKED		
342.	Unnecessary slow driving	132	$85.00
342.1	Unnecessary slow driving—community safety zone	132	$120.00
343.	Disobey officer directing traffic	134(1)	$85.00
343.1	Disobey officer directing traffic—community safety zone	134(1)	$120.00

Item	Column 1	Column 2 Section	Set Fine
344.	Drive on closed highway	134(3)	$85.00
344.1	Drive on closed highway—community safety zone	134(3)	$120.00
345.	Fail to yield—uncontrolled intersection	135(2)	$85.00
345.1	Fail to yield—uncontrolled intersection—community safety zone	135(2)	$150.00
346.	Fail to yield to vehicle on right	135(3)	$85.00
346.1	Fail to yield to vehicle on right—community safety zone	135(3)	$150.00
347.	Disobey stop sign—stop wrong place	136(1)(a)	$85.00
347.1	Disobey stop sign—stop wrong place—community safety zone	136(1)(a)	$120.00
348.	Disobey stop sign—fail to stop	136(1)(a)	$85.00
348.1	Disobey stop sign—fail to stop—community safety zone	136(1)(a)	$150.00
349.	Fail to yield to traffic on through highway	136(1)(b)	$85.00
349.1	Fail to yield to traffic on through highway—community safety zone	136(1)(b)	$150.00
350.	Traffic on through highway—fail to yield	136(2)	$85.00
350.1	Traffic on through highway—fail to yield—community safety zone	136(2)	$150.00
351.	Fail to yield—yield sign	138(1)	$85.00
351.1	Fail to yield—yield sign—community safety zone	138(1)	$150.00
352.	Fail to yield from private road	139(1)	$85.00
352.1	Fail to yield from private road—community safety zone	139(1)	$150.00
353.	Fail to yield from driveway	139(1)	$85.00
353.1	Fail to yield from driveway— community safety zone	139(1)	$150.00
354.	Fail to stop at crossover	140(1)(a)	$150.00
354.1	REVOKED		
355.	Fail to stop at crossover—community safety zone	140(1)(a)	$300.00
355.1	REVOKED		
356.	Pass stopped vehicle at crossover	140(1)(b)	$150.00
356.1	REVOKED		
357.	Pass stopped vehicle at crossover—community safety zone	140(1)(b)	$300.00
357.1	REVOKED		
358.	Fail to yield to pedestrian on roadway	140(1)(c)	$150.00
358.1	REVOKED		
359.	Fail to yield to pedestrian on roadway—community safety zone	140(1)(c)	$300.00
359.1	REVOKED		
360.	REVOKED		
360.1	REVOKED		

Item	Column 1	Column 2 Section	Set Fine
361.	REVOKED		
361.1	REVOKED		
362.	REVOKED		
362.1	REVOKED		
363.	REVOKED		
363.1	REVOKED		
364.	REVOKED		
364.1	REVOKED		
365.	REVOKED		
365.1	REVOKED		
366.	REVOKED		
366.1	REVOKED		
367.	REVOKED		
367.1	REVOKED		
368.	Pass front of vehicle within 30 m of crossover	140(3)	$150.00
368.1	Pass front of vehicle within 30 m of crossover—community safety zone	140(3)	$300.00
369.	REVOKED		
369.1	REVOKED		
370.	Pedestrian fail to yield at crossover	140(4)	$35.00
371.	Person in wheelchair—fail to yield at crossover	140(4)	$35.00
371.1	Cyclist—ride in crossover	140(6)	$85.00
372.	Improper right turn	141(2)	$85.00
372.1	Improper right turn—community safety zone	141(2)	$120.00
373.	Improper right turn—multi-lane highway	141(3)	$85.00
373.1	Improper right turn—multi-lane highway—community safety zone	141(3)	$120.00
374.	Left turn—fail to afford reasonable opportunity to avoid collision	141(5)	$85.00
374.1	Left turn—fail to afford reasonable opportunity to avoid collision—community safety zone	141(5)	$150.00
375.	Improper left turn	141(6)	$85.00
375.1	Improper left turn—community safety zone	141(6)	$120.00
376.	Improper left turn—multi-lane highway	141(7)	$85.00
376.1	Improper left turn—multi-lane highway—community safety zone	141(7)	$120.00
377.	Turn—not in safety	142(1)	$85.00
377.1	Turn—not in safety—community safety zone	142(1)	$150.00
378.	Change lane—not in safety	142(1)	$85.00

Item	Column 1	Column 2 Section	Set Fine
378.1	Change lane—not in safety—community safety zone	142(1)	$150.00
379.	Fail to signal for turn	142(1)	$85.00
379.1	Fail to signal for turn—community safety zone	142(1)	$120.00
380.	Fail to signal—lane change	142(1)	$85.00
380.1	Fail to signal—lane change—community safety zone	142(1)	$120.00
381.	Start from parked position—not in safety	142(2)	$85.00
381.1	Start from parked position—not in safety—community safety zone	142(2)	$150.00
382.	Start from stopped position—not in safety	142(2)	$85.00
382.1	Start from stopped position—not in safety—community safety zone	142(2)	$150.00
383.	Start from parked position—fail to signal	142(2)	$85.00
383.1	Start from parked position—fail to signal—community safety zone	142(2)	$120.00
384.	Start from stopped position—fail to signal	142(2)	$85.00
384.1	Start from stopped position—fail to signal—community safety zone	142(2)	$120.00
385.	Improper arm signal	142(4)	$85.00
385.1	Improper arm signal—community safety zone	142(4)	$120.00
386.	Improper signal device	142(6)	$85.00
386.1	Improper signal device—community safety zone	142(6)	$120.00
387.	Use turn signals improperly	142(7)	$85.00
387.1	Use turn signals improperly—community safety zone	142(7)	$120.00
388.	Fail to signal stop	142(8)	$85.00
388.1	Fail to signal stop—community safety zone	142(8)	$120.00
389.	Fail to signal decrease in speed	142(8)	$85.00
389.1	Fail to signal decrease in speed community safety zone	142(8)	$120.00
390.	Improper signal to stop	142(8)	$85.00
390.1	Improper signal to stop—community safety zone	142(8)	$120.00
391.	Improper signal to decrease in speed	142(8)	$85.00
391.1	Improper signal to decrease in speed community safety zone	142(8)	$120.00
392.	Brake lights—improper colour	142(8)(b)	$85.00
392.1	Brake lights—improper colour—community safety zone	142(8)(b)	$120.00
392.2	Fail to yield to bus re-entering lane from bus bay	142.1(1)	$85.00
392.3	Fail to yield to bus re-entering lane from bus bay—community safety zone	142.1(1)	$120.00
393.	U-turn on a curve—no clear view	143(a)	$85.00
393.1	U-turn on a curve—no clear view community safety zone	143(a)	$150.00
394.	U-turn—railway crossing	143(b)	$85.00

Item	Column 1	Column 2 Section	Set Fine
394.1	U-turn—railway crossing—community safety zone	143(b)	$150.00
395.	U-turn near crest of grade—no clear view	143(c)	$85.00
395.1	U-turn near crest of grade—no clear view—community safety zone	143(c)	$150.00
396.	U-turn—bridge—no clear view	143(d)	$85.00
396.1	U-turn—bridge—no clear view—community safety zone	143(d)	$150.00
397.	U-turn—viaduct—no clear view	143(d)	$85.00
397.1	U-turn—viaduct—no clear view—community safety zone	143(d)	$150.00
398.	U-turn—tunnel—no clear view	143(d)	$85.00
398.1	U-turn—tunnel—no clear view—community safety zone	143(d)	$150.00
399.	Improper stop—traffic signal at intersection	144(5)	$85.00
399.1	Improper stop—traffic signal at intersection community safety zone	144(5)	$120.00
400.	Improper stop—traffic signal not at intersection	144(6)	$85.00
400.1	Improper stop—traffic signal not at intersection—community safety zone	144(6)	$120.00
401.	Fail to yield to pedestrian	144(7)	$150.00
401.1	Fail to yield to pedestrian—community safety zone	144(7)	$300.00
402.	Fail to yield to traffic	144(8)	$85.00
402.1	Fail to yield to traffic—community safety zone	144(8)	$150.00
403.	Proceed contrary to sign at intersection	144(9)	$85.00
403.1	Proceed contrary to sign at intersection—community safety zone	144(9)	$120.00
404.	Disobey lane light	144(10)	$85.00
404.1	Disobey lane light—community safety zone	144(10)	$120.00
405.	Green light—fail to proceed as directed	144(12)	$85.00
405.1	Green light—fail to proceed as directed—community safety zone	144(12)	$120.00
406.	Flashing green light—fail to proceed as directed	144(13)	$85.00
406.1	Flashing green light—fail to proceed as directed—community safety zone	144(13)	$120.00
407.	Green arrow—fail to proceed as directed	144(14)	$85.00
407.1	Green arrow—fail to proceed as directed—community safety zone	144(14)	$120.00
408.	Amber light—fail to stop	144(15)	$150.00
408.1	Amber light—fail to stop—community safety zone	144(15)	$300.00
409.	Amber arrow—fail to stop	144(16)	$85.00
409.1	Amber arrow—fail to stop—community safety zone	144(16)	$120.00
410.	Amber arrow—fail to proceed as directed	144(16)	$85.00
410.1	Amber arrow—fail to proceed as directed—community safety zone	144(16)	$120.00
411.	Flashing amber light—fail to proceed with caution	144(17)	$85.00

Item	Column 1	Column 2 Section	Set Fine
411.1	Flashing amber light—fail to proceed with caution—community safety zone	144(17)	$120.00
412.	Red light—fail to stop	144(18)	$260.00
412.1	Red light—fail to stop—community safety zone	144(18)	$400.00
413.	Red light—proceed before green	144(18)	$260.00
413.1	Red light—proceed before green—community safety zone	144(18)	$400.00
413.2	Red light—vehicle owner fails to stop pursuant to section 207	144(18.1)	$260.00
414.	Turn on red light—fail to yield	144(19)	$85.00
414.1	Turn on red light—fail to yield—community safety zone	144(19)	$150.00
415.	REVOKED		
416.	Flashing red light—fail to stop	144(21)	$85.00
416.1	Flashing red light—fail to stop community safety zone	144(21)	$150.00
417.	Flashing red light—fail to yield	144(21)	$85.00
417.1	Flashing red light—fail to yield—community safety zone	144(21)	$150.00
418.	Pedestrian fail to use crosswalk	144(22)	$35.00
419.	Pedestrian disobey flashing green light	144(24)	$35.00
420.	Pedestrian disobey red light	144(25)	$35.00
421.	Pedestrian disobey amber light	144(25)	$35.00
422.	Pedestrian disobey "don't walk" signal	144(27)	$35.00
422.1	Cyclist—ride in crosswalk	144(29)	$85.00
423.	Disobey portable amber light—fail to stop	146(3)	$150.00
423.1	Disobey portable amber light—fail to stop—community safety zone	146(3)	$300.00
424.	Disobey portable red light—fail to stop	146(4)	$260.00
424.1	Disobey portable red light—fail to stop—community safety zone	146(4)	$400.00
425.	Disobey portable red light—proceed before green	146(4)	$260.00
425.1	Disobey portable red light—proceed before green—community safety zone	146(4)	$400.00
426.	Disobey portable red light—stop wrong place	146(5)	$85.00
426.1	Disobey portable red light—stop wrong place—community safety zone	146(5)	$120.00
427.	Disobey portable amber light—stop wrong place	146(5)	$85.00
427.1	Disobey portable amber light—stop wrong place—community safety zone	146(5)	$120.00
428.	Remove portable lane control signal system	146(6)	$85.00
428.1	Remove portable lane control signal system community safety zone	146(6)	$150.00
429.	Deface portable lane control signal system	146(6)	$85.00
429.1	Deface portable lane control signal system community safety zone	146(6)	$120.00
430.	Interfere with portable lane signal system	146(6)	$85.00

Item	Column 1	Column 2 Section	Set Fine
430.1	Interfere with portable lane control signal system—community safety zone	146(6)	$120.00
430.2	Fail to obey traffic control stop sign	146.1(3)	$85.00
430.3	Fail to obey traffic control stop sign—community safety zone	146.1(3)	$120.00
430.4	Fail to obey traffic control slow sign	146.1(4)	$85.00
430.5	Fail to obey traffic control slow sign—Community safety zone	146.1(4)	$120.00
430.6	Display traffic control sign—unauthorized person	146.1(5)	$85.00
431.	Fail to keep right when driving at less than normal speed	147(1)	$85.00
431.1	Fail to keep right when driving at less than normal speed—community safety zone	147(1)	$120.00
432.	Fail to share half roadway—meeting vehicle	148(1)	$85.00
432.1	Fail to share half roadway—meeting vehicle—community safety zone	148(1)	$120.00
433.	Fail to turn out to right when overtaken	148(2)	$85.00
433.1	Fail to turn out to right when overtaken—community safety zone	148(2)	$120.00
434.	Fail to share roadway—meeting bicycle	148(4)	$85.00
434.1	Fail to share roadway—meeting bicycle—community safety zone	148(4)	$120.00
435.	Fail to turn out to left to avoid collision	148(5)	$85.00
435.1	Fail to turn out to left to avoid collision community safety zone	148(5)	$120.00
436.	Bicycle—fail to turn out to right when overtaken	148(6)	$85.00
436.1	Bicycle—fail to turn out to right when overtaken—community safety zone	148(6)	$120.00
437.	Fail to turn out to left to avoid collision with bicycle	148(6)	$85.00
437.1	Fail to turn out to left to avoid collision with bicycle—community safety zone	148(6)	$120.00
438.	Motor assisted bicycle—fail to turn out to right when overtaken	148(6)	$85.00
438.1	Motor assisted bicycle—fail to turn out to right when overtaken—community safety zone	148(6)	$120.00
439.	Fail to turn out to left to avoid collision with motor assisted bicycle	148(6)	$85.00
439.1	Fail to turn out to left to avoid collision with motor assisted bicycle—community safety zone	148(6)	$120.00
439.2	Fail to leave one metre while passing bicycle	148(6.1)	$85.00
439.3	Fail to leave one metre while passing bicycle—community safety zone	148(6.1)	$150.00
440.	Fail to stop to facilitate passing	148(7)	$85.00
440.1	Fail to stop to facilitate passing—community safety zone	148(7)	$120.00
441.	Fail to assist in passing	148(7)	$85.00
441.1	Fail to assist in passing—community safety zone	148(7)	$120.00
442.	Pass—roadway not clear—approaching traffic	148(8)(a)	$85.00
442.1	Pass—roadway not clear—approaching traffic—community safety zone	148(8)(a)	$150.00
443.	Attempt to pass—roadway not clear—approaching traffic	148(8)(a)	$85.00
443.1	Attempt to pass—roadway not clear—approaching traffic—community safety zone	148(8)(a)	$150.00

Item	Column 1	Column 2 Section	Set Fine
444.	Pass—roadway not clear—overtaking traffic	148(8)(b)	$85.00
444.1	Pass—roadway not clear—overtaking traffic—community safety zone	148(8)(b)	$150.00
445.	Attempt to pass—roadway not clear—overtaking traffic	148(8)(b)	$85.00
445.1	Attempt to pass—roadway not clear—overtaking traffic—community safety zone	148(8)(b)	$150.00
446.	Drive left of centre—approaching crest of grade	149(1)(a)	$85.00
446.1	Drive left of centre—approaching crest of grade—community safety zone	149(1)(a)	$150.00
447.	Drive left of centre—on a curve	149(1)(a)	$85.00
447.1	Drive left of centre—on a curve—community safety zone	149(1)(a)	$150.00
448.	Drive left of centre within 30 m of bridge—no clear view	149(1)(a)	$85.00
448.1	Drive left of centre within 30 m of bridge—no clear view—community safety zone	149(1)(a)	$150.00
449.	Drive left of centre within 30 m of viaduct—no clear view	149(1)(a)	$85.00
449.1	Drive left of centre within 30 m of viaduct—no clear view—community safety zone	149(1)(a)	$150.00
450.	Drive left of centre within 30 m of tunnel—no clear view	149(1)(a)	$85.00
450.1	Drive left of centre within 30 m of tunnel—no clear view—community safety zone	149(1)(a)	$150.00
451.	Drive left of centre within 30 m of level railway crossing	149(1)(b)	$85.00
452.	Drive left of centre within 30 m of level railway crossing—community safety zone	149(1)(b)	$150.00
453.	Pass on right—not in safety	150(1)	$85.00
453.1	Pass on right—not in safety—community safety zone	150(1)	$150.00
454.	Pass—off roadway	150(2)	$85.00
454.1	Pass—off roadway—community safety zone	150(2)	$150.00
455.	Non-authorized driving on paved shoulder	151(5)	$85.00
455.1	Non-authorized driving on paved shoulder—community safety zone	151(5)	$120.00
456.	Drive wrong way—one way traffic	153	$85.00
456.1	Drive wrong way—one way traffic—community safety zone	153	$150.00
457.	Unsafe move—lane or shoulder	154(1)(a)	$85.00
457.1	REVOKED		
458.	Unsafe move—lane or shoulder—community safety zone	154(1)(a)	$150.00
458.1	REVOKED		
459.	Use centre lane improperly	154(1)(b)	$85.00
459.1	Use centre lane improperly—community safety zone	154(1)(b)	$120.00
460.	Fail to obey lane sign	154(1)(c)	$85.00
460.1	Fail to obey lane sign—community safety zone	154(1)(c)	$120.00
460.2	Improper use of high occupancy vehicle lane	154.1(3)	$85.00
460.3	Improper use of border approach lane	154.2(2)	$85.00

Item	Column 1	Column 2 Section	Set Fine
460.4	Driver in border approach lane—fail to stop	154.2(4)	$150.00
460.5	Fail to provide required document—driver	154.2(4)	$85.00
460.6	Fail to provide required document—occupant	154.2(4)	$85.00
461.	Drive wrong way—divided highway	156(1)(a)	$85.00
461.1	Drive wrong way—divided highway—community safety zone	156(1)(a)	$150.00
462.	Cross divided highway—no proper crossing provided	156(1)(b)	$85.00
462.0.1	Cross divided highway—no proper crossing provided—community safety zone	156(1)(b)	$120.00
462.1	Backing on roadway—divided highway	157(1)	$85.00
462.1.1	Backing on roadway—divided highway—community safety zone	157(1)	$120.00
462.2	Backing on shoulder—divided highway	157(1)	$85.00
462.3	Backing on shoulder—divided highway—community safety zone	157(1)	$120.00
463.	Follow too closely	158(1)	$85.00
463.1	Follow too closely—community safety zone	158(1)	$120.00
464.	Commercial vehicle—follow too closely	158(2)	$85.00
464.1	Commercial vehicle—follow too closely—community safety zone	158(2)	$120.00
465.	Fail to stop on right for emergency vehicle	159(1)(a)	$400.00
465.1	REVOKED		
466.	Fail to stop—nearest curb—for emergency vehicle	159(1)(b)	$400.00
466.1	REVOKED		
467.	Fail to stop—nearest edge of roadway—for emergency vehicle	159(1)(b)	$400.00
467.1	REVOKED		
468.	Fail to slow down and proceed with caution for emergency vehicle or tow truck	159(2)	$400.00
468.1	Fail to move into another lane for emergency vehicle or tow truck—if safe to do	159(3)	$400.00
468.2	Follow fire department vehicle too closely	159(4)	$400.00
468.3	REVOKED		
469.	Permit attachment to vehicle	160	$85.00
469.1	Permit attachment to vehicle—community safety zone	160	$120.00
470.	Permit attachment to street car	160	$85.00
470.1	Permit attachment to street car community safety zone	160	$120.00
471.	Draw more than one vehicle	161	$85.00
471.1	Draw more than one vehicle—community safety zone	161	$120.00
472.	Drive while crowded	162	$85.00
472.1	Drive while crowded—community safety zone	162	$120.00
473.	Disobey railway crossing signal—stop wrong place	163(1)	$85.00

Item	Column 1	Column 2 Section	Set Fine
473.1	Disobey railway crossing signal—stop at wrong place—community safety zone	163(1)	$150.00
474.	Disobey railway crossing signal—fail to stop	163(1)	$85.00
474.1	Disobey railway crossing signal—fail to stop—community safety zone	163(1)	$150.00
475.	Disobey railway crossing signal—proceed unsafely	163(1)	$85.00
475.1	Disobey railway crossing signal—proceed unsafely—community safety zone	163(1)	$150.00
475.2	Disobey stop sign at railway crossing—stop at wrong place	163(2)	$85.00
475.3	Disobey stop sign at railway crossing—stop at wrong place—community safety zone	163(2)	$150.00
475.4	Disobey stop sign at railway crossing—fail to stop	163(2)	$85.00
475.5	Disobey stop sign at railway crossing—fail to stop—community safety zone	163(2)	$150.00
475.6	Disobey stop sign at railway crossing—proceed unsafely	163(2)	$85.00
475.7	Disobey stop sign at railway crossing—proceed unsafely—community safety zone	163(2)	$150.00
476.	Disobey crossing gate	164	$85.00
476.1	Disobey crossing gate—community safety zone	164	$150.00
477.	Open vehicle door improperly	165(1)(a)	$300.00
478.	Leave vehicle door open	165(1)(b)	$300.00
479.	Pass street car improperly	166(1)	$85.00
479.1	Pass street car improperly—community safety zone	166(1)	$150.00
480.	Approach open street car door too closely	166(1)	$85.00
480.1	Approach open street car door too closely—community safety zone	166(1)	$150.00
481.	Pass street car on the left side	166(2)	$85.00
481.1	Pass street car on the left side—community safety zone	166(2)	$120.00
482.	Frighten animal	167	$85.00
482.1	Frighten animal—community safety zone	167	$120.00
483.	Fail to ensure safety of person in charge of animal	167	$85.00
483.1	Fail to ensure safety of person in charge of animal—community safety zone	167	$120.00
484.	Fail to use lower beam—oncoming	168(a)	$85.00
484.1	Fail to use lower beam—oncoming—community safety zone	168(a)	$120.00
485.	Fail to use lower beam—following	168(b)	$85.00
485.0.1	Fail to use lower beam—following—community safety zone	168(b)	$120.00
485.1	Prohibited use of alternating highbeam headlights	169(2)	$85.00
485.2	Prohibited use of alternating highbeam headlights—community safety zone	169(2)	$120.00
486.	Fail to take precaution against vehicle being set in motion	170(9)	$50.00
487.	Fail to have warning lights	170(10)(a)	$50.00
488.	Fail to use warning lights	170(11)	$50.00

Item	Column 1	Column 2 Section	Set Fine
489.	Interfere with traffic	170(12)	$50.00
490.	Interfere with snow removal	170(12)	$50.00
490.1	Offer tow truck services in King's Highway within 200 m of accident or apparent accident	171(1)(a)	$200.00
490.2	Offer tow truck services on King's Highway within 200 m of vehicle involved in accident	171(1)(b)	$200.00
490.3	Park tow truck on King's Highway within 200 m of accident or apparent accident —sufficient tow trucks available	171(2)(a)	$200.00
490.4	Stop tow truck on King's Highway within 200 m of accident or apparent accident —sufficient tow trucks available	171(2)(a)	$200.00
490.5	Park tow truck on King's Highway within 200 m of vehicle involved in accident —sufficient tow trucks available	171(2)(b)	$200.00
490.6	Stop tow trucks on King's Highway within 200 m of vehicle involved in accident —sufficient tow trucks available	171(2)(b)	$200.00
491.	Race a motor vehicle	172(1)	N.S.F.
491.1	Race a motor vehicle—community safety zone	172(1)	N.S.F.
492.	Race an animal	173	$85.00
493.	Fail to stop at railway crossing—public vehicle	174(1)	$85.00
494.	Stop wrong place at railway crossing—public vehicle	174(1)(a)	$85.00
495.	Fail to look both ways at railway crossing—public vehicle	174(1)(b)	$85.00
496.	Fail to open door at railway crossing—public vehicle	174(1)(c)	$85.00
497.	Cross tracks using gear requiring change—public vehicle	174(1)(d)	$85.00
497.1	Change gears while crossing railway track—public vehicle	174(1)(e)	$85.00
497.2	Fail to stop at railway crossing—school bus	174(2)	$85.00
497.3	Stop wrong place at railway crossing—school bus	174(2)(a)	$85.00
497.4	Fail to look both ways at railway crossing—school bus	174(2)(b)	$85.00
497.5	Fail to open door at railway crossing—school bus	174(2)(c)	$85.00
497.6	Cross tracks using gear requiring change—school bus	174(2)(d)	$85.00
497.7	Change gears while crossing railway track—school bus	174(2)(e)	$85.00
498.	Bus not used to transport adults with developmental disabilities or children, painted chrome yellow	175(3)	$85.00
498.1	Chrome yellow bus not displaying required markings	175(3.1)	$85.00
499.	Prohibited markings	175(4)	$85.00
499.1	Prohibited equipment—school bus stop arm	175(4)	$85.00
500.	Drive chrome yellow vehicle, not used to transport adults with developmental disabilities or children	175(5)	$85.00
500.1	Drive chrome yellow vehicle not displaying required markings	175(5)	$85.00
501.	Drive vehicle with prohibited school bus markings	175(5)	$85.00

Item	Column 1	Column 2 Section	Set Fine
502.	Drive vehicle with prohibited school bus stop arm	175(5)	$85.00
503.	Fail to actuate school bus signals	175(6)	$85.00
504.	Improperly actuate school bus signals	175(8)	$85.00
505.	Improperly actuate school bus signals at intersection controlled by operating traffic control system	175(9)(a)	$85.00
506.	Improperly actuate school bus signals at location, other than an intersection, controlled by operating traffic control system—at sign or roadway marking indicating stop to be made	175(9)(b)(i)	$85.00
507.	Improperly actuate school bus signals at location, other than an intersection, controlled by operating traffic control system—in area immediately before entering crosswalk	175(9)(b)(ii)	$85.00
507.1	Improperly actuate school bus signals at location, other than an intersection, controlled by operating traffic control system—within 5 m of traffic control system	175(9)(b)(iii)	$85.00
507.2	Improperly actuate school bus signals within 60 m of location controlled by operating traffic control system	175(9)(c)	$85.00
507.3	Stop school bus opposite loading zone	175(10)(a)	$85.00
507.5	Fail to stop for school bus—meeting	175(11)	$400.00
507.6	Fail to stop for school bus—overtaking	175(12)	$400.00
507.7	Fail to stop for school bus—owner	175(19)	$400.00
507.8	Fail to stop for school bus—owner	175(20)	$400.00
508.	Guard fail to properly display school crossing stop sign	176(2)	$85.00
509.	Fail to obey school crossing stop sign	176(3)	$150.00
509.1	Fail to obey school crossing stop sign community safety zone	176(3)	$300.00
510.	Improper use of school crossing stop sign	176(4)	$85.00
511.	Unauthorized person display school crossing stop sign	176(5)	$85.00
512.	Solicit a ride	177(1)	$50.00
513.	Solicit business	177(2)	$50.00
514.	Attach to vehicle	178(1)	$85.00
515.	Attach to street car	178(1)	$85.00
516.	Ride 2 on a bicycle	178(2)	$85.00
517.	Ride another person on a motor assisted bicycle	178(3)	$85.00
518.	Person—attach to vehicle	178(4)	$35.00
519.	Person—attach to street car	178(4)	$35.00
520.	Pedestrian fail to walk on left side of highway	179	$35.00
521.	Pedestrian on roadway fail to keep to left edge	179	$35.00
522.	Litter highway	180	$85.00
523.	Deposit snow or ice on roadway	181	$85.00
524.	Disobey sign	182(2)	$85.00
524.1	Disobey sign—community safety zone	182(2)	$120.00

Item	Column 1	Column 2 Section	Set Fine
525.	Disobey sign at tunnel	183(2)	$85.00
526.	Deface notice	184	N.S.F.
527.	Remove notice	184	N.S.F.
528.	Interfere with notice	184	N.S.F.
529.	Deface obstruction	184	N.S.F.
530.	Remove obstruction	184	N.S.F.
531.	Interfere with obstruction	184	N.S.F.
532.	Fail to remove aircraft	187(1)	N.S.F.
533.	Move aircraft improperly	187(2)	N.S.F.
534.	Aircraft unlawfully take off	187(3)	N.S.F.
535.	Draw occupied trailer	188	$85.00
536.	Operate air cushioned vehicle	189	$85.00
537.	Fail to maintain daily log	190(3)	$320.00
538.	Fail to carry daily log	190(3)	$320.00
539.	Fail to surrender daily log	190(4)	$320.00
540.	Driver in possession of more than one daily log	190(5)	$320.00
540.1	Permit person to drive commercial motor vehicle not in accordance with the regulations	190(6)	$320.00
540.2	Fail to produce proof of exemption	191(7)	$85.00
540.3	Drive motor vehicle—toll device improperly affixed	191.2(1)	$85.00
540.4	Drive motor vehicle—no toll device	191.2(1)	$85.00
540.5	Drive motor vehicle—invalid toll device	191.2(1)	$85.00
540.6	Engage in activity to evade toll system	191.3(1)	$85.00
540.7	Engage in activity to obstruct toll system	191.3(1)	$85.00
540.8	Engage in activity to interfere with toll system	191.3(1)	$85.00
540.9	Use device to evade toll system	191.3(1)	$85.00
540.10	Use device to obstruct toll system	191.3(1)	$85.00
540.11	Use device to interfere with toll system	191.3(1)	$85.00
540.12	Sell device designed to interfere with toll system	191.3(4)	$85.00
540.13	Offer to sell device designed to interfere with toll system	191.3(4)	$85.00
540.14	Advertise for sale device designed to interfere with toll system	191.3(4)	$85.00
540.15	Sell device intended to interfere with toll system	191.3(4)	$85.00
540.16	Offer to sell device intended to interfere with toll system	191.3(4)	$85.00
540.17	Advertise for sale device intended to interfere with toll system	191.3(4)	$85.00
541.	Fail to report accident	199(1)	$85.00

Item	Column 1	Column 2 Section	Set Fine
542.	Fail to furnish required information	199(1)	$85.00
542.1	Fail to report accident—specified location	199(1.1)	$85.00
542.2	Fail to furnish required information	199(1.1)	$85.00
543.	Occupant fail to report accident	199(2)	$85.00
544.	Police officer fail to report accident	199(3)	$85.00
544.1	Insurer fail to notify Registrar as prescribed re irreparable or salvage vehicle	199.1(4)	$400.00
544.2	Specified person ail to notify Registrar as prescribed re irreparable or salvage vehicle	199.1(5)	$400.00
544.3	Misclassify vehicle as irreparable or salvage in notice to Registrar	199.1(7)	$400.00
544.4	Fail to notify permit holder as prescribed re irreparable or salvage vehicle	199.1(8)	$400.00
544.5	Fail to return permit or portion of permit for irreparable or salvage vehicle to Registrar as prescribed	199.1(19)	$400.00
544.6	Drive or draw irreparable or salvage vehicle	199.1(19)	$140.00
544.7	Permit irreparable or salvage vehicle to be driven or drawn	199.1(19)	$140.00
545.	Fail to remain	200(1)(a)	N.S.F.
546.	Fail to render assistance	200(1)(b)	N.S.F.
547.	Fail to give required information	200(1)(c)	N.S.F.
548.	Fail to report damage to property on highway	201	$85.00
549.	Fail to report damage to fence bordering highway	201	$85.00
550.	Medical practitioner—fail to report	203(1)	$85.00
551.	Optometrist—fail to report	204(1)	$85.00
552.	Failing to forward suspended licence to Registrar	211(2)	$85.00
553.	Fail to surrender suspended driver's licence	212(2)	$60.00
554.	Refuse to surrender suspended driver's licence	212(2)	$60.00
554.0.1	Fail to assist in examination of commercial vehicle	216.1(1)	$310.00
554.0.2	Fail to stop commercial vehicle for examination	216.1(2)	$310.00
554.0.3	Fail to surrender documents	216.1(3)	$310.00
554.0.4	Fail to furnish information	216.1(3)	$310.00
554.0.5	Fail to comply with direction of officer	216.1(7)	$310.00
554.1	Cyclist—fail to stop	218(2)	$85.00
554.2	Cyclist—fail to identify self	218(2)	$85.00
555.	Obstruct officer	225(5)	$260.00
556.	Withhold record	225(5)	$260.00
557.	Conceal record	225(5)	$260.00
558.	Destroy record	225(5)	$260.00

SCHEDULE	OVERWEIGHT	PENALTY
SCHEDULE A *Highway Traffic Act* **Set Fine**	0-2,499 kg.	$4.00 per 100 kg. or part kg.*
	2,500-4,999 kg.	$5.00 per 100 kg. or part kg.
	5,000-7,499 kg.	$6.00 per 100 kg. or part kg.
	7,500-9,999 kg.	$8.00 per 100 kg. or part kg.
	Over 10,000 kg.	N.S.F.

* Regardless of the overweight, the penalty will not be less than $100.00

SCHEDULE	SPEED OVER THE MAXIMUM LIMIT	SET FINES
SCHEDULE B *Highway Traffic Act* **Speeding**	a) 1-19 kilometres per hour over the maximum speed limit	$2.50 per kilometre
	b) 20-29 kilometres per hour over the maximum speed limit	$3.75 per kilometre
	c) 30-49 kilometres per hour over the maximum speed limit	$6.00 per kilometre
	d) 50 kilometres per hour or more over the maximum speed limit	No out of court settlement
SCHEDULE C *Highway Traffic Act* **Speeding—Photo Radar**	a) 1-19 kilometres per hour over the maximum speed limit	$2.50 per kilometre
	b) 20-34 kilometres per hour over the maximum speed limit	$3.75 per kilometre
	c) 35-49 kilometres per hour over the maximum speed limit	$6.00 per kilometre
	d) 50-60 kilometres per hour over the maximum speed limit	$8.00 per kilometre
	e) 61+ kilometres per hour over the maximum speed limit	No Set Fine
SCHEDULE D *Highway Traffic Act* **Speeding—Community Safety Zone**	a) 1-19 kilometres per hour over the maximum speed limit	$5.00 per kilometre
	b) 20-29 kilometres per hour over the maximum speed limit	$7.50 per kilometre
	c) 30-49 kilometres per hour over the maximum speed limit	$12.00 per kilometre
	d) 50 kilometres per hour or more over the maximum speed limit	No out of court settlement
SCHEDULE E *Highway Traffic Act* **Speeding—Construction Zone**	a) 1-19 kilometres per hour over the maximum speed limit	$2.50 per kilometre
	b) 20-29 kilometres per hour over the maximum speed limit	$3.75 per kilometre
	c) 30-49 kilometres per hour over the maximum speed limit	$6.00 per kilometre
	d) 50 kilometres per hour or more over the maximum speed limit	No out of court settlement
SCHEDULE F *Highway Traffic Act* **Speeding—Construction Zone Worker Present**	a) 1-19 kilometres per hour over the maximum speed limit	$5.00 per kilometre
	b) 20-29 kilometres per hour over the maximum speed limit	$7.50 per kilometre
	c) 30-49 kilometres per hour over the maximum speed limit	$12.00 per kilometre
	d) 50 kilometres per hour or more over the maximum speed limit	No out of court settlement

Provincial Offence Notice, Provincial Offence Summons, and Part III Summons

B

A blank Provincial Offence Notice (PON), a blank Provincial Offence Summons, and a blank Part III Summons are reproduced on the following pages. Identifying numbers have been removed. All documents are white in colour unless otherwise marked in headings. Make photocopies of these pages and practise filling them out properly.

Provincial Offence Notice (Top Page), front (white)

ICON Location Code *Code d'emplacement du RIII*	Offence number *Numéro d'infraction*

Form 1, *Provincial Offences Act,* **Ontario Court of Justice, O. Reg. 108/11**
Formulaire 1, Loi sur les infractions provinciales, *Cour de justice de l'Ontario, Règl. de l'Ont. 108/11*

Certificate of Offence
Procès-verbal d'infraction

I, _____
Je soussigné(e) _____ (print name / *nom en lettres moulées*)

believe and certify that on the day of   Y / A   M / M   D / J   Time / *heure*
crois et atteste que le   2 0 | | | | | | | | M

Name _____
Nom _____ (family / *nom de famille*)

_____
(given / *prénom*)   (initials / *initiales*)

Address _____
Adresse _____ (number and street / *numéro et nom de la rue*)

(municipality / *municipalité*)   (P.O. / C.P.)   (province)   (postal code / *code postal*)

Driver's licence no. / *N° de permis de conduire*   Juris / *Aut. Lég.*

Birth date / *Date de naissance* Y / A M / M D / J	Sex / *Sexe*	Motor vehicle involved / *Véhicule Impliqué* ☐ N / N	Collision involved / *Collision* ☐ Y / O	Witnesses / *Témoins* ☐ Y / O

At _____
À _____ (municipality / *municipalité*)

Did commit the offence of _____
A commis l'infraction de

_____

contrary to _____   sect.
contrairement à   *l'art.*

Plate no. *N° de la plaque d'immatriculation*	Juris *Aut. Lég.*	Commercial *Utilitaire* ☐ Y / O	CVOR *IUVU* ☐ Y / O	NSC *CNS* ☐ Y / O	Code
CVOR No. - NSC No. / *N° de l'IUVU - N° du CNS*					

And I further certify that I served an offence notice   ☐ Or other service date of:
personally upon the person charged on the offence date.   *Autre date de signification, le :*
J'atteste également qu'à la date de l'infraction, j'ai signifié, en
mains propres, un avis d'infraction à la personne accusée.

Signature of issuing Provincial Offences Officer *Signature de l'agent des infractions provinciale*	Officer No. *N° de l'agent*	Platoon *Peloton*	Unit *Unité*

Set fine of *Amende fixée de* $ *$*	Total payable *Montant total exigible* $ *$*	Total payable includes set fine, applicable victim fine surcharge and costs. / *Le montant total exigible comprend l'amende fixée, la suramende compensatoire applicable et les frais.*

Summons issued. You are   Y / A   M / M   D / J   Time / *heure*
required to appear in court on   2 0 | | | | | | M
Assignation. *Vous êtes* | Ct. room / *Salle* | at the Ontario Court of Justice POA Office at / *à la Cour*
tenu(e) de comparaître devant | *d'audience* | *de justice de l'Ontario, Bureau des infractions provinciales au*
le tribunal le

Deemed not to dispute charge under s. 9(1)(a) of the *Provincial Offences Act.* Set fine imposed. / *Réputé ne pas*
contester l'accusation aux termes de l'alinéa 9 (1) (a) de la Loi sur les infractions provinciales. Amende fixée imposée.

Y / A   M / M   D / J
2 0 | | | | |

_____
Justice / *Juge*

POA 0847 (November 2, 2011 / 2 novembre 2011) CSD

Provincial Offence Notice (Top Page), back (white) (issued to accused)

Affidavit of service upon defendant

I, _____ , make oath and

say that on the _____ day of _____ yr 20 ____ , I personally

served the offence notice/summons* issued with the attached certificate of offence upon
the defendant named in the attached certificate of offence.

*(strike out inapplicable term)

The Corporate defendant named in the attached certificate of offence by leaving it with

_____
Person Served

_____ , at _____
Position   Address

_____
Signature of Provincial Offences Officer

_____   _____
Badge number   Unit

Sworn before me at _____

This _____ day of _____ yr 20 _____

_____
A Justice of the Peace/Commissioner for Taking Affidavits

Court Record

Date	Adjourned to	Requested by	on Consent

Date	Pleads:	
	☐ Guilty	☐ Failed to appear
	☐ Not Guilty	☐ Charge Withdrawn
	☐ Guilty to a substituted offence	

Finding of Court

☐ Guilty / Convicted   ☐ Suspended sentence

☐ Dismissed   ☐ Fine Imposed _____

☐ S.9.1 Conviction   Costs [s.60(2)] _____

☐ Quashed   Time to pay

Reasons: _____

The POA provides that the victim fine surcharge (s.60.1) and
certain costs (s.60(1)) are added administratively upon conviction.

For Prosecutor	For Defendant
Reporter	Clerk

_____
Justice

Defaulted fine enforcement

_____
Justice

Provincial Offence Notice (Second Page), front (yellow) (issued to accused)

ICON Location Code *Code d'emplacement du RIII*	Offence number *Numéro d'infraction*

Form 3, *Provincial Offences Act*, Ontario Court of Justice, O. Reg. 108/11
Formulaire 3, Loi sur les infractions provinciales, Cour de justice de l'Ontario, Règl. de l'Ont. 108/11

Offence Notice
Avis d'infraction

(print name / nom en lettres moulées)

believes and certifies that on the day of
croit et atteste que le

Y / A   M / M   D / J   Time / *heure*
2 0   M

Name
Nom
       (family / nom de famille)

(given / prénom)   *(initials / Initiales)*

Address
Adresse
    (number and street / numéro et nom de la rue)

(municipality / municipalité)   *(P.O. / C.P.)*   *(province)*   *(postal code / code postal)*

Driver's licence no. / *N° de permis de conduire*   Juris / *Aut. lég.*

Birth date / *Date de naissance* Y / A M / M D / J	Sex / *Sexe*	Motor vehicle involved / *Véhicule impliqué* ☐ N / N	Collision involved / *Collision* ☐ Y / O	Witnesses / *Témoins* ☐ Y / O

At
À
    (municipality / municipalité)

Did commit the offence of
A commis l'infraction de

contrary to   sect.
contrairement à   , *art.*

Plate no. *N° de la plaque d'immatriculation*	Juris *Aut. lég.*	Commercial *Utilitaire* ☐ Y / O	CVOR *IUVU* ☐ Y / O	NSC *CNS* ☐ Y / O	Code

CVOR No. - NSC No. / *N° de l'IUVU - N° du CNS*

And I further certify that I served an offence notice
personally upon the person charged on the offence date.
*J'atteste également qu'à la date de l'infraction, j'ai signifié, en
mains propres, un avis d'infraction à la personne accusée.*

☐ Or other service date of:
Autre date de signification, le :

Signature of issuing Provincial Offences Officer *Signature de l'agent des infractions provinciales*	Officer No. *N° de l'agent*	Platoon *Peloton*	Unit *Unité*

Set fine of *Amende fixée de* $ $	Total payable *Montant total exigible* $ $	Total payable includes set fine, applicable victim fine surcharge and costs. / *Le montant total exigible comprend l'amende fixée, la suramende compensatoire pour l'aide aux victimes applicable et les frais.*

Important:
You have 15 days from the day you receive this notice to choose one of the options on the back of the notice.

Important :
À compter de la réception du présent avis, vous avez 15 jours pour choisir une des options décrites au verso de l'avis.

POA 0848 (March 15, 2014 / *15 mars 2014*) CSD

Provincial Offence Notice (Second Page), back (yellow)
(issued to accused when no out-of-court settlement)

Important – If you do not exercise one of the following options within 15 days of receiving this notice, you will be deemed not to dispute the charge and a justice may enter a conviction against you. Upon conviction, additional costs will be added to the total payable. If the fine goes into default, an administrative fee will be added and steps will be taken to enforce your defaulted fine. For example, information may be provided to a consumer reporting agency and for certain offences, including speeding, your driver's licence may be suspended.

Important – Si vous n'exercez pas l'une des options suivantes dans un délai de 15 jours à compter de la réception du présent avis, vous serez réputé(e) ne pas contester l'accusation et un juge pourra inscrire une déclaration de culpabilité contre vous. Sur déclaration de culpabilité, des frais additionnels s'ajouteront au montant total exigible. En cas de défaut de paiement de l'amende, des frais d'administration s'ajouteront et des mesures seront prises pour faire exécuter le paiement de votre amende. Par exemple, l'information pourra être transmise à une agence de renseignements sur le consommateur et dans le cas de certaines infractions, dont l'excès de vitesse, votre permis de conduire pourra être suspendu.

OPTION 1

Plea of Guilty – Voluntary Payment of Total Payable: I plead guilty and make payment of the total payable is enclosed (follow the instructions on the "payment notice").

Plaidoyer de culpabilité – paiement volontaire du montant total exigible : Je plaide coupable et le montant total exigible est joint au présent avis (suivre les instructions figurant sur « l'avis de paiement »).

OPTION 2

Plea of guilty – Submissions as to Penalty: I want to appear before a justice to enter a plea of guilty and make submissions as to penalty (amount of fine or time to pay). **Note: You must attend the court office** shown below within the times and days shown. Bring this notice with you.

Plaidoyer de culpabilité – observations au sujet de la peine : Je désire comparaître devant un juge pour inscrire un plaidoyer de culpabilité et présenter des observations au sujet de la peine (montant de l'amende ou délai de paiement). Remarque : Vous devez vous présenter au greffe du tribunal indiqué ci-après aux dates et heures indiquées. Apportez le présent avis.

Ontario Court of Justice, Provincial Offences Office

Cour de justice de l'Ontario, Bureau des infractions provinciales

OPTION 3

Trial Option, Ontario Court of Justice, Provincial Offences Office

Procès, Cour de justice de l'Ontario, Bureau des infractions provinciales

Notice of intention to appear in court:

☐ I intend to appear in court to enter a plea of not guilty **at the time and place set for the trial** and I wish to have the trial conducted in the English language.

I request a _____ language interpreter for the trial. (Leave blank if inapplicable.)

Note: If you **fail to notify** the court office of address changes, you may not receive important notices, e.g., your Notice of Trial. You may be convicted in your absence if you do not attend the trial.

_____
Signature

Changes to your address (if applicable):

_____

Telephone Number:

Avis d'intention de comparaître devant le tribunal :

☐ *J'ai l'intention de comparaître devant le tribunal pour inscrire un plaidoyer de non-culpabilité à l'heure et au lieu prévus pour le procès et je désire que le procès se déroule en français.*

Je demande l'aide d'un interprète en langue _____ pour le procès.

(À remplir, s'il y a lieu.)

Remarque : Si vous omettez de prévenir le greffe du tribunal de tout changement d'adresse, vous pourriez ne pas recevoir d'importants avis (p. ex., votre avis de procès). Si vous n'assistez pas au procès, vous pourriez être déclaré(e) coupable en votre absence.

_____
Signature

Changement d'adresse (le cas échéant) :

_____

Numéro de téléphone :

FOR INFORMATION ON ACCESS TO ONTARIO COURTS FOR PERSONS WITH DISABILITIES: [Court to insert information]
POUR OBTENIR DES RENSEIGNEMENTS SUR L'ACCÈS DES PERSONNES HANDICAPÉES AUX TRIBUNAUX DE L'ONTARIO : [ajouter l'information]

POA 0848 (March 15, 2014 / 15 mars 2014) CSD

Provincial Offence Notice (Third Page), front (back is blank)

| ICON Location Code Code d'emplacement du RAI | | Offence Number N° d'infraction | |

Computer Input/Record Document
Entrées informatiques/Registre des documents

Believes and certifies that on the day of
Croit et atteste que le

(Print name/nom en lettres moulées)

Y/A   M/M   D/J   Time/ À (Heure)

2 0   M

Name
Nom

Family/Nom de famille

Given/Prénom   Initials/Initiales

Address
Adresse

Number and street/Numéro et nom de la rue

Municipality/Municipalité   P.O./C.P.   Province   Postal code/Code postal

Driver's licence No./*Numéro de permis de conduire*

Jur.lg Aut. lég.

Birthdate/*Date de naissance*

| | Y/A | M/M | D/J | Sex Sexe | Motor Vehicle Involved Véhicule impliqué | Collision involved Collision | Witnesses Témoins |
| 1 | 9 | | | | ☐ N/N | ☐ Y/O | ☐ Y/O |

At/À

Did commit the offence of:
A commis l'infraction de :

Municipality/Municipalité

Contrary to:
Contrairement à :

Sect./*L'art.*

Plate number N° de plaque d'immatriculation	Juris Aut. lég.	Commercial Utilitaire	CVOR/*IUVU*	NSC/CNS	Code
		☐ Y/O	☐ Y/O	☐ Y/O	

CVOR No. - NSC No. / *N° de l'IUVU - N° du CNS*

| And I further certify that I served an offence notice personally upon the person charged on the offence date. *J'atteste également qu'à la date de l'infraction, j'ai signifié, en mains propres, un avis d'infraction à la personne accusée.* | ☐ Or other service date of: *Autre date de signification, le :* |

| Signature of issuing Provincial-Offences Officer *Signature de l'agent des infractions provinciales* | Officer No. *N° de l'agent* | Platoon Peloton | Unit Unité |

| Set fine of *Amende fixée de* $ | Total payable $ $ Montant total exigible | Total payable includes set fine, applicable victim fine surcharge and costs. *Le montant total exigible comprend l'amende fixée, la suramende compensatoire applicable et les frais.* |

Summons issued. You are required to appear in court on

Y/A   M/M   D/J   Time / À (Heure)

2 0   M

Assignation.
Vous êtes tenu(e) de comparaître devant le tribunal le

Ct. room/Salle d'audience

Provincial Offence Notice (Fourth Page), front

| ICON Location Code / Code d'emplacement du RIII | | Offence Number / N° d'infraction | |

Provincial Offences Act Ontario Court of Justice
Loi sur les infractions provinciales *Cour de justice de l'Ontario*
Enforcement Agency Record/*Registre des documents de l'agence d'exécution*

Believes and certifies that on the day of
Croit et atteste que le   (Print name/nom en lettres moulées)   Y/A   M/M   D/J   Time/ À (Heure)   2 0 ▢M

Name / *Nom*   Family/*Nom de famille*
Given/*Prénom*   Initials/*Initiales*

Address / *Adresse*   Number and street/*Numéro et nom de la rue*

Municipality/*Municipalité*   P.O./C.P.   Province   Postal code/*Code postal*   Juris Aut. lég.

Driver's licence No./*Numéro de permis de conduire*

Birthdate/*Date de naissance*   Y/A   M/M   D/J   Sex/Saxe   Motor Vehicle Involved/*Véhicule impliqué*   Collision Involved/Collision   Witnesses/*Témoins*
1 9   ▢N/N   ▢Y/O   ▢Y/O

At/*À*   Municipality/*Municipalité*

Did commit the offence of:
A commis l'infraction de :

Contrary to:
Contrairement à :

Sect./*L'art.*

Plate number / N° de plaque d'immatriculation	Juris Aut. lég.	Commercial Utilitaire	CVOR/*IUVU*	NSC/CNS	Code
		▢Y/O	▢Y/O	▢Y/O	

CVOR No. - NSC No. / *N° de l'IUVU - N° du CNS*

And I further certify that I served an offence notice personally upon the person charged on the offence date. *J'atteste également qu'à la date de l'infraction, j'ai signifié, en mains propres, un avis d'infraction à la personne accusée.*   ▢ Or other service date of: *Autre date de signification, le :*

| Signature of issuing Provincial Offences Officer / *Signature de l'agent des infractions provinciales* | Officer No. N° de l'agent | Platoon Peloton | Unit Unité |

| Set fine of *Amende fixée de* $ | **Total payable** $ $ **Montant total exigible** | Total payable includes set fine, applicable victim fine surcharge and costs. *Le montant total exigible comprend l'amende fixée, la suramende compensatoire applicable et les frais.* |

Summons issued. You are required to appear in court on   Y/A M/M D/J Time / À (Heure) 2 0 ▢M
Assignation. *Vous êtes tenu(e) de comparaître devant le tribunal le*   Ct. room/*Salle d'audience*   at the Ontario Court of Justice P.O.A. Office at *à la Cour de justice de l'Ontario, Bureau des infractions provinciales au*

Provincial Offence Notice (Fourth Page), back

Enforcement Agency notes/*Notes de l'agence d'exécution*

Provincial Offence Notice (Fifth Page), front

Provincial Offences Act, Ontario Court of Justice
Loi sur les infractions provinciales Cour de justice de l'Ontario

Payment Notice/Avis de Paiement

To pay the total payable shown, forward your payment of the total payable with this notice and the offence notice to the address shown on this notice. Sign the plea of guilty on the offence notice (Option 1). **Complete the following information /** *Veuillez donner les renseignements suivants*

Pour acquitter le montant total exigible, faites parvenir votre paiement, accompagné de cet avis et de l'avis d'infraction, à l'adresse qui figure sur le présent avis. N'oubliez pas de signer le plaidoyer de culpabilité sur l'avis d'infraction (Option 1).

Name/*Nom*

Address/*Adresse*

Telephone/*Téléphone*

☐ Cheque/money order enclosed
Chèque/mandat joint   ☐ Visa   ☐ Master Card

Card number
Nº de carte

Card expiry date   (month)   (year)
Date d'expiration   *(mois)*   *(année)*

See back for mailing address and instructions / *Pour connaître l'adresse postale et les instructions, prière de voir au verso.*

OFFENCE NUMBER
Nº D'INFRACTION

Make cheque or money order payable to
The City of ▯

and write the number of the offence notice on the front of the cheque/money order. Do not send cash or post-dated cheques with your payment. If you have any questions, call **705-739-4291.**

Dishonoured cheques will be subject to an administrative charge and the amount may be referred to collection services.

Cardholder's name
Nom du détenteur de la carte

Cardholder's signature
Signature du détenteur de la carte

Faire un chèque ou mandat à l'ordre du
La Ville de ▯

et écrire le numéro d'avis d'infraction au recto du chèque/mandat. Ne pas envoyer d'espèces ou de chèques postdatés avec votre paiement. Pour plus de renseignements, composez le **705-739-4291.**

Les chèques impayés sont assujettis à des frais administratifs et les renseignements concernant le montant impayé peuvent être transmis au service de recouvrement.

Total Payable
Montant total exigible

$ ▯ $

Date of Offence:
Date de l'infraction :

Online Payment Option
www.paytickets.ca

Option de paiement en ligne
www.paietickets.ca

Provincial Offence Notice (Fifth Page), back

Remember to keep a record of this payment.
N'oubliez pas de conserver un reçu de paiement.

Sign the plea of guilty on the offence notice (Option 1) and mail
the offence notice with this payment notice to

*Veuillez signer le plaidoyer de culpabilité sur l'avis d'infraction
(Option 1) et adresser l'avis d'infraction accompagné de l'avis
de paiement à l'adresse suivante*

Pay to:

ONTARIO COURT OF JUSTICE
PROVINCIAL OFFENCES OFFICE

Payez À:

COUR DE JUSTICE DE L'ONTARIO
BUREAU DES INFRACTIONS PROVINCIALES

Provincial Offence Summons, front (pink)

ICON Location Code
Code d'emplacement du RIII

Form 7, *Provincial Offences Act*, Ontario Court of Justice
Formulaire 7, Loi sur les infractions provinciales, Cour de justice de l'Ontario

Summons
Assignation

(print name / *nom en lettres moulées*)

believes and certifies that on the day of
croit et atteste que le

Y / A	M / M	D / J	Time / *heure*
2 0			M

Name
Nom

(family / *nom de famille*)

(given / *prénom*)   (initials / *initiales*)

Address
Adresse

(number and street / *numéro et nom de la rue*)

(municipality / *municipalité*)   (P.O. / C.P.)   (province)   (postal code / *code postal*)

Driver's licence no. / *N° de permis de conduire*   Juris / *Aut. Lég.*

Birth date / *Date de naissance*			Sex / *Sexe*	Motor vehicle involved / *Véhicule impliqué*	Collision involved / *Collision*	Witnesses / *Témoins*
Y / A	M / M	D / J		☐ N / N	☐ Y / O	☐ Y / O

At
À

(municipality / *municipalité*)

Did commit the offence of
A commis l'infraction de

contrary to   sect.
contrairement à   *l'art.*

Plate no. / *N° de la plaque d'immatriculation*	Juris *Aut. Lég.*	Commercial *Utilitaire*	CVOR *IUVU*	NSC *CNS*	Code
		☐ Y / O	☐ Y / O	☐ Y / O	

CVOR No. - NSC No. / *N° de l'IUVU - N° du CNS*

This is therefore to command you in Her Majesty's name to appear before the Ontario Court of Justice. / *Pour ces motifs, il vous est enjoint, au nom de Sa Majesté, de comparaître devant la Cour de justice de l'Ontario.*

Officer No. *N° de l'agent*	Platoon *Peloton*	Unit *Unité*

	Y / A	M / M	D / J	Time / *heure*	
2 0					M
	Ct. room / *Salle d'audience*		at the Ontario Court of Justice POA Office at / *à la Cour de justice de l'Ontario, Bureau des infractions provinciales au*		

And to attend thereafter as required by the court in order to be dealt with according to law, this summons is served under Part I of the *Provincial Offences Act*.
Et d'être présent(e) par la suite selon les exigences du tribunal, afin d'être traité(e) selon la loi. La présente assignation vous est signifiée conformément à la Partie I de la Loi sur les infractions provinciales.

Signature of Provincial Offences Officer / *Signature de l'agent des infractions provinciales*

POA 0861 (March 17, 2011 / *17 mars 2011*) CSD

Provincial Offence Summons, back (pink)

Note to defendant

You are required to appear in court. You may appear personally or by representative.

When you appear you may:
- (A) Plead guilty to the offence
  or
- (B) Set a date for trial
  or
- (C) The trial may proceed.

If you do not appear:
- (A) The court may issue a warrant for your arrest
  or
- (B) The trial may proceed in your absence.

Remarque à l'intention du défendeur/de la défenderesse

Vous êtes tenu(e) de comparaître devant le tribunal. Vous pouvez comparaître en personne ou par représentant.

Lors de votre comparution :
- *(A) soit vous pouvez plaider coupable à l'infraction;*
- *(B) soit vous pouvez fixer une date de procès;*
- *(C) soit le procès peut avoir lieu.*

Si vous ne comparaissez pas :
- *(A) soit le tribunal peut décerner un mandat d'arrestation contre vous;*
- *(B) soit le procès peut avoir lieu en votre absence.*

For information on access to Ontario Courts

for persons with disabilities, call **705-739-4291**

Pour plus de renseignements sur l'accès des personnes handicapées

*aux tribunaux de l'Ontario, composez le **705-739-4291***

Part III Summons (yellow) (First Page), front

Form 104 · Courts of Justice Act · R.R.O. 1990 Reg. 200
Formule 104 · Loi sur les tribunaux judiciaires · L.R.O. 1990, Règl. 200

Ontario Court of Justice
Province of Ontario

Cour de Justice de l'Ontario
Province de l'Ontario

SUMMONS TO DEFENDANT
SOMMATION ADRESSÉE AU DÉFENDEUR
Under Section 22 of the Provincial Offences Act
Aux termes de l'article 22 de la Loi sur les infractions provinciales

You are charged with the following offence
Vous êtes accusé(e) de l'infraction suivant

On the
Le ____ day of _____ yr *an* 20 ____ at *à* _____   **M**

Name
Nom _____
Last/*Nom de famille*   First/*Prénom*   Middle/*Initiale*

Address
Adresse _____
Number and Street/*N° et rue*

At
À _____
Municipality/*Municipalité*   P.O./C.P.   Province   Postal Code/*Code postal*

Municipality/*Municipalité*

Did commit the offence of
Vous avez commis l'infraction suivante _____

_____

_____

Contrary to
Par dérogation à _____

Section
Article

Therefore you are commanded in Her Majesty's name to appear before the Ontario Court of Justice	À ces causes, au nom de Sa Majesté, vous êtes sommé(e) de comparaître devant la Cour de Justice de l'Ontario
At À _____	
yr *an* 20 ____ at *à* ____ **M**	On the *Le* ____ day of _____ Courtroom/*Salle d'audience* _____
and to appear thereafter as required by the court in order to be dealt with according to law.	et de comparaître par la suite chaque fois que le tribunal l'exigera de façon à ce que vous soyez jugé(e) selon la Loi.

Issued this day - *Délivré ce jour*

yr *an* 20 ____

Signature of Provincial Offences Officer
Signature de l'agent d'infractions provinciales

Summons confirmed
Sommation confirmée ☐

Summons cancelled
Sommation annulée ☐

this *le* ____ day of _____ yr 20 *an* ____ by *par* ____

A Judge or Justice of the Peace
Juge ou juge de paix

Driver's Licence No.   *N° du permis de conduire*   Juris / *Juri*   Class *Catégorie*   Cond *Restriction*

Sex *Sexe*   Birthdate *Date de naissance* D/J M Y/A   Plate No. *N° de plaque d'immatriculation*   Juris *Juri*   Commercial ☐ Y/O

CVOR *CECVU* ☐ Y/O   NSC *CNS* ☐ Y/O   CVOR No. - NSC No. / *N° du CECVU - N° du CNS*

Officer No. *Matricule de l'agent de police*   Unit *Groupe*   Code   Witnesses *Témoins* ☐ Y/O   P.I.   P.D.   D R P

Note   This summons is issued under Part III of the Provincial Offences Act.
Cette sommation est émise aux termes de la partie III de la Loi sur les infractions provinciales.

POA 0516 (rev. 08/07)

Part III Summons (First Page), back

Affidavit of Service of Summons Under Section
26(6) of the Provincial Offences Act
R.R.O. 1990, Reg. 200

Ontario Court
of Justice

I,_____, of_____ ,
a provincial offences officer make oath and say as follows, that on the
_____ day of _____ , yr 20_____ , I did serve
the summons in the manner indicated below:
(Check one)

(a) ☐   by delivering it personally on the defendant

(b) ☐   I could not conveniently find the defendant and left the summons for
him/her at his/her last known or usual place of abode with

_____

_____ ,an

inmate thereof who appeared to be at least sixteen years of age.

Sworn before me at _____
_____   ⎫   _____
                                    Signature
this_____ day of _____ , yr 20_____ ⎬ No. _____ Div. _____
_____   ⎭
A Justice of the Peace / Commissioner for Taking Affidavits

Part III Summons (Second Page), front

Form 104 / Formule 104	Courts of Justice Act R.R.O. 1990 Reg. 200 / Loi sur les tribunaux judiciaires L.R.O. 1990, Règl. 200

SUMMONS TO DEFENDANT
SOMMATION ADRESSÉE AU DÉFENDEUR
Under Section 22 of the Provincial Offences Act
Aux termes de l'article 22 de la Loi sur les infractions provinciales

Ontario Court of Justice
Province of Ontario
Cour de Justice de l'Ontario
Province de l'Ontario

You are charged with the following offence
Vous êtes accusé(e) de l'infraction suivant

On the / Le _____ day of _____ yr / an 20 _____ at / à _____   **M**

Name / Nom
Last/Nom de famille   First/Prénom   Middle/Initiale

Address / Adresse
Number and Street/N° et rue

At / À
Municipality/*Municipalité*   P.O./C.P.   Province   Postal Code/Code postal

Municipality/*Municipalité*

Did commit the offence of
Vous avez commis l'infraction suivante

Contrary to
Par dérogation à

Section
Article

Therefore you are commanded in Her Majesty's name to appear before the Ontario Court of Justice	*À ces causes, au nom de Sa Majesté, vous êtes sommé(e) de comparaître devant la Cour de Justice de l'Ontario*
At / À	On the / Le _____ day of _____
yr / an 20 _____ at / à _____ **M**	Courtroom/*Salle d'audience*
and to appear thereafter as required by the court in order to be dealt with according to law.	*et de comparaître par la suite chaque fois que le tribunal l'exigera de façon à ce que vous soyez jugé(e) selon la Loi.*

Issued this day - *Délivré ce jour*
yr / an 20 _____

Signature of Provincial Offences Officer
Signature de l'agent d'infractions provinciales

Summons confirmed / *Sommation confirmée* ☐   Summons cancelled / *Sommation annulée* ☐

this / le _____ day of _____ yr / an 20 _____ by / par _____   A Judge or Justice of the Peace / *Juge ou juge de paix*

Driver's Licence No.   *N° du permis de conduire*   Juris / Juri   Class / *Catégorie*   Cond / *Restriction*

Sex / Sexe   Birthdate / *Date de naissance*   D/J   M   Y/A   Plate No. / *N° de plaque d'immatriculation*   Juris / Juri   Commercial ☐ Y/O

CVOR / CECVU ☐ Y/O   NSC / CNS ☐ Y/O   CVOR No. - NSC No. / *N° du CECVU - N° du CNS*

Officer No. / *Matricule de l'agent de police*   Unit / *Groupe*

Defendant's Copy
Copie du défendeur

Note   This summons is issued under Part III of the Provincial Offences Act.
Cette sommation est émise aux termes de la partie III de la Loi sur les infractions provinciales.

Part III Summons (Second Page), back

Note to Defendant
You may appear personally, by agent or by counsel.

If you do not appear:
a) the court may issue a warrant for your arrest, or
b) your trial may proceed in your absence and evidence be taken, and
c) if you are convicted, you could be sentenced in your absence, and
d) depending on the offence of which you have been convicted, you could be sentenced to jail and a warrant issued for your arrest

If you do appear:
a) the trial may proceed; or
b) you, or the prosecutor, may ask the court to adjourn your case to another date. The court may grant or refuse such a request.

Remarque à l'adresse du prévenu
Vous pouvez comparaître personnellement, par mandataire, ou par un avocat.

Si vous ne comparaissez pas:
a) *le tribunal peut émettre un mandat d'arrestation à votre encontre,*
b) *votre procès peut se dérouler en votre absence et des témoignages entendus,*
c) *si vous êtes reconnu(e) coupable, votre peine pourrait être prononcée en votre absence,*
d) *selon l'intraction pour laquelle vous avez été condamné(e), vous pourriez recevoir une peine d'emprisonnement et un mandat d'arrestation pourrait être émis à votre encontre.*

Si vous comparaissez:
a) *le procès peut être tenu; ou*
b) *vous pouvez, vous ou le poursuivant, demander au tribunal un ajournement. Le tribunal peut accorder ou refuser cette demande.*

For information on access to Ontario courts For persons with disabilities, call **1-800-387-4456** Toronto Area **416-326-0111**

Pour plus de renseignements sur l'accès des personnes handicapées Aux tribunaux de l'Ontario, composez le **1-800-387-4456** Région de Toronto **416-326-0111**

Part III Summons (Third Page), front only (blank back)

Form 104
Courts of Justice Act
R.R.O. 1990 Reg. 200
Formule 104
Loi sur les tribunaux judiciaires
L.R.O. 1990, Règl. 200

SUMMONS TO DEFENDANT
SOMMATION ADRESSÉE AU DÉFENDEUR
Under Section 22 of the Provincial Offences Act
Aux termes de l'article 22 de la Loi sur les infractions provinciales

Ontario Court of Justice
Province of Ontario
Cour de Justice de l'Ontario
Province de l'Ontario

You are charged with the following offence
Vous êtes accusé(e) de l'infraction suivant

On the
Le _____ day of _____ yr *an* 20 ___ at *à* ___ **M**

Name
Nom
Last/*Nom de famille*   First/*Prénom*   Middle/*Initiale*

Address
Adresse
Number and Street/*N° et rue*

At
À
Municipality/*Municipalité*   P.O./*C.P.*   Province   Postal Code/*Code postal*

Municipality/*Municipalité*

Did commit the offence of
Vous avez commis l'infraction suivante

Contrary to
Par dérogation à _____

Section
Article

Therefore you are commanded in Her Majesty's name to appear before the Ontario Court of Justice	**À ces causes, au nom de Sa Majesté, vous êtes sommé(e) de comparaître devant la Cour de Justice de l'Ontario**
At *À*	On the *Le* _____ day of _____
yr *an* 20 ___ at *à* ___ **M**	Courtroom/*Salle d'audience*
and to appear thereafter as required by the court in order to be dealt with according to law.	et de comparaître par la suite chaque fois que le tribunal l'exigera de façon à ce que vous soyez jugé(e) selon la Loi.

Issued this day - *Délivré ce jour*

yr *an* 20 ___

Signature of Provincial Offences Officer
Signature de l'agent d'infractions provinciales

Summons confirmed
Sommation confirmée ☐

Summons cancelled
Sommation annulée ☐

this _____ day of _____ yr 20 ___ by _____
le *an* *par*
A Judge or Justice of the Peace
Juge ou juge de paix

Driver's Licence No.   *N° du permis de conduire*   Juris / *Juri*   Class *Catégorie*   Cond *Restriction*

Sex
Sexe   Birthdate
Date de naissance   Plate No.
N° de plaque d'immatriculation   Juris *Juri*   Commercial
D/J   M   Y/A   Y/O

CVOR
CECVU
Y/O   NSC
CNS
Y/O   CVOR No. - NSC No. / *N° du CECVU - N° du CNS*

Officer No.
Matricule de l'agent de police   Unit
Groupe   Code   Witnesses
Témoins
Y/O   P.I.   P.D.   D   R   P

Note   This summons is issued under Part III of the Provincial Offences Act.
Cette sommation est émise aux termes de la partie III de la Loi sur les infractions provinciales.

POA 0516 (rev. 08/07)

Part III Summons (Fourth Page), front

Form 104 / Formule 104
Courts of Justice Act
R.R.O. 1990 Reg. 200
Loi sur les tribunaux judiciaires
L.R.O. 1990, Régl. 200

SUMMONS TO DEFENDANT
SOMMATION ADRESSÉE AU DÉFENDEUR
Under Section 22 of the Provincial Offences Act
Aux termes de l'article 22 de la Loi sur les infractions provinciales

Ontario Court of Justice
Province of Ontario
Cour de Justice de l'Ontario
Province de l'Ontario

You are charged with the following offence
Vous êtes accusé(e) de l'infraction suivant

On the / Le ____ day of ____ yr / an 20 ____ at / à ____ **M**

Name / Nom
Last/Nom de famille | First/Prénom | Middle/Initiale

Address / Adresse
Number and Street/N° et rue

At / À
Municipality/Municipalité | P.O./C.P. | Province | Postal Code/Code postal

Did commit the offence of
Vous avez commis l'infraction suivante

Municipality/Municipalité

Contrary to / Par dérogation à

Section / Article

Therefore you are commanded in Her Majesty's name to appear before the Ontario Court of Justice	À ces causes, au nom de Sa Majesté, vous êtes sommé(e) de comparaître devant la Cour de Justice de l'Ontario
At / À	
yr / an 20 ____ at / à ____ **M**	On the / Le ____ day of ____ Courtroom/Salle d'audience
and to appear thereafter as required by the court in order to be dealt with according to law.	et de comparaître par la suite chaque fois que le tribunal l'exigera de façon à ce que vous soyez jugé(e) selon la Loi.

Issued this day - Délivré ce jour
yr / an 20 ____

Signature of Provincial Offences Officer
Signature de l'agent d'infractions provinciales

Summons confirmed / Sommation confirmée ☐
Summons cancelled / Sommation annulée ☐

this / le ____ day of ____ yr / an 20 ____ by / par ____
A Judge or Justice of the Peace
Juge ou juge de paix

Driver's Licence No. / N° du permis de conduire
Juris / Juri | Class Catégorie | Cond Restriction

Sex / Sexe | Birthdate / Date de naissance D/J M Y/A | Plate No. / N° de plaque d'immatriculation | Juris / Juri | Commercial ☐ Y/O

CVOR / CECVU ☐ Y/O | NSC / CNS ☐ Y/O | CVOR No. - NSC No. / N° du CECVU - N° du CNS

Officer No. / Matricule de l'agent de police | Unit / Groupe | Code | Witnesses / Témoins ☐ Y/O | P.I. | P.D. | D R P

Note This summons is issued under Part III of the Provincial Offences Act.
Cette sommation est émise aux termes de la partie III de la Loi sur les infractions provinciales.

POA 0516 (rev. 08/07)

Part III Summons (Fourth Page), back

Police Record - Court Disposition

Date _____ ☐ Guilty   ☐ Withdrawn
                                ☐ Dismissed

Sentence
_____
_____
_____
_____
_____
_____
_____
_____
_____
_____
_____
_____
_____
_____
_____
_____
_____
_____
_____

Suspect Apprehension Pursuits Regulation

C

O Reg 266/10 in force July 5, 2010

Interpretation

1(1) For the purposes of this Regulation, a suspect apprehension pursuit occurs when a police officer attempts to direct the driver of a motor vehicle to stop, the driver refuses to obey the officer and the officer pursues in a motor vehicle for the purpose of stopping the fleeing motor vehicle or identifying the fleeing motor vehicle or an individual in the fleeing motor vehicle.

(2) A suspect apprehension pursuit is discontinued when police officers are no longer pursuing a fleeing motor vehicle for the purpose of stopping the fleeing motor vehicle or identifying the fleeing motor vehicle or an individual in the fleeing motor vehicle.

Initiating or continuing pursuit

2(1) A police officer may pursue, or continue to pursue, a fleeing motor vehicle that fails to stop,

(a) if the police officer has reason to believe that a criminal offence has been committed or is about to be committed; or

(b) for the purposes of motor vehicle identification or the identification of an individual in the vehicle.

(2) Before initiating a suspect apprehension pursuit, a police officer shall determine that there are no alternatives available as set out in the written procedures of,

(a) the police force of the officer established under subsection 6(1), if the officer is a member of an Ontario police force as defined in the *Interprovincial Policing Act, 2009*;

(b) a police force whose local commander was notified of the appointment of the officer under subsection 6(1) of the *Interprovincial Policing Act, 2009*, if the officer was appointed under Part II of that Act; or

(c) the local police force of the local commander who appointed the officer under subsection 15(1) of the *Interprovincial Policing Act, 2009*, if the officer was appointed under Part III of that Act.

(3) A police officer shall, before initiating a suspect apprehension pursuit, determine whether in order to protect public safety the immediate need to apprehend an individual in the fleeing motor vehicle or the need to identify the fleeing motor vehicle or an individual in the fleeing motor vehicle outweighs the risk to public safety that may result from the pursuit.

(4) During a suspect apprehension pursuit, a police officer shall continually reassess the determination made under subsection (3) and shall discontinue the pursuit when the risk

to public safety that may result from the pursuit outweighs the risk to public safety that may result if an individual in the fleeing motor vehicle is not immediately apprehended or if the fleeing motor vehicle or an individual in the fleeing motor vehicle is not identified.

(5) No police officer shall initiate a suspect apprehension pursuit for a non-criminal offence if the identity of an individual in the fleeing motor vehicle is known.

(6) A police officer engaging in a suspect apprehension pursuit for a non-criminal offence shall discontinue the pursuit once the fleeing motor vehicle or an individual in the fleeing motor vehicle is identified.

Notice of pursuit

3(1) A police officer shall notify a dispatcher when the officer initiates a suspect apprehension pursuit.

(2) The dispatcher shall notify a communications supervisor or road supervisor, if a supervisor is available, that a suspect apprehension pursuit has been initiated.

Order to discontinue pursuit

4(1) A communications or road supervisor shall order police officers to discontinue a suspect apprehension pursuit if, in his or her opinion, the risk to public safety that may result from the pursuit outweighs the risk to public safety that may result if an individual in the fleeing motor vehicle is not immediately apprehended or if the fleeing motor vehicle or an individual in the fleeing motor vehicle is not identified.

(2) A police officer who receives an order under subsection (1) shall obey the order even if the officer is not a member of the police force of the communications or road supervisor who made the order.

Policies

5. Every police services board shall establish policies that are consistent with this Regulation about suspect apprehension pursuits.

Procedures for tactics

6(1) Every police force shall establish written procedures that set out the tactics that may be used in its jurisdiction,

(a) as an alternative to suspect apprehension pursuit; and

(b) for following or stopping a fleeing motor vehicle.

(2) Every police force shall establish written procedures that are consistent with this Regulation about suspect apprehension pursuits in its jurisdiction.

Use of firearm

7. A police officer shall not discharge his or her firearm for the sole purpose of attempting to stop a fleeing motor vehicle.

Pursuit in unmarked police motor vehicle

8. A police officer in an unmarked police motor vehicle shall not engage in a suspect apprehension pursuit unless a marked police motor vehicle is not readily available and the police officer believes that it is necessary to immediately apprehend an individual in the fleeing motor vehicle or to identify the fleeing motor vehicle or an individual in the fleeing motor vehicle.

Stopping a motor vehicle

9(1) During a suspect apprehension pursuit, a police officer shall consider the tactics for stopping a motor vehicle as set out in the written procedures of,

(a) the police force of the officer established under subsection 6(1), if the officer is a member of an Ontario police force as defined in the *Interprovincial Policing Act, 2009*;

(b) a police force whose local commander was notified of the appointment of the officer under subsection 6(1) of the *Interprovincial Policing Act, 2009*, if the officer was appointed under Part II of that Act; or

(c) the local police force of the local commander who appointed the officer under subsection 15(1) of the *Interprovincial Policing Act, 2009*, if the officer was appointed under Part III of that Act.

(2) A police officer may intentionally cause a police motor vehicle to come into physical contact with a fleeing motor vehicle for the purposes of stopping it only if the officer believes on reasonable grounds that to do so is necessary to immediately protect against loss of life or serious bodily harm.

(3) In considering the action mentioned in subsection (2), a police officer shall assess the effect of the action on the safety of other members of the public and police officers.

(4) Despite subsection (2), a police officer may cause a police motor vehicle to come into physical contact with a fleeing motor vehicle for the purposes of pinning it if the fleeing motor vehicle has lost control or collided with an object and come to a stop and the driver of the motor vehicle continues to try to use it to flee.

(5) Nothing in subsection (2) precludes police officers involved in a pursuit, with assistance from other police officers in motor vehicles, from attempting to safely position the police motor vehicles in a manner to prevent the movement either forward, backward or sideways of a fleeing motor vehicle.

(6) Every police force shall ensure that its police officers receive training about the intentional physical contact between motor vehicles that is described in subsection (2).

(7) The training must address the matters described in subsections (2) and (3).

Other procedures

10(1) Every police force shall establish written procedures on the management and control of suspect apprehension pursuits.

(2) The procedures must describe the responsibilities of police officers, dispatchers, communications supervisors and road supervisors.

(3) The procedures must describe the equipment that is available for implementing alternative tactics.

Supervision

11(1) If more than one jurisdiction is involved in a suspect apprehension pursuit, the supervisor in the jurisdiction in which the pursuit begins has decision-making responsibility for the pursuit.

(2) The supervisor may hand over decision-making responsibility to a supervisor in another jurisdiction involved in the pursuit.

Application of code of conduct

12. A police officer does not breach the code of conduct when deciding not to initiate or choosing to discontinue a suspect apprehension pursuit because he or she has reason to believe that the risk to public safety that may result from the pursuit outweighs the risk to public safety that may result if an individual in the fleeing motor vehicle is not immediately apprehended or if the fleeing motor vehicle or an individual in the fleeing motor vehicle is not identified.

Training

13. Every police force shall ensure that its police officers, dispatchers, communications supervisors and road supervisors receive training accredited by the Solicitor General about suspect apprehension pursuits.

Records

14(1) If a police officer engages in a suspect apprehension pursuit and the officer is a member of an Ontario police force as defined in the *Interprovincial Policing Act, 2009*, the police force of which the officer is a member shall ensure that the particulars of the pursuit are recorded on a form and in a manner approved by the Solicitor General.

(2) If a police officer engages in a suspect apprehension pursuit and the officer is appointed under the *Interprovincial Policing Act, 2009*, the officer shall report the particulars of the pursuit to the appointing official or local commander who appointed the officer under that Act and that person shall ensure that the particulars are recorded on a form and in a manner approved by the Solicitor General.

15. Omitted (revokes other Regulations).

16. Omitted (provides for coming into force of provisions of this Regulation).

Police Services Act, Code of Conduct

D

O Reg 268/10

Schedule
Code of Conduct

1. In this code of conduct,

"marital status" means the status of being married, single, widowed, divorced or separated and includes the status of living with a person in a conjugal relationship outside marriage;

"record" means any record of information, however recorded, whether in printed form, on film, by electronic means or otherwise, and includes correspondence, a memorandum, a book, a plan, a map, a drawing, a diagram, a pictorial or graphic work, a photograph, a film, a microfilm, a sound recording, a videotape, a machine readable record, any other documentary material, regardless of physical form or characteristics, and any copy of the record.

2(1) Any chief of police or other police officer commits misconduct if he or she engages in,

(a) DISCREDITABLE CONDUCT, in that he or she,

(i) fails to treat or protect persons equally without discrimination with respect to police services because of race, ancestry, place of origin, colour, ethnic origin, citizenship, creed, sex, sexual orientation, age, marital status, family status or disability,

(ii) uses profane, abusive or insulting language that relates to a person's race, ancestry, place of origin, colour, ethnic origin, citizenship, creed, sex, sexual orientation, age, marital status, family status or disability,

(iii) is guilty of oppressive or tyrannical conduct towards an inferior in rank,

(iv) uses profane, abusive or insulting language to any other member of a police force,

(v) uses profane, abusive or insulting language or is otherwise uncivil to a member of the public,

(vi) wilfully or negligently makes any false complaint or statement against any member of a police force,

(vii) assaults any other member of a police force,

(viii) withholds or suppresses a complaint or report against a member of a police force or about the policies of or services provided by the police force of which the officer is a member,

(ix) is guilty of a criminal offence that is an indictable offence or an offence punishable upon summary conviction,

(x) contravenes any provision of the Act or the regulations, or

(xi) acts in a disorderly manner or in a manner prejudicial to discipline or likely to bring discredit upon the reputation of the police force of which the officer is a member;

(b) INSUBORDINATION, in that he or she,

(i) is insubordinate by word, act or demeanour, or

(ii) without lawful excuse, disobeys, omits or neglects to carry out any lawful order;

(c) Neglect of Duty, in that he or she,

(i) without lawful excuse, neglects or omits promptly and diligently to perform a duty as,

(A) a member of the police force of which the officer is a member, if the officer is a member of an Ontario police force as defined in the *Interprovincial Policing Act, 2009*, or

(B) a police officer appointed under the *Interprovincial Policing Act, 2009*,

(ii) fails to comply with any provision of Ontario Regulation 267/10 (Conduct and Duties of Police Officers Respecting Investigations by the Special Investigations Unit) made under the Act,

(iii) fails to work in accordance with orders, or leaves an area, detachment, detail or other place of duty, without due permission or sufficient cause,

(iv) by carelessness or neglect permits a prisoner to escape,

(v) fails, when knowing where an offender is to be found, to report him or her or to make due exertions for bringing the offender to justice,

(vi) fails to report a matter that it is his or her duty to report,

(vii) fails to report anything that he or she knows concerning a criminal or other charge, or fails to disclose any evidence that he or she, or any person within his or her knowledge, can give for or against any prisoner or defendant,

(viii) omits to make any necessary entry in a record,

(ix) feigns or exaggerates sickness or injury to evade duty,

(x) is absent without leave from or late for any duty, without reasonable excuse, or

(xi) is improperly dressed, dirty or untidy in person, clothing or equipment while on duty;

(d) DECEIT, in that he or she,

(i) knowingly makes or signs a false statement in a record,

(ii) wilfully or negligently makes a false, misleading or inaccurate statement pertaining to official duties, or

(iii) without lawful excuse, destroys or mutilates a record or alters or erases an entry in a record;

(e) BREACH OF CONFIDENCE, in that he or she,

(i) divulges any matter which it is his or her duty to keep secret,

(ii) gives notice, directly or indirectly, to any person against whom any warrant or summons has been or is about to be issued, except in the lawful execution of the warrant or service of the summons,

(iii) without proper authority, communicates to the media or to any unauthorized person any matter connected with,

(A) the police force of which the officer is a member, if the officer is a member of an Ontario police force as defined in the *Interprovincial Policing Act, 2009*, or

(B) the police force with which the officer is working on a joint forces operation or investigation, if the officer is appointed as a police officer under the *Interprovincial Policing Act, 2009,* or

(iv) without proper authority, shows to any person not a member of the police force described in sub-subclause (iii)(A) or (B), as the case may be, or to any unauthorized member of that police force any record that is the property of that police force;

(f) Corrupt Practice, in that he or she,

(i) offers or takes a bribe,

(ii) fails to account for or to make a prompt, true return of money or property received in an official capacity,

(iii) directly or indirectly solicits or receives a gratuity or present without the consent of,

(A) the chief of police, if the officer is a member of an Ontario police force as defined in the *Interprovincial Policing Act, 2009,* or

(B) the person who appointed the police officer under Part II or III of the *Interprovincial Policing Act, 2009,*

(iv) places himself or herself under a pecuniary or other obligation to a licensee if a member of the following police force may have to report or give evidence concerning the granting or refusing of a licence to the licensee:

(A) the police force of which the officer is a member, if the officer is a member of an Ontario police force as defined in the *Interprovincial Policing Act, 2009,* or

(B) the police force with which the officer is working on a joint forces operation or investigation, if the officer is appointed as a police officer under the *Interprovincial Policing Act, 2009,* or

(v) improperly uses his or her character and position as a member of a police force for private advantage;

(g) Unlawful or Unnecessary Exercise of Authority, in that he or she,

(i) without good and sufficient cause makes an unlawful or unnecessary arrest,

(i.1) without good and sufficient cause makes an unlawful or unnecessary physical or psychological detention,*

(ii) uses any unnecessary force against a prisoner or other person contacted in the execution of duty, or

(iii) collects or attempts to collect identifying information about an individual from the individual in the circumstances to which Ontario Regulation 58/16 (Collection of Identifying Information in Certain Circumstances—Prohibition and Duties) made under the Act applies, other than as permitted by that regulation;**

(h) Damage to Clothing or Equipment, in that he or she,

(i) wilfully or carelessly causes loss or damage to any article of clothing or equipment, or to any record or other property of,

(A) the police force of which the officer is a member, if the officer is a member of an Ontario police force as defined in the *Interprovincial Policing Act, 2009,* or

(B) the police force with which the officer is working on a joint forces operation or investigation, if the officer is appointed as a police officer under the *Interprovincial Policing Act, 2009,* or

(ii) fails to report loss or damage, however caused, as soon as practicable; or

---

*   New s 2(1)(g)(i.1) comes into effect on January 1, 2017.

** New s 2(1)(g)(iii) comes into effect on January 1, 2017.

(i) CONSUMING DRUGS OR ALCOHOL IN A MANNER PREJUDICIAL TO DUTY, in that he or she,

(i) is unfit for duty, while on duty, through consumption of drugs or alcohol,

(ii) is unfit for duty when he or she reports for duty, through consumption of drugs or alcohol,

(iii) except with the consent of a superior officer or in the discharge of duty, consumes or receives alcohol from any other person while on duty, or

(iv) except in the discharge of duty, demands, persuades or attempts to persuade another person to give or purchase or obtain for a member of a police force any alcohol or illegal drugs while on duty.

(2) A police officer does not commit misconduct under subclause (1)(e)(iii) if he or she engages in the described activity in his or her capacity as an authorized representative of an association, as defined in section 2 of the Act.

(3) A police officer does not commit misconduct under subclause (1)(f)(iii) if he or she engages in the described activity in his or her capacity as an authorized representative of an association, as defined in section 2 of the Act, or of a work-related professional organization.

3. Any chief of police or other police officer also commits misconduct if he or she conspires in, abets or is knowingly an accessory to any misconduct described in section 2.

Relevant Legislation

Acts

Ambulance Act, RSO 1990, c A.19

Canadian Charter of Rights and Freedoms, Part I of the
Constitution Act, 1982, being Schedule B to the *Canada Act
1982* (UK), 1982, c. 11

Compulsory Automobile Insurance Act, RSO 1990, c C.25

Constitution Act, 1867 (UK), 30 & 31 Vict, c 3, reprinted in RSC
1985, Appendix II, No 5

Coroners Act, RSO 1990, c C.37

Courts of Justice Act, RSO 1990, c C.43

Criminal Code, RSC 1985, c C-46

Heritage Hunting and Fishing Act, 2002, SO 2002, c 10

Highway Traffic Act, RSO 1990, c H.8

Motor Vehicle Safety Act, SC 1993, c 16

Motorized Snow Vehicles Act, RSO 1990, c M.44

Municipal Act, 2001, SO 2001, c 25

National Capital Act, RSC 1985, c N-4

Photo Card Act, 2008, SO 2008, c 17

Police Services Act, RSO 1990, c P.15

Provincial Offences Act, RSO 1990, c P.33

Public Transportation and Highway Improvement Act, RSO 1990,
c P.50

Public Vehicles Act, RSO 1990, c P.54

Road Safety Act, 2009, SO 2009, c 5

Stronger City of Toronto for a Stronger Ontario Act, SO 2006, c 11

Toronto Municipal Code, 2015, c 915

*Transportation Statute Law Amendment Act (Making Ontario's
Roads Safer)*, SO 2015, c 14

Regulations Under the Highway Traffic Act

*Definitions and Requirements Under Section 142.1 of the Act
(Yielding Right of Way to Buses)*, O Reg 393/02

Demerit Point System, O Reg 339/94

Display Screens and Hand-Held Devices, O Reg 366/09

Drivers' Licences, O Reg 340/94

Equipment, RRO 1990, Reg 587

General, RRO 1990, Reg 596

Ignition Interlock Devices, O Reg 251/02

Long-Term Vehicle Impoundment Under Section 55.1 of the Act,
O Reg 631/98

Races, Contests and Stunts, O Reg 455/07

Safety Helmets, RRO 1990, Reg 610

Seat Belt Assembies, RRO 1990, Reg 613

Short-term Vehicle Impoundment under Section 55.2 of the Act,
O Reg 415/10

Vehicle Permits, RRO 1990, Reg 628

Regulations Under the Police Services Act

General, O Reg 268/10

Suspect Apprehension Pursuits, O Reg 266/10

Regulations Under
the Provincial Offences Act

Proceedings Commenced by Certificate of Offence, RRO 1990, Reg 950

Victim Fine Surcharges, O Reg 161/00

Regulation under
the Courts of Justice Act

Rules of Civil Procedure, RRO 1990, Reg 194

Glossary

A

actus reus the act or omission that is required to sustain a conviction

arrest results when a person's physical liberty is inhibited by conveying an intention to restrict the person's liberty; the actual restraint may involve physical force, although an arrest may occur without the use of force

B

bill of lading a receipt for merchandise that accompanies the merchandise when it is being transported from one place to another; it should provide detailed information about the cargo carried by a commercial vehicle

burden of proof describes the duty or obligation of a person to offer evidence to support or establish a fact

C

chain a surveyor's measure, consisting of a chain or line that is 66 feet long

consolidated statutes and regulations the current version of statutes and regulations that includes all amendments and revisions made to the original content; the printed consolidated version is current as of the time of publication, whereas the online consolidated version includes the most recent amendments and revisions; Ontario's e-Laws website lists the latest consolidation date for any statute, along with all previous consolidations

CVOR certificate the Commercial Vehicle Operator's Registration Certificate, which must be held by the operator of a commercial vehicle unless he or she is excluded or exempted under the HTA; requires commercial vehicle operators to comply with safety requirements under the HTA and other legislation

E

equestrian a person riding a horse

exigent requiring immediate aid or action

F

facts in issue all of the elements of an offence

forfeit to the Crown the government's right to seize property held or used illegally; the right is usually set out in a statute or regulation

G

gross weight the total weight of the motor vehicle, its trailer, and the load it is carrying; can be determined only by weigh scales used by the Ministry of Transportation

L

legal presumption the proof of one fact by the Crown means that a second fact is presumed to be true without the Crown having to adduce evidence to prove the second fact; however, the accused may present evidence to disprove the second fact, thereby rebutting the presumption

M

mens rea the mental element or intention that is required to sustain a conviction

motor vehicle includes an automobile, a motor-assisted bicycle (moped), or a motorcycle (including a motor scooter), unless otherwise indicated in the HTA, as well as any other vehicle propelled by anything other than muscular power; farm tractors, self-propelled implements of husbandry (such as reapers and combines), road-building machinery, and traction engines are not considered motor vehicles

O

oxidizer a substance that combines with oxygen, which may be quite volatile, flammable, or otherwise chemically active and therefore dangerous

P

prima facie a fact presumed to be true unless it is disproved

prohibition order made on conviction for a CC driving offence and disqualifies a person from driving a motor vehicle as defined in the CC

R

registered gross weight the weight of the vehicle and the load set out in the motor vehicle permit; the owner has prepaid the government to have the legal right to haul loads of that size in that vehicle on the highway

regulations rules made by Cabinet (although actually by ministry officials under the authority of a statute) that deal in more detail with matters covered by the statute itself. To be legitimate, the power to authorize and create a regulation must be found in a specific statute's regulation-making powers, usually set out at the end of a statute.

reverse-onus clause a provision in a statute that shifts the burden of proof from the person who normally bears it to a named person in a specific situation. For example, in criminal law, a reverse-onus clause may shift the burden of proof from the Crown to the accused, once the Crown proves a specific fact that triggers the shift of the burden of proof to the accused to rebut the presumed fact or prove a specific fact

Revised Statutes of Ontario and **Revised Regulations of Ontario** the printed versions of the government of Ontario's revised statutes and revised regulations as of the date of publication. Statutes and regulations repealed since the last revision are removed from the current version, and amendments and new statutes are added. With the advent of the Internet, revisions are no longer published in books but are posted to the province's e-Laws online database for statutes and regulations at <https://www.ontario.ca/laws>.

road allowance a continuous strip of land dedicated for the location of a public highway, usually one chain (66 feet) wide; the actual roadway may be considerably narrower, but the whole width of the road allowance constitutes the highway, within the meaning of the HTA

S

suspension may be made under the authority of the HTA for either a CC offence or an HTA offence; disqualifies a driver from driving a motor vehicle as defined in the HTA on a highway as defined in the HTA

T

total weight determined from *either* the gross weight of the motor vehicle, trailer, and load or the registered gross weight of the motor vehicle, whichever is more

towed weight the weight of the trailer and its load

V

valtag a vehicle permit renewal sticker that shows that a permit has been renewed and is up to date; must be properly affixed as required under the HTA

vehicle includes a motor vehicle, trailer, traction engine, farm tractor, road-building machine, bicycle, snowmobile, street car, or any vehicle drawn, propelled, or driven by any kind of power, including muscular power

voir dire a "trial within a trial" conducted by a trial judge to determine whether evidence to be tendered is admissible in the main proceeding; an officer may have to give evidence on whether the accused was given a warning and whether his or her statement was voluntary and not compelled or coerced

W

"will say" statements a brief description or summary from an officer's notebook of what the witness will say in court; its primary audience is the Crown attorney and defence counsel, who will likely see the statement under evidentiary disclosure rules

Index

Credits

The Marks of Safety (inside covers): Transport Canada © Her Majesty the Queen in Right of Canada, represented by the Minister of Transport (2016). This information has been reproduced with the permission of Transport Canada.

CHAPTER 1

Figure 1.1: MacBeth Publishing Ltd. *The Ontario Highway Traffic Act*, 2016. Reprinted with permission.

Figure 1.2: MacBeth Publishing Ltd. *The Ontario Highway Traffic Act*, 2016. Reprinted with permission.

CHAPTER 3

Sample Motor Vehicle Permit: Publications Ontario © Queen's Printer for Ontario, 2016. Reproduced with permission.

Sample Valtag: Publications Ontario © Queen's Printer for Ontario, 2016. Reproduced with permission.

Sections/Description of Offence table (pp 49-50): MacBeth Publishing Ltd. *Provincial Offences Wording and Fines*, 2015. Reprinted with permission.

MADD Canada (statistical findings; text). Reprinted with permission.

Short Form Wordings (box): Compulsory Automobile Insurance Act: MacBeth Publishing Ltd. *Provincial Offences Wording and Fines*, 2016. Reprinted with permission.

CHAPTER 5

Figure 5.1: Publications Ontario. Form 1, *Provincial Offences Act, Ontario Court of Justice O Reg 108/11 Certificate of Offence*. POA 0847 (November 2, 2011) © Queen's Printer for Ontario, 2011. Reproduced with permission. Form 3, *Provincial Offences Act, Ontario Court of Justice, O Reg 108/11, Offence Notice*. POA 0848 (March 15, 2014) © Queen's Printer for Ontario, 2014. Reproduced with permission. Enforcement Agency Notes. © Queen's Printer for Ontario. Reproduced with permission.

Figure 5.2: Publications Ontario. Form 6, Provincial Offence Summons Reg 950 POA-0861-rev0311 © Queen's Printer for Ontario. Reproduced with permission.

CHAPTER 6

Table 6.1: Hit and Run Offences: MacBeth Publishing Ltd. *Provincial Offences Wording and Fines*, 2015. Reprinted with permission.

Some Costs of Impaired Driving (box): MADD Canada.

Table 6.2: Based on Kurt M. Dubowski, University of Oklahoma, Stages of Acute Alcoholic Influence/Intoxication (table). Copyright © 2006 by Dr. Kurt M. Dubowski. All rights reserved. Reprinted by permission.

Table 6.3: MacBeth Publishing Ltd. *Provincial Offences Wording and Fines*, 2015. Reprinted with permission.

CHAPTER 7

Questioning Witnesses (Professional Practice box): Adapted from Laurence M. Olivo and Mary Ann Kelly, *Civil Litigation*, 3rd edition (Toronto: Emond Montgomery, 2014). Reprinted with permission.

Motor Vehicle Collision Report: Publications Ontario. Form #SR-LD-401 12-05 UNIT1-5. Reprinted with permission.

APPENDIX B

Provincial Offence Notice: Publications Ontario. Form 1, *Provincial Offences Act,* Ontario Court of Justice O Reg 108/11 *Certificate of Offence.* POA 0847 (November 2, 2011) © Queen's Printer for Ontario, 2011. Reproduced with permission. Form 3, *Provincial Offences Act*, Ontario Court of Justice, O Reg 108/11, *Offence Notice*. POA 0848 (March 15, 2014) © Queen's Printer for Ontario, 2014. Reproduced with permission. Enforcement Agency Notes. © Queen's Printer for Ontario. Reproduced with permission.

Provincial Offence Summons: Publications Ontario. Form 7, Provincial Offence Summons Reg 950 POA-0861-rev0311 © Queen's Printer for Ontario. Reproduced with permission.